THE CHRISTIAN MESSAGE
IN A
NON-CHRISTIAN WORLD

THE CHRISTIAN MESSAGE
IN A
NON-CHRISTIAN WORLD

BY

H. KRAEMER

PROFESSOR OF THE HISTORY OF RELIGIONS
IN THE UNIVERSITY OF LEIDEN (HOLLAND)

WITH FOREWORD BY

THE LATE ARCHBISHOP OF CANTERBURY

KREGEL PUBLICATIONS
Grand Rapids, Michigan

Library of Congress Catalog Card Number: 56-10732

SBN-8254-3002-X

First published 1938
Third edition   1956
Fourth printing 1958
Fifth printing   1961
Sixth printing   1963
Seventh printing . . . 1969

PHOTOLITHOPRINTED BY CUSHING - MALLOY, INC.
ANN ARBOR, MICHIGAN, UNITED STATES OF AMERICA

PREFACE TO THE THIRD EDITION

I want to express my gratitude that this new edition of my Tambaram book appears. I honestly believe that it is a good thing to do so. The book as to content and purpose is, I am convinced, still timely and relevant. Moreover, I have discovered that the demand for it is persistent.

This year my London publisher will bring out a new book written by me, entitled, "Religion and the Christian Faith." This new book will now and then touch upon the same subject matter as this present volume, but its content and range of discussion is quite different and new. It may, however, be useful to say here that at some places in the new book I have taken the opportunity of answering some of the main criticisms made regarding my "Christian Message."

I close by expressing the wish that all over the world this new edition may serve Christian thinking and action.

H. Kraemer

Union Theological Seminary,
New York, March 27, 1956

PREFACE TO THE SECOND EDITION

SINCE there have been requests from both Great Britain and the United States for the reprinting of this volume, now some years out of print, it may be useful to say a few words about my attitude towards this second edition.

Probably as much as my readers, I should have liked to re-write the book, particularly those chapters dealing with present conditions of the living religions. Since 1937, when the book was written and the estimate of these religions made, colossal changes have occured. However, I must confess that I am not able to do a satisfactory revision at present because of the impossibility of securing the necessary materials with which to work. With no other choice before me and with much regret, I deem it better to have a coherent picture re-printed which, at any rate, has the advantage of an immediate prewar background rather than to try to outline something based on inadequate information.

As to my position with respect to fundamental theological and missionary problems, it is essentially the same as when I wrote the book ten years ago. I know that, especially in America, many people have misunderstood my emphasis upon biblical realism as meaning a defence of literalism and fundamentalism. My standpoint has nothing to do with literalism and fundamentalism. I started and still do start from the evident fact that the Bible is the record of God's acts of revelation in history and that the Christian Church can only live by sedulously dealing with the Bible as such. The ways of biblical thinking are upsetting to other ways of thinking and demand that we be prepared to listen each time anew to the Christian message and to revise our judgments and attitudes in its light. The presupposition of this thinking is that the relation between God and man is fundamentally defective and that it can only be restored by divine initiative, the essence of which is the forgiveness of sins as God's sovereign act of grace through Christ.

It is my serious conviction that from this background alone can the Christian message get its newness and uniqueness and a real application to the situation of the contemporary world and its fundamental needs.

H. KRAEMER

October 29, 1946
Leiden, Holland

PREFACE

THIS book has been written at the request of the International Missionary Council in order to serve as material for the World Missionary Conference in 1938. Within the general plan of this Conference, which comprises five main themes, this volume has its place, according to the intention of those who proposed its preparation, under the second theme : The Witness of the Church. What is expected from it is that it will " state the fundamental position of the Christian Church as a witness-bearing body in the modern world, relating this to different conflicting views of the attitude to be taken by Christians towards other faiths, and dealing in detail with the evangelistic approach to the great non-Christian faiths." [1] Evangelism, or the witness of the Church in relation to the non-Christian faiths, has therefore to be the main concern of this book. When I decided to comply with the request of the I.M.C. to produce this study, I was quite aware that I had accepted an impossible task. Some reasons why this is so may be indicated.

To state the fundamental position of the Christian Church as a witness-bearing body in the modern world, and to deal in detail with the evangelistic approach to the great non-Christian faiths presupposes a clear and comprehensive knowledge of Christian theology and a not less clear and comprehensive knowledge of the rich and variegated world of non-Christian religions, and that at a time when the whole life of the world is in process of revolutionary transition and stupendous crisis. Even more, to treat the evangelistic approach to the great non-Christian faiths requires a fair and living knowledge of the many mission fields all over the world, as no help can be derived from an abstract approach to religions in the abstract, but only from a concrete approach to a concrete reality.

[1] Minutes of the *Ad Interim* Committee of the I.M.C., Old Jordans, 1936.

No single man is sufficiently qualified to perform such an arduous task, either spiritually or intellectually. This would be so even if he had more time for preparation and study than it has been my chance to have, and if he were given the opportunity of paying a research visit to all the great mission fields, which was not possible within the limited time at my disposal.

Yet, in spite of all these terrible limitations, I accepted the task allotted to me, for two considerations.

In the first place, the great missionary cause really needs in this crucial hour such a fundamental exposition of its evangelistic outlook and application, and when the cause calls one has to obey if there are at least some indications that one should do so. Utter inadequacy and natural hesitancy have then to give way to obedience to a necessary and urgent task.

In the second place, the kind of book this production has to be can be achieved in one or other of two different ways : either as a one-man job or as a symposium by a group of men, every one of whom is an expert on the subject with which he deals. Facing these alternatives the I.M.C. did wisely in choosing the former, because what is primarily needed now in this fundamental and central problem of evangelism is a concentrated conception and vision, which can only be offered, however inadequately and imperfectly, by one man.

The longer I have been absorbed in my task the more deeply have I become convinced that, especially in our time, when all fundamentals and principles have to be re-examined, the problem of " evangelistic approach to the great non-Christian religions " cannot remain confined to the field of the proclamation of the Word or the preaching of the Gospel to the fundamental and concrete realities of the different religious systems. The *entire* missionary enterprise in all its manifestations, activities and obligations has to envisage itself essentially as approach, as evangelistic approach, because all these manifestations can only legitimately be called Christian and missionary when they issue directly from the apostolic urgency of gladly witnessing to

God and His saving and redeeming Power through Christ. The Christian Church and the missionary enterprise to-day stand in dire need of coming back to this which is, as it were, the heart from which the life-blood gushes forth through all the parts of the body. All the ways in which the Church expresses and manifests itself in the non-Christian world, either in word or in deed, have to be impelled and inspired by its prime apostolic obligation of witness-bearing to the world.

This insight made my task still more arduous. Yet it could not be shunned. The result is that the way in which I have developed my subject often touches on the fundamental problems underlying the five themes of the Meeting in preparation for which this volume has been produced.

From all that has been said it will be clear that I offer this production with no illusions whatever as to its abiding value. The highest ambition I foster is that it may prove to be a helpful contribution to the Church's rediscovery of its apostolic nature.

For all the opinions expressed in the book the author alone is responsible. It is not to be taken as the expression of the position of the I.M.C. The object of the I.M.C. in planning this volume was to provide the Meeting with a focus and a point of orientation for the co-operative clarification of thinking and planning.

In preparing the book I had, of course, to work through a great deal of literature. I have rarely quoted this or alluded to it in notes, because the book would then have assumed a learned and ponderous aspect not suitable to the character of this production.

I am deeply grateful to the officers of the I.M.C. and its personnel, to many kind and helpful people in America, England and Germany, and to not a few missionary correspondents, for the gracious help they constantly offered me when I asked for it. I want to express my special thanks to Dr N. Macnicol, who was so kind as to undertake the task of correcting my faulty English.

H. KRAEMER.

FOREWORD

by

HIS GRACE THE ARCHBISHOP OF YORK *

THOSE who have had opportunity to become acquainted
with the leaders of the missionary enterprise of our
time have become accustomed to think of Dr Hendrik
Kraemer as one of the statesmen and seers of that enterprise.
His range of knowledge is immense, and is illuminated by
practical experience in one of those parts of the mission field
where many currents of tradition meet.

This volume is a product of his knowledge, experience
and vision. It is likely to remain for many years to come the
classical treatment of its theme—perhaps the central theme
for Christian thought in this age of multiform bewilderment.
It will bring new confidence to many who are perplexed,
and supply the principles of missionary policy for our
generation.

WILLIAM EBOR.

January 1938.

* (Later Archbishop of Canterbury, now deceased.)

CONTENTS

CHAPTER I

A WORLD IN TRANSITION 1

The necessity of a fundamental re-orientation of the Church in a planetary but really disunited world.

THE WESTERN CRISIS.—Relativism and pseudo-absolutes. The secularism of a world in which man is the measure of all things. Spiritual and social revolutions. The whole world as a mission field for the Christian Church.

THE EASTERN CRISIS.—The earthquake caused by the penetration of the West into the East. The machine as seismological centre. Resulting destruction and reconstruction. The meeting of the religions of the East with the thought-systems of the West.

THE CRISIS OF THE CHURCH.—The Church lives " between the times." The abiding tension and crisis within the Church. The shattering of the *Corpus Christianum* : the unity of Church, Community and State. The urgent necessity of fundamental re-orientation of the Church regarding its relation to the world and all its spheres of life. The Christian Church is confronted with essentially the same problem in East and West.

CHAPTER II

WHITHER MISSIONS ? 31

Criticism of the Church in the modern world. Negative and positive elements in the Church in the nineteenth and twentieth centuries. The missionary enterprise. Development. Edinburgh 1910 : the strategical outlook. Jerusalem 1928 : Christian service. The significance of the independent indigenous Churches. The relation of the Older to the Younger Churches in the future.

SOME DOUBTS DISCUSSED.—Grave realities in the home Churches. The material and financial basis of missions. Missionary education. The problem of religious liberty in the rising tide of nationalism. Gandhi and the blood-and-soil religion.

CONTENTS

CHAPTER V

THE NON-CHRISTIAN SYSTEMS OF LIFE AND THOUGHT

CHAPTER VI

THE NON-CHRISTIAN SYSTEMS OF LIFE AND THOUGHT

CONTENTS

CONTENTS

CHAPTER VIII

THE MISSIONARY APPROACH 284

CHAPTER IX

THE MISSIONARY APPROACH—continued . . . 336

CONTENTS

THE CHRISTIAN MESSAGE IN A
NON-CHRISTIAN WORLD

CHAPTER I

A WORLD IN TRANSITION

THE general trend of events in the world necessarily
affects one as gloomy and dark. As has been rightly
said, we are living " between the times." Such a period is
unavoidably attended by many upheavals, by great evils and
dreadful suffering and anxiety, whether secret or manifest.
Humanity is beset with great dangers. Different inter-
pretations of this are possible, and are actually given. Undoubtedly only a deeply prophetic spirit is in some measure
adequate to penetrate into the real background of our
present confusion and turmoil. For the Christian, however,
there is certainly one great cause for gratitude and joy amidst
all distress and anxiety. The whole situation is one loud
call to fundamental re-orientation. The tempest of contemporary history is forcing back the Christian Church to
fundamentals, to such a radically religious conception of life
as is revealed to us in the Bible. We are exploring again the
simple but revolutionary meaning of faith. The Christian
Church is awakening to its responsibility to give clear and
unequivocal answers to the questions that arise out of the
thunder of events. The œcumenical conferences at Oxford
and Edinburgh are indications of this.

The Church and all Christians, if they have ears to hear
and eyes to see, are confronted with the question : What
is its essential nature, and what is its obligation to the world ?
The Church is emphatically reminded that it, alone of all
human institutions in the world, is founded on divine commission. It is called upon to reflect on its position and

situation. This, however, can only be effectively done when the Church becomes conscious in a new way of its mission in the " Christian " and the non-Christian world, because of its being founded on a divine commission. The essential nature of the Church is that it is an *apostolic* body. It is this, not because its authority is derived from the apostles, for the apostles belong to the Church, but because in all its words and actions it ought to be a bearer of witness to God and His decisive creative and redeeming acts and purposes. To become conscious of its apostolic character is for the Church the surest way to take hold of its real essence and substance. And this, to take hold of its real essence and substance, has to be the object before us when we are thinking about the Christian Message in a non-Christian world or the fundamental position of the Christian Church as a witness-bearing body in the modern world. Therefore, re-orientation of the missionary enterprise is urgent, whether the outcome should be in some cases to perpetuate or in other cases to change radically what we are accustomed to say and do.

.   .   .   .

When we look at the world of to-day, on the surface we are struck by two seemingly contradictory facts. Never before in human history has the world and mankind been such a close unity, and never before has it been such a discordant disunity. Asia and Africa are no longer affecting the imagination with fascinating dreams or dim horror, but have become common realities in the thought of everybody. Not only in their geographical, but also in their historical dimensions the continents and peoples of the world have become an open book to be read by every intelligent reader. The modern means of invention and communication have provided uninterrupted intercourse between the different races of men. Knowingly or unknowingly, everybody is forced to think and live in terms of the world, and not only in terms of his own country or community. There is no sphere of life in which the different peoples all over the world are not interrelated to each other.

A hundred years ago it was in every respect quite immaterial to the Western world what happened in China, in Africa, in Japan or in the larger part of the Moslem world. The repercussion of events emanating from a certain centre had no world-circumference but a more or less restricted local influence. This localism or regionalism is definitely destroyed and abolished and has given way to a single planetary world. In political, economic, social and cultural respects the world has become one great body, in which the different parts are extremely sensitive to each other, and are interconnected by a web of very delicate tissue. This is a patent and all-important aspect of the present-day world, notwithstanding that the spirit of exclusiveness and self-sufficiency is as dominant a note of the human mind as ever. Every people of any importance not only shapes its life by its own political, economic or other decisions, but affects more or less the present and the future of many others. The printing-press, the wireless and the " pictures " constantly present the millions of the world with various trends of standardized ideas and ideals, stirring and moulding the minds and confusing or directing the thoughts of untold multitudes. The irresistible impact of Western patterns of life and behaviour on all parts of the globe produces an amazing uniformity of life. All the non-Western peoples of the world—and that is the largest part of it—have experienced in the last fifty years more radical changes and adjustments in their individual and corporate life and in their material and spiritual life than in all the preceding millennia together. All these changes and adjustments are tending towards a similar pattern and standard of reference and are therefore making for uniformity. This similar pattern and standard is, as is universally known, presented by the Western forms of political, economic and social organization and method. Nobody can ignore the fact that the tenacity of old cultural traditions and conceptions of life is still very great, and therefore nobody can tell with certainty where the real foundations of life are lying for all these peoples, whether in the old time-worn foundations or in the new superstructure. However, nobody can deny that this new superstructure moves with irresistible force towards uniformity and conformity.

It would be superficial to assume that this movement affects only the outward forms and not also the inner content of the life of the people in East and West. Form and content are too intimately intertwined in human life to admit of such a facile assumption. We are undoubtedly living in a time when a colossal and unprecedented process of material and spiritual interpenetration of life and of cultural change is taking place. This process realizes itself, even through or in spite of great antagonisms and conflicts. Therefore it is no marvel that, seeing this interpenetration of all spheres of life, many serious men and women are living in the expectation of a coming world-culture, and are already dimly discerning its hopeful contours. A unified world on the basis of a cultural synthesis, in which the vital and sublime elements of the various great civilizations of mankind will be blended together, is the vision that kindles their faith and hope. De Kat Angelino, the author of the most penetrating and ample philosophy of colonial politics that ever has been produced, builds his whole structure on the vision of the coming of a world-embracing cultural synthesis. Professor Baker of Chicago has even written a very interesting and provocative book on *Christian Missions and a New World-Culture*, in which missions become one of the instruments in the development of this evolving world-civilization.

It seems very doubtful whether this dream of a grand cultural synthesis, mainly as a result of conscious benevolent striving springing from goodwill, has any chance of becoming true. Some sort of unity certainly will emerge, although attended by great and unexpected difficulties. We have a foreshadowing of this in the fact that never before has the world offered such a disquieting spectacle of disunity. The contradiction between the tendencies towards unity and disunity is not so great as it seems. Although man has, through science and creative criticism, immensely progressed in the mastery of life by the organization of all human activity, the inner structure of his life has been imperceptibly but steadily undermined by forces of disruption and dissolution. For the West this is rooted in the development of the inner trends of its civilization in the last centuries. For the Eastern peoples it has come as a result of the impact of the Western peoples, which has uprooted the foundations of all primitive societies and is shaking the foundations and framework of the great Eastern civilizations. Unrest, the clash of old and new ideals, the conflict of spiritual and material interests, communalism, nationalism, absolutist and militant communism and many things more, are the inevitable consequences.

Man, mastering and conquering life on the earth and in the air, does not know how to master himself, because moral growth is a quite different thing from intellectual development or conquest of the world. The amazing thing is that even such determined and titanic efforts as are being launched by the various " totalitarian " systems with a view to overcoming the forces of disruption and dissolution, are at present the most fruitful sources of disunity, when viewed from the general standpoint of the condition of the world. The self-same masterful capacity of modern man to organize and order life in the present situation serves only to intensify disorder, enmity and destruction. Universalism is replaced by militant antagonisms. In a world in which all life has become interrelated and interdependent, autarchy and isolation have become ideals of a pseudo-religious quality. In the past, when the world was still divided up into self-contained regional worlds and had not yet become planetary, autarchy and isolation were mainly the religious justification of a given condition of life, and in this regionally-divided world were comparatively harmless. China and Japan before the European penetration are splendid examples of this. Primitive societies, as ethnological research and practical experience have taught us, can indeed only live when the principles of autarchy and isolation are integrally maintained. What, however, is harmless in a regionally-divided world turns out to be extremely harmful and dangerous in a unified and planetary world. The frightful tensions which are harassing the world of to-day issue from two unexpected consequences of the unification of the world. On the one hand it has acted as a dissolvent, on the other hand it has intensified the self-consciousness of the many regional worlds, and has fostered a spirit of aggressiveness for the sake of self-maintenance in them, whether they may be states, cultures or religions.

What are the deeper causes of the disruptive state of this world in transition? And what does it mean for the condition in which the Church finds itself, and for its re-orientation?

The Church being a world-wide community, for the sake of clarity we have to analyse these causes for the Western and for the Eastern world, and to determine the features which are common to West and East. This will pave the way for a deeper understanding of the fact that the Christian Mission in the non-Christian world must rightly be said to be confronted by a severe outward and inward crisis.

THE WESTERN CRISIS

The outstanding characteristic of our time is the complete disappearance of all absolutes, and the victorious but dreadful dominion of the spirit and attitude of relativism. This is not contradicted by the stupendous fact that mankind is literally wallowing in pseudo-absolutes ; rather the reverse is the case. Religion, morality, systems of life, standards, spiritual values, normative principles, social orders are all divested of any absolute character or significance. The political crisis with its constant threat and reality of war and destruction, the economic crisis with its ensuing terrible unemployment and instability of life, naturally breed a spirit of uncertainty and insecurity in the minds of men. This, however, is only an addition to a more fundamental uncertainty that eats at the vital centres of human life. The problem of religious certainty is *the* ultimate problem of modern man. And the problem of religious certainty is the eternal human problem of God ; always evaded, yet ever and ever again obtruding itself upon man. The still deeper tragedy of modern man, however, is that this is wholly true only in an objective sense. In a subjective sense it is only partly true.

Only a small proportion of modern men who have looked in the abyss of consistent relativism awaken to the fact that

the place to which they are destined to look is heaven, and
that heaven is not closed. The mortal but hidden wound
in the life of hosts of other people is that they are not aware
that the fundamental problem for them is their complete
lack of absolutes in life, their wholehearted surrender to
the dominion of their life by relativisms, their fundamental
and radical uncertainty about the meaning of life. They
accept it simply as a fact and seem rather satisfied with it,
especially in the domain of religion. They take it as a
foregone conclusion that God is dead, definitely dead, and
will not rise again. There is a dim but nevertheless all-
pervading conviction that religion, especially Christianity,
is a matter of history, doomed to die, meat for the weak,
and not for the self-reliant man of to-day. This life, with
all its confusing distractions and diversions, with its possibilities of creative mastery of nature, of society and its
problems, with its heavy demands on the strength and time
of man, with its tumultuous conflicts and many-sided
interests, leaves no room for a deeper and truer reality.
Eternity is crowded out by Time. God does not fit in in this
bustling world of ours. He is utterly irrelevant to this
world and this life. And many of those who still cling to
religion and God do not know how to demonstrate the
relevance of God and religion to real life. They are ultimately undermined by uncertainty although they keep to
their loyalties.

Society is moving on and shows great vitality, because
man is resourceful and draws great strength from his unquenchable thirst for life and his innate moral and intellectual
powers. Yet, viewed from the religious standpoint, the
fundamental fact stands that the objective moral standards
and religious realities which formerly were acknowledged
as the spiritual basis of all individual and corporate life,
and the openness to the realm of the Eternal which constituted
in all ages in some way the background of all great and
small civilizations and societies, have evaporated in the
modern world. Speaking in broad and general terms one
can legitimately say about the masses of mankind that the
spirit of secularism and relativism rules supreme notwith-

standing indications to the contrary. And those who consciously suffer under this rule and see its implications seem to be few.

Certainly there is spiritual hunger, but in most cases it is unconscious. The conscious hunger is for a more un-trammelled enjoyment of this life with all its possibilities, not necessarily in the bad sense but also in the nobler sense of the word. Of course there are ideals. The world bristles with idealisms, noble and ridiculous, pure and demonic, because man cannot live without them. He is an amazingly fertile creator of idealisms, for without them he starves and degenerates. Absolutes however there are not, only pseudo-absolutes. These pseudo-absolutes—race, nation, classless society, a " holy " or " eternal " country—clearly demon-strate that man cannot live on bread, on relativism, alone. When he has, consciously or unconsciously, abolished God, he makes another god, because the need for the divine " word " belongs to the essence of man's nature, for he was created by God and unto God. Notwithstanding that, the rule of the spirit of secularism and relativism is unbroken, the modern pseudo-absolutes are even the acme of this spirit, the most intense expression of it.

What does this radical spirit of secularism and relativism really mean and how has it grown so dominant in Western society ? As with all great movements in history, the spiritual movement that in our age has resulted in secularism and relativism, with its strange blend of self-confidence, resignation and despair, began as a gospel. It was the gospel of the autonomy of the human spirit and of its intellectual and moral judgment. It was the courageous and joyful discovery of man's innate powers, his worth and his high destiny to conquer the mysteries of life and nature. It was really a spiritual spring-time. Proudly and reverently at the same time man took the reins of life and destiny in his own hands, confident of finding the truth and the standards of life in the depth of his own divine-human being. Essentially, of course, this establishment of man involved the disestablish-ment of God. This implication, however, has only gradually become evident. The autonomy of man was actually preached as a gospel ; it was felt as a great liberation and emancipation of the spirit. It needs to be said in our time of indiscriminate cursing of humanism. rationalism and the like, which are admittedly or unadmittedly based on the fundamental conception of the autonomy of man, that viewed in the whole content of historical and human development, the raising of the banner of man's autonomy actually meant a great and in many respects beneficent liberation and emancipation of the human spirit. It has made for an enormous enrichment of life and has released a mighty stream of creative and energizing ability, which in the following centuries has radically changed the surface of the earth and the whole aspect of, and impact on, life.

The conquest of the world began, and is still going on. Man started on the adventure to unveil the mystery of life and to master its forces, in the power of his own innate abilities. An amazing amount of thought, investigation and invention has been the result. A great wealth of philosophies and life-theories has been added to the treasures of the documents of human yearning and seeking. The concept of disinterested scientific truth, constantly checked by verification in experiment or self-criticism, has become one of the most precious and most fruitful products of this new spirit. Politically and socially it has acted in many directions as a liberating ferment, creating new ideals and new experiments. We who are the heirs of this great movement recognize some of its outstanding achievements as belonging to the most precious truths bestowed on mankind.

Well understood, the ideals of this movement for the emancipation of the human spirit, expressed in terms of liberty of thought, tolerance, individualism, etc., are to a certain extent distorted and derived elements of Christianity. To be sure, the Christian Church can never have anything to do with this immanentist view of life with its belief in the autonomy of man, in which man ultimately is the standard and creator of all truths and norms and values. Whosoever lives under the authority of Christ must denounce it as wholly erroneous. Yet it has to be acknowledged that it is difficult to see, humanly speaking, by what other dynamite the equally impressive, but from the Biblical standpoint equally erroneous, mediæval conception of a fixed Christian civilization and a Christian social body and the external intellectualist conception of the authority of Christian revelation in post-reformation Protestantism, could have been exploded. When Leibniz in the eighteenth century rejoiced in the natural religion of China without revelation, priests and miracles, he certainly demonstrated an entire lack of understanding of the character of Christian revelation and a great misconception of the religion of China. Partly, however, it was a justified revolt of the human spirit against the intellectual bondage caused by the petrification of Christian truth. The triumphal march of man has ended, however, in the self-destruction of man, because it was not only an emancipation from a conception that obscured the reality of God and His word, but also from God Himself. Man, being rooted in God, destroys himself by destroying God.

Relativism and secularism which, against the background of an erroneously conceived absolutism of truth and sacralization of life, were apprehended as a liberation, revealed their innate consequences when this background was shattered. The triumphal march turned out to be a death-dance. That, it seems to me, is the outstanding characteristic of our time. Belief in man as the measure of all things ends in the ignoring or denial of God, and ultimately in the destruction of man. Where all has become relative, nothing is really worth-while, because it has no foundation in Eternity. Man cannot create for himself rules and standards and realities that are absolute, just because they are his own human creation. Vinet, the great Swiss thinker, wrote nearly a hundred years ago an article in which he made clear that all human thinking which ignores or does not know Christ is the endeavour of man to establish his own law. An impossible undertaking, because one's own creation never can be one's absolute authority. Developed to its last consequences autonomy of man must end in anarchy and lawlessness, because the only valid and indestructible law can be the Law from above and not from within.

The grand idealistic immanentist philosophical systems of the nineteenth century were built on the premise of the identity of thinking and being, or of consciousness and being. That is the premise of all philosophy that will grasp ultimate Reality in the act of thinking and will reach it by the conception of the Idea. Descartes took as his starting-point *cogito ergo sum*, for when God has abdicated the only starting-point left to human thinking is human consciousness. These identity-philosophies ultimately go back to the concept of the autonomy of man. To-day this immanentist thinking, with ruthless logic and with not less ruthless honesty, has drawn out its latent consequences, as appears in the representatives of existential philosophy. They have discovered that this identity of Thinking and Being or of Idea and Ultimate Reality is a fiction—a grand fiction, but still a fiction. Ultimate Reality, as a severe analysis of human consciousness teaches, always remains the object of our thinking, and consequently remains outside our grasp. It constantly recedes. Man, thus thrown back on himself, moreover having become acutely critical of the intricacies of the human mind by the discoveries of psychology, has become extremely sceptical about the really objective value of his thought-constructions. The quest for truth and certitude has driven him to the conclusion that all systems are somehow projections of tendencies of the human mind. He is alone in a howling wilderness. All his efforts are to be compared with Baron von Münchhausen's endeavour to draw himself by his own hair out of the swamp in which he is sunk.

This quest for truth of autonomous man, his passionate longing for an absolute and for certitude about Ultimate Reality and the meaning of life, are the basic indications that man has affinity with the order of absolute Truth and Ultimate Reality. The moving plight of man is that the fundamental fact of his existence is his being created unto the divine order of Ultimate Truth and Reality. Therefore the quest for Eternal Truth and Life is his prime life-necessity and by the nature of the case his prime obligation. Yet he cannot produce it by his own efforts. Karl Heim in his illuminating book, *Glaube und Denken*, to which I feel greatly indebted, justly says that the outcome of the deepest contemporary philosophy corresponds with the presupposition of the Gospel, namely, that man can never reach God (or, philosophically speaking, Ultimate Reality) and indestructible certitude about Him by his own powers. If man takes God seriously, and the fact that God, not he himself, has laid eternity in his heart, he never can be the creator and producer in the realm of ultimate Truth and Reality, but only the humble receiver.

The fundamental relativism and secularism in morals, religion and philosophy, and the resulting disintegration of life which we have shortly indicated, are not consciously felt by everyone. There are still many humanistic currents that are persistently and confidently striving for salvation by faith in man's possibility to attain truth and to realize the good life by means of his own resources.

Relativism is, however, *the* decisive and dominant reality of modern life, although to a great extent subconscious and subterraneous. The great tensions which Western civilization has to endure hereby become still more evident when we realize that the inner and fundamental disintegration is steadily being aggravated by the obvious disintegration of old social structures and loyalties as a result of the urbanization and complexity of life in the modern world. The World War, with its destruction of the political and economic equilibrium and its disturbance of the delicate international organization in commerce, finance and spiritual intercourse, has intensified the disintegration which was already disastrously playing havoc with the spiritual and social bases of life, and has opened the eyes of many people to it. Two great instances may suffice for our purpose to illustrate that relativism and secularism are the dominant notes of modern life.

The first is the attitude towards institutional and traditional religion, in this case especially Christianity. The disquieting fact which every earnest Christian must face is that religion has become irrelevant in modern life, because God has become irrelevant. We do not mean to say that modern man, generally speaking, is less religious by nature than man of any other age. Man is by nature a religious " animal " as well as a moral or an intellectual one. This remains true to-day. In diverse ways he is still seeking satisfaction for his religious instinct and he will always seek it. Religion, however, has been banished from the centre of life, whether individual or corporate life. This is the crucial point in the situation, because religion by the nature of the case must claim to be central.

In modern life religion is either a non-entity, an embellishment or an object of hate, seldom a central fact. From the standpoint of really vital religion, its being an object of hate is probably one of the most auspicious features in the whole scene.

Moreover, many factors conspire to atrophy the religious instinct. We have alluded once already to the overwhelming secular rush and aspect of life, which leaves no time or leisure for religion. Gilbert Murray in his *Five Stages of Greek Religion* gives excellent expression to a notion of religion that in all ages has been widespread among men. He says : " Religion essentially deals with the uncharted region of human experience." This erroneous—from the standpoint of true religion—but universal notion has always been supported by the unanimous testimony of the great institutional religions themselves. The important thing to note in man is that, although a religious " animal " by nature, he is at the same time deeply irreligious, if we take the word religion with the seriousness we have learnt from Christ. In primitive societies, which are admittedly integrally religious, religious and magical rites and practices are resorted to when knowledge and skill are insufficient to master situations of danger and uncertainty. " Popular " religion, which forms the broad understream of all great religions, Christianity included, provides us with many examples of this same tendency. No wonder that from Lucretius to modern communists voices have been raised affirming that religion has been begotten by ignorance and fear ; and it is, as already suggested, an indisputable fact that many sections in the wide field of religion rightly fall under this verdict. The critics of this irreligious religion, which utilizes the objects of religion irreverently for selfish ends, are sound judges. Now, one of the characteristics of the modern age is that scientific progress in the domain of nature, society and psychology has enabled man to find solutions and master life by his own wits where formerly the authoritative wisdom or consolation of religion fulfilled his needs. So gradually religion has slipped out of the life of untold masses, and God and His Reality, being usually identified with religion, has constantly been driven further back from the field of life, either evaporating to the vanishing point, or being kept in reserve for man's still unanswered questions, or forming his last resort in times of extreme need and impotence. The relevance of God to the actual problems of life remained obscure and the Church rarely saw its way to bring the necessary light. The representatives of religion themselves, because of their own diluted conception of religion, have contributed to this rise of the notion of God's irrelevancy.

The result of scientific investigation into foreign civilizations and religions and the growth of the historical mind, which necessarily strengthened the relativist temper, have influenced slowly but irresistibly the general mind. The windows of the mind were opened on all sides. The result has been an enormous enrichment in knowledge and insight, but also confusion and uncertainty. With a note of indifference or plaintive resignation thousands have learned to ask : What is truth ? From this atmosphere the often unformulated notion has soaked into the general mind that there are evidently more possibilities of religious truth than that offered by Christianity. In the first stages of adjustment many entertained the conviction that all religions were equally true and equally important. The general atmosphere of relativism and the steadily-growing conviction of the irrelevancy of religion, however, evoked the notion that all religions were probably equally unimportant and equally erroneous, which in its turn reinforced the relativist and secularist temper.

The second illustration of the reality of the underlying

atmosphere of relativism and secularism is afforded by the cataclysmic spiritual and social revolutions as manifested in Communism, Fascism and National-Socialism.

The World War, its accompanying circumstances and its aftermath, undoubtedly have an important share in the shape and spirit in which these revulsions have expressed themselves. In their political and economic aspects they are gigantic efforts, inspired by universalist or nationalist ideas, to master the anarchy of our social and political world. Their peculiar characteristic, however, is that they are primarily creeds, philosophies of life and religions of an extremely intolerant and absolutist type. They consequently develop mythologies, doctrinal systems, catechisms, " churches," " priests," " prophets," " saints," and " mediators." All the paraphernalia of a full-fledged religion are virtually present. They even make gods—for the race, the ideal communist society, and the State assume a distinctly God-like position. Absolute allegiance to these gods is demanded with religious fervour. Absolute devotion to their service is the ultimate standard of moral life, and releases in many individuals, as all ultimates do, marvellous manifestations of self-sacrifice, discipline and creativeness. These " religions " impetuously claim dominion over life in all its ramifications. They intolerantly persecute other religions that do not subordinate their specific allegiance to the absolute one that is only due to their " god." Tillich justly remarks that the disintegrated masses, sensing the meaninglessness of life, hunger for " new authorities and symbols." The totalitarian systems satisfy this hunger, and millions of men gladly sacrifice their political, economic and spiritual autonomy.

If we still need evidence that man, even de-religionized modern man, is a religious and metaphysical animal, here it is. Is not one of the most paradoxical facts in modern life this strange coincidence? In the field of philosophy and religion the conception of absolute truth or authority, embodied in a system, is entirely discredited. The once much-debated problem of the absolute character of Christianity has become silent, and is continued on a different plane.

One observes, however, the startling fact that what is discredited in relation to religion and philosophy is emphatically assumed as self-evident in relation to the deified state, nation or community.

This frantic fanaticism is only to be explained by the background of fundamental relativism and secularism that has been indicated. It is a desperate endeavour to overcome relativism by *self-made* absolutism. The absolute is a life-necessity for man. Therefore when he has annihilated God, man, the inveterate god-maker, creates new gods or makes himself god. However, just because the absolutism of these new " religions " is self-made, it is void and false. The salutary unbreakable law for man is that real absolutes can only be received by him as a gift ; those he makes are pseudo-absolutes. Consequently these religions are pseudo-religions. They remain in the secular sphere, for, fundamentally speaking, they unconsciously exploit man's capacity for absolute devotion, which is essentially religious, for worldly ends, namely to unify and fortify the State or the Community or the Nation. Man and his ends and his desires, noble as well as ignoble, remain the standard of reference. It is therefore significant to note that these secularist efforts, which assume religious quality and put forward religious claims, are, properly speaking, a reversion to tribal religion and tribal morality. Both, of course, assume huge dimensions, for their commandments and prohibitions are determined, as in the primitive tribe, by the rule of what promotes or what damages the life, stability and power of State, Nation or Community.

Certainly the modern world is extremely puzzling. Primitive civilizations are breaking down all over the world at the onslaught of Western civilization, because tribal religion, on which those civilizations are based, crumbles away under the pressure of a widened outlook. At the same time the West is inventing magnified tribal religions to invigorate its crumbling systems of life and its anarchic social and political order.

Nothing can demonstrate more clearly that *the Christian Church, religiously speaking, in the West as well as in the East is*

*standing in a pagan, non-Christian world, and has again to consider
the whole world its mission field, not in the rhetorical but in the literal
sense of the word.*

THE EASTERN CRISIS

The Eastern crisis we can treat even more succinctly than
the Western, because its primary cause lies in the penetration
of the West into the East.

Why did this Western penetration effect such a tremendous
crisis and revolution in the life of the primitive as well as of
the highly civilized East ? This is a legitimate question, for it
is not the first time in history that great imperial nations and
civilizations have spread their rule over a wide territory,
inhabited by peoples of different civilizations and religion.
Take one of the great instances of this, the Hellenization of
the whole Mediterranean world and a part of Asia and
Europe, resulting from Alexander the Great's expedition and
continued by the Roman conquest. In examining this we
state that its effect, unlike what is happening to-day, was not
a general upheaval of social, cultural and religious life, but a
steady penetration, a leavening and intermingling of life-
conceptions. Yet, just as in the case of Western penetration
to-day, it did not merely mean a peaceful religious and
cultural penetration, such as for instance Buddhism accomplished in Japan and China, but also a political, social and
cultural conquest.

Why this remarkable difference between the influence
of the Roman Empire and the modern Western " Empire "
and that exercised by Buddhism in Japan and China ?

Buddhism, being of Indian origin, represented a civilization
and a religion of which the fundamental ideals and life-
patterns were utterly different from the natural endow-
ments and propensities of Japan and China. Yet
these two peoples, notwithstanding their sharply-defined
cultural physiognomy and their strong self-consciousness,
absorbed it without much difficulty and even with great
profit. It became a thoroughly naturalized Chinese and
Japanese religion and type of civilization. It did not remain
foreign. Why, then, is " foreignness " still the indelible

mark that attaches to the Western penetration? On this question one might answer that in the case of Buddhism in Japan and China we have the advantage of looking back over a long period, whereas we are still in the midst of the Western penetration, having no brief to speak for the future. This is true, and we are certainly entitled to suspect that in view of the inevitable external unification and the resulting equalization of political, economic, social and cultural levels and implementations, which practically means the adjustment towards Western patterns, the "foreignness" of the Western penetration will more and more disappear.

Yet there remains a deep difference, the same difference as with the process of Hellenization in the Roman Empire. The essential reason for the "foreignness," and the disturbing effect—in the good sense of the word as well as in the bad—of Western penetration appears to be that never before in the history of the world has there been a meeting between worlds so radically and irreconcilably different as East and West. The metaphor of the earthquake is the only appropriate one to suggest what has happened to the East by the penetration of the West. In religion, in outlook, in attitude towards life, fellow-man and the world, in customs, in modes and appetites of life, in political and social systems and idealisms, in economic organization, in technical equipment, they were and are worlds asunder. The only thing they seemed to have in common when they had the first contacts with each other was their common manhood. Each party at that time felt the other to be utterly foreign.

We must leave aside here the fascinating topic of what were the reasons why these Western "newcomers" on the stage of world-history were able to impose themselves so imperiously on these ancient "aristocratic" civilizations of the East. The crucial fact is that in the nineteenth century the machine, as the symbol of the inventive and organizing capacity of the West, appeared on the scene. In it the creative urge and intelligence of the Westerners had shaped a marvellous but fateful tool to express and multiply their creativity infinitely, even to the degree that the creator became the servant and victim of his own invention. The ensuing industrial revolution, which now found at its disposal tools more highly perfected than ever before, and the liberation of life from its old fetters, made the conquest of the world inevitable. So the machine, as the expression of the methodical spirit of the West, may be called the seismological centre for the earthquake in the East.

The agricultural East with its age-old established spiritual and social orders, which seemed unchangeable laws of life, was exposed to the vigorous impact of this dynamic Western world with its technical implements that, by their indisputable superiority, intensified its dynamic power to an incredible degree. Because the spiritual and material foundations of life are always indissolubly intertwined with their corresponding forms of expression, this could but mean a complete revolution for the East. Its whole conception of life and its political and social structure were thoroughly disturbed and are still disturbed. The West with its radically different attitude towards life, with its entirely different conceptions and methods in the political, social, economic and cultural realm, imperiously led the way along which the East had to move.

The outcome, as we see it, has been destruction and reconstruction. The perplexity of the situation is that both are so entirely and indiscernibly intermixed. The degree and the nature of destruction, the trend of and the advance towards reconstruction, are very different amongst different communities. Primitive peoples, the Moslem world in its various and variegated components, India, China, Japan, each presents a different picture.

Primarily, the process of destruction and reconstruction is everywhere a response and reaction to some Western stimulus, as Professor Toynbee has shown so vividly in relation to the Near and Middle East in his book, *The Western Question in Greece and Turkey*. The crisis of life in the West and in the East includes both a complete and a drastic re-shaping of all spheres of life and is therefore in many respects full of similar effects and problems. In a very dramatic sense East and West are both worlds in transition. Yet the deep difference in their respective situations of crisis is that in the West the crisis is the result of its own inner development ; in the East the process has been set in motion by causes operating from without. This lends a different colouring to the two pictures, although in the East as well as in the West this period of turbulent transition is marked by the same kind of defensive, reconstructive and aggressive nationalism.

True as it may be, however, that the process of destruction and reconstruction in the East is primarily a response and a reaction to a heterogeneous cause, this must not prevent us from seeing that we have entered on a very important new phase in modern history, which we call by the name of the meeting of East and West. The Western penetration was in the nineteenth century an expression of the Western hegemony in the affairs of the world. During that period the East reacted to it either with sullenness or with eager enthusiasm for the vision of a new world which was inaugurated by the dynamic powers of the West. Both attitudes were essentially reactions in the passive sense of the word. The West was the determining and directive force. The only notable exception was Japan, whose decision to liquidate its splendid isolation was the well-considered result of its determination to remain the master of its fortune and the maker of its own destiny. Once awakened to the inevitability of being drawn into a larger world, it acted with an amazingly sensitive and clear-sighted national and spiritual self-consciousness. The other parts of the East, however, were slower in their response. They endured the Western penetration rather than digested it. They long remained largely victims and not actors.

The great change that has come in the twentieth century is that, to use the same expression, the victims have become actors. Mainly passive impulsive reaction has become conscious action. Essentially speaking, this universal awakening of the East to resolute action may still fall under the category of defence, the defence of its own identity, the resolve to remain itself and to remain that energetically. Within the content of the course of events this means that the East rides again the horses of its own destiny. The

Western hegemony in the affairs of the world belongs to the past. The East, which not very long ago played only a passive or negligible rôle in the determination of the course of world history, has become now a factor as influential as the West.ʼ Probably there is no fact more fraught with consequences for the shaping of the future of humanity than this passing of the European world hegemony. It not only fundamentally changes the whole political and economic outlook of the world but—more significant to note for those who are engaged in the great missionary cause—all prognosis about the future religious and spiritual development of mankind will have to adjust itself to the new fact that all great religions and conceptions of life may become world-wide in their effects and possibilities. Islam, Buddhism, the great Eastern idealistic systems are no longer confined to definite sections and regions of the world. Their latent dynamics, whether spiritual or political, may become world-factors.

The thoughtful observer of human history has ample food to reflect how inscrutable and mysterious are the ways of history. The indomitable energetic Westerners, inspired by a feeling of superior intelligence and ability, drove in an exultant and victorious mood the seemingly lethargic East into the arena of world history, intent on using it for their own ends and purposes. But they turn out to be the instrument of wholly unpremeditated effects and ends. The East, with its colossal spiritual and material resources, has definitely come upon the stage, and helps to shape the world's destiny. So little does this marvellous creature, man, know what he does !

Dr S. K. Datta, in his *Asiatic Asia*, treats in a very lucid way the inner and outer transformation, the social, political, economic and cultural revolution which is implied in the active response of the East to the impact of the West. He rightly defines this active response as the endeavour towards national reconstruction in all spheres of life. The problems of spiritual, political, social and economic reconstruction, the questions of communism, socialism, capitalism, fascism, totalitarianism in their doctrinal and practical aspects, are therefore as vital to the East as to the West, although they are fought out against very different backgrounds.

The conception of nation as the integrating idea is entirely new to the East, with the exception of Japan to a certain degree. National reconstruction, therefore, means a radical break with the past and an equally radical re-evaluation of the value and the position of all classes and conditions of men. All Eastern conceptions of life are at one in this, that the corporate forms of life are sacred orders, that is to say, that they are dependent upon and integrated in a wider spiritual order of divine quality. National reconstruction, however, inspired by modern incentives and modern ends, aims at the creation of a human order subordinate to self-devised human standards. In other words, the problem of secularism, though in a particular setting, is as burning in the East as in the West. The nationalist movement in India, which in its romantic period was steeped in religious sentiment and seemed under the suggestive leadership of Gandhi to be the struggle for a " holy people " in a " holy country," is becoming under the leadership of Jawaharlal Nehru increasingly and consciously secular. " The Three Principles " of Sun Yat-sen—nationalism, democracy and socialism— are a clear expression of the same trend. Japan presents in many respects the parallel to the totalitarian currents in Europe. Making national consolidation the ultimate value of life, it established a pseudo-absolute in the deification of the Emperor, founding its secular imperialism on the religious basis of the idea that Japan is destined to be the world-embracing theocracy. One has to wait to see whether in other Eastern countries the same tendency will emerge toward using inherited religious systems to cement national reconstruction and consolidation. The future alone can tell.

The mass-disintegration, which is so conspicuous in the West, becomes more and more operative in the East. There, as well as here, it follows in the wake of industrialization. Rural and urban proletariats are steadily growing ; and the old sacred bonds of family and clan, with which are bound up so many moral and religious values, are becoming weaker and weaker. Not individualism, but what one might call atomism, is taking their places.

Relativism in relation to the problem of absolute truth is not such a burning problem in the East as in the West. It certainly exists, but for some obvious reasons it is not so severe. The first reason is that the Eastern world, with the sole exception of Islam, has, in the field of religion and philosophy, virtually always lived on the theory of the relativity of all truth as formulated by man. This theory served in the East to justify, sanctify and consolidate every existing form of religion. In the West, characteristically, the relativist spirit has always exercised a revolutionary and explosive influence on the life of positive religion, because Christianity, *the* religion of revelation, stands for absolute truth and cannot treat religious scepticism or rejection as comparatively innocent things. For the same reason religious scepticism and relativism cannot leave Christianity unassailed. The East is deeply convinced that Ultimate Reality and Absolute Truth are utterly ineffable. All religions and philosophies are differently-graded approaches to this unfathomable Mystery. Only some lonely travellers on the road to the highest gnosis do find it, or, more properly expressed, do become it, throwing away the crutches embodied in the various religious systems. Also, religious relativism and scepticism are quietly accepted as long as one conforms to religious customs and practices.

The second reason arises from the exigencies of the present situation. In many respects the modern forms of rationalism and humanism, in which the West has discovered or is beginning to discover the danger of disintegrating relativism and their inadequacy to meet the deepest crises of life, are still liberating tonics for the East. Hence the deep influence of men like Dewey and Bertrand Russell. The deadening grip of religion, with its systems of degrading and life-stifling beliefs, customs and institutions in the lives of millions of human beings, is such a dreadful reality that the philosophy of progress, emancipation and self-reliance sounds like a gospel of liberation ; and in the existing circumstances it actually is so. Against this background Hu Shih's militant humanism is quite intelligible. It is the voice of a man who fights with noble passion a mighty enemy, when he says in his article on *The Civilization of the East and the West* that " civilization, which makes the fullest possible use of human ingenuity and intelligence in search of truth in order to control nature and transform matter for the service of mankind, to liberate the human spirit from ignorance, superstition and slavery to the forces of nature and to reform political and social institutions for the benefit of the greatest number, such a civilization is highly idealistic and spiritual."

The contact with the Western mind, however, the wholesale destruction of old values that for ages were accepted unquestioned, the confusion caused by the many conflicting theories of life, the repeated experience of their untrustworthiness, make relativism a much more painful problem for many than it has been in many ages. Besides, because the dominant tendency of the East has always been to present a relativist attitude towards positive religion as a sign of intellectual aristocracy, and because the hidden relativism of modern humanism will certainly, once it becomes manifest, be viewed in the light of the conception that certainty about Truth is man's prime life-necessity, the problem of relativism is one of the most fundamental in Eastern life.

Seeing the vehement and deep-going crisis of life in which the East is caught at the present time, it would be nothing to marvel at if in many parts of the East a desperate surrender to false absolutes should ensue in order to master a situation which, in order to be overcome, needs more than the traditional attitude of aristocratic relativism of the East.

THE CRISIS OF THE CHURCH

Just as the crisis of life in the world of to-day is the coming to the surface of a long and slow process which is at present becoming acute, so it is also with the crisis of the Church. Strictly speaking, one ought to say that the Church is always in a state of crisis and that its greatest shortcoming is that it is only occasionally aware of it. The Church ought always to be aware of its condition of crisis on account of the abiding tension between its essential nature and its empirical condition.

According to its essential nature it is not one of the many religious and moral institutions that exist in the world. It is a divine-human society, which always and not only in periods of worldly crisis is living " between the times "— the time of its foundation by the Holy Spirit, when the redemptive Reign of God as revealed in Jesus Christ entered the world as a working reality ; and the time of the consummation of God's Reign, the coming of which is in the hand of the Father. The abiding tension in which the Church ought to live, but in which it rarely lives, is implied in the fact that this divine-human society enters the world as an empirical human institution, and cannot enter it otherwise. It is called to constant witness and opposition to the world, to which it itself belongs, because this world is dominated by the forces of evil and is the object of the divine wrath ; at the same time it is called to constant witness and service, because this self-same world is God's creation and the object of God's saving grace. The abiding tension and crisis in which the Church ought to live, if it were constantly conscious of its nature and mission, is not the tension between the ideal and the real, but the same religious and ethical tension and crisis in which every individual Christian ought to live, if he takes seriously his real calling as a Christian. If the Church and the individual Christian understood rightly the Revelation in Christ, they would be conscious that within the empirical, imperfect, finite and sinful order of the world and this life, their life is founded upon and rooted in a new divine order of life that has been brought to light by Christ and His work and has become by Him a living reality. This new divine order is the foundation of the life of the Church and of the Christian, and at the same time their never-ending task and their deep expectation. That is the really abiding tension and crisis of the Church, or, at least, it ought to be so.

In actual fact this tension and crisis are rarely active in the consciousness of the Church. There are two important indications of this. In the first place, the Church too often has become reconciled to its being merely a religious and moral institution, whether a highly influential or a neglected one. In the second place, according to the testimony of history, it has always needed apparent failure and suffering in order to become fully alive to its real nature and mission. This has to be kept in mind in order to get the right perspective of the present situation of the Church.

Viewed against the background of the last five centuries, the Church in its present crisis has to face two principal facts.

First, the whole cultural, political and social development of those centuries has meant the secularization of life in steadily increasing degree. The dynamic force in this progress has been the creed of the autonomy of man in the sense we have already indicated. When this process started, the Church was what is called the *Corpus Christianum*, that indissoluble unity of Church, Community and State which is the outstanding characteristic in the mediæval period of European history. That was the time when Europe knew a " Christian " state, a " Christian " society and a " Christian " civilization under the leadership of the Church as the Representative of Christ. Viewed from the standpoint of human achievement it was in many respects a grand synthesis of different spheres of life and civilization, just as Buddhism in Japan or the theocratic civilization of Islam has been and still is to some degree. From this same standpoint it was also a great educational experiment. The fact that, empirically speaking, notwithstanding all attacks and weakening forces, Christianity in form and in substance is still a living force in the totality of Western life is to a great extent due to this achievement of the Middle Ages. For great historical achievements have a long life. Fundamentally speaking, however, from the standpoint of the Church as the divine-human community, it was an anticipation and a blurring of the vision by which it ought to live. In this world we can only speak about a Christian society and a Christian civilization in a very attenuated and diluted sense. The sense in which it is commonly used, and which is implied in the term *Corpus Christianum*, is highly secularized. The facile idealization with which this term often is treated leaves entirely out of account that, essentially, it is dangerously mixed with the pagan ideal of religion, namely, that religion is a cult which is recognized by the community (or state) as its basic foundation, and which therefore is valid for and obligatory on every member of the community. This pagan conception, with which the Primitive Church fought its life or death struggle, constantly meets the Church in the modern missionary enterprise and confronts it in the totalitarian creeds, but in the mediæval ecclesiastical ideal it was blended with the Christian idea of the Church.

The steadily growing slow progress of secularization in the cultural, political and social spheres, of which we have already spoken, has meant the gradual shattering of this *Corpus Christianum*. Protestantism in its different forms (although it is, on account of its " churchism " and its breaking away from the authority of the Mother-Church, rightly accused by Roman Catholic writers of complicity in this destruction) in many respects virtually held the same idea, but on a territorial scale. The territorial Protestantisms only slowly and under compulsion recognized that it was inevitable to let this conception go. Many remnants are still alive and are even still of great importance. The " sects " helped actively to destroy it in their struggle for religious and ecclesiastical freedom.

What, put positively, can be formulated as the present dominion of secularism and relativism, is, put negatively, the fact that the shattering of the *Corpus Christianum* has nowadays become a patent situation, and that religion and the Church seem so largely irrelevant to the bulk of man. It would require a whole chapter to describe the vicissitudes of the life of the Church in this whole situation, its shameful defeats, its silent victories, its lack of discernment, its ignoring of its real nature and mission, and its groping for light. For our purpose it suffices to say that there are signs of its awakening to the real fundamental issues. Suffering and seeming defeat are again the instruments for this awakening, for example, the attack on the Church in Germany and the determination of the Church to obey God rather than man or man-made ultimates ; and also the persecution of Christian believers in Russia. Moreover, we are reminded by it that despite relativism, secularism, persecution and campaigns for the extinction of the Church with their resultant destructive effects, the real divine-human community is indestructible, because it is God's.

The confusion in which the Church finds itself, since its meeting and conflict with modern culture, modern thinking and modern organization of life, is from the view-point of the history of civilization the consequence of this gradual shattering of the *Corpus Christianum*. The Church has thereby lost its " recognized " or " established " position in the conscience of man, although the remnants of this " established " position are still alive in the structure of modern society. This loss of the " recognized " position in the conscience of man constitutes the present crisis of the Church as to its position in the world. The disintegrated masses, in their hunger for new authorities and symbols to give meaning to life, did not think for a moment of turning to the Church, but turned away from it. That is the first principal fact the Church has to face.

A fundamental re-orientation regarding its relation to the world and all its spheres of life has therefore become the urgent need of the hour. And that is the second principal fact which looms up before the eye in the present crisis. In the divine commission and mission of the Church the problem of its relation to the world and its sphere of life is inherent, because the Church exists in and for the sake of the world. The shattering of the *Corpus Christianum* implies the ruin of a definite and very remarkable endeavour to construe and realize a system of life in which the problem of the relation to the world found a temporary solution. This problem has therefore to be considered in its entirety—in its entirety and not only fragmentarily. All the reactions of the Church on the whole complex of modern life in the last hundred years, which have emerged in the contest between faith and science, Christianity and culture, Christianity and the social problem, including Christian Socialism, the Social Gospel, etc., were *fragmentary* endeavours to solve the problem of the relation of the Church to the world. The special characteristic of the present time is that that trend of events has gone so far as to allow us no longer fragmentary, and therefore half-blind, approaches to its solution. The problem in its totality presses itself upon us. Here lies the real significance of the present theological revolution. Therefore the discussion inevitably is driven back to the root-problems of revelation, of God and His character, of man and his place in the world, of natural theology, *i.e.*, the meaning and value of nature, of history, of the relation of the Church to State, Nation and Community.

The frightful tensions to which modern life in all its spheres is exposed, the crumbling of the old foundations and frameworks, as well as the mysterious resurgence of vital, instinctive forces in the life of many peoples which we are witnessing to-day, are calling forth the ideal of the State as the absolute, stabilizing power to which all other agencies have to be subservient. The conflict of " Church " and " State " issuing therefrom in a very acute form makes the problem of the relation of the Christian Church to the world a matter of life or death. A noteworthy fact therefore is that the call for the integral reconsideration and solution of this problem of the relation of the Church to the world arises not only from the critical condition of the Church in its endeavour to re-define its essential relations and obligations towards the world and its different spheres of life, but also is forced upon the Church by the dominating life-tendencies in the world itself. Everywhere over the world Christianity and the Church—even religion in general— are being more and more thoroughly tested on their negative or positive value for the reconstruction of human life as this is at present understood. The dominant views apply a pragmatist standard, measuring the significance of Christianity from the view-point of their own ends, namely, their own ideals of life and culture. Does it, from this standpoint, work well on the whole ?

Communism weighs it and finds it " opium " and an obstacle on the way to an ideal society. Nationalism in its different forms surveys Christianity with the question in its mind whether it can be an important ally in the rebuilding of the nation and the reconstruction of national life and destiny, or not. In many cases the answer is in the negative. But, whether the answer is positive or negative, the important point is that Christianity and the Church are scrutinized as to their value for the shaping of life. This movement of scrutiny, moreover, is literally world-wide. The other great world-religions, Islam, Buddhism, Hinduism, are subjected to the same test. In the non-Christian world the question is universal : are the huge traditional systems of religion and life still to be utilized for the great dynamic purposes of cultural reconstruction and national rejuvenation and consolidation ? To mention only a few instances—Turkey has for the present dismissed Islam as not being a serviceable instrument to realize its new vision of national life ; Japan manufactures for its national purposes a religious stimulus of its own, and follows a very complicated policy towards its other religious forces, a policy wholly inspired by the evaluation of their significance to the power of the nation and the State.

Summing up, we may be justified in concluding that the Christian Church in the West and in the East, despite the difference in background and history, is virtually confronted with the same fundamental problem : the relation to the world and all its spheres of life, and the same danger lest it solve it in the wrong way. For the different concrete conditions there will certainly be no one solution. But one demand universally emerges from the situation everywhere, that is, back to the recapturing of the vision of what God in Christ meant the Christian Community to be—a fellowship of believers, rooted in God and His divine redemptive order, and therefore committed to the service and the salvation of the world ; going to the bottom in its criticism of and opposition to the evil of the world, but at the same time going to the bottom in its identification with the sufferings and needs of the world.

CHAPTER II

WHITHER MISSIONS ?

IN this world of transition, confusion, antagonism, dis-integration and reconstruction the missionary enterprise of the Christian Church has to be accomplished. It is necessary to keep this constantly in mind in order to see things in the right perspective. The transitional character of the present time is particularly evident in the fact that, as never before, new extraordinarily militant world-conceptions, all deeply tinged with religious quality, force millions of men under their sway, claiming their absolute allegiance. They certainly will disappear, because they are the result of a spasmodic crisis of the mass-mind, sensing the spiritual abyss which mankind has approached through the dissolution and disintegration of the strong old foundations of life ; but just for that reason they are the clearest symptoms of turbulent transition. It is quite natural that the missionary enterprise should also be affected by the storm, and that in its ranks, at home as well as abroad, there should be confusion and a manifold cry for re-orientation and clarification. The coming World Conference at Madras in December 1938 will not achieve anything worth-while unless it achieves a deepened sense of direction and a renewed consciousness of the meaning and purpose of the Christian Mission in the world under *any* circumstances, whether quiet and evolutionary or turbulent and revolutionary.

It has become the custom to speak in tones of severe criticism and condemnation about the Christian Church and the way it has behaved in the midst of the process that is known as the rise of the modern world. The severest critics are not its enemies, but representatives of the Church itself. Both these phenomena, the severe condemnatory criticism and its being pronounced most trenchantly by

31

Christians themselves, are signs of health. They demonstrate that the prophetic spirit and the capacity for " dreaming dreams and seeing visions " has not left the Church. This fierce self-criticism is an indispensable life-necessity. To a shamefully high degree the Church, in the confusion of the times, has become confounded about its nature and mission. It has become a segment and reflection of modern society with all its respectabilities, entrenched interests, prejudices and hypocrisies, only in a somewhat more dignified while more antiquated manner, and often also in a vulgar bourgeois way. It has not been the clear witness and guide to the divine redemptive order of life for time and eternity that God has revealed in Jesus Christ our Lord ; but it has suffered itself to become mainly the refuge of people with " other-worldly " interests and needs. Even when in sundry movements and individuals it has evinced an acute sense of obligation toward its mission in the world, it has often gone astray because many of these movements and individuals found the clue of the situation in adjustment to the dominant philosophies and demands of the hour. The Christian Faith had to be justified before the tribunal of science and philosophy or to be reconciled to them. To harmonize Christian ideas with influential philosophies of the day was considered up-to-date and genuine interpretation of the Gospel. So-called pre-scientific elements of Christianity, among which belonged cardinal tenets of the faith, were readily sacrificed for the sake of being in tune with the time. Christian ethics, on account of the sincere desire to meet the situation, were subordinated to or expressed in terms of the dominant moral idealisms of personality as the highest good. Christian thought took up the attitude of defence. Before the overwhelming forces of the deluge of modern life this was not at all strange. The really weak point in the situation was that Christian thinking resigned itself to this defensive attitude and nearly lost the consciousness that the object of Christian faith and thought, the Gospel, is primarily announcement, proclamation of salvation and victory in the name of God and not in the name of cultural purposes or ideals. Orthodoxy fled before the storm behind the fortifications of creed and dogma, acting as the guardian of the spiritual credits of the Church, but lamentably prone to treat them as frozen credits, not as liquid ones.

Thus severe criticism is entirely justified. Nevertheless, there is another side to the picture. The history of Christian thought in the nineteenth and twentieth century is not only one of weak surrender and dilution, but also of honest integrity and creative profundity. Many endeavours towards adjustment to the conditions and needs of the time sprang from a deep desire to be " living epistles of Christ." Many a one recognized the spiritual tempest of the times as a much-needed purification of faith and life, so coming to know in a new fashion that " for those who love God all things are working together for good." Several cleansing revivals swept through the ranks of the Christian Church, and actualized that ethical passion, which is peculiar only to the ethics of Christianity, namely, the yearning desire, inflamed by the love of Christ, to pour out one's life for the benefit of the seemingly most hopeless and forlorn of men.

One of the most conspicuous signs that the Spirit of God continued to move in the Christian Church has been and is the modern missionary enterprise. Latourette in his book, *Missions To-morrow*, rightly calls attention to this fact in saying that " the missionary movement of the past century has been the most notable outpouring of life, in the main unselfish, in the service of alien peoples which the world has ever seen." Pearl Buck in *Fighting Angel*, which is a searching criticism of missions even to the degree of distortion, yet finds striking words of vindication for the older generation of missionaries, who are nowadays so often misrepresented as chiefly models of narrow-minded bigotry. Her pronouncement is worth quoting : " The early missionaries were born warriors and very great men, for in those days religion was still a banner, under which to fight. No weak or timid soul could sail the seas to foreign lands and defy death and danger unless he did carry religion as his banner under which even death would be a glorious end. To go forth, to cry out, to warn, to save others, these were frightful urgencies upon the soul already saved. There was a very madness of necessity, an agony of salvation." The missionary enterprise was and is and will be a work full of human faultiness, error, limitation and sin. It has constantly to place itself under the judgment of God, to expose itself to incessant self-criticism, and to remain sensitive to much justified and even to much unjustified criticism from outside. Otherwise it becomes tasteless salt, fit only to be thrown away and trodden on by the feet of men, for in this corrupt world the corruption of the best is the worst.

The fact stands, however, that the awakening since the eighteenth century of the missionary spirit in the Church is one of the most amazing movements in the history of the world. The Churches as official institutions have only gradually become aware of their essential missionary character. Even to-day only a minority of the membership consciously participate in this life-function of the Church. Individuals and groups of individuals, in the teeth of keen opposition or deadening indifference, were kindled to missionary activity by the imperative urge to translate into action, by word and deed, God's ever-active yearning for the salvation of the whole world. The apostolic consciousness of the Church which, as is evident from the most superficial perusal of the New Testament, is and must be one of its primary characteristics, had gone to sleep inside the crust of the all too creedal conception the Church had of its nature. In the missionary movement it broke through the fetters in which the Church was bound by its identification of itself with the idea of " Christendom," that is, the domain of Western " Christian " civilization. The Church conceived of itself almost exclusively as a body to conserve values and maintain a once-attained position. This static and worldly view was swept aside by the arising missionary movement with its prophetic and apostolic recapturing of the witnessing, militant and therefore suffering and triumphing Church. From the standpoint of world history this movement, especially in its formative period, is so amazing because it offers the unique spectacle of groups of men and women, many of them of lowly condition, who, gripped by the vision of Christ's universal Redemption and His Kingship of

life and the world, and moved by the idea of the Christless-
ness of the non-Christian world, marched forth to unknown
continents expecting great things from God and attempting
great things for Him. To them it was no human heroism, but
the simple and joyful obedience of faith. No other religion
offers a parallel to this overwhelming compassion and
solicitude for distant and utterly foreign fellow-creatures
which has manifested itself for generations in the sustained
prayer and giving of the missionary church at home, and in
the obedience to the call of those who went abroad. All the
common human admixtures of romanticism, love for adventure
or for the exotic, and the subconscious desire for self-realization, do not wipe out the fact that this movement drew and
draws its inspiration from the vision of " the city which hath
foundations, whose maker and builder is God." Most
people will call this a fiction, with contempt or with some
admiration. They cannot do otherwise, because this " city "
can only be discerned by the eye of faith, and is revealed to
the human mind by the action of divine grace.

The missionary movement began its course, led by
simple faith and burning love, in an isolated world of
stagnant religions and civilizations. Moreover, it is not
sufficient to say that it was ignorant about this world in
which it acted ; it even approached it with a host of misconceptions and wrong notions. It had a very chequered
and unexpected career. It went through high hopes, deep
disillusionments and triumphant successes. At present the
Christian Church, although everywhere in greater or
smaller degree a minority and grievously divided into
sectional groups, is planted in all the continents and seas
of the globe. For the first time in its history the Christian
Church is in fact a world-wide community, a universal
Church. The missionary movement has been instrumental
to that purpose. Now the Church stands in the present
world in the face of an enormous and steadily growing task,
and at the same time puzzled and baffled by the complexity
of the situation. The swift movement of events and of outlook
can be gauged by comparing some important landmarks in
the history of missions in the last decades.

The Conference of Edinburgh in 1910 focused its chief attention on a strategical review of the whole mission field throughout the world. It was the first act of united and co-ordinated reconnoitring of the non-Christian world, accomplished by the concerted action of Protestant missions. It seemed as if the non-Christian world was spread out before the eye as a world to be conquered. It was not only the eye of faith, but also the eye of the Westerner, who subconsciously lived in the conviction that he could dispose of the destiny of the world, because the absorption of the Eastern by the Western world appeared to come inevitably. The Jerusalem Meeting in 1928 moves in a quite different atmosphere. The faith in the cause as such is firm as ever. However, the mood is more introspective and observant than strategical. Faith and natural Western self-confidence have become more differentiated by the purifying fire of reality and experience. The unequivocal disavowal at Jerusalem of all spiritual imperialism is one of the clearest symptoms of this change. The Laymen's Report was a reflex of the rapidly declining fervour of missionary interest at the home base, and an effort to present the missionary cause as the expression of the responsibility of the West towards the emergence of a new Eastern world by making its spiritual contribution in the shape of Christian service. As it announced itself as an endeavour to " rethink missions " and especially invited attention to its basic principles by the statement that the Report would stand or fall with its theology, it evoked heated discussions. Its theological position manifested a remarkable mixture of sincere devotion to the missionary cause as a Christian obligation with a very weak sense of apostolic consciousness.

These three instances suffice to show how rapid the change in reaction is in the present transitional world. The critical situation in which the missionary enterprise of the entire Christian Church, younger and older Churches included, finds itself outwardly and inwardly may be described as follows.

The call to the Church to missionary expression in the non-Christian world is more urgent than ever. From the standpoint of the Church and its essential nature and obliga-

tion towards God and the world it is always urgent. This
inherent urgency, however, may not always be applicable.
The concrete situation of the non-Christian world and of the
centres of Christian faith and life that have been the outcome of the missionary labours of the last 150 years all over
the non-Christian world make the application at present
self-evident. The unification of the world and the resultant
process of world-wide interpenetration in its material and
spiritual aspects, apparently tending to some kind of common
world-culture, create a quite new situation for the Christian
Church. The awareness of this new situation has been
apprehended by but a small group of thinking Christians.
It has not at all penetrated the mind of the Church, not even
in the ranks of its broader leadership. We may talk occasionally about a planetary world ; in reality, however, the
Christian Church as a whole continues to think in regional
terms. Those who have more intimate contact with the
missionary enterprise have an inkling of it, but even this
minority neither realize the implications of the alignment of
the political, economic and spiritual forces in the present
unified world, nor the significance that the existence of the
newly-founded Christian Churches and the radiating forces
of missionary activity in the non-Christian world have for
the Church of Christ as a whole. Unconsciously people live
on the deep-rooted assumption that missionary work is a
kind of colonizing activity of the Christian Church in foreign
parts. It finds its parallel and pattern in the political
thinking in the home countries of colonizing peoples. The
larger majority of those peoples persist in considering the
parts outside the home country as foreign, notwithstanding
the most striking evidences of the interdependence and
inter-relation of the different parts of the " Empire." So
mission fields, although, of course, connected with a host of
purer associations of religious and moral quality, involuntarily—this must be stressed, because it makes it all the more
important—take on in the mind the aspect of religious
colonies. The state of ecclesiastical independence and
autonomy to which many mission fields have now attained,
and the growing habit of speaking about indigenous Churches,

fortunately help to destroy this instinctive turn of thought that naturally arose in a past period when there was no unified world and when the results of missionary work were still meagre.

The new situation which emerges out of the unification of the world and the independent significance the indigenous Churches have in the universal Christian Church and its missionary enterprise, is far-reaching in its consequences for the future. The whole complex of religious and spiritual life in the large non-Christian world with all its possibilities will be no longer merely an object of study, curiosity or indifference ; it will have its share in the shaping of the spiritual life of mankind, and its influence on the course of the history of the Christian Church. *Mutatis mutandis*, one might say that the situation of the Christian Church in the world at large begins to resemble that in which it was placed in the world of the Roman Empire, in the midst of an official State-cult and a great mass of local cults and mystery-religions. The comparison must not be stressed too hard, because one of the most marked differences is the important fact that in all sorts of ways, perceptible and imperceptible, Christian influences for centuries have moulded the life and the outlook of the " Christian " world. Nevertheless, the comparison can do good service in guiding the imagination. Theosophy, Anthroposophy, Indian philosophical influence, the impression made by Tagore and Gandhi, etc., are some small portents of what may happen perhaps in the future on a wider scale. In the fields of philosophical speculation, of psychological analysis and penetration into uncharted depths of human consciousness—systematized, for instance, in the different forms of *yoga*—of religious expression, of art, to mention only these, the possible influences that may flow from the East through the world are not at all exhausted.

The existence of comparatively small but vigorous Christian Churches and of centres of radiating influence is a fact that is seriously to be taken account of in Africa and Asia. Christianity, and what it represents in its attitude towards life and its activities, is, despite its numerical smallness when compared with the hundreds of millions that still belong to the non-Christian religions, a recognized and influential factor in the life of Japan, China, India, Central and South Africa, to mention only the chief instances. This, of course, places a very heavy responsibility on these Christian Churches and groups in the East and in Africa. Not on them only, however, but also on the Christian Church at large, or the so-called older Churches. This is so for some obvious reasons.

The older Churches by their missionary initiative and activity are the parents of these Churches and the cause that Christianity in the non-Christian continents has established itself and has attained there to a position of new and great responsibility. Sheer loyalty to their own work should compel them in any case to cherish the achieved results and develop them. There are, however, still weightier reasons. The newly-founded Churches are the adult children of the older Churches. As parts of the universal Christian Church, and having to represent the Gospel, its gifts and its claims, in this turbulent non-Christian world so full of tensions and danger-situations for the Christian Church, they have an extremely difficult position and an arduous task. That task is fraught with the possibilities of ruin as well as of victory, because, humanly speaking, their numerical, material and spiritual strength is entirely inadequate to the demands of the situation. As the adult children of the older Churches they have a natural claim on the continuous brotherly interest of their parents. As particularly exposed parts of the Universal Christian Church they have a very urgent and special claim on the effective solidarity of the parent Churches that created this position for them. And finally, the new situation which arises out of the unification of the world and the responsible and influential place which the Christian Church occupies in the non-Christian world, strongly suggests that Church history apparently *will* and *must* be written in the future in the life-books of Africa and Asia, and that these new chapters will be of decisive importance for the life and the development of the Christian Church in its older domains.

Oscar Buck, in his stimulating book *Christianity Tested*,

expresses the same view in even such strong words as these : " It is in Asia—not in America, or Europe or Africa—that the future of the Christian religion will be determined, is being determined." This pointed expression serves remarkably well to impress upon the mind the startling novelty of the world situation in which the Christian Church has to steer its course. All the evidence, compressed in the foregoing line of reasoning, drives irresistibly to the conclusion *that the Christian Church is not at the end of its missionary enterprise in the non-Christian world, but just at the beginning. The independence and autonomy of the daughter-churches in the non-Christian world does not mean a gradual withdrawal of the missionary activity of the parent Churches. On the contrary, the fact that the Christian Church actually has become a world-wide community, the responsibility this involves, and the solidarity in faith and love and hope in which the older and younger Churches have been thereby bound together, point to the obligation of renewed missionary consecration and activity.*

SOME DOUBTS DISCUSSED

We have approached the point where it becomes necessary to direct an inquiring glance at the realities of the Church and of the missionary enterprise in its empirical background and results in order to compare these with the exigencies of the total world situation as outlined above. It has recently become a custom to insist upon " sober," " realistic " judgment. Deep disillusionment has naturally led man in the present day to cry for " realism." He has a dread of being deceived. This fear has in many cases, however, become such a strong emotion that the " sober," " realistic," " matter of fact " judgment is often apt to become a cynical or pessimistic judgment, although served up as " realistic," excluding all deceptive illusions. The " realism " that we really need is of a far deeper quality. It is a radically honest openness to total reality, which leads on to a plane different from mere optimism or pessimism or even a well-balanced equilibrium of both. As such it is an essentially Christian virtue. The Gospel itself, in the tension of its two paradoxical poles, is the example of divine realism, and therefore its teacher. Its divine realism is that it takes man and God radically and seriously : man in his high origin and destiny as well as in his utter corruption and frustration ; God in His radical rejection and condemnation of man, and in His never-weakening faith in and saving grace for man. Here we can learn the right and saving kind of realism that looks realities honestly in the face and exposes them to the light of the divine judgment. We learn from the Gospel that God is not to be treated as an appendix—usually a rather disconnected one—to our human reasonings and analyses, but as the all-pervading centre in total reality.

The realities of the Church and of the missionary enterprise in their present empirical background make a rather grave impression. One may legitimately say that the condition of the Church and its present position in the world seem to make it anything but properly equipped for renewed missionary consecration and activity. In great parts of the world the Church is beginning to be impeded in its liberty of decision and action to a degree that amounts to the impossibility of any action. The inestimable contribution of German Christianity to the great missionary enterprise is constantly in danger of being wiped out or so maimed as to reduce it to a very small fraction of what it has been.

In the countries where the liberty of action of the Churches is still safeguarded, an enormous work has still to be done in order to introduce the majority of the constituencies of the Church to a real grasp of the new situation of the Universal Christian Church in the present world ; especially to a grasp which springs from the intelligence of faith. For it goes without saying that the Church and missionary leaders of to-day cannot and may not resign themselves to the fact that, great comparatively as the missionary activity of the Church in the past may have been, the missionary cause is the cause of a decided minority in the Churches, and that only a part even of this minority shoulders its share in the missionary task with the real intelligence of real faith. They, the Church and its missionary leaders, may not and cannot resign themselves to this for two reasons. In the first place, because it is a life-interest of the first rank for the

Church itself to be really alive to its missionary obligation in the whole world—" Christian " and non-Christian—and to its fraternal privileges and obligations as a part of the one universal Christian Church. A Church which is not really alive to that is also largely ineffective and oblivious of its obligation in its own environment. The majority, not merely the minority, must get a real grasp of this vision, in order that the Church indeed may be a living body.

In the second place, the Church cannot accept this situation on account of some purely practical considerations. In a great part of the sending home countries, especially in the Anglo-Saxon countries which bear the bulk of the missionary task, a large amount of the money that has been put at the disposal of missions has come from large gifts of extremely wealthy individuals. Missions are, humanly speaking, deeply indebted to these large-hearted donors. Yet the full recognition of this fact may not blind us to the problem that this has not been a right foundation. The missionary cause, in the nature of the case, is the cause of the Church, not of a group of interested individuals. The financial crisis and the repercussion of the economic confusion, with their consequences for missionary giving, have had at any rate this beneficent result, that they have served as eye-openers to this situation. The lesson that we have learned, and that we have to work out in practice now, is to educate the membership of the Church in quite a new way as to its missionary vision and task. The task as it arises now out of the situation can only be done by the *entire* Church. An intensified accumulation of small and moderate gifts, coming from the total membership, must now become the material basis of the enterprise instead of a budget that was accustomed to lean so heavily on huge gifts. Practically speaking, as well as spiritually, it is the only sound foundation of the missionary enterprise. Practically speaking, because the times in which the huge gifts sustained a very substantial part of the missionary enterprise apparently belong to the past. From an essentially religious standpoint one might say, with all due recognition and gratitude, that this change is a fortunate one ; although this does not mean that, on account of a mechanical love of system, large gifts should now be excluded. The only basis on which to build the material foundation of the missionary task in the present time is the universal and regular contribution of the total membership. Upon this foundation only it can be built, because there is no other. Spiritually speaking, it is the only sound one, because only then does the missionary task become the natural and self-evident expression of the nature of the Church. Only then is the secret, deep-rooted conviction in the Christian world demolished, that the missionary enterprise—or to put it more correctly, the apostolic attitude towards the world around and far-away—is a special interest of a group of Christians with a special turn of mind, but not at all an ordinary attribute of the Christian life. At the same time it delivers missionary education and " propaganda" from an aspect which is secretly one of its great impediments, namely, the widespread conviction that the essential end of all missionary propaganda is to raise financial contributions. For when the missionary appeal does not aim, as is so often the case, at arousing the greatest possible amount of enthusiasm which issues in financial contributions, but is founded on the persistent reminder of the membership of the Church that it is invited to partake in the objective, God-given commission and mission of the Church and not simply to pour its enthusiasm and devotion into a good human cause, then the financial contribution becomes what it really ought to be : the expression of faith, love and hope. Missions are then serving the Church in a deeply spiritual manner.

This readjustment and re-orientation of missionary education is already under way, but one of the present features of the Christian Church and the missionary enterprise is that it is only in its incipient stage. This must be faced realistically. Everywhere through the missionary world there is a feverish questioning of missionary principles, methods and results. To a certain degree that has always been the case, because the foreignness of the world in which the work was done, insufficient experience and the failures and disappointments that attend all human work, made this indispensable. At present, however, that questioning is done on a far wider scale, partly from outward, partly from inward reasons. The colossal transition which now marks the life of the peoples of Africa and Asia necessitates a complete overhauling of missionary principles and methods. The disintegration of the primitive peoples ; the necessity to develop not only an " anthropology of change " but also a " missiology " of change ; the disastrous aspect the race problem increasingly assumes ; the quite new evolution in the forms of nationalism from a defensive to an aggressive and imperialistic form ; the complete change in the position and influence of missionary education and social work on account of the fact that the State everywhere takes the lead in these fields and dictates its policy ; the new tasks of reconstruction that in all African and Asiatic lands rise up before our generation : these are some of the outward reasons for drastic re-thinking and overhauling.

There is still another category of outward reasons, which are partly inward, calling for serious reflection. The problem of religious liberty is rapidly becoming a burning issue for Christianity and Christian missions. The liberty of religious opinion and of religious " propaganda " is going to be threatened all over the world. The argument used to restrict or even to strangle this liberty is invariably national consolidation. In some cases this need for national consolidation proceeds from the ardent nationalist desire to rebuild a new state and to make all powers and functions of national life subservient to this ideal, because in the midst of the many disintegrating tensions and forces which disrupt modern life concentration appears the command of the hour. In other cases it is not only the desire for rebuilding, but also for a powerful, commanding position in the world engendering the attitude that the State cannot suffer any institution that does not subordinate itself, soul and body, to the service and the glorification of the State, which is the ultimate end of life. The totalitarian States in East and West are examples of this type.

In the Islamic world either all propaganda of a " foreign " religion is forbidden, as in Turkey, or it is made ineffective by the rule that one is only allowed to remain what one is or to become a Moslem. Egypt has no clause for religious liberty on its Statute Book. In Iran the situation is uncertain and at times difficult. In Fleming's book, *Ethical Issues*, one can find an impressive array of facts on this subject. Cohesion and consolidation in political and social life is the regulative principle, and liberty of religious opinion and propaganda is conceded or withdrawn according as it is found in con- formity with or in contradiction of this principle. This tendency towards spasmodic national contraction is stirring virtually all over the world even in States and countries where the old political principle of religious liberty still stands. There are even signs in these countries that point to the possibility of alteration in this attitude. Much of the liberty still conceded under these regimes is given on the basis of the tacit assumption that the Church must strictly keep to its business, to preach and to serve as a centre of harmless edification.

A very noteworthy phenomenon, which is connected with this problem of liberty of religious expression and propaganda, is Gandhi's protest against conversion (i.e. against missions), because conversion is deemed to be " invading the sacredness of personality." This protest and the argument for it find a reverberation in the mind of many an Eastern and Western Christian, who, by the subtle relativism that pervades his whole religious outlook and by the noble desire to respect the religious life and personality of the adherents of other religions, has become very sensitive to this appeal. The chapter on the Aim and Scope of Missions in the Laymen's Report is a testimony to this condition of mind. Not only is the fact overlooked that the presupposition of the Gospel is the necessity of conversion for everyone—even the finest and the noblest personality— and that this is God's way really to " respect " personality, but also the fact is left entirely out of account that in reality Gandhi's motive is primarily nationalistic. Gandhi's notion about religions is that they are products of the national soil, *Swadeshi*-products, and that therefore it is incumbent on everyone to keep to his " national " religion. The universal character of real religion and the problem of truth are entirely disregarded in this conception, in which Gandhi comes dangerously near to the opinion of the adherents of the blood-and-soil religion. *Bien étonnés de se trouver ensembles.*[1]

A very important outward reason for a reconsideration of missionary principles and methods is the resurgence of the great non-Christian religions. Everywhere, in Islam, Buddhism, Hinduism, Sikhism, etc., there is manifest in the Eastern world to-day, along with the general national revitalization, a movement towards a heightening of religious group consciousness, embodying itself in movements for reform, reorganization, propaganda, consolidation and concerted opposition to Christian missions. In discussing the present condition of the non-Christian religions we shall have occasion repeatedly to draw attention to these facts.

The inward reasons for a reconsideration of the Christian mission are, of course, subtler and deeper. In Germany the deep experiences of the World War and what followed in its wake and the vigorous theological revolution have issued in a radical re-thinking of missionary principles and methods. Its general trend is a deepened Christian self-consciousness, a fundamental break with all thinking that takes its standard of reference from evolutionary principles or from the leading ideas of comparative religion. At the same time, naturally deeply affected by the spiritual and national revolution in Germany, it treats with unusual thoroughness the problems which are enshrined in the existence of the non-Christian religions and in the real nature of communal life and its specific forms of expression and ethos.

In America, which takes a large share in the world-wide missionary enterprise at home and abroad, the scene is much more confusing. The relativistic spirit of a Christianity which in the case of thousands of people is all too much assimilated to a humanistic conception of life undermines the missionary understanding of Christianity. If it were not for the fact that the American temperament, for natural and historical reasons, is youthfully aggressive and prone to a crusading type of idealism, the missionary tempera-

[1] Translation : Very much surprised to find themselves in the same company.

ture in the Churches of America would be still lower than it is. To be sure, there is to be observed a turning away from the roads of subjectivistic idealism and an expectant returning to the bed-rock verities of historic Christianity. The rank and file in the Churches, however, are wholly at sea about the Christian faith and the Christian obligation to the world. An all-pervading pragmatist attitude, which naïvely takes the practically-demonstrated value of a certain attitude in life as the standard of reference for truth, naturally causes a very diluted conception of what religion and Christianity really are. This is the more easily so because the religious and moral quality of life of many of those who think in this line is strikingly pure and noble and is still emotionally centred around the Personality of Jesus Christ. However, if there should not occur in the future a real re-discovery of Biblical Christianity, the next generation certainly will lack this emotional connection with the realm of Christian faith and worship, and become definitely unchristian and anti-christian.

The activistic and optimistic trend of the American character is the legitimate and natural outcome of one of the elementary facts in American history. America practically was an unoccupied country that had to be conquered and subdued by the discipline of the combined efforts of the human intellect and the human will. Besides others, not to be treated here, this has been one of the chief causes why the American conception of the missionary task has always been deeply tinged by the spirit of conquest and reform. Missions meant the specially Christian endeavour for the transformation of life into a kingdom of righteousness. Expressions such as—the Christianizing of the political and social order, the realization of the Kingdom of God, the marshalling of all the forces of goodwill for the benefit of inaugurating a new world-order in which war, inequality, race-prejudice and despotism are crushed out and righteousness and progress shall reign, easily therefore became equivalents for the missionary purpose. The non-Christian religions gradually assumed more and more the aspect of real or potential allies in this glorious crusade, and lost the aspect of domains of life outside Christ and His Revelation which had to be claimed for Him and to be brought to exclusive surrender to Him.

The international missionary discussions in which this missionary ideal came to grips with the more fundamentally Christian position of the continental missionary people, resulted more often in the strengthening of this attitude than in the reverse. For special historical reasons and by way of reaction, the continental attitude was set in such an exaggerated mood of quietist and pessimistic approach to the problems of the social and international order that the Anglo-Saxon mind strongly and justly suspected there a derailment in the field of Christian ethics.

This same activistic, optimistic idealism became one of the chief causes of a deep disappointment in the value and truth of the Christian religion. As D. J. Fleming has expressed it in *The Church through Half a Century*, in the last ten years there developed " a deep discontent with the achievements of Christianity itself in dealing with social, economic and international relations, which weakened the sense of Christianity's value to the world." Unawares the aim of missions had become this worldly reform. This ideal collapsed before the stern atrocious realities of the present world. " Christianity " as it was conceived proved a weak reed and not an invincible sword in the holy war for world reconstruction. The subversion of Christianity into a noble this-worldly idealism blocked the entrance to the only position where its unassailable truth and eternal strength could be vindicated. This position is the really Christian conception of the Kingdom as that is to be found in the New Testament in its entirety, and not in a misinterpreted Sermon on the Mount. The Kingdom is there the undying and infallible hope of the Christian and a reality that works already in many manifest and latent ways in the Community of Christ, but it can never be the direct object and achievement of our labours, because it is in the hand of the Father. The vision of it and the actual participation in it through the ever-active work of the Holy Spirit inspire men to go out into the world in order to claim it for

Christ and His divine, saving and regenerating order of life ; but if the claim is ignored the messenger is not disillusioned or broken, but goes on indefatigably, loyal to his prime duty to be God's obedient servant, whether there are results or not. Of course he is fully alive to the importance of " success " or " results," but neither successes nor the realization of self-defined programmes are the standard for his missionary perseverance. This standard is only the apostolic obligation towards God and the world, which is implied in the fact that God sent Jesus Christ into the world as the Way, the Truth and the Life. The failure to realize this is, it seems to me, the background of the Laymen's Report and the essential cause of the confusion in American missionary thinking.

Other inward reasons for the present questioning of missionary principles and methods are the disappointment about the meagre results that apparently have been achieved in the field of the naturalization and indigenization of Christianity, combined with the general feeling that these problems ask very urgently for a solution. Finally, to finish this incomplete list of burning problems, the autonomy and independence of the indigenous Churches have created a new situation, in which theological problems, questions of building up real Church life and the problem of the unity of the Churches are becoming far more prominent than ever before.

Surveying this whole situation in the present missionary world it is not to be marvelled at that many voices are heard affirming that, viewed on the whole, the progress of the colossal missionary effort of the last 150 years is disappointing and that this is due to wrong methods and wrong purposes. The recent and important discussions about group-conversion ; the search for new missionary motivations, such as " sharing religious experience " ; Oscar Buck's interesting book, *Christianity Tested*, in which he tries to answer the questions why Christianity has worked miracles in Asia in moral and social respects, and yet as a religion is generally neglected even by Asia's best representatives, and how the Christian Message may be made " so comprehensible to the non-Christian that there is left no room within him for hostility based upon misapprehension " ; the many books that are written to defend or re-interpret missions—all these and many more are indications of a searching spirit or of disappointment, though combined with an unwavering belief in the rightness of the cause and the obligation to Christian action and religious expression in the non-Christian world.   The need to re-think the approach of Christianity to the non-Christian systems of life has therefore become widely realized.

.   .   .   .

Is the progress of Christianity in the non-Christian world, with all recognition of the achieved results, justly called disappointing ?   Naturally such a question can be answered in the main only in a subjective way.   It is possible to contend that the results are disappointing and that they are amazing, and in both statements there is a great deal of truth.

I will attempt here to give shortly some brief answer because it affords an opportunity to lay bare some essential features of the present situation.

In the first place, then, to avoid a too unbalanced attitude, we must keep in mind that the modern spirit of continuous critical investigation and review and the methodical application of it, enormously facilitated by the modern technical means to get a co-ordinated survey of the world, incite to more frequent endeavours for fact-finding and appraisal than formerly could be the case.   This has its great advantages that should be utilized constantly.   But it easily causes us to forget such simple facts as, for example, that it took four centuries before Belgium, three centuries before the Frisians, and more before Germany were wholly " Christian-ized," despite the overwhelming cultural prestige and political preponderance which the Christian Church had in the Middle Ages as the continuator of the civilization of the Roman Empire.   Nor ought one to be blind to the fact that Islam, whose victorious power is always pointed out in comparison with Christianity, after ten centuries has not at all succeeded in removing Hinduism from its dominant place. Islam is still the religion of the minority in India, although it was, for centuries, politically paramount and exploited this position thoroughly for proselytizing ends. And Buddhism, for all its deep influence on the life of Eastern Asia, has in more than a thousand years not succeeded in supplanting the great indigenous conceptions of life in China and Japan. Confucianism, Taoism, Shinto, have remained powerful forces up to the present day.

Evidently the change of religious allegiance in great and self-conscious civilizations, which are embedded in a religious view of life that transcends the narrow tribal view of " primitive " religions, is a process of many centuries ; this is so in every case, and not only in the case of Christianity.

In the second place, as we have pointed out in the first chapter, Western penetration into Africa and Asia distinguishes itself from all previous occurrences of the same kind in history by the fact of the total and radical difference between the Eastern and Western world. Leaving aside the fact that the missionary urge of the Christian Church is the primary cause of the movement, and viewing the missionary movement from the standpoint of world history in the last two centuries, the missionary movement has to be taken as one of the many aspects of Western penetration. As such it entered an utterly foreign world, of whose foundations and intricacies it had no notion whatever. Properly speaking, it had only wrong notions and misconceptions. With a characteristically individualistic conception of religious life it met a world in which religion was only understood as a communal affair. This disregard of the communal conception of religion in the East was not only the natural consequence of the fact that the essentially Christian conception is wholly contradictory to that involved in the communal conception in the East. It was as much, or perhaps still more, in most cases an expression of modern individualism, which is entirely different from the personalistic attitude which is to be found in the Bible. It took a very long time to awaken men to the importance of this basic fact and of the conclusions that have to be derived therefrom for the manner of approach, of method of work, of treating converts and building up a Christian community. It is no exaggeration to say that we are only beginning to learn this lesson.

In its evangelistic fervour the missionary movement did not realize in the least that it had to do not with individuals, who as human beings simply were placed before the alternative to answer positively or negatively to the Message and the appeal of the Gospel and act accordingly, but with societies and highly integrated forms of life, having through their great antiquity an unquestioned authority and command over the life of these individuals. Even at present the insight is but slowly dawning on most minds that the great and ancient civilizations of the East in which missions are at work are solid blocks of social and spiritual life of extraordinary strength and tenacity. In the eighteenth and nineteenth centuries, the early period of modern missions, they were even more than that, namely, huge systems of organized and religiously-sanctioned conservatism and immutability. Besides, the people which lived under the unbroken sway of these systems were just then in a period of increasing fossilization, whilst the currents of their creative energy were deeply hidden. It required the highly explosive strength and the concentrated effort of Western penetration to destroy this placidity. The West, being itself in a period of continuous and creative change, drunk with its own love of initiative and progress, was not in the right psychological mood to see through this strange world. Therefore, not only had missions to take a long time in getting the right angle of view, but the entire West in all its activities, as, for example, political administration and economic exploitation, slowly learnt its lesson and is still learning.

One is justified, therefore, in concluding that the modern missionary enterprise must also be seen as a period in which there had to be developed the eyes to see clearly, the ears to hear well, and the tongue to speak rightly. To put it in a more homely fashion, the past period of missionary work has been one of learning the "job." The real meeting between Christianity and the Eastern systems of life has not yet taken place, and is still a matter of the future. All the work that has been done is preliminary, and nobody can tell how long this stage will last. This enormous spiritual distance between the agent and the object of missions, as just indicated, has been a retarding factor of great significance. However, there were many others, especially when this period of missionary activity of the Christian Church is compared with previous periods.

History teaches unequivocally that the change in religious belief of whole peoples and civilizations is not and cannot be, in this complicated world of still more complicated human beings, the pure result of religious and moral persuasion alone. Religious life, institutions and aspirations being inextricably intertwined with all the other domains of life, with religious change it is the same. Political, cultural, and economic factors and motives, either consciously or unconsciously, have always played a very influential rôle in the process of religious change. In the history of all great religions, at the crucial moment political decisions and occurrences always turned the scales of religious change in a definite direction. Constantine's world-historical turnover in 312, the decisions of West European kings and popular assemblies in the Middle Ages, the acceptance of Islam by the Mongolian peoples, the introduction of Buddhism into Japan under Prince Shokotu, the Japanese and Buddhist "Constantine," are some very conspicuous examples. This implies that it is always *mass-conversion* which raises a religion in a certain period from the status of a conviction of many scattered individuals or various groups to that of the recognized, formative agency of the religious and cultural life of a whole nation or group of nations. It is this last objective that all people have consciously or unconsciously in their minds when they speak about the efforts of missions for the Christianization or evangelization of the non-Christian world and of their apparently disappointing results.

Roman Catholic Missions in India during the period of Portuguese-Spanish colonization and in Japan in the sixteenth century consciously took this lesson of history to heart and made it the guiding principle of their work. They thereby outwitted history, because what in history in most

cases was a normal consequence of long-range development became in this case political coercion, consciously
applied with all the means that could be used. A glance
at the correspondence of Francis Xavier with Joâ III of
Portugal affords ample evidence. This conscious and
methodical application of a lesson of history was, it is interesting to note, an adulteration of the usual historical process.
The outstanding aspect of the course of events, as can be
observed in the great historical instances of mass-conversion
—which means the decisive acceptance by a whole nation
of a definite religion as its spiritual home—is that the change
occurred, fundamentally speaking, as the largely natural,
and not the artificial, outcome of the co-operation of political,
cultural and religious motives.

How utterly different in the modern missionary period
are both the objective position and the subjective attitude
of Protestant missions ! As already mentioned, Protestant
missions spurned all consideration for the communal understanding of religion in the Orient. The situation was in
some measure similar to that of the Church in the first
centuries, when all extension of the faith occurred through
individual conversion, and when the stubborn opponent the
Church had to meet was communal religion in various
forms. In some measure only, because the great difference
is that the Christians in the first centuries were children of
their own environment, learning to express their faith by
conflict and commingling with this environment ; whereas
the modern missionary is a foreigner, bringing Christianity
in a very definite form which was a product of a long and
complicated historical development.

The Christian faith and Western civilization in the
nineteenth century had a much more complicated and subtle
relation to each other than had Christianity and civilization
in the Middle Ages. In the mediæval period Christianity
and civilization were co-terminous, because the communal
conception of religion then prevailed. Christianity, so to
speak, was then inescapable. In the modern period Christianity and autonomous Western civilization have virtually
separated. This departmentalization of the religious and

the other spheres of life, which is typical for the modern West, was very confusing for the mind of the East, which only knows of a communal conception of religion. Christianity impressed the East not only as a foreign religion, but also as a very strange religion. It was the religion of the Westerners and yet the foreign " Christian " Governments sedulously strove to emphasize their detachment from it, and the average European in the East seemed indifferent or hostile to Christianity !

This divorce of Christianity from the State and Community, and the ensuing secularization of life and hostility to Christianity, were all intelligible to the observer of Western history, but not to the Eastern mind. The effect was that modern missions had to work in an atmosphere and under conditions entirely different from what has been known in previous periods. To be sure, there was a period when Christianity, progress and the seemingly victorious power of Western civilization were identified by missionaries as well as by Eastern onlookers. This period lasted, however, only a short time. Christianity counted as the hidden source of Western power and success. World events saw to the collapse of this fallacy, but missions and Christianity share heavily in the discrediting of Western civilization, just because of this identification.

The divorce of religion from other spheres of life involves also the fact that the political powers which emanated from the " Christian " West did not and could not behave as the exponents of a unified civilization, that was universally the case in the West till the modern age, and always has been and still is the deeply-ingrained life-pattern of the East. This new fact finds its expression in the policy of neutrality, the only possible policy for the modern autonomous State, and also the only sensible policy in countries with many religions. Yet, in practice it often means a cold and over-prudent reserve, which confuses the mind of the average Easterner, who, being himself still a member of a unified world, does not understand this methodical differentiation of spheres of life. It has put Christianity in an ambiguous position for the Eastern mind, and this ambiguity has worked repellently on the whole. Yet, on the other hand, just because of his natural inclination to treat life as a unified whole, the average Easterner persists in identifying Christianity and Western civilization. To become a Christian means to his mind to become a European, and this idea, too, works repellently, because he feels it is contradictory to the laws of nature and history for him to do so.

Many volumes have been written about the successive endeavours to spread Christianity in Asia (Nestorian missions, the different missionary undertakings of the Roman Catholic Church in India, China and Japan from the sixteenth till the eighteenth century), with the question in mind—Why did they not succeed? Many writers, especially those who are not personally interested in Christianity, have confidently offered as the solution that the Eastern mind is constitutionally disinclined to accept Christianity and therefore never will. Many missionary writers tend to make a too-lenient syncretistic missionary method responsible for the many abortive endeavours, especially that of the Nestorians and the Jesuit missions in China in the seventeenth and eighteenth century. About Nestorian missions we know far too little to hazard such assured opinions. Moreover, what is considered in the case of Nestorian missions the reason of their failure is by many writers adduced as the reason of the success of Buddhism. It is much more probable that political reasons have been the main cause, as certainly is the case with the Jesuit missions. We have no room here to discuss this important and complicated question and have to restrict ourselves to a few remarks.

Both answers appear to be over-simplifying the problem. It is not alone the Eastern mind that is constitutionally disinclined to accept the Gospel, but the human mind everywhere; because the Gospel is " a stumbling-block to the Jews " and " foolishness to the Gentiles," that is, to all mankind. And the process of Christianization is far too vast a thing to admit of one cause, such as syncretism, explaining its frustration.

Yet, the problem of the reaction of the great Eastern civilizations to Christianity poses itself imperiously, because it enables us to take a more intelligent, long view of the missionary enterprise. In this connection it is essential to make the following observations. The three great Eastern civilizations of China, Japan and India have manifested through all the ages a truly remarkable toughness, self-consciousness and a consistent tendency to remain true to their original type. The strongest evidence of this phenomenon we have mentioned already in alluding to the minority position of Islam in the midst of a Hindu environment— the only instance in the history of Islam of a country that had to accept the political domination of Islam but refused its religious domination—and to the peculiar way in which China and Japan assimilated Buddhism without giving up their allegiance to their indigenous conceptions of life and the world. The tempestuous process of Western penetration apparently is met also by the same fundamental mood and attitude of determination to remain true to type, to assimilate and yet to remain itself. R. Kjellèn, the great Swedish political philosopher, has shrewdly remarked that China and especially Japan, despite all Westernization, probably ultimately will not really amalgamate with Western culture but will use it to provide its changeless spiritual type with a new " coat of armour." Precarious as such speculations may be, the obstinate tendency to remain true to the original type certainly is an evident characteristic of these great civilizations and helps much in understanding the breathless struggle that has to be fought in order to win these worlds for Christ. The deepest reason of this obstinate tendency we shall analyse at another point.

This whole discussion strongly suggests the following considerations. Having regard to the peculiar conditions under which modern missions are labouring and the false tracks that have been followed through ignorance and blindness, the results are in many respects amazing. Unlike all previous missionary periods in the history of the Church— with the exception of the first centuries of Church history— missions have to work now by purely religious and moral persuasion. And again, unlike all previous periods, that of the Primitive Church included, Christianity has to be planted in a cultural world of an unparalleled continuous longevity and radically different from the cultural world in which Christianity originally grew up and became the dominant religion of the West. Christianity took its first steps in a world of which it was, historically speaking, the offspring. In the Middle Ages it established itself as the religion of Europe, representing at once superior religion and superior culture for the peoples of Europe. In the modern missionary period, for the first time in Church history, it sets out upon an entirely new adventure, that of leaving the cultural sphere, in which it rose and along with which it developed to what it is now in all its various aspects, and entering that peculiar spiritual hemisphere of mankind which has been the exclusive and characteristic creation of the Eastern mind. Finally, unlike what happened in the Christianization of Europe, modern missions do not aim at planting Christianity by identifying religion and community. The Christianization of Europe meant the building up of the *Corpus Christianum* in which State, Church and Community became identified. The dissolution of this *Corpus Christianum* and the chastening lessons which the Christians of the modern age have learnt thereby have made this a deflated ideal. And even if it had remained the ideal, the modern divorce of " Church " and " State," that in different degrees is maintained in the modern States in West and East, would make it impossible. The real motive, however, of working on the assumption of the non-identification of Church and community is that the Church must be a community in which faith, worship and life are not expressions of " custom," but in which the truth revealed in Christ is the criterion of faith and life, transcending all other criteria and authorities. This inevitably leads continually to conflicts with the general communal attitude towards religion in the East. Because Christianity has always, when there is a conflict, to urge the pre-eminence of loyalty to religious truth above loyalty to the rules and requirements of the community, it necessarily acts as a disturbing element in ordinary Eastern life. This well-considered purpose of modern missions to plant a Church that lives in and with the community, but which is always distinct from it by its inward autonomy which again is founded on obedience to God, is one of its peculiar characteristics.

The situation in which modern missions have to perform their task may therefore justly be called without parallel.

CONCLUSIONS

To work by purely religious and moral persuasion is, as we have seen, from the standpoint of history a comparatively new aspect of the missionary enterprise. To the Christian and missionary mind of to-day it has become a self-evident maxim and ought to continue to be so. Starting from this maxim and reminding ourselves of the different aspects of the missionary situation as discussed in this chapter, what conclusion can be drawn ?

This seems to be the same conclusion which crops up from the consideration of the situation of the Church in the storm of modern life. Back to fundamentals ! Surveying the missionary problem at the home base and in the field all indications point in one direction : the call to consecrate ourselves anew to the great missionary task by fundamental re-thinking of missionary principles and methods, enlightened by past failures and successes, drawing support from what deepened knowledge through modern research can teach us, but above all re-discovering the true missionary motive and purpose.

The whole trend of development, one discovers with awe, seems to confront the missionary movement with its original missionary motive, that is, the certitude of having the apostolic obligation towards the world of witnessing to Christ and His new Kingdom. For all subsidiary arguments or motives, that have often usurped practically the place of the primary motive, are smitten to pieces under the hammer of the times. Recommending Christianity as the bringer of enlightenment and freedom, as a capital national and social tonic to make powerful nations, as the infallible guide to progress, has come to naught. It has even proved a great danger, because it rouses expectations and offers promises which often will not be fulfilled, and therefore necessarily entails disillusionment. Enlightenment may lead as well to freedom of the spirit as to sceptical relativism. China and Japan know that there are other very fertile sources from which to draw strength for nation-building. The spell of the erroneous identification of Christianity and the progressive West is broken, and, still deadlier, the prestige of Western culture has decreased enormously. To promise that Christianity will dispel economic misery and social disturbance is to invite inevitable disillusionment, because economic misery and social disturbance are caused and cured by many factors entirely outside the control of Church or missions. Sharing religious experiences, even service to men, "christianizing" the social, economic and political order, although necessarily included in the living act of manifold missionary expression, cannot be the real motive and ultimate purpose. The real motive and ultimate purpose are not founded in anything that men or civilizations or societies call for. As Kagawa has said, the starting-point of missions is the divine commission to proclaim the Lordship of Christ over all life ; and therefore a return to the pristine enthusiasm for evangelism and a new vision of what this implies in word and deed in the present complicated world are needed.

This leads us to the question, What is the Christian faith ? For a crisis of missions is a crisis of faith.

CHAPTER III

THE CHRISTIAN FAITH AND THE CHRISTIAN ETHIC

IN the midst of the cataclysmic events of the modern world
and the meeting with the great non-Christian religions
in their state of partial disintegration and partial reconstruction, the Christian Church needs a clear consciousness
of its faith. A translation of this faith and its rich content
in relation to the present condition of the world and of men
in their various settings is one great need of the hour.
However urgent and important this translation may be in
order that the Church may really speak to the man of to-day,
it is still more urgent and important for the Church to know
its original faith. A faithful and compelling translation is
only possible through a vital knowledge of the original.
This is especially the case with the Christian faith, because
in its real substance it does not go back to a connected
series of religious and moral ideas, such as a theistic and
personalistic conception of God or a pessimistic or optimistic
evaluation of the world, but to the revelation of a connected
series of divine acts. This revelation, this repeated divine
initiative has in the course of history engendered many ideas,
concepts and experiences that are subject to the vicissitudes
of ordinary human development ; but they are never
adequate to or to be identified with the revelation from which
they flow. The ideas and concepts are derivations from
and not the genuine content of this revelation. By the
nature of the case, this world of divine revelational acts
cannot be explained in terms of human evolution as ideas
that have developed, but can only be stated in the form of a
story. The only legitimate source from which to take our
knowledge of the Christian faith in its real substance is the
Bible. Therefore to the Bible we will turn, because there
the witness of the prophets and the apostles is to be found on

which the Church is built. In addition to this fundamental reason for turning to the Bible there is still another one, founded in the modern situation. One of the greatest blessings in disguise that has come to the Christian Church in the last hundred years is the searching and critical investigation to which the Christian faith and the Christian ethic have been subjected by friend and foe. Their historical setting, their validity, their truth, their uniqueness have been the objects of assiduous research and attack, springing from the quest for truth, honest doubt, profound or ill-advised attempts for defence, complete misunderstanding or outspoken enmity. It can confidently be asserted that never before in the history of mankind has a religion been exposed to such a relentless procedure of analysis, comparison and testing as Christianity has in the last centuries. This procedure is still going on. The Christian faith has been summoned before the tribunal of reason and history and has been tested severely. Many efforts have been made and are still made to insert it in the great immanent process of human creativity in the field of religion ; for it can be safely said that all investigations in the origins of Christianity, all endeavours to explain it as the outcome of religious development in the Jewish and Hellenistic world and to demonstrate its kinship to the mystery-religions, aim at making Christianity the result of the immanent process of history. It is one of the most fascinating things to notice that Christianity, the religion of revelation, constantly eludes these endeavours. Deepened investigation tends to reveal more and more not only its originality but also its refractoriness to this reducing treatment. The origins of Christianity are irreducible.

The blessing in disguise that we have alluded to is the fact that through the impact of this crucial searching the Christian Church has been forced more deeply than ever before to delve into the treasures that have been entrusted to it. A deeper and purer awareness of the peculiar character and object of the Christian faith has been the result. In regard to other religions, the same critical method of investigation and of disinterested understanding has developed the attitude that the only way to understand these religions

and to be just to them is to take them according to their
peculiar fundamental motives and meaning. This rule
applies also to the Christian faith, and this naturally leads
again to the Bible as the source of the most valid answer to
the question, What is the Christian faith ?

To be an honest and open-minded reader of the Bible is
not so easy a matter as it seems. The reason for this is
obviously that the religious and moral universe which we
enter in the Bible is radically different from what we meet
anywhere else and also from our natural habits of thinking,
even our so-called " Christian " thinking. The peculiar
character of the Bible is that it is radically religious. We
need constantly to remind ourselves of this as this is really
very unusual. The Bible is also intensely ethical ; but it
is more an indication of our modern propensities and habits
of thought and feeling than of our clear-sightedness if we
constantly stress the highly ethical character and motivation
of the Bible. The ethical is always in the Bible submerged
in, derived from, and subordinated to, the religious, because
the Bible is radically theocentric. God, His holy Will, His
acts, His love, His judgment, is the beginning and the end of
all. Man and the world are brought in direct, immediate
relation to this God, who always takes the initiative. Strictly
speaking, not only at the beginning but in all cases and
circumstances He is and remains the Creator ; that is, the
eternal initiative-taker, because He is really God. That is
something wholly different from an Ultimate Cause or
Ground of Existence. In calling the Bible a radically theocentric book, we simply mean to say that the Bible takes in a
radically serious fashion the fact that God is God, that He
is the Absolute Sovereign and the only rightful Lord, with
all the consequences that are implied herein for the world,
human life and the position of man. In this point consist
the originality and uniqueness of the Bible ; also its perennial
strangeness and newness to us, however intimate we may be
with it. Real contact with the Bible mean a constantly-
recurring process of conversion of our " normal " thinking
and judgment. The Bible protests its revelational character
by the fact that everyone who reads it with the eyes of faith

continuously makes the experience that it again and again is a new revelation to him. It is a book of infinite spiritual discovery.

The trend of our " normal " thinking is to treat the Bible as an embodiment of universal and sublime truths and ideals. Although we know that Christianity is a religion and intends to be that and nothing else, we are constantly prone to present it as a specimen of religious or moral philosophy. We are constantly preoccupied with endeavours to bend the Christian faith and its content to the ways and structures of rational coherent thinking. This craving in man for rational coherence is natural and legitimate, but the intention to provide the Christian faith in this way with an adequate organ of expression is fallacious. A rationally coherent system of thought is the legitimate but perennially elusive object of philosophy. The Christian faith is indifferent to rational coherence in this philosophical sense, not because it is incoherent or necessarily irrational, but because, as the divine order of life revealed in Jesus Christ, it has a coherence and rationality of a quite different order, and is therefore, when formulated in the terms of a definite philosophy, only partly expressed and for a part strangled or distorted.

The Bible offers no religious or moral philosophy, not even a theistic or Christocentric one. It is rebellious against all endeavours to reduce it to a body of truths and ideals about the personality of God, the infinite value of man, the source of ethical inspiration. To be sure, a personal God, the infinite value of man, the call to a life of never-relaxing devotion to high purposes and therefore a theistic conception of God, a deeply-personalistic idea of man and a vigorous ethos, are conceptions and ideas *derived* from the Bible and the Christian faith, and as such have their great significance. It is, however, an adulteration of the concrete and radical religious realism of the Bible and the Christian faith to take these derivations as the essential and abiding invariables of the Gospel. This intense religious realism of the Bible proclaims and asserts realities. It does not intend to present a " world view," but it challenges man in his *total* being to confront himself with these realities and accordingly take decisions. It does not ask for agreement with world- and life-views, not even with " Christian " views of life and the world. Pascal, that acute and great mind, discovered the revolutionary and revealing character of this Biblical realism in the night of his conversion. In his famous " Mémorial," written down in that night, he says : " Dieu ! Dieu d'Abraham, d'Isaac et de Jacob ! Dieu de Jésus Christ, non des philosophes ou des savants," [1] and Pascal knew what he was talking about, as he is admittedly known as one of the most brilliant philosophical and scholarly minds that have ever appeared in human history. It could not be better expressed that the essential message and content of the Bible is always the Living, eternally-active God, the indubitable Reality, from whom, by whom and to whom all things are.

Nor is the Christian faith a specimen of theology. The radically religious character of the Bible and of the Christian faith, the Biblical realism we alluded to, rebel against that also. Of course, just as philosophy is a natural and therefore inevitable and legitimate concern of the human mind, so is theology. It is indispensable for the Christian Church. Yet theology is a treatment of the data of the Christian faith and the Biblical revelation, tending by nature to a greater or lesser degree of rationalization. The Bible in its direct, intense realism presents no theology. It presents the witness of prophets and apostles.

Even the Apostle Paul, surely the profoundest and greatest theologian the world has ever seen, cannot appro- priately be characterized as the creator of a theology. His legacy is too rich for that. The most elaborate ex- positions or the seemingly most simple ethical exhortations in his letters are always the outcome of the thinking of a man who is apostle, missionary, pastor of souls and theological thinker in indissoluble unity. He does not try to systematize or to produce rational coherence ; but with a singular sensitivity, born of a deep apostolic consciousness, he

---

[1] " God ! The God of Abraham, Isaac and Jacob ! The God of Jesus Christ ! *Not* the God of the philosophers and the scholars ! "

registers, describes and witnesses to God's creative and redemptive dealing with man and the world. His sweep and structure of thinking manifest a peculiar religious and moral logic of imposing consistency. This radically religious way of thinking, this Biblical realism in St Paul, is the reason why he is so inexhaustibly rich, paradoxically combining religious and ethical view-points that defy " normal " rational thinking, even " normal " religious thinking. Yet in the realm of the new life in Christ, they impress the mind with the force of sheer religious logic. The deeper one penetrates into his world of thought, the more one becomes impressed by the fact that this radical religious realism does not mean extremist one-sidedness, but by its vital touch with the fundamental realities of divine life and human life evinces a sanity and balance of thought and discernment in comparison with which all philosophical and theological striving for equilibrium and rational coherence fade away. This religious realism is also the reason why all theologies, even the greatest, have been and are minor elaborations of some of St Paul's fundamental lines of thought. A real comprehensive elaboration of St Paul in his totality would presuppose the same intense religious apprehension which is the hall-mark of the apostolic and prophetic mind.

To take Biblical realism as the fundamental starting-point and criterion of all Christian and theological thinking exposes all problems to an unexpected and revealing light. A few illustrations may elucidate this.

In the discussion with other world-views and with the great religions, especially the mystical ones, there always crops up the problem of divine transcendence and immanence in relation to the world. To Biblical realism this problem is quite irrelevant. It springs from quite a different background, different either from that of pagan religious naturalism, in which it remains vague whether " God " and the " world " are ultimately one universal stream of life or whether they are distinct ; or from the background of religious philosophy, which always has some sort of religious monism as its starting-point. This religious monism ultimately is derived from the pagan religious naturalism just mentioned.

The mistake often made is that in discussing the question of God's transcendence and immanence in the Bible and in the Christian faith, one approaches it unconsciously from this entirely different naturalistic or philosophical background. The result is then always either a vindication of mystical elements and tendencies in Christianity or the effort to state a fairly satisfying concept of a God who is outside as well as inside the world and man. Virtually, however, it amounts to an adjustment of the Christian faith and its content to a quite different conception of life and the world, which serves as the standard of reference in the whole process. The Bible and the Christian faith know in their own characteristic and realistic way about transcendence and immanence. God is the sovereign Creator of the world and of man ; He is the Lord of history. This transcendence is not the derived transcendence of a divine essence (mark this unbiblical word) that essentially is a part of the entire world process, but is absolute, primary transcendence, founded on the fact of God's Godhead. God works in history and in man, speaks to him and in him, saves and regenerates him, communes with him and dwells in him through the Holy Spirit, invites him to a life of fellowship with Him. This essentially religious immanence is radically different from the concept of immanence as current in religious philosophy with its ontological colouring. It is the immanence of personal fellowship with and active participation in the life of the world and of man ; the fellowship of the Father, but the Father who is in *Heaven*. Hence an exposition of this Biblical realism is of greater advantage to the elucidation of the Christian faith than the inevitably abstract discussion of the relation of immanence and transcendence in God as commonly understood.

Another illustration is the problem of creation. The age-long conflict between philosophy and science and the religions of prophetic character has been with reference to the problem of creation. It is assumed that the characteristic conception of the Christian faith in regard to the origin of the universe is the *creatio ex nihilo*. This is a misconception, arising out of the neglect of Biblical realism. Again, the problem, Is the world eternal or created out of nothing? derives from the same background of religious naturalism as was mentioned in relation to the problem of transcendence and immanence. It found this peculiar setting in Greek philosophy, which in its fundamental presuppositions never has become emancipated from its original naturalistic starting-point. Biblical realism by its theocentric character, which relates everything directly to the living God who is fully and wholly God, is not interested in the *creatio ex nihilo* but in this, that the world and man have been created by God's *Will*. Not an abstract philosophical *creatio ex nihilo* dominates Christian faith and thought, but the holy, sovereign Will of God. Man, the world, nature, history are products and objects of God's Will. That is radically different from the problem of the eternity or non-eternity of the world as commonly stated, and that was in the Middle Ages one of the great points of contest between the scholastic theologians and the philosophers. By the nature of the case, the philosophical problem of the eternity or non-eternity of the world will perennially remain unsolved. The solution will always occur in one or the other direction according to some axiomatic presupposition one has about God. The realism of the Bible and the Christian faith, however, although freely witnessing to divine acts, decisions, purposes, leaves every metaphysical problem aside. It simply takes seriously, on account of a robust and sane intuition, the fact that God is God, and that if He is God, His Will is the Ground of all that is.

These two illustrations may suffice to make clear why a continuous confrontation with this Biblical realism is the best and safest way really to know what the Christian faith is, and to guarantee a theology which really does what its name implies, that is, tells a tale about God.

THE CHRISTIAN FAITH

As the Bible is religiously, and not metaphysically or philosophically or even theologically, interested, it has no theory about anything. It has therefore no theory about revelation. Yet revelation is the presupposition on which the prophetic and apostolic witness of the Bible is built. Therefore, something must be said about it.

Revelation as a formal concept is not at all an exclusive Christian idea or Biblical presupposition. It is a universal religious conception. All religions know about mysteries that have to be revealed and which cannot be known except through revelation. This is not made less true by the fact that the word revelation is so often used in a very loose and improper sense, when what is called revelation properly should go by the name of enlightenment, a sudden intuitive insight, a luminous idea, or knowledge about so-called occult facts. Revelation in its proper sense is what is by its nature inaccessible and *remains so, even when it is revealed.* The necessary correlate to the concept of revelation is therefore faith. It lies in the very nature of divine revelation that the only organ for apprehending it is faith ; and for the same reason faith, in this strictly religious sense, can only be appropriately defined as at the same time a divine gift and a human act.

The characteristic clearness and purity of the Christian conception of revelation become manifest just at this point. Nowhere has revelation been taken in such a radical and absolute manner as in the sphere of Biblical realism. Nowhere is it so radically true that " what no eye has ever seen, what no ear has ever heard, what never entered the mind of man, God has prepared all that for those who love Him. And God has revealed it to us by the Spirit, for the Spirit fathoms everything, even the depths of God " [1] (1 Cor. ii. 9, 10).

Nowhere has the inherent correlation between revelation as the act of God and faith as the corresponding organ of

[1] The quotations from Scripture are given according to Moffatt's translation, except when stated otherwise.

human apprehension and as the gift of God been grasped so fully. Nowhere is the genuine meaning of revelation maintained so consistently. When Peter confesses : " You are the Christ, the Son of the living God," Jesus answers : " You are a blessed man, Simon bar Jona, for it was my Father in heaven, not flesh and blood that revealed this to you " (St Matt. xvi. 16, 17). God was truly revealed in Jesus Christ, but at the same time He hid and disguised Himself in the man Jesus Christ. The universal revulsion from and protest against the Incarnation at all times is a clear indication of how completely hidden God's revelation remains from the natural eye of man. Neither flesh nor blood can reveal it, only God Himself. If flesh and blood could reveal it, then it would be no revelation, but human intuition or power of apprehension. The essential, absolutely unique feature in the revelation of God in Christ is that, contrary to all human conceptions, God's revelation is an offence to man. If we follow the usual way of human thinking, revelation of God is always represented as blissful. It certainly is, but the Bible sternly and unequivocally teaches that this bliss is hidden in the offensive guise of the Incarnation.

The Christian revelation testifies to the self-disclosure of God in Jesus Christ, the Crucified and Risen Lord, which is a " stumbling-block " to the Jew, " sheer folly " to the Gentiles, and only adorable and saving mystery to the eye of faith. Revelation in Christ is a free divine act of redemptive irruption into the life of man and of the world. This is an offence to man, because all philosophy, all idealistic religion, all consistent mystical religion, all moralism meet in one point. They constitute various endeavours for self-redemption, and instinctively reject the truth that God and God alone can work redemption.

God's revelation in Christ, according to Biblical realism, is therefore not only the revelation of God, but also of man. Man is revealed as a being who in his deepest instincts and desires wants to be god. The supreme expression of this fundamental conviction in man is to be found in the idea, so widely prevalent in diverse philosophies and religions, that God or the Eternal Mind comes to self-consciousness in man when he retires into the inner recesses of his being. The revelation of God in Christ the Crucified is therefore at the same time an act of divine salvation and of divine judgment. In the Cross, God reveals His loving heart, and through the same Cross man shows his blindness to God's revelation ; because natural man without exception refuses to recognize that the divine grace, as manifest in Christ, means the divine judgment on man. This is the stern teaching of Biblical realism. The heart of man may go out to the Christ of gentleness, humility and of miraculous help, but this does not necessarily imply that it recognizes Him as God meant Him to be, the Christ of *sinners*. Hence Paul said that the mysterious Wisdom of God has not been understood by the powers of this world, for " if they had, they never would have crucified the Lord of glory " (1 Cor. ii. 8). Nock in his book, *Conversion*, calls attention to the fact that amongst the Christians of the first centuries not the unique attractiveness of Jesus in the Synoptics, which is a one-sided modern interpretation of the Synoptics, but the superhuman divine Christ was always emphasized.

How difficult it is for the human mind to grasp the essential meaning of the Christian revelation appears from the many misinterpretations that have been put upon it. It is usually conceived in an intellectualistic way, as a special way to knowledge, as a communication of divine truth about different things, as an extraordinary form of epistemology. The knowledge man cannot attain by the powers of his own mind is acquired by revelation. This is a conception belonging in the non-Christian sphere, where the inherent correlation between revelation and faith is substituted by that between revelation and gnosis, and revelation becomes a supernaturally prolonged gnosis. The Roman Catholic Church has canonized this intellectualist and non-Christian conception in its doctrine about the natural order of religious facts which the human mind has acquired by its strenuous efforts, and the supernatural order of truths which have come down to us from heaven. Faith then inevitably becomes the intellectual assent to a

series of " revealed " truths and propositions, and acquires
the character of a sacrifice of the intellect (*sacrificium in-
tellectus*). This intellectualist distortion of faith, which is
the besetting sin of all doctrinal orthodoxy, is the obvious
implication of the intellectualist conception of revelation,
and is one of the most disastrous misinterpretations of the
Christian faith. Its opponents are right if they contend that
it entails a blameworthy sacrifice of the intellect. They
are wrong in taking it as the expression of the meaning of
revelation in Biblical realism.

In the Gospel, however, revelation is always meant in a
radically religious sense, a tale about " the wonderful things
God has done " (Acts ii. 11) [1] which remain " wonderful "
and incomprehensible despite their being told. Therefore,
the other thing besides faith, inherently correlated to revelation, is witness. Christianity is in a very emphatic sense a
witnessing religion, because it is *the* religion of revelation
and faith. Witness, faith and revelation are indissolubly
connected. The one cannot exist without the other. A
body of " revealed " truths may be divulged or kept secret.
All religions and conceptions that remain caught in the
wrong correlation of revelation and gnosis tend to the
aristocratic attitude. When, however, revelation means
God's doing redemptive and saving acts to realize the
restoration of mankind and the world, the only appropriate
thing to do for those who have apprehended it by the
eye of faith is to bear witness to it, to become apostles,
ambassadors, messengers. " You will be My witnesses "
(Acts i. 8), said Jesus Christ in His parting mandate to
His disciples. The ever-recurring tone in the missionary
speeches of Peter and Paul can be expressed in this sentence :
" This Jesus, who has been rejected and crucified by His own
people and who was raised by God from the dead, we bear
witness to."

Still another characteristic feature of the Christian
revelation ought to be mentioned, in which it manifested
that the Christian faith stubbornly refuses to be treated as
a specimen of religious speculation, as a set of ideas about

[1] Revised Version.

God, man and the world, which afford an explanation of the world and life. Just as in the case of creation the crucial point is that man and the world are products of the *Will* of the living God, the Lord of the Universe, so in the case of salvation God has made known to us " the mystery of His *Will* " (Eph. i. 9) in order to restore in accordance with His merciful purpose the whole creation in its one Head, Christ. Not the mystery of His being or Essence is revealed, because that remains God's exclusive domain, but His redemptive Will towards mankind. God's saving Will, become manifest in divine action, is what is revealed in the Christian faith. Therefore it is quite natural that the God who wills and acts is the God who commands, and that the appropriate correlate to the divine command is human obedience. The mystery of God's Essence, as is demonstrated in all ages and all religions, is to be concealed, to be hedged around by the shuddering awe of inaccessibility ; the mystery of the divine Will, as lies in the nature of the case, has to be announced. The missionary command and urge in Christianity thus burst forth from the heart of God.

.   .   .   .

What is the heart of the Christian message? What are the essential and characteristic features of the Christian faith ? How are we to describe it ?

Various ways are possible, because the richness of the Gospel is inexhaustible. It is quite legitimate to say : Christianity is *the* religion of the Incarnation. The Word became flesh, God became real man ; this surely is one of the central aspects of the Christian faith. " God loved the world so dearly that He gave up His only Son, so that everyone who believes in Him may have eternal life instead of perishing " (St John iii. 16). The Incarnation accentuates in a marvellously clear way that the background of the world of Christian faith, that which makes it possible, is an unthinkable *act* of divine revelation, becoming a fact in a given moment of history ; and also an act of true revelation, because there is no more emphatic way than the Incarnation to express that what is revealed remains always, by its nature, a mystery, an adorable mystery. God becoming man : it will always remain incomprehensible, but yet it is the saving mystery. John, who was the first to express what happened in Jesus Christ in terms of the Incarnation, stressed this in his remarkable words : " The real light which enlightens every man was coming then into the world ; He entered the world, the world which existed through Him, yet the world did not recognize Him " (St John i. 9, 10).

The truly amazing thing about the Incarnation is that this doctrine of God really becoming man is proclaimed precisely by that religion which affirms an indelible distinction between God the Creator and man His creature, while all religions that assume the essential identity of God and man indignantly reject it.

The Incarnation states that the decisive moment in world history is the moment in which God revealed Himself in Christ as the holy and loving Travailer for the redemption and restoration of the world. Therefore, in the Incarnation God is not only revealed, but in it is also implied that empirical man and the empirical world are realities of infinite worth and objects of such deep concern to God that He surrenders Himself in Christ to the Cross.

Another effective way to outline the Christian faith is to say that it means justification by faith. This is no outmodish dogma, but one of the grandest expressions of what the Christian faith means. It surely belongs to the core of the Christian faith. The first eight chapters of the Epistle to the Romans are the still unsurpassed characterization of the meaning of the Christian revelation in its profound and revolutionary significance. There Biblical realism rises to its greatest heights. Nowhere in the world are man in his greatness and in his misery, and God in His holiness, righteousness and incomprehensible love, taken with such desperate reality and seriousness as there. Nowhere is the problem of God and man looked so squarely and honestly in the face. The presupposition of these chapters is that the moral perfection of God requires the moral perfection of man ; a presupposition that answers to the deepest and truest instincts of the human mind. Whosoever penetrates into these chapters begins to understand why Christ must be called the crisis of all religions and philosophies, because in the light of Paul's radical unveiling of the insoluble root problem that lies at the bottom of man's relation to God, all religions and systems of thought appear in the light of clumsy or magnificent evasions ; and the sublimer a religion or a system of thought is, the greater the evasion. This root problem is : How can sinful man really walk with God, the Holy and the Righteous, in unbroken and undefiled fellowship ?

The answer is : It is impossible, because man even in his best efforts to realize this deep-seated necessity of his life only demonstrates again the root cause of the impossibility, namely, his wilful maintenance of self in the face of God, his rightful Lord and Judge. God Himself can only make possible the impossible by His sovereign, creative act of salvation in Jesus Christ.

It is only after such radical questioning and such a radical answer that it is possible to assert such a radical religious certitude as Paul avers in the end of his exposition, when he says : " I am certain that neither death nor life . . . nor anything else in all creation will be able to part us from the love of God in Christ Jesus our Lord " (Rom. viii. 38, 39).

One is also fully justified in saying that Christianity is *the* religion of reconciliation and atonement. The unalterable background of all Biblical thinking is—it has constantly to be reiterated—that God is really God and man is really man. God is not the first cause of the world, the Absolute Mind, the Universal Life, the Eternal Law of the Universe, the Pure Essence of the undifferentiated One, but He is God, that is, the holy, righteous and merciful Lord, to be worshipped, loved and served by His creatures. Man is not a being in whom the Absolute Mind comes to self-consciousness or the meaning of whose life is to realize his essential unity with God, but man is of God's making ; he is destined to be the master of all creation and God's child, because God wills it so.

The actual condition of man is contradictory to this ; he is fallen. The Bible describes this inexplicable but patent fact with the words that man wanted to be " like God." Man, whose natural relation to God, His Lord and Maker, is obedience and love, has become a rebel. Reconciliation and atonement are a very pertinent way of saying that God, being the only One who can restore the destroyed natural relation, has taken the initiative. Nobody else can take the initiative in this situation, for man cannot make good his rebellion. It can only be made good by forgiveness. Enmity cannot be annihilated without real reconciliation ; guilt can never be removed without real atonement. The message of the Gospel is that God by His creative act of reconciliation and atonement in Jesus Christ, reconciling the world unto Himself, not imputing men's trespasses unto them, opened a way of reconciliation when there was no way. There is no way, because man, taken in the fundamental position of sin and guilt in which he finds himself in the face of God, can neither claim nor even imagine, if he deals radically and in earnest with this fundamental position, a way of reconciliation. It is with reconciliation and atonement as with incarnation and justification by faith. These classical terms express in a vivid way the real purpose of God's revelation in Jesus Christ.

It is very noteworthy that the famous Greek scholar, U. von Wilamowitz Moellendorf, when he enumerates in the second volume of his book, *Der Glaube der Hellenen* (i.e. The Faith of the Greek), the causes which according to his opinion effected the victory of Christianity in the ancient world, expresses one of those causes in the following way. Christianity taught a quite new relation to God. Individual man must come to God and He will help him. It is God's will that man lives according to God's moral commandments, but He knows that man is weak and He forgives him if man is not able to do so, and helps him to do what is good. The noteworthy thing about von Wilamowitz's opinion is that this brilliant scholar and intellectual aristocrat entirely misunderstands the core of the Biblical conception of forgiveness. This radically religious conception of forgiveness of sin, in which divine holiness and divine love, divine judgment and divine forgiveness are a vital and indissoluble unity, becomes under his hands a tame, external moralism and compassion with human weakness. It is no marvel that a self-respecting and self-reliant humanist considers this moralism too vulgar.

It is also very appropriate to say that the content of the Christian faith is the announcement of the Kingdom of God. The root of all evil, of the brokenness and disorder of the world, is the disavowal of God's will as the supreme and only-valid rule of all life. The reign, the Lordship, the dominion of God is rejected. That is the problem to which all problems in all spheres of life can and must be reduced in order to be realistic and true to the facts in their bare nakedness. Again, the Gospel is a radical answer to this fundamental need. " Repent, the Kingdom of God is near," was the message of Jesus. Here again it is God who takes the initiative, because He is the only one who can. Man, caught in his rebellion, confusion, sin and finiteness, cannot create the Kingdom of God. Even, on account of the same reasons, he cannot create an ideal society. The message of the Gospel is that God has begun in Jesus Christ a new divine order of life, of which Christ is the centre and the head. By His saving Will He commences the restoration of the original and normal divine life-order, in which the worship of God and the joyful doing of His will are the *natural* life. The time of Christ's coming in the world is the fullness of the ages, because in Him the turning-point in human history has appeared. Men are invited again into a fellowship where God is the Lord and His will the law of life. For " he who does the will of God remains for ever " (1 John ii. 17).

The Christian faith can also be described as a new way and quality of life. In the Acts of the Apostles more than once there are mentioned people who ask for explanation about the new way. When we look in the New Testament, it is amazing how various and seemingly contradictory this way of life is. It is the way of the Cross, of giving up all self-assertion and self-regard, the way of conflict with the world, of martyrdom and ruin ; it is also the life of victory, of a new creation in Christ, of faith and hope and love, the way of absolute trust in the reality of God, His acts and promises in Christ, for " if God is for us, who *can* be against us ? " (Rom. viii. 31). It is the way of " obedience to the faith " and fellowship with Christ, of joy and of service, of living by divine forgiveness and therefore loving God and loving man, for " if God had such a love for us we also ought to love one another " (1 John v. 11).

But in describing the Christian faith as a way and quality of life, we must never forget that, judged by the essential character of the Christian revelation, we are then virtually describing the reflex upon this revelation, the new kind of life and the new possibilities that have been made possible by the acts of God, who created in Jesus Christ the beginning of a new order. As God the Creator stands at the beginning of all things, so God the Redeemer and Renewer with His saving acts of renewal stands at the beginning of the Christian faith. Christianity in the dynamic sense of the word is not a set of sublime religious and moral ideas and ideals, nor is it a body of circumscribed truths which bind a man's mind, but it is the divinely-wrought objective reality of a newly established relation between God and man in which is opened up the possibility of a life of real fellowship with God. To proclaim the Gospel means to entreat men, in God's name, to participate in this divine reality of new life, and faith means obedient receptivity to this reality. In the first Epistle of Peter this is expressed in words ringing with the joy of salvation : " Blessed be the God and Father of our Lord Jesus Christ. By His great mercy we have been born anew to a life of hope through the resurrection of Jesus Christ from the dead " (1 Peter i. 3).

Probably one of the best ways to give shortly an impression of the basic structure of the Christian faith is to take as a starting-point the answer of Peter after his first missionary speech when many people asked him : " What are we to do ? " He answered : " Repent, let each of you be baptized in the name of Jesus Christ for the remission of your sins " (Acts ii. 37, 38). Jesus Christ and the forgiveness of sins are the divine elements ; repentance is the human element in the structure of the Christian faith.

Divine forgiveness is the wonderful tidings that constantly rings through the Gospel. Here again the Bible is very radical in its conception, quite different from ordinary conceptions. To forgive is not a matter-of-course in God. Voltaire's well-known phrase, " C'est son métier de pardonner" (It is his job to forgive), is a great blasphemy. That Christ came to seek sinners, and not the righteous, is what is revolting to current human conceptions. Forgiveness is, according to the Bible, the incomprehensible miraculous result of God's free and sovereign grace. It is the great miracle of God, which changes the entire situation. That is why the Gospel is full of joy. The whole New Testament overflows with deep and varied tones of this grateful joy.

Why is the Bible such a radical and to ordinary human thinking exaggerated and even misguided conception of the divine forgiveness ? Is not ordinary human thinking inclined to agree with Voltaire ? God is love, perfect love, and is then forgiveness not the most obvious thing to happen ? It is not. At any rate not if one wants to be radical and earnest as the Bible is, which disregards all our human diluted conceptions of love, of forgiveness, and of God. God's love is holy love, and therefore radical love. Because God loves man, the sinner, radically, He condemns him radically. His holy condemnation of sin and the sinner is a sign of His love, because disregarding the reality of sin would be indulgence, not love. It would mean destroying holiness, on which depends the validity of all moral life. The note of joy and gratitude for the divine forgiveness in the Bible springs from the conviction that a miracle has happened, because God, the rightful and holy Judge of man, has manifested Himself in Jesus Christ as the forgiving and merciful Saviour.

Only if one takes holiness seriously can one take sin seriously and understand that sin is, by its nature, irreparable. The parable of the Prodigal Son suggests this very vividly. When he was resolved to return home, he says : " Father, I have sinned against Heaven and before you ; I don't deserve to be called your son any more ; only make me as one of your hired men " (St Luke xv. 18, 19). To be " children of God " is not a birthright ; it is a gift and a grace. Because the Bible takes both holiness and sin seriously, it speaks so emphatically about the miracle of forgiveness. Jesus constantly pressed upon the minds of His hearers that He had the authority to forgive sins, and that this was His most important function, far exceeding the power to work miracles of healing. His opponents rightly sensed this as a claim to divine rights, because God the Holy is the only One who can really forgive. The message of the Gospel is that He not only can forgive but that He does forgive in Jesus Christ.

Parallel to the fact that Jesus always emphasized the forgiveness of sins as His characteristic business is the other fact in the Gospels, that Jesus represents His own person and work as central in His whole message.

Without these two facts, the Gospel would become a mere sample of partly prophetic, partly didactic and partly apocalyptic literature, and Jesus would be a prophet, a teacher and a fervent popular preacher. It is solely through these two facts that the Gospels get their true depth and revolutionary significance. This Man, who called to gentleness and humility of heart, who made the naive simplicity of children an object of emulation and who did not come to be served but to serve, claimed confidently this central place in God's plan for the world. He it is who ushers in the Kingdom of God ; He claims as a right from His followers that they be witnesses to His name and be gladly prepared to suffer on His behalf ; He represents Himself as the Messiah whom the prophets announced ; He placed beside and above the injunctions of the Law His " But I tell you." He knows that He is the Confidant of the Father and the Instrument in His dealing with the world and with mankind. He tastes death, but it is no martyr-death, nor is it a heroic death, or a serene death. Socrates and many more have died more heroically and more serenely. He performs it as a Messianic act, and yet suffers it, with its preceding struggles, as a common deathlike death, full of anxiety that weighs on man, so hungry for life full and abundant in the face of this enigmatic and revolting extinction of life. It is finished. World history seems to have passed its inexorable judgment on the life of this attractive and yet so strange Man, who was full of prophetic fervour, whose heart was moved with pity over the multitudes because they were like sheep which have no shepherd, who did not break the broken reed, nor quench the smouldering flax, whom the demons addressed as God's Holy One, who declared Himself the Lord of the Sabbath and who claimed as His brother and sister and mother all those who obeyed His Father in heaven. It was not finished. He rose from the dead, because He, the Son of Man and the Son of God, conquered death by tasting death. And since that day His followers became the witnesses to His resurrection, to the divine victory over sin and death, inviting everyone to believe in Him and thereby share in this victory and in the new life in the Spirit. They again and again expressed their wonder and gratitude at God's manner of acting by saying to the multitudes, " *God* has made Him both Lord and Christ, this very Jesus whom *you* have crucified " (Acts ii. 36).

His greatest apostle would describe this whole career in the following words : " Though He was divine by nature He did not set store upon equality with God, but emptied Himself by taking the nature of a servant ; born in human guise and appearing in human form, He humbly stooped in His obedience even to die, and to die upon the Cross. Therefore God raised Him high and conferred on Him a name above all names, so that before the name of Jesus every knee should bend in heaven, on earth, and underneath the earth, and every tongue confess that ' Jesus Christ is Lord ' to the glory of God the Father " (Phil. ii. 7–11). " Jesus is Lord " became the apostolic testimony. A Lord has a Kingdom. This Kingdom is the real Church, the community of those who are united in the unity of faith, of love and of worship towards Him, who is their Head ; who as children of the divine grace and forgiveness are re-born into a new life created by the Holy Spirit, which impels to a life of strenuous moral endeavour in a spirit of deep humility, gladly and obediently serving God's purpose for man and the world. The character of this Kingdom is that it is a living, working reality and yet not realized. It is " between the times," the time of God's beginning with Christ of a new chapter in the life of mankind and the time of the consummation of God's hidden purpose in history. We have remarked already that the meaning of incarnation and reconciliation is not only the salvation of individual men and women but the restoration of the normal, original, divine order of life, in which the worship of God and the joyful doing of God's holy will become the *natural* life. Now we need to add that this restoration took in Christ its beginning. His coming in the flesh marks the inauguration of the first term in God's work of redemption and reclaiming. The joyful doing of the holy will of God is not yet our natural life. We have understood through Christ that it ought to be so, but the powers of sin and confusion contend in us against it as long as this world stands. The integral realization of this new order, of the Kingdom of God, is the object of expectation. The community, the *Koinonia* of those who live in Christ, is waiting with longing expectation for the coming of the Kingdom. In the radical religious realism of the Bible this expectation is a real longing. It is not a resigning of oneself to the *status quo*, but a stretching of the soul towards its sure manifestation. To live by the Christian faith means to have the light of eternity in one's eyes, and to stand in the world, the object of God's saving and renewing activity, as His co-worker in service and love.

This short and very incomplete sketch of the Christian faith has but one aim, to suggest some essential and fundamental features of the Christian faith *as it appears in the radical religious realism of the Bible*. That this method of presenting a succinct outline of the Christian faith is the most valid one is beyond question. Religious and scientific considerations mutually corroborate each other to show this. Besides that, however, this method is in our opinion the need of the hour all over the world. Everywhere in the Christian Church, in the West and in the East, there arises the cry for theology, real theology, in order to give a new and much-needed sense of direction and consistency to Christian thinking, feeling and willing. Really good Christian theology will never emerge, in this time of world-wide confusion, without an open, honest and courageous *religious confrontation with and orientation upon the concrete realism of the Bible*. The Christian faith floats in the present time amidst the surging waves of numerous conflicting and vigorous world-views and of the great massive systems of non-Christian religion. A clear and vigorous conception of what the Christian faith is and stands for is a matter of life or death. It ought therefore to be repeated with the strongest emphasis possible that the prime necessity in this situation is a *religious* confrontation with and orientation upon the radical religious realism of the Bible. This means to expose the totality of our being to the claim of the Biblical revelation for absolute allegiance to it—half-hearted allegiance means no allegiance at all—and then to take decisions.

Another advantage of this method of presentation is that it is the only way to suggest sufficiently strongly the inherent incommensurableness of the religion of Biblical realism with all other specimens of religious life. This religion of Biblical realism is void of all speculative, metaphysical and philosophical trends of thinking. General religious and religio-philosophical ideas, as, for example, a theistic conception of God, can be and have been deduced from it, and naturally will be deduced in the future, because to do so is one of the natural necessities of the human mind. What, however, is not permitted and is utterly misleading is to substitute these deductions for the purely religious data of Biblical realism. In our time of decisive confrontation with various world-views and with the great non-Christian systems of life, all permeating the atmosphere with subtle, inevitably suggestive forces, a strong reminder of this is needed. The radical religious realism of the Biblical revelation, in which all religious and moral life revolves around one point only, namely, the creative and redemptive Will of the living, holy, righteous God of Love, the exclusive ground of nature and history, of man and the world, has to be the standard of reference. A very impressive feature of our present situation is that the painstaking work of scientific Biblical research enables us to have an open eye for this Biblical realism and its peculiarity, and to make the confrontation with it therefore more feasible ; for orthodox people and for " liberals," for doctrinal-minded and undoctrinal-minded alike.

One point more, in connection with our short and incomplete sketch of the Christian faith, must be touched upon. This sketch has merely been a selection of some essential points. The question, however, arises, Is there no variety of religious doctrine and experience ? How far is this variety legitimate, and how far is it not ?

In the New Testament itself there is a rich variety of approach, expression and experience. Various accents of various intensity are to be found. John's emphasis on love in God, and, as response to that, in man ; the characteristic expressions of the writer of the Epistle to the Hebrews of Christ's significance under the aspect of the fulfilment of what had been foreshadowed in the religious institutions of Israel ; Peter's moving emphasis upon the inestimable joy in the new hope by God in Christ, and upon Christ's holiness and patience as patterns of emulation for Christians ; James with his emphasis upon actions as evidence of the faith and his championship of the poor and oppressed ; the great masterful strokes with which Paul delineates the faith : these are only some few examples of this variety of expression and experience. Such variety is not only legitimate ; it is inevitable and natural, founded on the rich content of the revelation and on the rich variety of the human mind, the recipient organ and the responding agent for the divine revelation.

Yet one highly important point ought to be noted. Notwithstanding the many varying, individual accents, there is in the whole range of apostolic preaching and expression a surprising amount of unity, because *their orientation point is the same*, namely, the radical realism of Biblical revelation. The God they meet and respond to, each in his way, is always the Creator, the Lord and Judge of man and the world ; the God of holiness and righteousness who travails in His incomprehensible mercy for the salvation of mankind. The Christ they proclaim is always the incarnate Son of God, whose life and work meant the execution of God's plan of salvation for mankind ; whose death and resurrection effect reconciliation with God and open the new æon of life.

The Holy Spirit to whom they testify is always the creator and sustainer of the new life in Christ, and the guarantee of God's direct dealing with those who are new creatures in Christ. Naturally, the emphases and accents in their ethical attitude and exhortations are various ; but by the same orientation towards the same God, the same Christ and the same Spirit, and on account of the same experience of salvation and participation in the same expectation, the unity is unmistakable. Much more could be mentioned, but it is superfluous here.

Therefore in regard to the problem of the legitimate variety of expression and approach in the Christian faith, which in the Younger Churches and the mission field is a problem of fundamental importance, because it crops up inevitably through the natural fact of the different backgrounds, heritages and mentalities, we find our point of reference again in the indisputable and continuous confrontation with and orientation upon the radical realism of the Biblical revelation.

THE CHRISTIAN ETHIC

The dominant point in the Christian ethic is the same as in the Christian faith. It is embedded in the same sphere of concrete religious realism, and is, like the Christian faith, radically religious and theocentric. Consequently it is, just like the Christian faith, entirely incommensurable with all other ethics in the world.

When this dominant point is lost sight of, a radical misconception and misconstruction of the Christian ethic is the inevitable result. The neglect of this dominant point for the Christian faith has led to the substitution for the prophetic and apostolic message of the Gospel of various religious world-views and philosophies with more or less Christian colouring. So in the case of the Christian ethic it has resulted in the production of many ethics, which are specimens of a philosophy of cultural life, shot through with stronger or weaker Christian threads. In these cases other ethical systems, all fundamentally anthropocentric and not theo- and Christocentric, were the points of orientation while the Christian ethic only contributed elements, a procedure which resulted in an adjustment of the Christian ethic to other ethics. The rising Christian Churches in the great world of non-Christian religions and cultures will have to face the same problems and the same danger.

All ethics in the world, except the Christian ethic, are some form of eudæmonism, this word not being meant in a disparaging but in a purely descriptive sense. The central question is always, What is for man the highest good, the *summum bonum* in life? in order to obtain happiness by striving after it and attaining it. This eudæmonistic ethic manifests itself in various, deeply different forms. They may be of exceedingly noble and idealistic quality, and may even be mixed with slight or strong ascetic touches, as in the case of the Platonic, Stoic, Kantian, Hindu, or Buddhist ethic. They may be of a lower grade, such as sensualist or utilitarian ethics. They are all individualistic, except the ethics in primitive societies that are collectivist, but whose *summum bonum* is also the happiness of man by the maintenance of the equilibrium of life as authoritatively established by the ancestors.

The Christian ethic, as contained in Biblical realism, is neither eudæmonistic nor individualistic nor collectivistic. In stating this it is not intended to suggest that human happiness or values are to be despised or deemed irrelevant to life. That would be preposterous. The desire for happiness is a vital and legitimate instinct in man, a sign of his being created for perfect harmony. As long as mankind lives it will have to create and preserve values. The vitality and significance of cultural life will always be dependent on the kind of values that are created or preserved. Therefore to speak about values and to aim at preserving or developing them is a natural and necessary pursuit. The ways of the Christian ethic and the ethics of " values " and " goods " part company, because the latter takes the creation of values as the immediate and highest object of ethical striving, while the former does not aim directly at the creation of values, but at the fulfilment of God's will from which various values derive as fruits and results. It is not intended to say that human happiness, human misery and human values are not a deep concern for those who recognize the Christian ethic as the really valid one. The history of the Christian Church demonstrates clearly that it always felt the ministry to human need as a distinctly Christian obligation, and for the Christian Church at the present time one of the most urgent tasks is to learn great new lessons in the application and interpretation of this ministry.

What, however, is meant to be affirmed here is that the Christian ethic as contained in Biblical realism neither has its prime motive nor its ultimate end in a *summum bonum* or in the happiness of man. The happiness of man is or can be a fruit, a result, but fundamentally speaking never the direct object. The deep reason why this is so is that the Christian ethic is radically religious and theocentric and Christocentric. Its prime motive and ultimate end, as shown in both the Old and the New Testaments, is to do the will of God. This motive and end is brought into practice by obedience to the will of God. The Christian ethic is therefore never abstract ; it is never the application of abstract principles belonging to a moral order, of which God is the Custodian and Maintainer, but the concrete doing of the will of the living, ever-active God. Here lies the root of its amazing and perplexing freedom, which Augustine sensed in his famous expression, *Ama Deum et fac quod vis* (i.e. love God and do what you like !). Hence the prophets impetuously brush aside all the zeal in religious observance, feasts, sacrifices, even propitiatory sacrifices, as worthless in God's eyes, and speak in the name of the Eternal : " O man, He has *told* you what is good ; what does the Eternal *ask* from you but to be just and kind and live in quiet fellowship with your God ? " (Mic. vi. 8). Hence Jesus says : " Whosoever does the will of my Father in heaven, is my brother, sister and mother " (St Matt. xii. 50) and " It is not everyone who says to me ' Lord, Lord ! ' who will get into the Kingdom of heaven, but he who does the will of my Father in heaven " (St Matt. vii. 21). Even the criterion

by which to find out the truth of His message, He makes
dependent on the doing of God's will : " My teaching is
not my own but His who sent me. Anyone who chooses to
do His will, shall understand whether my teaching comes
from God or whether I am talking on my own authority "
(St John vii. 17). The Sermon on the Mount is not a high-
flown ethic of idealistic principles or an interim ethic, but
the Law of the Kingdom of God, the concrete application
of God's will. Just because of this intense concreteness the
application is free and eternally changing, while the criterion,
God's will, remains eternally fixed. The fact that this
criterion is the will of God and of the *holy* God gives to it
its character of absolute validity and authority. The fact
that it is the will of the *living* God provides it with an ever-
changing, while ever-living, flexibility. In the light of this
criterion such opposites as enjoining the love of parents and
at the same time the " hate " of parents for His sake are
indissolubly one.

This radically religious, revolutionary ethic upsets all
human thinking, and just as the Christian faith is the crisis
of all religions, so the Christian ethic is the crisis of all ethic
and ethics. Through the inveterate legalistic turn of the
human mind in all questions regarding morals it is often
called rigorism, because of its entire negation of natural
self-regard and self-assertion. This is a radical misconception.
The Christian ethic lies outside the sphere of the current
ethical rubrics. In the sphere of Biblical realism, to do the
will of God is a spontaneous act and a decision of loving
obedience, because God's will is love and can only be done
in free, spontaneous love. To do it otherwise means to do
it not at all. The Christian ethic, well understood, is the
opposite of rigorism ; it is the joyful liberty of the pure-
hearted children of God.

The motivation in the Christian ethic points always to
God and His will. Love, for God loves ! Be righteous, for
God is righteous ! Be perfect, for your Father in heaven is
perfect ! There is no word about confidence or diffidence
in man as the motive for an ethical injunction. Neither is
there a word about the inherent worthiness or unworthiness

of man to be loved by his fellow-man. Man has no inherent worthiness or unworthiness. He is a great and a miserable being ; he is great because he is God's creature and has had " conferred " on him the right of being God's child through Jesus Christ, not because he is of the same divine nature with God ; he is miserable because he is a fallen rebellious creature, disobedient to the will of God, incapable of doing God's will as it only can be done in the free spontaneous obedience of love. Because of his greatness and his misery it is wholly justifiable to talk about the infinite value of man, but it is wholly unjustifiable in the sphere of the Christian faith and ethic to declare this value to be the prime motive for love or obligation towards man. Our fellow-man as such has infinite value because he is God's creature, and he is to be loved because of this fact and because it is God's will. Therefore the love of enemies and of the most disgusting and hopeless men is, in the sphere of this radically theocentric ethic, as natural as the shining of the sun.

In contrast with the natural inclination to interpret this Christian ethic as a specimen of moral heroism with all the tension and contortion so easily adherent to it, it breathes an atmosphere of complete, serene freedom. For no small reason Paul speaks with deep emotion about the religious and ethical " liberty of the children of God." It really depicts the normal divine order of life in which the worship of God and the joyful doing of His will is the *natural* life. Therefore every idea of merit is radically annihilated. The employer in the twentieth chapter of Matthew, who hires men for his vineyard at different hours of the day and yet pays them the same wages, meets the obvious protest of empirical man, who in the past and to-day instinctively calculates on the basis of merit and of achievement, by saying : " My man, I am not wronging you. Can I not do as I please with what belongs to me ? " The Kingdom of God is the realm of God's sovereign grace, and there all usual human evaluations are deflated and irrelevant. The religious and ethical act of surrender to God's will and living on that basis cannot be computed in terms of more or less ; it is or it is not. Its radical theocentricity frees ethical life, according to the ethics of the Kingdom of God, from all possibility of thinking or judging in human terms of merit, achievement or boasting. One of the deepest roots of Paul's doctrine of justification by faith lies here, which illustrates, by the way, the essential unity of faith and ethic in the Bible.

The love of fellow-men is motivated by and naturally implied in the love of God. The first great commandment, " Love the Lord your God with your whole heart " precedes and determines the second, " Love your neighbour as yourself," which is " like it." The apostolic moral exhortations to love, to be kind, to be humble, to display all sorts of " excellencies " are always based on the will of God in Christ or on the Spirit that was in Christ, who is the embodiment of God's will, or on the fact that God loved us first and forgave us and Jesus underwent death for us.

The ethic of the apostolic writings is as radically religious and theocentric as that of the Gospels. With Paul and all the other apostolic writers, faith and works, religion and ethics, or to put it dogmatically, justification and sanctification, are as intimately and vitally related to each other as inhalation and expiration. The divine gift of salvation and new life and the corresponding human answer in living the new life are connected with each other as salvation and gratitude, as being transplanted by God through Christ into eternal life and consequently yielding " fruit to God " in the newness of the Spirit. This intertwining of the religious and the ethical is expressed pregnantly in the well-known verse, " Work strenuously at your salvation with reverence and trembling, for it is God who in His goodwill enables you to will this and to achieve this" (Phil. ii. 12, 13). The German theologian, P. Althaus, has made the very fine remark, that there is always in Paul's thinking an absolute unity of the religious, divine indicative with the ethical, human imperative. The divinely-wrought salvation in the death and resurrection of Jesus Christ and God's creative opening up of the new æon for those who are in Christ, is the basis and incentive of the whole ethical life of the Christian. Because you are made new, constantly renew yourself—that is the underlying maxim of all apostolic religious and ethical thinking, and they are so intimately combined that they cannot even be separately treated. Because sin is dead, strive to make your members " weapons of righteousness."

The objective reality of God's doing is the basis of Christian ethical life. In the Epistle to the Ephesians the first three chapters deal with the subject that the salvation and restoration of man and the world in Christ has been the eternal purpose of God's love, and that equally Jews and Gentiles are " called " to enter into this new " one " humanity. In the fourth chapter the natural and intimate connection of ethics with God's acts and with faith breaks through shiningly when a couple of chapters full of ethical exhortations are introduced by the words : " I then beg you to live a life worthy of your calling." This intimate connection between the divine, religious indicative and the human imperative or between faith and works, *both* made possible by the divine, religious indicative, is the backbone of the Christian ethic.

It is only on this foundation that one can justly speak about the possibility of a " victorious life " for a Christian ; not on that of the misconception of the Christian ethic as the sublimest form of moral heroism by which the " victorious life " can be achieved. The latter conviction, although fascinating and able to inspire with great enthusiasm, is ultimately always doomed to failure and wrecking dis- illusion, because it remains in the sphere of aristocratic and heroic moralism as expressed in the Kantian maxim : *Du sollst denn du kannst* (you must for you can), with the important difference that Christ is then made responsible for *du kannst*. The victorious life, as depicted in Romans v., in its joy and its hope, rests on the objective reality of salva- tion wrought by God ; on the peace, the being a child of God, on the reconciliation, that have become effective and real in Christ. " We triumph even in our troubles, knowing that trouble produces endurance, endurance produces character, and character produces hope, a hope which never dis- appoints, *since God's love floods our hearts through the holy Spirit*" (Rom. v. 4, 5). In this sphere no moral virtue, be it love, self-sacrifice, humility or what not, ever becomes an end, but always is but an expression of a new condition of life. And, very important to note, religious experience thus gets its due place too. It is neither an end, nor a treasure to be cherished ; nor the ground and motive power of our faith. It is the condition of mind that accompanies the state of newness of life, launched by God's initiative.

Just as in Biblical realism no dogmatic theology in the usual sense is offered, so here it has to be stated that neither is there to be found in it anything like ethical theory. All ethical reasonings and decisions in the apostolic writings, especially in those of Paul, arise out of concrete practical situations and are concrete decisions. The missionary, the thinker and the pastor of souls pronounces his opinions, thereby handling only one criterion—the new world, revealed in Jesus Christ ; and hence knowing only one judgment, the judgment of faith, born from the new way of looking at all things and situations, through the faith in Jesus Christ. The first letter to the Corinthians, to mention only one instance (the epistles of John and Peter offer also a wealth of material) is, it seems to me, to every attentive reader an inexhaustible mine of information, from which can be learned how occupation with the trite but perennial problems of human life becomes the occasion for an amazing depth, freedom and sagacity of ethical decision, because all decisions emanate from the radically religious basis of faith.

Now, at last, in the light of the Christian ethic as contained in Biblical realism we have to touch one of the most burning problems of the present day. In Chapter I we stated that the Christian Church to-day has to face the problem of its relation to the world and to revise this relation drastically. The human relationships, the political and social reality ; what has the Christian ethic to say in these spheres of life in our time of revolutionary transition ? In other words : what is the Christian social ethic ?

The following conclusions that may be justly deduced from our preceding discussion are at the same time a short answer to these questions.

In the first place, from this radically religious ethic,

of which the two poles are God's will and the loving, spontaneous obedience of man, no ready-made political and social or international programme can be derived. Social and political programmes and life-systems belong to the relative sphere of historic human life. The Kingdom of God is a transcendental, supra-historical order of life. Identification of a so-called Christian social order, Christian State or Christian culture with the Kingdom of God signifies making what is by its nature relative (social order, state, culture) absolute, and making the absolute (the Kingdom of God) relative. This is so because the tension inherent between the sphere of relative human history and that of the transcendent realm of God, the ethic of the Kingdom of God, of the complete fulfilment of the will of God, can never be annihilated in this dispensation. Therefore the Kingdom of God can never be realized in any social, economic, political or cultural order. If it were it would amount to saying that the absolute and perfect can be adequately expressed in the relative and imperfect. To "christianize" the social or other spheres of life can only legitimately mean their being influenced and tamed by Christian influences and standards. Whoever expects more confuses the relative realities of life, where self-assertion and self-regard remain active because of the reality of sin and human finiteness, with the realm of God's will that is not to be realized, but *works as a ferment and an explosive* in these relative spheres.

In the second place, although Christianity, on account of its prophetic spirit and origin, is exceedingly ethical—more ethical than any other religion—and although it is concerned with a "Kingdom" and with a new order of life, in the New Testament there is no definite guidance in regard to the political, social, cultural, and economic spheres of life. It was no social, but a radically religious, movement. Surveying the material of ethical nature in the New Testament we have to state that nearly exclusively the individual moral life and the relations between men and women, parents and children, masters and slaves are treated. To say on account of this that the ethic of the New Testament is individualistic would be wholly erroneous, for it is just the opposite, namely, the ethic of a new Kingdom, of a new order of life. The community of the believers in Christ look expectantly for the manifestation of this new order and feel already its forces working in their members. However, the problems of individual ethics and of pastoral care for the building up of the congregations that have been founded absorb nearly all attention. There is no concern at all, or only casual concern, with the world and its great spheres of life ; the real concern is other-worldly, the transcendental Kingdom of God.

This, it must be emphasized, is not a matter for disappointment but for gratitude. It means not a defection from or an imperfection of the Christian ethic. It is just what should be expected in a book whose mission is to reveal fundamental backgrounds and needs of human life from the purely religious standpoint of their confrontation with God's holy perfect and saving Will. It would have been a defection if the New Testament had left its radically religious standpoint and presented us with seemingly universal principles and programmes. The relative, ever-changing character of historical and cultural life requires ever-changing programmes. Universal principles can only be formal. The essential in them, namely, the content, is not at all unchangeable, but is wholly dependent on the interpretation given in the concrete historical moment. There is, for example, universal agreement of opinion as to the value of man, the sanctity of righteousness, etc. Agreement of opinion on these universal principles in the abstract, however, does not carry far. The crucial point is, what is concretely meant by it, and on what foundation is the validity of this concrete interpretation built ? The depth and the greatness of the New Testament is that it takes quietly for granted this paradox, that the universal can only be concrete and not, as usually thought, abstract and rational. The radical concreteness of the Christian ethic excludes all general, immutable principles and programmes and hinges entirely on the concrete decision over against God's will. This ever-active and ever-new Will is, properly speaking, the sole universal principle in all ethical life. It very distinctly precludes taking any ethical decision or prescription in the New Testament as a law for all times, and so opens up the way for an inestimable freedom and flexibility, devoid of the least trace of legalistic moralism. The besetting sin of the Christian Church in all ages has been the legalistic and rationalistic maltreatment of the New Testament ethic, be it by Tolstoian or correctly orthodox legalists and ethical rationalists. The inescapable logic, however, of this ethic of concrete obedience of God's will is that every generation has the right, no, much deeper, has the precious *obligation* to seek its own solution for its peculiar problems in the light of the concrete obedience to God's will. By the same logic it is clear that it is not permitted to use the New Testament for definite social or political theories, whether conservative or radical. In no way whatever is the New Testament a handbook for immutable and general doctrines about the state or society.

In the seeming weakness of the Christian ethic, its so-called unpractical " other-worldliness " (to speak according to ordinary human understanding) lies its strength. By this elasticity of ever-new confrontation and decision inherent in its prophetic and radically religious character, it is the only ethic that, well understood, can really give trustworthy guidance. This is all the more so because the same prophetic character of this ethic, with its intrinsic relatedness of all life to God's holy Will which can only be fulfilled in loving freedom, brings the moral temperament to the utmost intensity and precludes all possibility of moral nihilism. As experience teaches, man is so accustomed by the " natural " bent of his mind to take moral life as meaning laws and duties, that he sees as its sole alternative moral nihilism in the form of libertinism. This moral nihilism, that denies the validity of any moral law and obligation, is nevertheless a child of the same inveterate legalistic thinking. In the New Testament all legalism, the nihilist form included, is radically transcended. God, the Creator, and man, His creature, are vitally and intimately connected with each other, for man is created unto God and the doing of

His Will, which is the meaning of man's life and hence its real fulfilment. The atmosphere of radical freedom, in which alone this ethic of God's holy Will and man's fulfilling it in loving obedience can be performed, is therefore at the same time the atmosphere of the highest ethical passion.

This atmosphere is the dominant one in the New Testament, which, when speaking concretely, gives mainly decisions on points of individual moral life and very rarely pronounces definite guidance as to political and social problems. This, we repeat, is not a matter for disappointment but for gratitude, because it shows the realism of the New Testament ethics. The apostles and the Christians of the first century were children of their time and situation, and *as such* the prophetic ethic of God's revelation in Christ finds them and challenges them. It is the clearest indication that the New Testament ethic will always remain rebellious against all efforts, though these are continuously made, to reduce it to a kind of moral law.

The apostles and the first Christians were, as are all human beings, children of their time. This is evident in their opinions about the position of women and slavery. The widespread habit of emphasizing this point with a tone of apology seems to me a symbol of our confused thinking. Everyone who has learnt to think historically will understand its obviousness. The apologetic note which usually occurs in this statement is apparently caused by the fact that many people are still insufficiently historical in their thinking. The really amazing and revealing thing in this instance of the ideas about women and slavery is rather that the apostles, while naturally holding to the current opinions of their day as to the position of women and slavery, under the influence of the prophetic ethic of God's will and guided by the judgment of faith, manifest a depth and a delicacy of feeling as to the real worth of women and slaves that rises triumphantly above the moral presuppositions of any juridical or sociological structure, whether ancient or modern, because the purifying love of Christ enlightens their judgment. To grasp this, one need only read the seventh chapter of the

First Epistle to the Corinthians on marriage and sexual intercourse, and mark the delicate and deep mutual respect of love which Paul assumes in all relations of married people ; or penetrate into the entirely new spirit of freedom and self-respect that breathes in Paul's exhortations to slaves : " Do God's will from the heart like servants of Christ, by rendering service with goodwill as to the Lord and Master, not to men " (Eph. vi. 7).

These are only some examples to illustrate that the concrete form of the decisions of faith in the Christian naturally change according to the concrete circumstances and historical situations in which the decisions of faith have to be given, but they illustrate also that a real decision or judgment of faith reflects in its inner spirit a gleam of the eternal lustre of the transcendent sphere of God's holy Will.

The apostles were also children of their time and circumstances in their attitude towards the spheres of political and social life. These first missionaries of a new, unknown faith, with only a handful of followers, were not interested in the political and social problems of their day. They were interested in their job, to proclaim the new Kingdom of God and Christ. They did not see, and in the circumstances could not possibly see, the implications of the prophetic Christian faith and ethic for the political and social realm. Taking into account their tiny number and their dominant interest, it would be preposterous to suppose that they could even have dreamed of programmes for political and social reconstruction ; while the questions of the individual moral life inevitably obtruded themselves upon them and therefore had to be solved in the light of faith in Christ as they *concretely presented themselves* in their situation. For us who are living to-day and belong to a world-wide Christian community with millions of members, it is the concrete duty, involved in the one principle of the Christian ethic, namely, the concrete obedience to God's Will, to discover the implications. The well-known verses of the thirteenth chapter of the Epistle to the Romans are therefore not to be taken as unalterable principles of political ethics. They were exhortations regarding a matter in which Paul was interested for special reasons. If used to-day, they need radical re-thinking.

The freedom and flexibility of the Christian ethic in regard to social ethics thus consists in three points. Firstly, the ethic of the Will of God contains very important implications for social and political and cultural life. Secondly, the concrete application of these implications will have to be concretely found through the judgment of faith in the different concrete situations of life and history, and yet will always, on account of sin, remain imperfect and broken. Thirdly, the decisions and pronouncements in the New Testament are, by virtue of the nature of the Christian faith and ethic, never laws for any other generation of Christians. They are temporary solutions, full of suggestions to us, who have to live out the Christian ethic in a different period of history.

It will be clear now that quietist sanctioning of the *status quo* in the political and social order, which has so often been taken as inherent in the " other-worldly " Christian ethic, is a radical misconception of this ethic. It is especially harmful in the present day.[1] To-day the problems of the human relationships, of the political, social and economic order, of war and international justice, of humanity and liberty, are the pressing problems of mankind. Hence it is the most patent Christian duty of the present Christian Church—which is not as in the first century an insignificant handful of men and women still groping for its way, but a great body intimately related to the present world-structure—to seek with utmost diligence how to express its concrete obedience to God's Will in regard to these spheres of life. In this respect we, Christians of the present age, are groping for our way. The Conference at Oxford in 1937 on Church, Community and State is an example of this groping. The result, as said already, will never be a Christian social or international order in the full sense of the word Christian ;

---

[1] In the past, and also at present, although the Church has seldom had an adequate insight into the real character of the Christian ethic, it has leavened and is leavening the life of the community to a considerable degree. This ought to be mentioned in order to avoid misunderstanding, even if it can only be in passing.

still less the realization of the Kingdom of God, because that works in this dispensation as a ferment and an explosive, and on the other hand is an object of faith and expectant hope. The result must be in the first place a Church that courageously and perseveringly brings the minds of men and the conditions and the spheres of life under the moulding influence of its prophetic ethic. What the result will be on the world and its spheres of life can never be predicted. It may be—and it is our duty to hope and strive for that— of deeply purifying quality ; it may be hardly of any avail, because the Church, like every human agency, has no power to foresee or regulate the ultimate causes of social, economic or political conjunctures, and therefore has no right to pretend to " christianize " the spheres of life. What the Church can actually do is to instil the influence of concrete Christian lives into the general life. A " Christian " social, political or international order would mean a way of life in which all coercion had vanished and everything happened in the freedom of love.

Thus, although results are extremely important, in its relation and obligation to the world and its spheres of life, the Church, if true to its vocation, can never work except for the sake of obedience to God's Will.

And now we must turn to another aspect of the Christian ethic, which follows also from its prophetic and radically religious character. While on the one hand it implies strenuous devotion to the tasks of life and of the world because all is done in direct obedience to God and not to men or to principles, on the other hand it produces a great soberness of judgment and attitude and keeps Christians in constant conflict and tension. The arid words " the relative reality of historic human life " mean concretely that the world and all its spheres of life, the Church and individual Christians included, are full of sin and perversion, often to a satanic degree. Unavoidable human ignorance and finiteness and the complexity of the world add to the difficulty. In this world the Christian is called to live as a man or woman who is primarily sensitive to the Will of God and the Spirit of Jesus Christ. His practical decisions, despite his belonging to Christ, will mostly turn out to be what must be honestly called, in the light of the Christian ethic, exceedingly poor approximations. To be sure, this does not signify a pessimistic attitude towards the world. A Christian is, properly speaking, neither pessimistic nor optimistic about the world, but trusts joyfully to God in trying as well as in hopeful periods, being His co-worker in this world, which God loved so dearly that He gave up His only Son.

Yet we ought never to forget that the natural drag of mankind, and also of the Christian and the Christian Church, is towards resignation to or conformity with things as they are. Therefore, we stand in all the greater need of being constantly reminded rather of the vigorously dynamic character of the prophetic Christian ethic, which places the world and all it contains under the judgment of God's Will and calls for strenuous and inspired action, than of the painful inevitability of our poor approximations. For Christians, in rightly emphasizing the brokenness of life and the small measure of our approximations to the Christian life in the full sense of the word, find it so fatally easy to forget that the brokenness in this dispensation is painful. They take it often as a pretext for making wholly inoperative the obligation towards concrete obedience to God's Will in every sphere of life, which is always and everywhere incumbent on the Christian Church. This disavowal of the prophetic character of the Christian ethic in the deceptive guise of humble piety must be deemed exceedingly more fatal than its distortion by the perfectionists, who violently try to " seize the Kingdom of God by force."

Where is the never-dying source of inspiration and humility ? In the mind of God, who willed the salvation and restoration of the world, not sparing His Son, who revealed the heart of the Father in the compassion that moved His heart when He saw the multitudes as sheep without a shepherd. The multitudes of Asia and Africa surely need this divine quality of compassion.

CHAPTER IV

The Attitude towards the Non-Christian Religions

THE Christian religion in its real sense, that is, as the revelation in Christ with all that that involves as to faith and ethics, revolves around two poles.

The first pole is knowledge of God of a very special kind that upsets all other conceptions of God or of the Divine. The God revealed and active in Christ is the holy, reconciling God. He is the God who, in His act of reconciling the world and man unto Himself, manifested His holiness as well as His love. He set a new course so as to re-establish His rightful dominion of men on the foundation of a new relation of " love which has no dread in it."

The second pole is a knowledge of man, also of a very special kind and revolutionary in comparison with any other conception of man. Man, in the light of the revelation in Christ, is God's creature, destined to be His child and co-worker, hence of great worth and great qualities. His nature and condition, however, have become perverted by a radical self-centredness, explained in the Bible as the will to be " like God, knowing good and evil," the root of sin and death in the world. Man's God-rooted origin and end, and his splendid God-given qualities, assert themselves still in the ways in which he tries to master and regulate life, as manifested in his great achievements in the field of culture, art, science, political, social and economic life. The perversion of sin, which permeates all his achievements with the will that makes for god-likeness, causes that in all things, not excepting the greatest and sublimest in any sphere of life, man is trying to evade his fundamental problem, namely, this perversion of sin. Yet at the same time, in these evasions he is trying to overcome and conquer—though unsuccessfully —by his own devices this his fundamental problem. Therefore human life in all its manifestations, abject as well as sublime, lies under the judgment of God and can only be redeemed and fundamentally renewed by recognizing whole-heartedly this judgment and the love and faith of God which are embodied therein. The whole-hearted recognition and acceptance of God's judgment and love by man is called faith, and the life built on that kind of faith is called the new life of the Spirit.

Those two poles have been discussed in the preceding chapter. Now it is our task to determine against this background our attitude towards the non-Christian religions.

The problem of this attitude is, for various reasons, one of the greatest and gravest which the Christian Church all over the world and the missionary cause have to face at the present time. Properly speaking, it is part of the root-problem which occupies us through our whole discussion—that is, the Christian Church and the Christian religion in their relation to the world and its spheres of life. The question behind this root-problem is always in some form or another : What do you think about man, his nature, his possibilities, his achievements ? It is very pertinent to remind ourselves of this, for two reasons.

First, the non-Christian religions are not merely sets of speculative ideas about the eternal destiny of man. The departmentalization of religion in the modern world as a result of the secularist differentiation of life-spheres strongly forces this erroneous conception of religion on the general mind. These non-Christian religions, however, are all-inclusive systems and theories of life, rooted in a religious basis, and therefore at the same time embrace a system of culture and civilization and a definite structure of society and state. To pronounce from the standpoint of the Christian faith upon our attitude towards the non-Christian religions necessarily means to pronounce upon the relation of the Christian faith to culture, state, society—in short, to the world and its spheres of life.

Secondly, the course usually followed—and which we shall follow too—when discussing the attitude of Christianity towards the non-Christian religions is that of expressing the whole problem in terms of the problems of general revelation and natural theology. This theological limitation of the discussion is all to the good, because it concentrates thought on the fundamental religious problems, effecting thereby a greater clarity of insight. It ought, however, constantly to be kept in mind that it is embedded in the all-embracing problem of the Christian religion or the Christian Church in its relation to the world. The great advantage that is to be derived from sticking to this commanding view is that the burning missionary problem of the attitude towards the non-Christian religions is a specimen of the great problem with which the Christian Church all over the world in different ways is inescapably confronted. In the condition of universal transition and revolutionary revision of culture, structure of state, society and economic order in which the world of to-day finds itself, the Church has to state anew its position in and obligation towards these spheres of life and their *present* pre-suppositions, pretensions, tendencies and values.

The confusion left behind in many minds from the discussion in the Jerusalem Meeting of the I.M.C. in 1928 of the papers on the values of the different religions was due to the fact that the value of those religions was discussed in a too-isolated way and the religions were not therefore given their appropriate setting. The questions that, from the Christian point of view, i.e. the view-point of revelation, lie at the back of such terms as general revelation and natural theology may be expressed as follows. Are nature, reason and history sources of revelation in the Christian sense of the word ? If so, what is the relation of the Christian revelation and its implications to the body of human self-unfolding which takes place in philosophy, religion, culture, art, and the other domains of life ? Whether the answer of the Christian Church is in the terms of a resolute renunciation of the world, as in the first centuries, or in those of a form of co-operation as in the Middle Ages, or is still different, depends wholly on the concrete circumstances of a given period and which aspect of its obligation as a Church, which lives by only one supreme loyalty, has to be operative in this given period.

There are, however, two conditions never to be lost sight of. In the first place, Christianity, under all circumstances, must always be aware that it is built on the prophetic and apostolic witness to a divine, transcendental order of life that transcends and judges by virtue of its inherent authority the whole range of historical human life in every period.

In the second place, whether the attitude is one of renunciation, of reserve or of intimate relation, it has to be essentially a *positive* attitude, because the world remains the domain of God who created it. After its rebellion against Him, He did not let it go but held it fast in His new initiative of reconciliation. It must be a positive attitude also because the Christian Church, as the witness to and representative of the new order of salvation and reconciliation, has been set by God *in* this world in order to be and work for the sake of this world. Jesus taught us to pray, " God's will be done on earth as it is in heaven," and this petition will always be the Magna Charta of the Church's obligation to occupy itself strenuously and positively with the world and its spheres of life, including the non-Christian religions.

The two conditions just mentioned indicate clearly the dialectical relation in which Christianity, if true to its nature and mission, ought to stand to the world—the combination of a fierce " yes " and at the same time a fierce " no " to the world : the *human* and *broken* reflection of the divine " no " and " yes " of the holy God of reconciliation, who held the world under His absolute judgment and at the same time claimed it for His love.

. . . .

Such are the perennial terms of the problem of the relation of Christianity to the world, which in every period of history require their peculiar expression and application. Now in turning to the great missionary problem of the attitude towards the non-Christian religions as a part of this all-inclusive problem, there are some considerations that ought to be continuously present in our mind when discussing it. The reason why we stand so badly in need of clarification about this problem is that the spiritual atmosphere of the present world makes it for the Christian Churches " at home " and in the non-Christian countries and for the vitality of the missionary cause a question of life or death. The " younger Churches " are living in a numerically overwhelming non-Christian world and in a not less overwhelming non-Christian atmosphere. To define their attitude towards these non-Christian religions is, on one hand, an indispensable necessity to them in order to develop the right sense of direction and certitude ; on the other hand, it implies a judgment and evaluation not only of the *religious* life and heritage of their own people in the restricted sense of the word, but also of the whole cultural, social and political structure and heritage of the people of whom they physically and spiritually are a living part. At least, if they want to penetrate into the real meaning of the Christian religion and become conscious of its implications for their task in their environment, they need light as to their attitude. But even if they did not feel this desire, the present state of the non-Christian world with its social, political and cultural upheaval presses the problem in this all-inclusive form very urgently on their minds.

In addition—and this applies not alone to the Younger Churches but as much to the Christian Church in general and the missionary enterprise as such—the problem of the attitude towards the non-Christian religions as representative and massive structures of religious life has a setting quite of its own in the modern world in which we live, and a tone of particular gravity. A few centuries ago the attitude all over the world was to assume, as a matter of course, the unquestionable and unquestioned superiority and validity of one's own religion. The increasing contact which the different civilizations and religions have with each other, and the accompanying rise and development of the scientific study and comparison of religions, has radically changed this atmosphere and has made this attitude impossible. By painstaking research, by efforts to get an insight into the historical and psychological development of the different religions, we have to-day a knowledge of these religions more accurate and extensive than ever before. Amazing similarities and not less amazing dissimilarities in them have come to the light, and the result has been that the religious uncertainty and lack of a sense of direction, already flowing from other sources, have enormously increased. The question, What is truth in religion ? is more urgent and more obscure than ever. This question is particularly urgent for Christianity, because it claims as its source and basis a divine revelation which at the same time is claimed to be the standard of reference for all truth and all religion. " I am the Way, the Truth and the Life. No one comes to the Father except through me " (John xiv. 6). "There is no salvation by anyone else, nor even a second Name under heaven appointed, for us men and our salvation " (Acts iv. 12). This question of truth is particularly urgent for the missionary cause, because missions inevitably must lose their vital impetus if this conviction becomes thin or turns out to be invalid, or is held with an uneasy conscience and a confused intellect. The psychological, cultural, social and moral value of Christianity may be rich and impressive ; yea, it may even be still richer than can be demonstrated by historical research and clear reasoning, but this argument carries us only to the point that Christianity is an extraordinarily valuable asset of historic human life, and in all probability will continue in the future to be so. From the standpoint of human history and culture this is highly important, but it ignores entirely the claim for truth which is the core of all real religious life and especially of Christianity, the religion of God's sole incarnation in Jesus Christ.

The argument of value does not coincide in any way whatever with that of truth. The non-Christian religions can just as well as Christianity show up an impressive record of psychological, cultural and other values, and it is wholly dependent on one's fundamental axioms of life whether one considers these non-Christian achievements of higher value for mankind than the Christian. The weakness of the value-argument in relation to the problem of ultimate and authoritative truth is still more patent if one remembers that from the standpoint of relative cultural value fictions and even lies have been extraordinarily valuable and successful. To-day we are taught unforgettable lessons on this score. Learned, ingenious, enthusiastic apologies for Christianity or religion, which shun the problem of truth because of its difficulty and satisfy themselves with important secondary motivations, are bred in ambiguity. A pragmatist position means ultimate scepticism or agnosticism and involves the surrender of the problem of truth. At the end the problem of truth stares us always sternly in the face, because man's deepest and noblest instincts refuse to extinguish the mark of his divine origin, namely, his thirst for and want of imperishable truth. The subjectively-motivated superiority of religious truths, experiences and values can never substantiate the claim for truth or justify and keep alive a missionary movement. The only possible basis is the faith that God has revealed *the* Way and *the* Life and *the* Truth in Jesus Christ and wills this to be known through all the world. A missionary movement and obligation so founded is alone able to remain unshaken and undiscouraged, even when it is without visible result as, for example, is so largely true in the case of Islam.

And how are we to justify this faith? The only valid answer, which is at the same time according to the character and nature of faith, is that it will become justified in the end when God will fulfil His purpose. For " Faith is a well-grounded assurance of that for which we *hope*, and a conviction of the reality of things which we do *not* see " (Heb. xi. 1). To demand a rational argument for faith is to make reason, that is, man, the standard of reference for faith, and ends in a vicious circle. Ultimate convictions never rest on a universally lucid and rational argument, in any philosophy and in any religion, and they never will. To adhere to a certain view of life and of the world has always meant a choice and a decision ; not a rational step in the sense of being universally demonstrable as a mathematical truth. Religion and philosophy deal with different things from mathematics and physical science. They deal with man and his desires, his passions and aspirations ; or

—to put it more adequately—loving, hating, coveting, aspiring man tries to deal with himself in religion and philosophy, and this involves every moment ethical and religious choices and decisions. The Christian's ultimate ground of faith is : " The Spirit bears witness along with our own spirits that we are children of God " (Rom. viii. 16) ; and he can die for that.

It has to be emphatically stated that the science of comparative religion, which brought and brings this confusion and anxiety, has exercised in many respects a highly salutary influence on religious life and our notions of it. Many fruits of the great humanistic movements of the last few centuries have made for a noble quest for truth, and for the liberation and widening of the human mind. So the science of comparative religion has effected in many directions a beneficent purification of religious insight. This remains true notwithstanding the many misguided notions and aberrations that it naturally entertained as being an occupation of human beings. In God's Hand it has become a means to unveil the stupendous richness of the religious life of mankind, in the good sense of the word as well as in the bad ; to foster a spirit of openness and honesty towards this alien religious life ; to undermine the unchristian intellectualistic and narrow-minded arrogance towards these other religions ; to open the eyes to the often all-too-human element in Christianity in its historical development and reality, often as degrading as the baser elements in the other religions ; to make aware of the petrification of faith and church-life into which the Christian Church slips as easily as other religions fall short of their original stimuli. Whosoever has learnt, with the aid of the science of comparative religion, to look honestly in the face the empirical reality of Christianity—I am not now speaking about the Christian revelation and its reality— and of the other religions, and has understood that Christianity as an historical religious body is thoroughly human, that is, a combination of sublime and abject and tolerable elements, will feel deeply that to speak glibly of the superiority of Christianity is offensive. Of course, there

are many traits in which Christianity in its historical manifestation is superior to other religions ; but of other traits
the same can be said in regard to the non-Christian religions.
The truly remarkable thing about Christianity as an historic
and empirical reality, which differentiates it from all other
religions, is rather that radical self-criticism is one of its
chief characteristics, because the revelation in Christ to
which it testifies erects the absolute superiority of God's
holy Will and judgment over *all* life, historical Christianity
included.

The feeling of superiority is essentially a cultural, and
not at all a religious, product ; and decidedly not a Christian
one. A feeling of superiority can only thrive on a definite
consciousness of achievement. The famous student of
religion, Troeltsch, who declined the Christian claim of
representing the ultimate, exclusive truth as revealed in
Jesus Christ, yet who nevertheless maintained a so-called
relative absoluteness for Christianity, was virtually giving
expression to his innate feeling of Western cultural achievement. There is no reason why a Hindu or a Chinese, being
nurtured in his particular atmosphere, should not claim,
after a comparative survey of the cultures and religions of
the world, the same relative absoluteness with regard to
his religion.

In the light of the Christian revelation, however, it is
impossible and unnatural to think in terms of achievement,
whether ethical or religious ; for the heart of the Gospel is
that we live by divine grace and forgiveness, and that
God has *made* Jesus Christ for us " wisdom from God,"
" righteousness," " sanctification " and " redemption " in
order that " he who boasts, let his boast be in the Lord "
(1 Cor. i. 30, 31) and not in any achievement of his own.
Speaking strictly as a Christian, the feeling of superiority is
the denial of what God meant and did through the Gospel.
That in Christianity and in the mission field the superiority-
feeling has so many victims indicates the intellectualist
distortion of the Gospel into which pious Christians can
lapse, by forgetting that to be a Christian means always
and in all circumstances to be a forgiven sinner and never

the *beatus possidens* of ready-made truth. In one of the preparatory papers for the Oxford Conference, Niebuhr makes the acute observation, which is pertinent to this attitude : " The final symbol of the perennial character of human sin is in the fact that the theologies, which preach humility and contrition, can nevertheless be vehicles of human pride."

   .   .   .   .

Three points of crucial importance have now become clear. In the first place, the attitude towards the non-Christian religions is to be seen in the context of the general problem of the relation of Christianity to the world and its spheres of life. To define our attitude towards these religions virtually means to affirm our conception of man and his faculties, to pass judgment on our fellow-man and his aspirations, attainments and aberrations.

Secondly, it confronts us with the question of normative truth. In both cases it is clear that for a Christian the only standard of reference can be the new and incommensurable world which has been revealed and made real by God in Jesus Christ and His life and work, and which is accessible to faith alone, that is, the free affirmative answer of man to God's " wonderful deeds." Christ, as the ultimate standard of reference, is the crisis of all religions, of the non-Christian religions and of empirical Christianity too. This implies that the most fruitful and legitimate way to analyse and evaluate all religions is to investigate them in the light of the revelation of Christ.

In the third place, the character of this faith and the nature of the divine truth of revelation consists not in general ideas but in fundamental conditions and relations between God, man and the world. Strengthened by the liberating work of the science of comparative religion, it excludes all feeling of superiority, requiring an honest recognition of our common humanity with adherents of other religions, as well in religious attainments as in religious defects. A missionary or a Christian who harbours the tiniest spark of spiritual arrogance and boasts of " his " superiority by being a Christian and " having " the truth, grieves the Spirit of Christ and obscures his message, because the foundation of the Christian life is to " boast in the Lord " and to rejoice gratefully and humbly in *His* mercy.

We must, however, go still further. From the standpoint of the Christian revelation, what answer can be given to the question : Does God—and if so, how and where does God—reveal Himself in the religious life as present in the non-Christian religions ?

This question is more difficult than it appears. Surveying human endeavour towards spiritual expression over the whole range of life, the obvious statement to be made is that all religions, the so-called " higher " as well as the so-called " lower " ones, all philosophies and world-views, are the various efforts of man to apprehend the totality of existence, often stirring in their sublimity and as often pathetic or revolting in their ineffectiveness. So philosophy is this effort towards apprehension by way of knowledge ; religion is the same effort by way of the heart ; theology, as, for example, Moslem theology or Ramanuja's bhakti-theology, is an effort to reflect in a system of coherent thinking the religious apprehension of existence. This universal effort towards the apprehension of the totality of existence being the effort of man, it is quite natural that there should be an amazing amount of concurrence as to the aspirations, ideas, institutions, symbols and intuitions in all the religions and philosophies of mankind, despite their great variations caused by differences of environment, mental structure and historical development. There is a universal religious consciousness amongst men of all ages and climes and races, which evidently produces in very different forms and concatenations many similar data and symbols of religious and ethical insight. Hence the well-known fact that, whether we live with peoples of " higher " or of " lower " religions, we so often recognize our own religious or ethical aspirations or insight, and that many a religious handbook, which has fame and authority with the followers of the religion which produced it, is equally valued by followers of other religions. Take, for example, the *Tao*

Teh King, the *Bhagavadgita*, the *Kural* of Tiruvalluvar, the *Imitatio*, and some Moslem handbooks of religion and ethics. Another well-known fact is that again and again people arise who try to construe out of these concurring religious and ethical evidences the " normal," " natural " religion of mankind. This endeavour, although quite intelligible on account of the mentioned similarities, is false. It confuses concurrent but widely scattered, unevenly distributed, differently graded and differently motivated religious and ethical notions, with a supposedly coherent system, governed by some leading general ideas which the creators of this " natural " religion arbitrarily put upon it. As scientific research and critical thinking both teach, there is no " natural " religion ; there is only a universal religious consciousness in man, which produces many similarities. Besides that, there are concrete religions, each with its peculiar structure and character.

Man's dangerous condition is that he is a dual being. He is of divine origin, and he is corrupted by sin and constantly prone to assert his self-centred and disordered will against the divine will. In a magnificent way Pascal has expressed this in his *Pensées*. He says : " Quelle chimère est-ce donc que l'homme ! Quelle nouveauté ! quel monstre, quel chaos, quel sujet de contradiction, quel prodige ! Juge de toutes choses, imbécile ver de terre, dépositaire du vrai, cloaque d'incertitude et d'erreur, gloire et rebut de l'univers." (What a chimera man is ! What a novelty, what a monster, how chaotic, how full of contradictions, what a marvel ! Judge of all things, a stupid earthworm, a depository of truth, a heap of uncertainty and error, the glory and refuse of the universe.) This fundamental disharmony is also manifested in all the spheres of life in which man moves, and in his cultural and religious achievements. His divine origin and his great gifts make him a creature that masters and regulates life in many ways, and that develops great cultures and civilizations. The development and progress which can be traced in their history are the manifestation of the deep urge of his splendid faculties and of his destiny " to subdue and master the earth and all that is in it " (Gen. i. 28).

In the domain of the religious consciousness man's

possibilities and abilities shine in the lofty religions and the ethical systems that he has produced and tried to live by. The non-Christian world in the past and the present offers many illustrious examples. His sin and his subjection to evil and to satanic forces, however, corrupt all his creations and achievements, even the sublimest, in the most vicious way. The mystic, who triumphantly realizes his essential one-ness with God or the Divine, knowing himself in serene equanimity the supreme master of the universe and of destiny, and who by his marvellous feats of moral self-restraint and spiritual self-discipline offers a fascinating example of splendid humanity, commits in this sublime way the root-sin of mankind, " to be like God " (Gen. iii. 5). The splendid results of human mastery of the laws of nature and of human inventiveness become the instruments of the most barbarous and monstrous violations of elementary humanity. The world of development and progress is at the same time the world of degeneration, decay and destruction. The doom of death, corruption and demonic self-destruction is always hovering over this splendid world of man and nature. Hence the universal religious consciousness of man has everywhere produced also the most abhorrent and degrading filth that perverted human imagination and lust can beget. This fundamental and horrid disharmony, this dialectical[1] condition of man is called by the Christian revelation, as contained in Biblical realism, sin, guilt, lostness past recovery except by God Himself ; and no other religion does this in such unmistakable and consistent terms. The universal religious consciousness of man itself nowhere speaks this clear language, because it is confused and blinded by its inherent disharmony.

The Christian revelation places itself over against the many efforts to apprehend the totality of existence. It asserts itself as the record of God's self-disclosing and re-creating revelation in Jesus Christ, as an apprehension of existence that revolves around the poles of divine judgment

---

[1] To avoid obscurity the reader is informed that by " dialectical " is meant this condition, inherent in man, of saying at the same time yes and no to his true destiny and his relatedness to the eternal.

and divine salvation, giving the divine answer to this demonic and guilty disharmony of man and the world.

THE PROBLEM OF NATURAL THEOLOGY

This fact of the universal religious consciousness of humanity and of its products and achievements has been a serious problem for Christianity since the beginning. For a very simple and obvious reason. Christianity as *the* religion of revelation is necessarily at close grips with the problem of truth. The Apologists and Fathers of the first Christian centuries propounded two opposite solutions to the problem ; either they assumed the operation of diffused reason (*logos spermatikos*) in the non-Christian world or they denounced the non-Christian religious world as the product of demonic influences.

The most massive attempt to embrace the religious life of mankind and the Christian revelation in one harmonious system of thought has been Aquinas's hierarchical system of the sphere of natural and rational religious truth and that of the supernatural and superrational realm of revelation, on the assumption that the first grade of natural theology has the function of a *præambula fidei* and a *præparatio evangelica*. The main objection to this imposing system is not that it is rationalistic. Its value lies rather in its legitimate endeavour to recognize the rights of reason and of the undeniable human urge for ordered and progressive life, and so to vindicate that rationalism within due proportions has a valid and important place in human life and thinking. Thomas Aquinas did not aim at rationalizing the data of revelation. He was too good a Christian not to maintain the mystery of revelation, for in his opinion a " vetula " (an old uneducated woman) who lived by the mysteries of the Christian revelation had deeper knowledge and certitude about the fundamental problems of existence than his beloved philosophers of antiquity.

The fundamental weakness of Thomas's system is, from the standpoint of Biblical realism, a religious one. Under the influence of Aristotelian philosophy he entertained an intellectualist conception of revelation, considering it to offer a set of supernatural truths, inaccessible to reason (for example, the Trinity). This conception is a denial of the existential [1] and dynamic character of Biblical revelation. Further than that, in order to construe his harmony he made the order of grace and revelation a perfected stage of nature and of reason. *Gratia non tollit sed perficit naturam* (grace does not abrogate but perfects nature), was his maxim. In doing this he destroyed the insuperable barrier between natural and supernatural truth that he previously erected, and ignored—a fundamental religious mistake—the fact that, according to Biblical realism, the opposite of grace is not nature or reason, but sin. The real cause of this unpardonable mistake is that his starting-point is the ontological conception of Greek philosophy about God, that God is Pure Essence and the Unity of all Being—and not the prophetic voluntaristic conception of the Bible. The urge for rational unity of thought was the impelling force in his ontological hierarchy and drove him into the arms of philosophical monism, setting the religious life of mankind and the revelation in Christ in the relation of horizontal grading to each other. The revelation in Christ, however, is vertically related to all human religious life and wisdom, because it is the " wisdom of God " which is " sheer folly " to the Greeks, and not the perfection or crown of human reason or religion. In Thomas's system revelation and its content becomes, logically speaking, a much-needed supplement to the insufficiency of reason in the realm of supernatural truth, and not the crisis of all religion and all human reasoning, which it is in the sphere of Biblical realism.

The Roman Catholic conception of " natural theology " is therefore from the standpoint of revelation a failure and an error. The unique character of Biblical religion, which it intends to maintain, is imprudently sacrificed to the exigencies of all-inclusive harmonistic thinking.

The opposite standpoint is the subject of vigorous theological debate in the last ten years. Karl Barth's theology is an energetic endeavour to assert and lay bare the exclusive

---

[1] By " existential " is meant that which lays bare the elemental roots of reality.

nature of Biblical religious truth as wholly *sui generis*. Its outstanding merit in the present deluge of relativist thinking is that it states the problem of revelation as a matter of life or death for Christianity and theology. It is deeply sensitive to the radically religious character of Biblical realism and proclaims it with prophetic aggressiveness and fervour. Its voice deserves the most serious attention to-day, because this theology offers a much-needed purification of Christian thinking. To appreciate this, one ought to have in mind the whole development of theological thinking in the last two centuries.

In the eighteenth century the representatives of the enlightenment fought—as periodically occurs and has to occur in human history—a partly legitimate and salutary battle for the rights of human reason. As their self-chosen opponents were intellectualist orthodox theology and the external authoritative conception of religious truth in the Roman Catholic Church, revelation appeared to them to be synonymous with unworthy suppression of the light of human reason. Believing in the autonomy of man, their eyes were naturally blinded to the peculiarly religious and unique character of Biblical realism ; and orthodox theology in this matter was then a blind guide of the blind. The conception of " natural religion " as the " normal " and " standard " religion became paramount, and in their humanist theology the light of reason became *the* organ of revelation. " Natural theology " was conceived to be the only true kind of theology, a liberation from the fetters of current theology ; and " general revelation " was the introduction to it. Current theology and " special revelation " either got the position of specifications and additions, or, more logically, were deemed unnecessary, as, for instance, by Toland. The standard of reference for religious truth was found in the essence of religion, supposedly derived from natural theology. " Special revelation," that is, the Christian message and its claims, appeared more and more in this atmosphere of thought as irrational or anti-rational, and consequently irrelevant.

Lessing's story of the three rings in *Nathan the Wise* and

his well-known words : " *Zufällige Geschichtswahrheiten können nie der Beweis ewiger notwendiger Vernunftswahrheiten sein* " (Accidental historical truths can never be the evidence for eternal and necessary rational truths), are the classical expression of this authoritative position of natural and rational religion. He tried to reserve within this realm of reason a special place for Christianity by conceiving the whole religious process of mankind as an experiment of divine pedagogy. However, this conception of divine pedagogy —even to-day a favourite idea with many—becoming manifest in the ever-evolving progress of human religiosity, wholly misconceives the peculiar character of revelation. To be a pedagogue, to educate, means to assist in the development of innate forces ; and applied to religion it means to render help in making man conscious of his divine nature and possibilities. Nobody can deny that in religious education we certainly have to do with innate forces, favourable and unfavourable, and with possibilities and dangers ; but to conceive God primarily as the Pedagogue, who fundamentally does not create anything new but assists in and guarantees the self-unfolding of the human spirit in the sphere of religion, is a complete disavowal of revelation, which means God's sovereign Will creating an entirely new situation. The abstruse Hamann, probably the most profound Christian thinker of the eighteenth century through his deep sense of the peculiar nature of the historical revelation in Christ, rightly said that, properly speaking, Kant's moralism meant the deification of the human will and Lessing's rationalism the deification of human reason. To reject the God of revelation inevitably means to erect man in some form as god.

The relativism which is inherent in this " deification " of what is by nature relative and limited, but which is hidden as such because of the faith in " abstract," " eternal " ideas, came to the surface in the nineteenth century. The strong positivist turn of mind, an increasing knowledge of the many religions, and more critical philosophical thinking, demolished the mirage of a " natural " standard religion, of which the positive religions are lower grade specifications. In the first place it was contradicted by the facts, and in the second place it became understood that " abstract," " eternal " ideas and the " natural " standard religion are creations of the human mind and as such relative, falsely claiming absoluteness.

Comparative religion became aware of the peculiar, typical character of every religion, and abandoned more and more all evolutionary schemes for explaining the religious reality of mankind. The present situation in comparative religion is that, having no standard of reference as norm, all religions are conceived as more or less worthy vehicles of divine revelation. Virtually, this means the denial of all revelation, because the fundamentally relativist trend of modern thinking excludes all possibility of taking the idea of revelation really seriously. Honest and courageous thinking requires this conclusion. The reason why this inescapable conclusion is evaded is that relativist thinking instinctively fears its own destructive consequences, and at the same time instinctively suspects its fallacy, because the human mind is created for ultimate and indestructible truth and cannot live without certitude and a conviction that there is a stable point. All the discussions about the absoluteness of Christianity or about its " provisional " absoluteness—a rather strange and contradictory concept—are intelligible as defences against the flood of relativism, but they are misguided as interpretations of revelation in the radical sense of Biblical realism.

Barth's theology is a merciless war-cry against this persuasive and omnipresent relativism. The great service he renders to all the world, and not only to the continent of Europe, is that he reminds us of the real meaning of revelation. Revelation is an act of God, an act of divine grace for forlorn man and a forlorn world by which He condescends to reveal His Will and His Heart, and which, just because it is revelation, remains hidden except to the eye of *faith*, and even then remains an incomprehensible miracle. This is the Biblical and the only valid idea of revelation, because a revealed mystery in the sense of a mystery that has become comprehensible by the act of revealing is no mystery. Revelation is no object but an action, a divine movement. In this connection " general revelation," in the sense of God revealing Himself with compelling lucidity in nature, history and reason, is a contradiction in terms, for what lies on the street has no need to be revealed. By its nature revelation is and must be special. It affirms that God paves the way, not man. The remark of D. F. Strausz, " *Die Gottheit liebt es nicht in ein Exemplar ihre ganze Fülle auszuschütten und gegen alle andere zu geizen* " (The Deity does not like to pour out Its complete fullness in one specimen and be niggardly towards others), is a frivolous ignoring of what it means that God is really God.

The opinion is often heard that it would be detestable pride on the part of a Christian and a sample of mean thinking about God to suppose that He has " limited " His revelation to Israel and left the other peoples destitute. This issues partly from a justifiable indignation at the all-too-common sin amongst Christians of behaving themselves as the proud and superior possessors of truth, becoming guilty thereby of that " boasting " which Paul so emphatically denounces as anti-christian. It arises partly also from a noble generosity and honesty of mind that will gladly recognize the lofty elements in alien religious life and the active dealing of God with all mankind. Yet, although this indignation and generosity are to the point, those who hold this opinion are labouring under a radical misconception of revelation in the Biblical sense. The relevant question is not, Who owns revelation? Neither Christians, nor Jews, nor non-Christians can pretend or boast to be in possession of it. Revelation is *eo ipso* an act of divine condescension. The real Christian contention is not : " We have the revelation and not you," but pointing gratefully and humbly to Christ : " It has pleased God to reveal Himself fully and decisively in Christ ; repent, believe and adore."

In the midst of the atmosphere of relativism Barth's concern is deeply religious. By the right desire to maintain integrally that the revelation is solely God's act and that it is exclusively His grace that creates the new situation for man and the world, he rejects radically any shadow of synergism in the realm of faith, and on the same grounds also anything like natural theology.

He does not deny that there must exist something common between God and man, which makes it possible for man " to hear God's Word." However, to avoid the danger of making human religious experience and effort a preamble of faith, which would imply making the realm of revelation and grace continuous to the realm of human religious effort, he refuses to move one inch further. Afraid of the pitfall into which Aquinas has fallen with his harmonious system of natural and supernatural theology, he rightly asserts the discontinuity of " nature " and " grace " or " reason " with " revelation " by rejecting all natural theology. He will not and cannot deny *that* God works and has worked in man outside the Biblical sphere of revelation, but *how* this has happened he refuses to discuss.

This, it seems, savours too much of theological and logical consistency and breathes not sufficiently the free atmosphere of Biblical realism. This self-willed refusal to move further will in the long run appear to be untenable. Although at the present moment it is a religiously-inspired, drastic unmasking of the implications of relativism, it will be dangerously open to the dreary fate of sterile intellectualism if the chief attention remains focussed, as it tends to do, on "pure doctrine." History and the psychology of mankind teach lessons of terrible moment in this connection. Biblical realism is wholly absorbed in God's acts and the apostolic concern to confront *men* with them, that they may believe ; not in " pure doctrine." The problem of the relation to the world and all its spheres of life and that of the attitude towards other religions and how God works in them cannot be constantly passed by in silence or left untouched. Common sense and the reality of life revolt against this. Biblical realism requires us to wrestle with it, for the world is still the creation of God " who does not abandon the works of His hands," but continues working in it. Even in this fallen world God shines through in a broken, troubled way : in reason, in nature and in history. Otherwise the urge for truth, beauty, goodness and holiness, stirring in science, philosophy, art, religion are incomprehensible. The community of the believers in Christ belongs to this world and lives and works in it, and even for the sake of self-comprehension it needs light on the subject of this world as it is and its relation to God.

It seems that the problem of synergism versus monergism [1] does not have in the sphere of Biblical realism, with its indissoluble unity of faith and ethics, that strained aspect which it often has in theology. Faith is ethics and ethics are faith, because both are rooted in and sustained by divine grace. The universal religious consciousness of man and the results of his endeavour to obtain an apprehension of the totality of existence cannot be dismissed as outside discussion. The testimony of the Bible in the Acts and the Epistles breathes a freer, more human, more positive spirit, despite its uncompromising attitude towards the world. The perception of Divinity (*sensus divinitatis*) operative in mankind, asserted by Calvin, is in the religious realism of the Bible no object of discussion, but a working hypothesis that goes without saying. Here lie the necessity and legitimacy of Brunner's protest, and of his combat in favour of a critical and right kind of natural theology ; for, although beset with many possibilities of error, we must somehow try to talk about it. Vital and genuine faith is in the long run more endangered by a too-exclusive concentration on " pure doctrine " than by the inescapable endeavour, however subject to error, to try to speak in the light of the revelation in Christ about the religious reality of man outside the sphere of " special revelation." In the present stage of the discussion all contributions must be tentative and preliminary, because as our eyes have become sharpened again for the unique and *sui generis* character of the realm of revelation and salvation, we must learn to talk in a new way about the realm of fallen creation (nature and reason)—that is to say, in a deeper, more realistic, freer way than has been the case in the past.

[1] The question whether in salvation the human soul collaborates with God or is the object of the sole act of God.

The great advantage of this discussion about natural theology, which is still in its first stages in Europe and on which the different schools of thought will probably separate, is that it engenders a healthy purification of thinking, also of our missionary thinking. Though the future must still bring clarification, the following results may at present be stated. The terms " general revelation " and " natural theology " cannot forthwith be used in the customary loose way. It will no more be permitted to call, as so often is done undiscerningly, sublime religious and moral achievements the pure and unmistakable evidences of divine revelation of the same sort and quality as the revelation in Jesus Christ. Not—it ought to be said with all possible emphasis—because one grudges, from a narrow-minded and unchristian attitude, the non-Christian world the real experience of divine revelation. Whosoever by God's grace has some moderate understanding of the all-inclusive compassion of God and of Christ rejoices over every evidence of divine working and revelation that may be found in the non-Christian world. No man, and certainly no Christian, can claim the power or the right to limit God's revelatory working. The reason, however, why it is undiscerning to dub religious and moral achievements, because they impress us as sublime and lofty, revelations of the same quality as the revelation in Christ is that—it may be said with all reverence—it has pleased God in His plan of world-redemption to exercise self-limitation by becoming flesh in this special, historic man, Jesus Christ, and so to express clearly and exclusively in Christ's life and work His judgment on and purpose for man and the world.

The way in which this special revelation in Christ contradicts and upsets all human religious aspiration and imagination is an indirect indication of its special and *sui generis* quality and significance. The protest which all philosophies and religions have raised, raise and will raise against the cardinal elements of the Christian faith demonstrates that the God of the philosophers and the scholars, however lofty their conception may be, is *not* the God and Father of Jesus Christ, as Pascal said.

Likewise it will no more be permitted to consider undiscerningly the glimpses of revelation and the religious intuitions of mankind as a preceding and preparatory stage for the full revelation in Christ. Natural theology of that sort, which conceives the Gospel as essentially the fulfilment, the highest development and budding forth of the religious forces and seeds in mankind, overlooks—we repeat—the *sui generis* character of the revelation of Christ. It ought to be said again with all possible emphasis that having placed oneself under the authority of God's revelation in Christ does not mean that one disregards and despises the religious life of mankind outside the Christian revelation. Whosoever, by God's grace, has gone into the school of Jesus Christ and has beheld the Master's large-hearted praise of the faith of the Roman officer, the like of which He had not met in Israel, and His tender shrinking from " breaking the crushed reed " and " quenching the smouldering flax "—all things which are also included in *His function of revealing God*—has learnt another lesson.

Fulfilment, then, is not the term by which to characterize the relation of the revelation in Christ to the non-Christian religions. To use it engenders inevitably the erroneous conception that the lines of the so-called highest developments point naturally in the direction of Christ, and would end in Him if produced further. The Cross and its real meaning —reconciliation as God's initiative and act—is antagonistic to all human religious aspirations and ends, for the tendency of all human religious striving is to possess or conquer God, to realize our divine nature (*theosis*). Christ is not the fulfilment of this but the uncovering of its self-assertive nature ; and at the same time the re-birth to a completely opposite condition, namely, the fellowship of reconciliation with God. Moreover, in Biblical realism fulfilment means always the fulfilment of God's promises and of His previous preparatory doings. As ever, it remains consistent in its theocentric emphasis. To be sure, in many men and in the religions of mankind there stir deep aspirations, longings and intuitions which find their fulfilment in Christ, for man " is groping for God," as Paul said on the Areopagus. Because of that, many a convert to Christianity has had this experience of liberating fulfilment. Nevertheless, as the revelation of God in Christ transcends and contradicts all human wisdom by its divine folly, and all human aspiration and expectation by its entirely unexpected way of fulfilling them, it is wrong to use the term fulfilment. Conversion and regeneration would be truer to reality. At any rate, the term fulfilment, in the customary sense of bringing to perfection what had already naturally grown to a more or less successful approximation to the life and the truth revealed in Christ, is not applicable to the relation of the non-Christian religions to the revelation in Christ.

Some illustrations may serve to clear up this point. All over the world propitiatory sacrifices are known. Their practice points to the fact that man has an inkling of his ultimate insufficiency before God, in moral or ceremonial respects. He suspects that atonement is needed. To a certain degree one has the right to say that Christ is the fulfilment of this dim inkling, though it is often smothered in matters of detail that have practically become chief concerns. Nevertheless, on closer investigation and experience it appears that this non-Christian idea of propitiation and atonement virtually springs from the awareness of the ultimate indigence of man in his efforts to appease the superhuman forces. It is an ultimate measure of insurance, and therefore of self-assertion. There is no road from that to the reconciliation in Christ, which revolves around the poles of radical divine judgment on sin as self-assertion, and of exclusive divine effort to reclaim man. To talk here of fulfilment would mean to destroy all insight and discernment.

The longing for and the expectation of a world of perfect harmony and bliss, of a " Kingdom of God " and of a Divine Saviour and Mediator to bring and realize it, is universally known in very different forms in all the religions of the world. Christ and His Kingdom of God may be called in a certain sense the fulfilment of these expectations. Nevertheless, this " fulfilment " brings quite the reverse of all expectations, for His Kingdom is a " *Umwertung aller*

Werte " (re-casting of all values) ; it is realized in the suffering and self-abandonment of the Saviour and can be entered, not by miraculous mythical deliverance, but by faith alone, that is, by obedience to the Will of God.

General revelation can henceforth only mean that God shines revealingly through the works of His creation (nature), through the thirst and quest for truth and beauty, through conscience and the thirst and quest for goodness, which throbs in man even in his condition of forlorn sinfulness, because God is continuously occupying Himself and wrestling with man, in all ages and with all peoples. This " general revelation " can only be effectually discovered in the light of the " special revelation." Here Biblical realism demonstrates again its deep and sound sense of reality, because it testifies that God's revelation in " general revelation " is just as well an object of faith as that in " special revelation." " By *faith* we understand that the world was fashioned by the Word of God " (Heb. xi. 1). The function of natural theology will henceforth be, not to construe preparatory stages and draw unbroken, continuous lines of religious development ending and reaching their summit in Christ, but in the light of the Christian revelation to lay bare the dialectical condition not only of the non-Christian religions but of *all* the human attempts towards apprehension of the totality of existence. Or, to put it differently, to uncover in the light of the revelation in Christ the different modes of God-, self- and world-consciousness of man in his religious life.

This dialectical condition, as we have already sought to show, issues from the fundamental and demonic disharmony of man, which stares everyone in the face, and which is the most disquieting riddle of history and mankind. On the one hand, man's sublime faculties and accomplishments in the realm of intellect, culture, art, morals, religion, mastery of life, and, on the other hand, man's apparently constitutional blindness, even in his sublimest moments, to God as He is in Jesus Christ, and his perversion and corruption. Biblical realism is fully aware of this fundamental and demonic disharmony, and therefore has a dialectical attitude towards it, at the same time saying yes and no. It holds that God still works in this disharmony, shines dimly through it and performs His judgment over it and in it, for in the light of Biblical realism the disharmony in man is not only fundamental and demonic, but also and above all guilty. Above the dialectical unity of yes and no, however, there rises triumphantly an ultimate divine yes in God's saving Will towards mankind and the world.

An exhaustive discussion of the material in Biblical realism regarding its dialectical attitude towards the fallen creation is impossible. Some hints only can be given to corroborate what has just been said, and to vindicate the claim that the assumption of God's speaking in nature and conscience is in Biblical realism not an element in a conscious systematic effort for natural theology, but is clearly regarded as self-evident. The well-known passages in Romans i. and ii. about God's " being plain " in His creation and in the conscience of man seem to suggest the following lines of thought. God's everlasting power and Godhead, ever since the world was created, is clearly visible and intelligible through His works. God has made it plain to man, but through his impiety and iniquity man has suppressed and suppresses this plain truth. He is therefore inescapably subject to religious and moral confusion and divine judgment. At the same time, however, Jews and Gentiles, that is, all mankind, know by nature the law written in their hearts and consciences and often obey it.

It is not intended to treat the content of these chapters in their extraordinary richness and depth. That would mean a treatise on the Christian philosophy of history. What we aim at is merely to illustrate the dialectical attitude of Biblical realism. God works in man and shines through nature. The religious and moral life of man is man's achievement, but also God's wrestling with him ; it manifests a receptivity to God, but at the same time an inexcusable disobedience and blindness to God. The world fails to know God even in its highest wisdom, although it strives to do so. Man seeks God and at the same time flees from Him in his seeking, because his self-assertive self-centredness of will, his root-sin, always breaks through. God's anger is revealed towards the iniquity of man as manifested in his religious and moral depravity ; but nevertheless the entire creation is eagerly longing for the revelation of the " glorious freedom of the children of God " (Rom. viii.). Such was and is the contradictory condition of the world, and of the religious and moral life of the world in its different forms, and the dialectical relation of God to it. To indicate systematically and concretely where God revealed Himself and wrestled and wrestles with man in the non-Christian religions is not feasible. Every effort to do so is hazardous. Personal concrete experiences, the meeting of spirit *with spirit* and illumined divination can alone lead on the right track.

The attitude of the missionary and the Christian towards the non-Christian religions has therefore the same quality. When his mind is schooled by Biblical realism and has the humane openness that ought to be natural to one whose life-task is to have apostolic interest in man, the missionary knows of the dialectical condition of non-Christian religious life and takes both sides seriously.

Paul and Barnabas in Lystra vehemently protested against the idolatrous nature and habits of the men who tried to treat them as gods, for the zeal for the sole Lordship of God filled their hearts, they being no mere speculative monotheists. So in their speech of protest they said : " In bygone ages God allowed all nations to go their own ways, though as the Bountiful Giver He did not leave Himself without a witness," expressing in these words at the same time the working of the divine judgment and of the continuous divine solicitude for the religious life of mankind. When Paul entered Athens his mind was stirred within him when he noticed that the town was full of idols, because to his apostolic mind to go astray in the worship of God is a very serious matter. Next, in his speech on the Areopagus, he recognizes frankly that men are seeking and groping for God, as God has meant them to do ; but, standing in the light of the revelation of Christ, in the same breath he says with quiet assurance of the philosophy and

religion of the Greek, the philosophical light of the world :
" God has overlooked the ages of ignorance." That is
the glorious freedom and courage of faith. In Ephesus
he won many over to the faith, of whom " numbers who
had practised magic arts collected their books and burned
them in the presence of all " ; yet he appears to have known
that witness to God and Christ and rejection of idolatry
do not imply disparagement of religious sentiment, for
the secretary of the town testifies that these men were " no
blasphemers of our goddess." Peter, impressed by Cornelius'
religious life, declares with gratitude : " I see quite plainly
that God has no favourites, but that he who reverences
Him and lives a good life in any nation, is welcomed by
Him " ; but his letters show that he certainly agreed with
Paul when he declared before Agrippa that entering the
sphere of the revelation in Christ means to " turn from
darkness to light, from the power of Satan to God," for
it is " remission of sins," which is not to be found but in
Jesus Christ.

Inspired by this Biblical realism, the attitude towards
the non-Christian religions is a remarkable combination of
down-right intrepidity and of radical humility. Radical
humility, because the missionary and through him the
Christian Church is the bringer of a divine gift, not something of his making and achievement ; and what he has
received for nothing, he gives for nothing. Downright
intrepidity, because the missionary is the bearer of a message,
the witness to a divine revelation, not his discovery, but
God's act. In this light, not in the light or by the virtue of
his religious achievements, he has the freedom and obligation
to maintain, in the face of the highest and loftiest religious
and moral achievements in the non-Christian religions, that
they need conversion and regeneration as much as the
" ordinary " sinner needs it ; because the meaning of Christ
is that He makes *all* things new, and that, according to
Jesus' word, " the least in the kingdom of Heaven is greater
than John the Baptist," who was greater than anyone
" among the sons of women."

If the revelation in Christ is well understood, the eye is

opened for the depravity and the perversion of human religious life which occur in the non-Christian religions and in empirical Christianity, and no weak or meek judgment will be pronounced. The eye is also opened for the deep aspirations and longings and magnificent embodiments of these longings and aspirations. Nevertheless, in the light of this revelation in Christ and of what *God* has wrought through it, all things necessarily undergo a drastic re-evaluation and re-creation. One will often meet representatives of the non-Christian religions who justly fill one with deep reverence, because they represent in their whole life an extraordinary degree of devotion to the reality of the world of the spiritual and eternal. Nevertheless, in the light of Christ's revelation it is a disturbing thing that such highly-developed spiritual personalities often do not show the least comprehension of the greatest gift of Christ—forgiveness of sins.

Paul is an illuminating example of one combining a high appreciation of religious life outside the sphere of God's revelation in Christ with the fundamental rejection of it for Christ's sake. In the third chapter of the Epistle to the Philippians he enumerates the high privileges and values of his religious past. He was a son of Israel, a Jew of sincere piety and immaculate life, a God-fearing Pharisee ; and we know that the Pharisees could be splendid examples of what man is able to achieve as to religious and moral attainments. Paul does not despise it, he values it. Even when he has forsaken it, he values and respects it highly. " But," he says, " for Christ's sake I have learnt to count my former gains a loss ; indeed, I count anything a loss, compared to the supreme value of knowing Christ Jesus my Lord."

To sum up, from the standpoint of Biblical realism the attitude towards the non-Christian religions, and likewise the relation of the Christian Church to the world in all its domains, is the combination of a prophetic, apostolic heraldship of truth for Christ's sake with a priestly apostolic ambassadorship of love for His sake. The right attitude of the Church, properly understood, is essentially a missionary one, the Church being set by God in the world as ambassador of His reconciliation, which is the truth that outshines all truth and the grace that works faithful love.

POINTS OF CONTACT

Whenever the problem of the missionary attitude towards the non-Christian religions is discussed, the " point of contact " inevitably appears on the scene. The task of a good missionary is naturally considered to be that of eagerly looking for points of contact. Every missionary who has his heart in his work is all his life deeply concerned about points of contact. His apostolic and missionary obligation and desire to reach men with the Message, to stir a response, to set the chords of men's inner conscience vibrating, to find an entrance for the Gospel into their minds, to " make the way ready for the Lord," foster this concern. This concern is legitimate and should not be weakened by the knowledge that no mortal man can work faith in God and in Christ in another man, and that it is the Holy Spirit alone that can work faith and " convince of sin, righteousness and judgment." Its legitimacy and necessity are founded on a host of considerations,[1] of which the chief must be mentioned.

Man is, even in his fallen condition, God's creature, in whose heart God " has laid eternity." He knows about God ; therefore he seeks God and at the same time in his seeking tries to run from Him. This tragic contradictory position is his deepest problem and testifies to his indestructible relatedness to God. The quest for God, even when man tries to kill it in himself, is the perennially disturbing and central problem of man. Therefore, there is here undeniably a point of contact for the Message of the Gospel. To deny it is virtually to deny the humanity of man.

[1] The discussions about the problem of the " point of contact " are, like those on " natural theology," a part of the general revival of fundamental theological discussion that is going on all over the world, but especially in Germany. In this latter country the discussions are peculiarly profound and radical, because the German Church is in a life and death conflict over the same problems (the relation of the Church to the spheres of life, such as state, nation, people, community and the new paganism) as in many respects the Younger Churches (mutatis mutandis) have to face. To treat all these problems exhaustively would require a special volume and the literature is indeed overwhelming. In this book, of course, we can select only the main points.

In Biblical realism God is presented as deeply and strenuously concerned about man and the world. So deeply and so strenuously, so movingly humane is this concern, that in all ages all dignified philosophical and religious thinking has been shocked by the passionate anthropomorphism of prophetic Biblical religion ; and has always tried to mitigate and normalize it by a decent scheme of an immutable divine essence, arrayed with exalted divine attributes. God's deep and strenuous concern goes to the length of the Incarnation. If there is any meaning in it, it means that God wants, even passionately wants, contact with man, and thus through the act of His revelation shows His belief in the possibility of contact. Stronger argument than this for the existence of the point of contact in man there cannot be. The apostolic nature of God's revelation in Christ pre-supposes it. No human reasoning can wipe this out, unless it wants to make the Gospel void and meaningless.

Still another serious consideration is that our common humanity, our common capacity for religious and moral experience, effort, achievement and failure, our common aspirations, needs and dreads, and the fact that the Christian faith has to function and move through this common psychological apparatus, strongly point to a point of contact as a given fact.

Nevertheless, the curious thing is that there is always confusion in the atmosphere surrounding the problem of the point of contact. This confusion is particularly nervous at present, because Barthian theology, true to its vocation to be a purifying storm, has acted like a thunderstroke by the sentence : " There is no point of contact." Barth himself does not, of course, deny that there is a point of contact between God and man ; because the fact that faith in God's revelation occurs pre-supposes that it can be communicated to man and apprehended by him as revelation coming from God. Nevertheless, he puts outside the domain of theology the question as to what this point of contact is and how man can act in regard to it. It belongs entirely in the field of psychology and pedagogy. Therefore the sentence : " There is no point of contact " is asserted with fierce emphasis.

Preaching, religious education and instruction, missions, theological discussion and instruction, which are felt as natural, indispensable and even as very stringent obligations of the Christian Church, seem to assume a rather absurd aspect in the light of this absolutist sentence. Consequently reason and conscience remain deeply dissatisfied and disturbed.

Another reason for the confusion surrounding the problem is the secret conviction that a surer grasp of points of contact would ensure a greater and easier missionary result. This conviction has, properly understood, much truth in it ; but it has, of course, the same tendency as all human instruments, to induce us to entertain a delusive trust in these points of contact as the real *agents* of missionary results in the sense of previously unbelieving people coming to believe in Christ. The sole *agent* of real faith in Christ is the Holy Spirit.

The absolute sentence just mentioned affords an excellent opportunity to clear up somewhat the whole problem of the point of contact as a general and theoretical problem. It springs from the same background as the resistance offered to " general revelation " and " natural theology." Intent on maintaining integrally the unique character of the Christian revelation as God's sovereign, condescending act, what it says is that there are no bridges from human religious consciousness to the reality in Christ, and that it is exclusively God's grace and no human contribution or disposition whatever that effects " the falling of the scales from the eyes."

This is wholly true. Its being said with aggressive vehemence and passion in our atmosphere of loose relativist thinking renders the inestimable service of purging our thinking of many delusions. For example, the delusion of building too great hopes on our methods ; that of expecting success surely to come from our psychological and theological approaches or our dogmatic correctness or liberalism ; that of taking the term " point of contact " in the sense of an idea or disposition in the religious consciousness from which faith and conversion to Christ and His gifts and demands can be developed. It calls us vigorously back to the fundamental fact expressed in Jesus' word : " The wind blows where it wills, you can hear its sound, but you never know whence or where it goes ; it is the same with everyone who is born of the Spirit " (John iii. 8) ; and reminds us that man can only do the planting and the watering, " neither planter nor waterer " counting, " but God alone who makes the seed grow " (1 Cor. iii. 7).

Nevertheless, it must be repeated once again, the exclusive concern for theological consistency, although deriving from a deeply religious motive, too much ignores the not less patent religious interests and the apostolic nature of the Gospel. Here, again, Brunner's protest is justified. Out of exclusive zeal for the right contention that God and not man himself in any sense whatever is the Saviour and Redeemer, it disregards what is really at stake in the problem of the " point of contact " ; that is to say, the fact that man can respond to the call of God and consequently is held responsible for his doing so or not. Besides, it ignores the fact that the three considerations which we presented in order to elucidate the legitimacy and necessity of the irresistible concern for a point of contact cannot for ever be silenced, for theological and religious reasons. By eluding these realities, it easily loses vital touch with the free and humane atmosphere of Biblical realism. Once again, purity of truth or of doctrine is never an end, pursued in isolation in Biblical realism. The deep concern for " the building up of the Church in Christ " includes solicitude for preaching the right Gospel and for the right response in faith and life.

No theological problem can be merely treated by systematic theological reasoning, because its object is the divine reality of the living God and the religious and moral reality of living man. This applies more strongly to the problem of the " point of contact," because it is a vast pastoral problem as well. The vital unity of proclaiming and interpreting the truth with concern for souls, while constantly subjecting oneself to the testing of Biblical realism, offers in the long run a better guarantee for purity than does the isolated occupation with purity. The remarkable paradox in the life of every religious worker who is called to recommend the Gospel to the consciences of men is that it is his plain obligation and privilege to exert himself to the utmost and to utilize every means that experience and knowledge and talent put at his disposal, seemingly working as if all depended on his sincere devotion to the task ; and yet that he has to be deeply and reverently aware that it is " God who makes the seed grow " and that only " the Day will show what the nature of his work is." This paradox produces a deep tranquillity and at the same time opens the way for a humorous modesty in regard to one's work. This same dialectical structure is the core of the whole problem of the point of contact : divine grace and human responsiveness are its components ; yet the fact of human responsiveness does not impair the exclusive causality of grace in the whole process.

After these general considerations on the " point of contact " as a general problem, the question remains : Where, for the missionary in the various religious conditions in which he finds himself, are the concrete points of contact to be found ? When the different religions are treated later, more will be said about this matter. Here some remarks will be ventured in an endeavour to see this question of the concrete points of contact in its due perspective.

The insistent demand for concrete points of contact is quite natural. It springs from the normal desire to see one's way and from the apostolic desire, mentioned above, to reach men with the Message. However, in this matter of concrete points of contact, it is easy to entertain fallacious hopes and reasonings. Somehow the conviction is alive that it is possible and feasible to produce for every religion a sort of catalogue of points of contact. This apparently is a misguided pursuit. Such a catalogue, based on the similarities between Christianity and the non-Christian religions, for example, on such subjects as the idea of God and of man, the conception of the soul or of redemption, the expectation of an eternal life or the precedence of the community over the individual, etc., is an impossible thing. The reasons are twofold.

In the first place, religion is nowhere in the world an

assortment of spiritual commodities, that can be compared as shoes or neck-ties. This sounds frivolous, nevertheless it is a point of such overwhelming importance that it can hardly be over-estimated. It ought never to be forgotten in the treatment of religious subjects—but it constantly is—that religion is the vast and desperate effort of mankind to get somehow an apprehension of the totality of existence, and therefore every religion is an indivisible, and not to be divided, unity of existential apprehension. It is not a series of tenets, dogmas, prescriptions, institutions, practices, that can be taken one by one as independent items of religious life, conception or organization, and that can arbitrarily be compared with, and somehow related to, and grafted upon, the similar item of another religion.

Every religion is a living, indivisible unity. Every part of it—a dogma, a rite, a myth, an institution, a cult—is so vitally related to the whole that it can never be understood in its real function, significance and tendency, as these occur in the reality of life, without keeping constantly in mind the vast and living unity of existential apprehension in which this part moves and has its being. It is only for the sake of scientific analysis that we are allowed to break up a religion into conceptions about God, man, sin, redemption, soul, etc. This scientific method, properly speaking, is a great distortion and disregard of living and actual reality. It is, however, indispensable to get an *intellectual* command of the material and is therefore, at least to a certain extent, necessary as an instrument. As a guide for the adequate apprehension of religion as a living and thriving reality it is less than useless.

Now, missions have to do with religions as thriving and living realities, and in the problem of concrete points of contact to keep this incessantly in mind is the key of the whole matter. The many false hopes and reasonings that have been and are entertained on this subject in missionary circles are due to the neglect of this point. Many attempts made in missionary literature to build up various points of contact with different religions proceed on this intellectualist and analytical line of approach, which is applied by science in her own way and for a different and more legitimate end.

In doing this the all-decisive point in the whole matter is entirely left out of account. This point is that one does not know what the real force, value and function of the idea of God or of redemption or of faith or of the soul or of anything else is, if one does not primarily take into account what is the fundamental existential apprehension of the totality of life which dominates this whole religion, and what place and significance God, redemption, the soul or faith or anything else has in this existential apprehension.

Thus, a real insight is possible only if one applies this " totalitarian " approach to a religion and its constituent parts ; only so, therefore, can the problem of the concrete points of contact be approached with intelligence. Opposition to the use of catalogues therefore is not intended to imply that there is nothing to be said about points of contact, but that intellectualist and sterile ways should be abandoned.

In the second place, there is a still deeper reason than the " totalitarian " comprehension of religion for abandoning false hopes set on composing catalogues. This brings us back to a point already indicated more than once. The dialectical tension in which all human life, and consequently all religious life and all religions, are caught, and the dialectical view that Biblical realism accordingly entertains about it, were discussed under the subject of " natural theology." When this view-point is applied to the problem now under discussion, we are led still deeper. In the illuminating light of the revelation in Christ, which lays bare the moving and grand but at the same time distressing and desperate reality of human religious life, as reflected in the various religions, all " similarities " and points of contact become dissimilarities. For the revealing function of this light is that, when exposed to it, all religious life, the lofty and the degraded, appear to lie under the divine judgment, because it is *misdirected*. This is the dialectical " no " of the revelation in Christ to all religious life, and therefore also to every point of contact in the sense of its being one that, if it were properly developed, would end in the sphere of the revelation in Christ. At the same time, however, this revealing light means a dialectical

" yes," a comprehension of religion and the various religions that is deeper and more adequate than their understanding of themselves, because it uncovers the groping and persistent human aspiration and need for " the glory of the children of God " in the misdirected expressions of religious life.

In order to elucidate this line of thought some illustrations may be adduced.

Elaborate reasonings have been produced to demonstrate that the Chinese " high-god," Shang-ti, in various places in classical literature and in some phases of Chinese religious history had personal traits, such as might appear to offer a point of contact for the preaching of the personal God of the Christian religion. This surely was a mistake for many reasons. In the first place it is, as pointed out, always arbitrary to take one element from a whole living system of religion and to use this artificially-isolated element as a point of contact. No element of a living system of religion or culture can ever be taken in isolation, as if a culture or a human soul is a laboratory of spiritual chemistry. The value and significance of such an element is entirely dependent on the more or less vital and predominant place it holds in the totality of such a life-system. What we outsiders deem, for some reason external to such a life-system, interesting or important, may be of very minor significance in the system itself. Therefore this was a sterile, intellectual way of construing a point of contact.

In the second place it took for granted that the characteristic nature of the God and Father of Jesus Christ can be described as theistic ; even if we do not urge the fact of the very feeble " theistic " quality of Shang-ti. Our sketch of the conception of God in Biblical realism has shown that this is a misconception.

In the third place, this construing of a point of contact secretly started from the naïve evolutionist and rationalistic pre-supposition that the " theistic " conception of God in Christianity could be grafted upon the Chinese idea of Shang-ti, and that the clearer and sharper theistic and personalistic physiognomy of the Christian " idea " of God would induce people after some instruction to recognize gratefully the higher stage of development which this represented in comparison with the vague figure of Shang-ti. This reasoning was wrong and naïve, because the whole soul of Chinese culture cares very little for personality in the Divine. No neat and intelligent reasoning can awaken this ; it can come only by confrontation with Jesus Christ.

To take another example. Buddhism in its original inspiration and purpose is probably the greatest among the non-Christian religions. It takes, with such radical seriousness as is to be found in no other religion or philosophy, one of the elementary and fundamental facts of existence of man and the world, namely, its transiency. Where do we find such a tremendous sincerity in the face of the facts of death, sickness, decay and ultimate annihilation of all human endeavour ? The Christian Middle Ages knew also with realistic clarity of this transiency and wrote above all things the grave sentence : *Mundus transit et concupiscentia ejus* (The world and its desire pass away). Buddhism, however, drew ruthlessly and radically all consequences that can possibly be drawn from this deep conviction of the transiency of everything. Is this not a sublime point of contact ? Does not Biblical realism majestically proclaim that " all men are grass and all their glory like a flower in the field " ? Is not Christianity dominated by the poles of the transiency of the temporal and the exclusive permanency of the eternal ? Is this not a splendid opportunity of relating the Gospel to a living and existing spiritual reality ? It is not, unless a radical conversion of the Buddhist conception of transiency takes place first, and the Buddhist apprehension of the totality of existence, in which this conception of transiency is rooted, is entirely changed.

There are two conditions which exclude the possibility of making the Buddhist conception of transiency—however grand and soul-stirring it may be—the stem on which can be grafted the conception of transiency as implied in Biblical realism. The unbridgeable gulf between the two is at once clear if it is considered that Buddhist transiency has meaning only on the background of a void, God-less universe ; whereas Biblical realism proclaims the transiency of men on the background of a real world, which passes " because the breath of the Eternal blows upon them."

These examples, which could easily be multiplied, illustrate graphically some points of crucial importance in regard to the problem of the concrete points of contact.

The main conclusion that follows from them and from the reasoning that preceded these illustrations is that, in the light of the dialectical situation of all religious life and of all religions, and in the light of the dialectical view of this religious life in Biblical realism, points of contact in the real, deep sense of the word can only be found by antithesis. This means by discovering in the revealing light of Christ the fundamental misdirection that dominates all religious life and at the same time the groping for God which throbs in this misdirection, and which finds an unsuspected divine solution in Christ. It is clear from all that has been said that this antithetical way of establishing points of contact is not meant as a negative way of condemnation, but as a deeply positive way of dealing realistically with the dialectical reality of the religion of mankind.

Another conclusion is that the quest for concrete points of contact can only be sharp-sighted and realistic and yield fruit for missionary practice if the mind remains free from intellectualist delusions and is aware of the necessity to have a " totalitarian " interpretation of religion.

In order to avoid a fatal and all-too-probable misunderstanding, it must be stated with the utmost emphasis that neither this dialectical approach nor this " totalitarian " conception of religious life means the measuring of these religions with the rod of current Christian dogmatism and dogma. That would be one of the worst forms of intellectualism. The combination of the two approaches explained above presupposes a permanent condition of openness in the missionary himself to the criticism and guidance of the Christian revelation, and a not less permanent openness to the reality of the non-Christian religion with which he has to deal.

This leads us to another point of great significance in the problem of concrete points of contact. It is in large measure a matter of individual religious sensitivity. If the word is not misunderstood, the missionary has to be a religious artist. Here we approach the pastoral aspect of our problem, and enter the field of psychology, of pedagogy and of knowledge of the human heart. But it is a regenerated and purified psychology, pedagogy and knowledge of human nature, because baptized into a sense of the conditions of all men by the Spirit of Christ.

One might state this important aspect of the problem of concrete points of contact in this somewhat unusual way : that there is only one point of contact, and if that one point really exists, then there are many points of contact. This one point of contact is the disposition and the attitude of the missionary. It seems rather upsetting to make the missionary the point of contact. Nevertheless it is true, as practice teaches. *The strategic and absolutely dominant point in this whole important problem, when it has to be discussed in general terms, is the missionary worker himself.* Such is the golden rule, or, if one prefers, the iron law, in this whole matter. The way to live up to this rule is to have an untiring and genuine interest in the religion, the ideas, the sentiments, the institutions—in short, in the whole range of life of the people among whom one works, *for Christ's sake and for the sake of those people*. Whosoever disobeys this rule does not find any real point of contact. Whosoever obeys it becomes one with his environment, and has and finds contacts. Obedience to it is implied in the prime missionary obligation and passion, to wit, preparing the way for Christ and being by God's grace a pointer to Him. Only a genuine and continuous interest in the people as they are creates real points of contact, because man everywhere intuitively knows that, only when his actual being is the object of humane interest and love, is he looked upon in actual fact, and not theoretically, as a fellow-man. As long as a man feels that he is the object of interest only for reasons of intellectual curiosity or for purposes of conversion, and not because of himself as he is in his total empirical reality, there cannot arise that humane natural contact which is the indispensable condition of all real religious meeting of man with man. In these conditions the door to such a man and to the world he lives in remains locked, and the love of Christ remains for him remote and abstract. It needs translation by the manifestation of the missionary's genuine interest in the whole life of the people to whom he goes.

The problem of the concrete points of contact is thus in its practical aspect to a very great extent a problem of missionary ethics, and not only a problem of insight and knowledge.

Later when discussing the problems of approach and adaptation we shall return to this whole subject.

CHAPTER V

THE NON-CHRISTIAN SYSTEMS OF LIFE AND THOUGHT

IT is neither necessary nor feasible to give in this book a sketch of the historical development and of the content of the living non-Christian religions. Many excellent handbooks are available, which can enlighten on these subjects. A rapid survey of well-known material—and more would not be possible—would merely prove cumbersome and superfluous. We will try to indicate some fundamental conceptions that are particularly vital in their relation to the Christian revelation.

Surveying the whole field of the living religions of mankind, various possible ways of specifying them according to their nature present themselves. Thus, Saviour-religions may be differentiated from legalist or ceremonial religions ; while another way to obtain some convenient grouping is to distinguish between " primitive " or nature-religions and " civilized " or culture-religions. So also it is possible to divide the religions into mystical and moralist.

The most pertinent division is that into prophetic religions of revelation and naturalist religions of trans-empirical realization. Under the first heading fall Christianity, Judaism, and, as being historically and by its nature related to the Christian and Jewish background, to a certain degree also Islam. All the other religions can be brought under the category of naturalist religions of trans-empirical realization. This division does not imply that the second kind of religions are entirely ignorant of revelation. In a more external sense all religions, not excepting the " primitive " ones, can be called religions of revelation, because all religions rely upon some sort of sacred book or sacred text that is more or less distinctly considered a revelation. As Malinowski has demonstrated in a very lucid way, in primitive religions myth is the account of a primeval revelation, in which a god or ancestral spirits or culture-heroes create and mould the universe and manifest their will and power to man. It is a statement of primeval reality that justifies by precedent the existing order. In Hinduism the *Vedas* are " seen " by the divine rishi's. The *Dharma* in Buddhism and the *Adigranth* of Sikhism, to take only some instances, have the rank and connotation of divine revelations. Even with Shankara the way of knowledge (jñāna mārga) becomes known through revelation.

Nevertheless, the facts justify us in distinguishing between the three mentioned religions of revelation and the other naturalist religions of trans-empirical realization.[1] In these latter religions the centre of gravity does not lie in the fact or notion of revelation ; it is a subsidiary notion, introduced because revelation is such an essentially religious concept that no religion whatever can do without it. But revelation is not at all characteristic of them, and moreover, what they consider to be revelation is of a quite different character from what the religions of revelation understand by it. In these naturalist religions, which are all mystical in their core, revelation consists of what are in some sense supreme moments of religious experience. The three religions of revelation belong all within the periphery of Biblical realism and have their centre of gravity wholly in revelation. This is especially true of Christianity in the most intense way that can be imagined. It is a prophetic religion, wholly theocentric ; and the God who is the all-dominant and all-radiating centre is the personal, living God, who creates, speaks, commands, comforts, acts and saves ; He is above nature, time and history and yet works mightily in nature, time and history. Revelation in this Biblical realism means always an objective act of God, in which *His* will and *His* mind in regard to the condition of man and the world and their need become revealed and claim absolute and unique validity. The

---

[1] By the expression "trans-empirical realization" is meant that man conceives all his efforts of meditation, religious practices, concentration, asceticism, etc., as means towards realizing and grasping the identity of his real self with divine reality.

religious experience which is the human correlate of this divine initiative and aggression remains wholly in the position of a human correlate, and becomes never an end in itself. The search for supreme religious experience is utterly foreign to Biblical realism, because the emphasis falls exclusively on what God does and reveals, and the correlate religious experience is secondary in the strongest sense possible. Far from being necessarily " supreme," we can learn from the great prophets that they seldom experience God's revealing activity as a blissful immanence of the divine, never as the supreme moment of deification, but often as a being overpowered by God's imperative claim on the whole of life.

Of Islam all this can be said only in a very reduced and very qualified sense, but still it can be said. Christianity has been discussed already in the third chapter. To Judaism and Islam we shall devote special sections at the end of the present discussion. Now we shall turn to all the other living non-Christian religious systems with which Christian missions are confronted, and deal with some essential and fundamental features of their apprehension of the totality of existence.

From what has been said in the preceding chapters on the dialectical and " totalitarian " approach, it will be understood that in describing some fundamental traits in the non-Christian religions the question of emphasizing the light sides or the dark sides is, properly speaking, irrelevant. Prepossessed by an intellectualist dogmatic outlook, the Christian Church and its emissaries formerly were in the habit of pronouncing a merely condemnatory judgment on non-Christian religious life. It behoves us, who belong to another generation and who have learned to adopt a more " dialectical " attitude, not to express our scorn of this standpoint too rashly. Our forerunners belonged to a time which understood all truth, philosophical and religious truth, in an intellectualist way. Under their intellectualist armour, however, there burned in most cases a living faith, ready to sacrifice all things for the sake of the " supreme knowledge of Jesus Christ." Moreover, in their day the world of non-

Christian religions was largely unknown and was in many respects in a state of torpor and decay. In the present time, however, missions and missionaries have no excuse whatever for taking the attitude that is born from intellectualist religious narrow-mindedness towards other religions. The drastic testing of Christianity as to its real content and its empirical embodiments in history requires justly from us a more discerning, a more really " Christian " attitude towards ourselves and the religious life of mankind as manifest in the other faiths.

In the nineteenth century Christian theological thinking not only has undergone a purging from intellectualism ; alien religious life has become better known and our view of it has become less unduly prejudiced and prepossessed. We have also, fortunately, unlearned the rash and erroneous identification of empirical Christianity with the revelation in Christ in consequence of which this empirical Christianity, which belongs to the relative sphere of history, was wrongly regarded and treated as of absolute character. At the same time we have learnt—or at least ought to have learnt—that empirical Christianity is just as much an example of religion in general as the other religions are. We have acquired the freedom to apply to empirical Christianity the same dialectical and " totalitarian " view as to other religions, and honesty requires us to do this courageously for the sake of the benefit to Christianity itself. There is only one great difference between empirical Christianity and the other faiths. Empirical Christianity has stood and stands under continuous and direct influence and judgment of the revelation in Christ and is in virtue thereof in a different position from the other religions.

After our eyes became opened to the richness and significance of alien religious life there occurred, quite understandably, a reaction in certain quarters of the Christian Church. The harsh external judgment of dogmatism was supplemented by a generous judgment, full of delight over the religious depth and beauty of alien faiths. This was, and in many respects is, an inevitable reaction, because there is amazing depth and beauty in these faiths, and a missionary ought to view the life of non-Christian religions with open, unprejudiced eyes and with an open, unprepossessed heart. He, indeed, even more than any other, because as a Christian missionary he labours all his life to see man and the world through the eyes of Christ.

Dogmatic narrowness and generous large-heartedness, however, both appear to be prejudiced, if one is really concerned about *truth* and not about one's own attitude. The generous large-heartedness which characterizes the attitude of the so-called " liberal " missionary towards alien faiths is entirely intelligible as a reaction, and is in many respects a paying off of our debt of neglected justice towards these faiths as being very remarkable products of human religious and ethical experience and endeavour. The prime and principal question for a Christian and a missionary, however, is to try all his life to see the non-Christian faiths under the light of the revelation in Christ ; and then the highest commandment is not to be generous or ungenerous, to be tolerant and sympathetic or intolerant and harsh, but to be obedient to the light that shines in Christ, who is " grace and truth " from God but whom " the world " does not recognize intuitively.

Scientifically speaking, the most fruitful way to acquire true insight into a religion is the " totalitarian " approach, namely, to take a religion as one whole body of religious life and expression, of which all the component parts are inseparably interrelated to each other and animated by the same apprehension of the totality of existence peculiar to it. Speaking from the standpoint of the revelation in Christ, who is the Measure of all things, the " dialectical " approach, which is included in the view that the revelation in Christ has of all human existence, is the only right one by means of which to acquire a true and adequate insight. In this view the loftiest heights and the basest depths of all religious life are laid bare with radical realism and meet their due recognition or judgment, because only in the light of the revelation in Christ are the greatness and misery of man adequately unveiled.

Dealing then with some essential and fundamental traits

of the non-Christian religions that do not belong to the category of the religions of revelation, we will constantly keep in mind the " totalitarian " approach and take as our guide the realism of the " dialectical " view of Biblical revelation. This can only be an attempt, because man remains all his life a humble and stumbling learner of what the revelation in Christ really implies, and accordingly remains also continuously a learner in the field of the great faiths of mankind.

THE NATURALIST RELIGIONS

In writing about those religions which in a long development of thousands of years have dominated the lives of the peoples of Asia and Africa, one ought always to be aware that they not only represent different concrete bodies of religious theory and practice, but at the same time are cultures and civilizations. This simple truism must constantly be reiterated, because for modern man, to whom religion is an isolated and in most cases entirely negligible department of life, it is very difficult to get hold of this important and normal fact. His own abnormality in this respect blinds his eyes to the normality of the all-permeating position of religion and of the merging of religion and civilization. Those religious cultures and civilizations we are considering comprise a great number of tribal culture- and life-patterns in Africa and Asia and also the great civilizations of India, China and Japan. The Indian and the Chinese civilizations along with Western civilization are the three great and representative creations of the human spirit in the history of mankind, each one revealing a fascinating and very characteristic aspect of the human mind and its endless possibilities. Japanese civilization, although it has a quite peculiar and characteristic type and value of its own, from the standpoint of cultural history belongs to the Indian, and especially to Chinese civilization.

There have been pointed out deeply interesting similarities in the outward rhythm of development of these three great civilizations, by, for example, the French philosopher Masson-Oursel in his book, *La philosophie comparée*. All over the world the " higher " civilizations manifest an alternation of creative and of digestive, systematizing periods, attended by social and political situations of similar structure and physiognomy. One of these great alternating rhythms is that of brilliantly creative, critical and searching thought and of massively scholastic and synthetical systematization. The West, India and China have known more than once this alternating rhythm. Apart from this similarity of outward rhythm, however, there is a deep-going difference between the civilization of the West and the civilizations of India and China. The two latter are marked by an unbrokenness of continuity that is entirely foreign to Western civilization. Speculating on this imposing continuity, especially of Chinese civilization, a Westerner, knowing himself the child of a civilization of a more violent and broken rhythm, often feels fickle. This continuity cannot be explained only by the geographical difference between India and China on one hand and Europe on the other. It has deeper reasons as well. One of the chief reasons—there are many, but they will be left out of discussion here—is that Western civilization in its history has repeatedly taken the all-decisive step of breaking *on principle with the authority of tradition*. The civilizations of India and China, which are of an amazing depth, width and wealth of expression, never have. Perhaps nowhere in the history of the world has the human spirit soared so high and enjoyed its omnipotence with such superb self-confidence and serene placidity as it has some-times in the civilizations of India and China,[1] yet the authority of tradition has remained throughout their history one of their immovable foundations.

This leads us to another point and to the subject of religion. The civilizations of India and of China appear, on close investigation, to be colossal and fascinating develop-ments of the " primitive " apprehension of the totality of existence. One of the many traits by which they demon-strate this marvellous continuance and development of the " primitive " apprehension is just this unbroken sway of

[1] I am thinking of what is told of the great masters of Vedanta and Yoga, of the Taoist Wu-wei and of the great masters of Zen-Buddhism.

the authority of tradition. India and China, each for itself, represent, of course, a distinct and unique type of life that must be interpreted by virtue of its own presuppositions, and are, so to speak, autonomous worlds of culture. But these two civilizations are at one in this respect, that they are the two classic examples of the phenomenal outgrowth of the " primitive " apprehension of life.

Although it is perhaps superfluous, to avoid misunderstanding we emphasize that the term " primitive apprehension" does not imply any value-judgment. Throughout our whole book we use the word " primitive " not in the sense of the initial stage of cultural life or the primeval condition of man. The use of the word " primitive " in this sense is justly becoming more and more discredited, for very obvious reasons. First, the " primitive " civilizations in the restricted sense of the word appear more and more, as scientific research teaches, to be the opposite of representing an " initial " or " primeval " stage ; they are highly complex. Second, we have become more modest and prudent in the evaluation of our knowledge of " primeval conditions," since prehistoric man begins to present us with new mysteries. Third, all facile evolutionary theorizing is, on philosophical and scientific grounds, untenable. The sense in which we use the term " primitive " is that of one of the great representative human apprehensions of life. There are three of them : this " primitive apprehension " ; the rational apprehension that first broke through in the Greeks and was continued and developed in Western civilization ; and the prophetic apprehension of Biblical realism.

What usually are called " primitive " religions we term " tribal religions," to avoid all confusion. By the term " primitive apprehension " we simply try to express the fact that the Indian and Chinese civilizations in all their rich and variegated manifestations never made a definite break with the fundamental presuppositions of the " primitive " apprehension of the totality of existence. The starting-point in this whole matter, contrary to common misguided notions, is just that this " primitive " apprehension thus appears to possess such an elasticity as to produce those gorgeous systems of civilized life that Indian and Chinese civilizations represent.

What, then, are the main features of the " primitive apprehension " of life which governs the various tribal religions and patterns of life ? Each tribal religion and each tribal system of life is, of course, an autonomous living unity with many characteristics peculiar to it. Differences of environment, of historical circumstances, of natural aptitude, and, by virtue of that, differences in adjustment and in the way the crucial problems of life are conceived, are the reasons why all tribal religions, although rightly put in one category, have their own distinct type and interest. The varieties among the many tribal religions regarding the nature and complexity of their social systems, the wealth or the poverty in mythology, their different religious and cere-monial emphases, etc., are bewilderingly great. Nevertheless, it is allowable to make the following observations on the main features of the primitive apprehension of the totality of existence. In doing this, we make no attempt to enumerate them in the form of a causally connected chain, because this is naturally a matter of dispute.

One of the basic facts in all primitive life-systems is the absolute interdependence of all the spheres of life—the economic, the social, the religious—and consequently the total absence of conscious differentiation and specialization. The religions we usually call " primitive " are always the soul of a system of life that is to a very high degree marked by its static and isolated condition. A considerable infringe-ment of this isolated condition, indeed, is in most cases the cause of its disintegration, an event that we can witness to-day all over the world as a result of the impact of the highly differentiated and dynamic Western civilization on these tribal life-patterns. This inter-relatedness of all spheres of life with its absence of all real differentiation is governed and maintained by the rigid and unassailable authority of tradition. The eye is turned to the past and to the authoritative example and doctrine of the ancestors.

All primitive religions, by their rites, their myths and their manifold regulations of life aspire towards justifying the existing order, towards strengthening tradition and heightening its authority. Tribal life, therefore, is permeated by a deep sense of being taken up into an all-embracing " order," affecting in undivided unity the world at large, tribal and social life, and the individual. This is expressed in the highly corporate character of primitive life. The dominating interest of life is to preserve and perpetuate social harmony, stability and welfare. Religious cults and magic practices have chiefly this purpose in view. Everyone who has lived with a " primitive " people and has tried to immerse his mind in theirs knows the deep-rooted dread they foster towards any disturbance of the universal and social harmony and equilibrium, and the intimate interdependence they assume as existing between these two. A violation of this harmony and equilibrium, whether this issues from the universal sphere—for example, by an unusual occurrence in nature—or from the social—by a dangerous transgression of tradition or by a disturbing event such as the birth of twins—calls forth a corporate and strenuous religious activity towards restoring the harmony and thereby saving the fertility of their fields, their health, the security of their families, the stability and welfare of their tribe from becoming endangered. Thus, social and religious matters are an inextricable unity, and in the execution of his duties in respect to them the individual has his predestined place.

This undifferentiated and interdependent pattern of life is animated and borne up by a peculiar type of thinking that, in different degrees and in different states of completeness, is characteristic of the peoples of Asia and Africa. Ethnological research of the last decennia demonstrates this with increasing clearness. This type of thinking can be expressed in the following terms. It is " totalitarian," it is classificatory and it is steeped in a cosmic-mythological view of the totality of existence. It is a type of monistic thinking, which is more adequately understood when it is conceived as the primitive pattern of philosophy and science than as religion. It is religious too, of course, because everything in primitive theory and practice is indivisibly connected with religion, that is, with the existential apprehension of reality ;

but its intrinsic trend and tendency of mastering the world
prompt one to call it by the name of philosophy and science.
The colossal development of this totalitarian, classificatory
and cosmic-mythological thinking in India and China into
intricate systems of religiously-tinged philosophy and science
is the best justification for this nomenclature.

By " totalitarian " thinking is meant that in an un-
reflective, spontaneous way it starts from the conception of
totality and of unbroken, primeval unity, which comprises
and dominates the whole range of reality in nature and
human life with all its distinctions, nuances and correspondences.   This thoroughly synthetic and concrete way
of thinking has the opposite tendency from the analysing,
isolating way of modern, scientific thinking.   One might
therefore more adequately call it emotional thinking, because
thinking is in this case not yet the abstract, differentiated
activity of the human mind as we, not wholly correctly,
assume it to be in philosophical thought ; but it is the activity
of the thinking, willing and feeling animal that man is in
common life.   Its dominant interest is not to analyse and
isolate, but to arrange and classify, to determine the place
and rank that everything has in the totality of things as this
is conceived.   Here again it appears why it is legitimate and
to the point to call this " totalitarian " and classificatory
thinking the primitive form of philosophy and science ;
for in it gods and men, natural phenomena and social
institutions, the sexes and the social classes, animals and
plants, water and land, mountains and plains and so many
things more, have their place and rank and defined inter-
relation in the whole cosmic-human order.   It is, like every
other kind of philosophy and science, a great attempt to
master the world, doing it in this case by classificatory
systems.   One of the fundamental laws in this type of
thinking is that the macrocosmos (the world, " nature,"
as we would say) and the microcosmos (man) are correlative
entities that co-exist in an uninterrupted process of living
inter-relations and inter-correspondences.   The world of
nature, or the cosmos in all its operations, and the world
of human social relations, are thus inter-related and inter-

dependent. When one takes notice of the thorough, radical way in which this is elaborated concretely, one becomes convinced of the strong sense for systematic mastery of the world in the primitive mind.

Other universally-known principles of this cosmic, classificatory thinking are the division of reality according to dualistic principles, such as masculine and feminine, light and dark, cold and hot, etc., these being all very obvious and constant opposites ; and that of classifying and determining reality as manifest in the manifold life of nature and man within the terms of five or nine cosmic regions, derived from the centre and the four or eight points of the compass. The centre represents totality and the points of the compass represent the relatively independent, but ultimately dependent regions of life, which are rigidly inter-related.[1] Five and nine, therefore, belong to the most sacred numbers of this section of mankind.

An essential characteristic of this concretely-monistic and synthetic thinking is that there are no really antagonistic and opposite principles and realities. There are, of course, contrasts (masculine and feminine, light and dark, good and evil, etc.), but no absolute or irreconcilable ones. The contrasts are taken up and discounted in primeval totality, and have their *due* and *legitimate* place in this totality, which justifies them all and makes for harmony. An outstanding feature of all tribal civilizations, that is connected with this view, is the deep-rooted desire to solve problems of clashing interests by conciliation and laborious and patient endeavour so as to come to decisions founded on mutual agreement. This is usually explained as an evidence of " primitive " democracy. Although in practice it issues in relations and conditions that may be loosely termed democratic, in reality this explanation is utterly wrong. This spirit of conciliation and this predilection for solving conflicts (e.g. legal cases) by mutual agreement, derive from that intrinsic tendency towards harmony which is implied in the primitive apprehension of existence. As in so many cases, Confucian

---

[1] A wealth of examples could be adduced from all over the world, but we must content ourselves with this general sketch.

civilization has elaborated this conciliatory tendency in a classic way.

The fundamental importance of this primitive apprehension of reality is obvious. Under those peoples which are called primitive in the restricted sense because they are confined to tribal life, the theoretical implications of this apprehension of reality remain to a great extent undeveloped. The civilizations of India and China, however, are its profound and cómplicated elaborations, while the great monistic philosophies of the Eastern and Western world are the critically purified and emancipated metamorphoses of it. It is much more than a *bon mot* to maintain that Hegel's absolute idealism is the highest and most systematically-thought-out version of the primitive apprehension of totality in modern life.

In the light of this primitive monism it becomes at once evident that in the roots of its being this whole world of naturalistic religions that we are dealing with is, religiously speaking, *relativistic*. In this monistic atmosphere of inter-related and counter-balancing entities no religious or ethical absolute, that is a really irrevocable absolute, is possible. The importance of this is immediately clear when we think about holiness or sin in the terms of Biblical realism, or realize that, if our contention is right, the prophetic nature of the religion of Biblical realism is thus utterly foreign to the whole tendency of existential apprehension as represented by this primitive apprehension of totality in its higher and more developed forms. To mention, in passing, an illustration from another field of life than religion, in the same light it is quite obvious why the great religious civilizations of Asia never have produced anything that belongs to the category of real tragedy, although these civilizations have been so superbly creative in the different branches of artistic expression. Tragedy presupposes the mystery of absolute contrasts, developed in Greece, where the autonomous individual matched himself against fate or the mysterious moral world-order. Tragedy is not possible in prophetic Biblical realism either, but for a reason quite opposite to that of the naturalist religions. The absolutely holy Will of the God of Love remains always, even when incomprehensible, the object of trust and obedience, and so a really " tragic " conflict can never arise. This becomes still more evident in the sphere of the divinely-wrought reconciliation in Christ.

We must dig still deeper. What is the reason for this spontaneous primitive monism that has blossomed out in such magnificent and stately forms in the civilizations of India and China ? Apparently it is this, that all non-prophetic thinking in the world is in one form or another *naturalistic and vitalistic*. It starts from the fundamental assumption, regarded as self-evident, that man and nature are essentially one ; man in his whole being and possibilities is a part of nature, equivalent to other parts of it. For this reason we call it naturalistic. Vitalistic it may be termed for another not less fundamental reason. The naturalistic core of primitive apprehension of reality meets in a very natural way the most imperative urge in human life : the desire for life. Religion is not for a mean reason expressed in terms of the human quest for life eternal. In the sphere of the naturalistic monism of the primitive apprehension of reality the perpetuation and strengthening of individual and corporate life, which are virtually concretions of the immanent vital urge of the universe, become *the* object of religion and its practice. This elementary vitalism of all naturalistic religions has two important consequences. On the one hand religion becomes thereby a magnificent and noble quest for eternal, imperishable life. This is embodied in the many forms of " higher " mysticism. In this context ethics as one chief instrument in this quest often assumes the character of a titanic moralism. of which many grand examples are present to the mind of everybody who knows this world of naturalist religions by experience. On the other hand, by this elementary vitalism religion becomes the cloak for the crassest materialism and sensualism. How dominant is this elementary vitalism in religious life appears clearly from the important part " higher " mysticism and material-istic religion play in empirical Christianity also.

An important thing to note is that, given these natural-istic and vitalistic presuppositions, gods with personal traits can easily and abundantly occur ; but a personal God in the real sense of the word can never be seriously conceived in this atmosphere. It can be a useful religious "idea" but not a definite reality. The relation of man and the Divine, also, can never be seriously conceived as a fellowship. It is and remains essentially an inter-relation of forces.

The key to the understanding of the deepest roots of the primitive apprehension of the totality of existence—in somewhat crude forms, at least to us, among primitive peoples in the restricted sense, and in highly developed and elaborate forms in the naturalistic religious systems of India and China—is this *naturalistic monism*. In it nature and its cyclic course is the perennial pattern and source of the interpretation of life and its problems.

Here it appears in a new way why there are no absolute contrasts in this primitive apprehension of existence. The course of nature is cyclic, it is eternal recurrence, a swinging between the two poles of life and death, which are opposite, but only in a relative sense. Life really springs from death because there is no real death, for there are actually only *aspects* of totality.

A fundamental relativism is therefore a constituent part of naturalistic monism. And because of its vitalistic character, *eudæmonism* in some form or another puts its stamp on all forms of religious and ethical life in the naturalistic religions. By eudæmonism is meant that religion and ethics, in this vast world of naturalist religions, in principle are always the means to an end, namely, to the *summum bonum* which consists in absolute happiness through the *summum* realization of life. Therefore, it can signify in practice an ethic of noble asceticism and admirable self-conquest as well as a sensualistic or even libertinistic conception of moral life.

The light that this naturalistic monism sheds on the structure and tendency of the primitive apprehension of existence makes it still more intelligible that the respect for tradition and the impressive and aristocratic conservatism, which the great civilizations of India and China have always betrayed, are also founded on this inherent identification with nature and its cyclic law of life. Nature means eternal recurrence and repetition.

The conclusion we derive from this short discussion of the fundamental components of the primitive apprehension of existence and from the principal traits of tribal religions is as follows. Looking at the undifferentiated, static, corporate and traditional character of these tribal religions and their being related to and founded on a cosmic-mythological view of primeval totality and classificatory division, we are impressed by the overwhelmingly *social* aspect of this type of religious life. In the tribal religions and in the great religious civilizations of China and India religion has a strongly corporate or social connotation. The social order is a reflex of the universal order and is correlated to it. The reverse is also the case. Religion means a system of practices to preserve the harmony of the social and universal order, and conformity to this system of practices is thus a fundamental and indispensable law of life. Looking, however, at the naturalistic monism which lies at the bottom of the primitive apprehension of existence, we understand its deeply *naturalistic* aspect. Nature and its course are *the* pattern. These two aspects, the social and the naturalistic, will guide us when surveying some essential elements of the great religious civilizations of India, China and Japan.

Before doing this, one point still deserves to be touched upon. It is clear from what has been said about the characteristics of the primitive apprehension of existence that, in its totality and natural tendency, it stands entirely outside and opposite to the world of Biblical realism, with its radical insistence on God as God, the Living Lord and Creator of man and the world, and in which sin and holiness are taken radically as what they are, namely, the disobedient human will and its resistance against the pure and perfect divine Will.

In the light of Biblical realism and of the dialectical view of human life which it includes, we do not conceive this primitive apprehension of existence nor any other form of apprehension of existence simply to be one of the available human psychological structures as is done by some leading authors in this field. Of course, each of the various forms of apprehension of existence, which appear to occur in the world according to modern structural psychology, are psychological structures and types of thinking. But if that alone is said, the least important thing is said. They are not only types of the ordering of the plurality of the universe by a definite method of thinking, in our case the synthetic, concrete thinking of the primitive apprehension of existence. The essence of man is not that he is a neutrally thinking being, but that he is a willing, desiring and striving being, which means a being who chooses and decides. This existential fact logically and actually implies that man is a responsible being. This points above man himself and vividly suggests that man and his life and the whole drama of history are meaningless if they have not their source and end in eternity and in responsibility towards God. Every form of apprehension of existence, the primitive one included, is therefore not " merely " a type of thinking or of psychological structure, but is a choice and decision in the face of the totality of existence. These choices and decisions must be placed in the judging and saving light of the revelation in Christ.

From what has been said in preceding pages about our attitude towards the non-Christian religions it will be clear that exposing the religious life of mankind, empirical Christianity included, to the light of the revelation in Christ, does not mean that we ignore or deny the richness and quality of religious and ethical achievement which are, humanly speaking, manifest in it. What these " rich heritages " mean in connection with the Christian mission will be discussed when the problem of adaptation is dealt with. Our present pre-occupation is to attempt to picture in some of their fundamental outlines the naturalist religions in the light of the " totalitarian " approach of science and the dialectical approach of Biblical realism.

HINDUISM

It is often said to be impossible to define Hinduism, and rightly so. It is a vast jungle of religious cults, sects, institutions and tendencies, including every possible variation of human religious expression : the serene ecstatic experience of oneness with the attributeless Pure Essence of the heroic, lonely mystic ; the exuberant loving worship of the devotee or *bhakta*, who exults in the deliverance wrought by Ishvara ; the elaborate ritual that accompanies the many phases of life ; the village-cults and feasts, partly touching and partly repulsive, because steeped in a confusing and degrading atmosphere of polytheism, dæmonism and magic. One could go on endlessly and still not succeed in giving an adequate impression of the content of the religious complex that goes by the name of Hinduism.

This polymorphous complexity becomes still more bewildering if one realizes that the seeming absence of all consistency is even manifest in its foundations. In Hinduism itself it is generally accepted that all forms of religious life that are recognized as belonging to Hinduism agree in two fundamental things. Every Hindu belongs to a caste and has to live according to its *dharma* (*dharma* means the peculiar type of behaviour that is one's cosmically and socially predestined lot). There are hundreds of castes and *dharmas*. However, all Hindus, although exceedingly different in cult-objects, rules of life and religious aspirations, are one in accepting the *Vedas* as the authoritative sacred literature of Hinduism in its polymorphous totality. Now the bewildering thing about this sacred authority, on which Hinduism is considered to go back, is that the *Vedas* in the strict sense of the term are almost entirely ignorant of the central Hindu gods such as Shiva and Vishnu, and on the other hand extol gods—for example, Indra and Varuna—that are entirely forgotten in Hinduism as it has lived for 2000 years. The sacredness of the cow, one of the pillars of modern Hindu *dharma*, is unknown in the *Vedas*. One can hardly meet a literature that is more frankly life- and world-affirming than the four *Vedas*, while the ferment that pervades Hinduism and the *Upanishads* in its roots and its branches is a radical life- and world-denying temperament.

So Hinduism is full of paradoxes, and one cannot make any general statement about any phenomenon without having to place some limitations upon it. The bewildering variety, the endless range of religious experience and practice, comprising the highest peaks and the basest depths of human experience, the paradoxical contrasts in the field of doctrine where pantheism, theism, atheism and a thousand sorts of polytheism are alike possible and recognized, become clear, however, at once if one realizes that Hinduism is the outstanding and characteristic embodiment of the primitive apprehension of existence and of naturalistic monism. It is as wide, as polymorphous, as full of fierce contrasts and fine shades, as capricious, as Nature is. With this in mind it becomes at once clear as daylight why in Hinduism every cult, every doctrine, every form of worship is received with gracious and literally inexhaustible hospitality. All have their proper place. There is no immutable criterion of truth, and the power of absorption, reception and production in Hinduism is endless. Of course this is so, for Nature is inexhaustibly hospitable ; it is eternally absorbing and producing; it knows no criterion and cannot know a real one, because all is contained in and issues from its womb, and it knows only the difference of grades and shades, because there is no absolute standard of reference above or outside it.

We have noticed that the sole endeavour in Hinduism to erect an authoritative standard and source for its system has been to declare the *Vedas* divine and sacred revelation, but that the *Vedas* either ignore or contradict in letter and spirit the most fundamental tenets of Hinduism as we know it through more than two millennia. This curious fact is, as will be clear now, not an indication of inconsistency. Startling as it may seem, it is a lucid example of really *Hindu consistency*. The capricious and careless disregard of the real character of a criterion which this doctrine manifests —for capricious it is—is the most lucid expression of the naturalist-monistic spirit by which Hinduism in all its manifestations is ultimately animated or affected. It reflects the capriciousness and the lack of any criterion in nature. Just as Nature is not interested in truth, but in manifestation, in realizations, in shades, so Hinduism is not really interested in religious truth but in the endless possibilities of religious realization and expression. Who would dare to deny that Hinduism stands unmatched in wealth and variety of this expression ? Therefore it need not take even the authority of its own sacred criterion of truth and revelation seriously, because its dealing in practice rather lightheartedly with its own authority is an expression of its inherent criterionless naturalist-monistic nature.

Miss B. Heimann has rightly made the fundamental thesis of her extraordinarily illuminating book, *Studien zur Eigenart des Indischen Denkens*, that Indian civilization, religion and thinking in its entire rich development never abandons the magic circle of the innate assumption that man is essentially one with all the other parts of Nature. Yet, Hinduism does, of course, use criteria, but all relative ones. It is therefore very significant to note that there are only two criteria which Hinduism takes seriously as limitations of its amorphous religious universality—the one natural and the other social, namely, the biological fact of being born a Hindu, and the social fact of belonging to a caste. This again clearly indicates that Hinduism is essentially a polyphone expression of the primitive apprehension of existence and a continuation of the social conception of religion amongst tribal peoples. In its aristocratic contemplative acosmic mysticism of *advaita* and *kaivalya* it becomes the extremest expression of religious individualism, leaving all limitation and relativism of nature or history, race or country behind. Why not ? In the sphere of naturalistic monism every form of expression is legitimate and possible. The terms *kaivalya* and *advaita* mean absolute separateness from all duality or plurality of existence and a return to the primordial Oneness of Totality. To attain that is *moksha* (deliverance, salvation). The highest ideal of India, and also of the great religious civilizations of China and Japan, thus appears to return to one of the cardinal centres of the primitive monistic apprehension of existence, namely, the return to Totality as the primordial condition of all existence, conceived as the serenest possible bliss.

Nevertheless Hinduism remains always deeply rooted in the social conception of religion that is typical of primitive religion. Its versatile naturalistic monism, that is modelled on the versatility of Nature, is only impotent in one respect, namely, to do anything which implies a radical contrast, an irrevocable breaking away, a raising of the voice : " Hear, O *heavens*, and listen, O *earth*, it is the *Eternal* who speaks " (Isaiah i.). Therefore, despite the stirring quest for truth that one constantly meets with in the annals of Indian religious history, the rules that one is Hindu by birth and that the most characteristic and indispensable attribute of a Hindu is to live according to the *dharma* of his caste, have never become dissolved even a little, and never can be unless Hinduism becomes thoroughly emancipated from its ingrained naturalistic monism.

Because Hinduism is so deeply rooted in naturalistic monism it never has eliminated or vanquished magic. Nor have the other great naturalistic religions done this. The only religion that, on principle, has eliminated magic from religion and has done this radically, is the prophetic religion of Biblical realism. The bizarre Tantric cults with their sexual aberrations become entirely intelligible in the light of naturalistic monism. This same monism, however, produces also the great methods of salvation, replete with religious and ethical fervour. So to identify Hinduism either with Tantrism or with these great religious phenomena is not feasible.

Hinduism has admittedly been very prolific in the production of gods. Of course, for this reflects the fertility of nature. Everything can virtually be *made* an object of worship. The emphasis on " made " is important, for in Hinduism it is unhesitatingly admitted that " gods " are the projections of our human will, desires and thoughts. And it is quite in order that this admission is not made shamefacedly. Moreover, the great natural gifts for speculation in India have developed this god-creating quality in diverse directions. The wealth of conceptions of the Divine is simply stupendous. However, the most important thing to note is that the many gods, exalted ones or repellent ones, belong within the sphere of the cosmic and natural process. They represent always some aspect of cosmic and natural totality. That is the reason why gods never are fundamentally different from man. They are mortal just as man is; they are subject to the law of *karma* ; the only difference is that they enjoy, as a result of a good *karma*, a finer and longer state of bliss than in the human category is possible. This is not an absurd conception of the gods ; in the sphere of naturalistic monism it is wholly logical. The power above all powers is never a god, but *karma*, the tyrannical lord and creator of all existence ; or ultimately, *avidya* (the state of ignorance about the real nature of man and the universe). *All* forms of polytheism all over the world, including popular saint-worship, are the fruits of a still vigorous or not yet vanquished naturalistic monism. All ideas or conceptions of God, whether theistic or pantheistic, remain in Hinduism steeped in an atmosphere of immanence, because the cosmic natural process does not permit an idea of real transcendence. They are all, fundamentally speaking, auxiliary constructions to aid in the adventure for deliverance or the fulfilment of certain wishes. Besides this soteriological necessity, they have virtually no other necessity to exist or function. Basic Hindu-naturalistic monism really—and in doing this it is loyal to its nature—treats God-ideas as ideas, that is to say as ways in which the human mind conceives the Divine. They never are pointers to an objective living Reality, who in full earnest is the Lord and the God of man. In the religious philosophy of Vedanta all conceptions of the Divine, however moving they may be, belong to the sphere of *maya* (the delusion by which man takes the unreal world as real). This is a logical deduction from the " totalitarian " tendency of the primitive apprehension of existence. If the Ultimate Reality is the Primeval Oneness of Being in the Totality, the plurality of the cosmic and natural process naturally tends to become the unreal. The conception of *maya* and that of the imperishable, absolute, attributeless, inactive Pure Essence are the most consistent developments of the primitive apprehension of existence and therefore the truly Hindu conception of the world and the Divine. All theistic conceptions of God in Hinduism, however deeply they may stir the emotions in practical religious life, must, when the problem of their objective reality and truth is considered to be the paramount problem, necessarily impress the mind as affected with unreality. This is so, first because it is in Hinduism considered to be a *conception* of God, one of the many that are possible. It lies, however, in the nature of the case that the personal God of authentic theism is the real, sole, objective, divine Being, or He is nothing. Second, the theistic Ishvara in Hinduism belongs ultimately to the sphere of *maya*. It must be so, for He remains in the category of the plurality of existence and not in that of the immovable primeval Oneness.

The well-known Hindu *caturvarga* (the four ends of human life) of *artha, kama, dharma, moksha* is a very convenient and terse expression of the view of life and the world as contained in Hinduism. Human life has four aspects. *Artha* means man seen from the angle of his being an acquisitive being and of the economic consequences and obligations that this involves. *Kama* envisages man in his sensual and natural needs and demands. *Dharma* indicates the order of life in which man is subject to a definite set of rules which regulate his social and ritual behaviour, founded on the sacred authority of tradition. Each man and each group of men has his or its peculiar *dharma*, which cannot be abrogated. Hinduism is often called *sanatana dharma* (eternal *dharma*). Caste and the all-important category of *dharma* are indissolubly connected with each other. This enormous significance of the conception of *dharma* makes Hinduism a religion that conceives religion primarily as a social matter and religiousness as conformity to one's *dharma*.[1]

These four aspects of human life are of different grading, but each within its sphere has an absolute right. Each has its criterion in itself, as is obvious in the naturalistic atmosphere of Hinduism. This opens an insight into another important implication of fundamental naturalistic monism as apparent in Hinduism. We have indicated already that naturalistic monism necessarily implies a predisposition towards a relativistic attitude to truth and an eudæmonistic attitude to ethics. The whole religious history of Hinduism affords a vivid illustration of this. Relativism never became

[1] For *moksha* see pp. 161, 165.

a conflict full of dangerous tension as, for example, in Christianity. It could not, because the naturalistic background implies that relativism in the realm of religious truth is not felt as a matter of life or death, but on the contrary as a symptom of delightful richness.

The great ways of *moksha* are lofty forms of life- and mind-training, means to the great end, deliverance or salvation, and therefore noble examples of eudæmonistic ethics. This eudæmonistic flavour is still more accentuated, because what is aimed at is deliverance from *samsara*, from the suffering of existence. Here also lies the root of the great maxim of *ahimsa* (abstaining from giving pain to others in thought, word or deed). This maxim has permeated the purer forms of Hindu and Buddhist ethical sentiment with a truly marvellous aroma of benevolence, gentleness and regard for the whole kosmos. To see it in its right perspective, one must, however, envisage its soteriological roots. The goal of individual deliverance from the suffering of existence engendered the meticulous desire to lessen the chances of re-birth by avoiding the infliction of suffering, but in the long run it became, psychologically speaking, positive benevolence towards all beings.

Here we have to add another implication of naturalism, namely, a fundamental *anthropocentric* tendency in religion. This becomes very evident if we observe somewhat more closely the domain of *moksha* in Hinduism, because there this religion has realized in the sublimest and deepest forms its religious and ethical capacity.

The masses of the common people in India live, as do also those in China and Japan, their everyday religious life in the sphere of that universal religious materialism which makes religion and magic, its rites and practices, a means whereby weak, ignorant, helpless, yet life-hungry and coveting men satisfy their worldly interests of welfare and happiness, or better their chances of future re-birth. Fortunately, this distressing picture, which again and again arouses the feeling of their being sheep without a shepherd, has many redeeming touches because of the glimpses of sincere and pure religious insight and experience that shine through.

Moksha, deliverance, is the end pursued by a minority, not by a majority. This minority, however, has imprinted on Hinduism the indelible character of a soteriological religion. Its great systems of *yoga*, with their astounding wealth of psychological knowledge and insight, are virtually huge and ingenious techniques of deliverance. Deliverance always means, as said already, deliverance from the transiency of existence (*samsara*). The haunting sense of the transiency of life and the world runs deeply in the veins of Hinduism. By its system of re-birth and of *karma*, the ever-fertile seed of re-birth, it has even magnified and accentuated to a bizarre degree this transiency, for this endless process of re-birth produces an oppressive intensification of transiency. This deep-seated complaint of the transiency of existence is the inverted form of an intense desire for life, imperishable life. This is the reason why the soteriological systems of Hinduism are such passionate, resolute combats for deliverance (*moksha*), and why the ways of deliverance (*marga*) are so many and so arduous. Nowhere in the world have so many people so intensely believed in the possibility of self-deliverance and so unwaveringly and courageously striven and toiled for it as in India. To reflect on this inevitably means to become awestruck. In unbroken connection with the " totalitarian " apprehension of existence, the root of all error and misery in the world is conceived to be *avidya*, ignorance about the sole reality of the Primeval Oneness of Totality (Sat) and about the deceptive unreality of the plurality of the cosmic and natural process (*maya*). Deliverance comes by knowledge (*Jñana*) which means the evaporation of this ignorance. The result is the bliss (*ananda*) of the ineffable experience of oneness with this Primeval Oneness (Brahman Atman), in which man realizes his deepest reality.

In this highest moment of serene ecstasy man, properly speaking, does not find God, but the reality of the mystery of his own being asserts itself supremely. The inevitable consequence of the innate naturalistic monism in Hinduism is that God or the Divine never really exists. At the end the only thing that appears to exist really in this whole mirage of existence is human consciousness moving in sovereign solitude over the void abyss of void existence. The daring illusionist speculations of the Shunyavada school in Mahayanist Buddhism are the logical outcome of this. Therefore Hinduism is the opposite of a theocentric apprehension of existence. It is, speaking fundamentally, radically anthropocentric. The sole theocentric apprehension of existence is given in the prophetic religion of Biblical realism, because there any trace of naturalistic monism is entirely absent. There not the womb of nature but the hand of God is the cause of all things. Because Hinduism, despite its fertile creativity in the field of god-making, in its roots and branches is anthropocentric, its ethics are, in principle, eudæmonistic, for its ethics never embody the expression of a God-willed, authoritative new order of life, but are the means for man, his training-endeavours, to achieve deliverance, which is in its different connotations the *summum bonum*. All asceticism, however important its developments may be for the cultural life of India, is, seen in this light, essentially training for *moksha*, a moral athleticism to conquer salvation. Kant's maxim : *Du sollst denn du kannst* (you must, because you can) betrays in the first words, *Du sollst*, still the influence of the prophetic background of Christianity, for Kant knew about *das radikal Böse* (the radical moral evil). The more radical moralism of the Indian roads of deliverance lives virtually by the maxim : *Du kannst, denn du willst* (You can because you have the will). In the sphere of naturalistic monism the truth remains hidden that sin can only be forgiven, but can never be effaced by conquering it.

Such is the aristocratic mysticism of liberating gnosis, to which the select few adhere and to which Shankara has given philosophical expression. Max Weber, in his excellent studies in the sociology of religion, rightly points out that " enlightened " Asiatic thinking, in India, China and Japan, finds the belief in a personal God, an ethic of absolute difference between good and evil, the attitude of faith as personal fellowship between the worshipper and the Worshipped, a second-rate and absurd apprehension of existence. This must be so because the ontological presuppositions of naturalistic monism rebel against the voluntaristic apprehension of prophetic religion, which proclaims a God of judgment and fellowship and not an Essence that is grasped in the bliss of ecstasy or in the orgiastic enjoyment of God-intoxication.

To anticipate what has to be said about China and Japan, in these countries, by reason of the same fundamental naturalistic monism that underlies the different Chinese and Japanese apprehensions of life, we find there in the august development of Taoism which is embodied in the Tao Teh King, in Zen-Buddhism and in many schools of Buddhism, either in a speculative or in a more emotional form—and of course with a quite different colouring from Indian mysticism—the same aristocratic mysticism, founded on the contrast of the Total Oneness and of Plurality, which is virtually no contrast, because Plurality is unreal phantas-magory. The anthropocentric nature of this monistic apprehension is very clearly expressed in the way in which Zen-Buddhism formulates its purpose, namely, to realize Buddhahood in oneself and to discover it in everything.

We find in these three great religious civilizations of Asia in different ways not only forms of aristocratic mysti-cism, but also representative forms of soteriological mysticism, which revolve around faith, a Saviour and a Mediator. These soteriological mysticisms are not the " ways " of the few select, but of multitudes of men and women who desire comfort and strength in the struggle of existence. They are great examples of pietistic religion, exuberantly fervid and prolific in their modes of expression. In India these are the many forms of *bhakti*-religion. In Chinese Buddhism there is similarly the Pure-Land or Ching-tu school and in Japanese Buddhism the Yodo-shu sects or Amidism. Because of their many startling similarities with Christianity, which is the *prophetic* soteriological religion, these types of religious life need closer investigation.

Rudolf Otto, in his *India's Religion of Grace and Christianity*, has given an excellent introduction to this pietistic religion of faith. We call it a pietistic religion of faith, because in the Vishishtadvaita-system of Ramanuja, the great *bhakti*-theologian, the crucial points are his passionate protest against the absolute monism of Shankara ; his vindication of fellowship with and loving faith in the personal living Ishvara, who is a reality and not as in Shankara's system a fiction which, while belonging to the sphere of *maya* and *avidya*, is necessary in the stage of lower gnosis ; the proclamation of divine grace, and not speculative gnosis, as the means of salvation. Further, the moving experience of sin and grace, of conversion, the many revivals and the wealth of conversion-stories and many more similar traits remind us vividly of Christian Pietism. Even more, we are often as vividly reminded of Protestant Reformation theology. The combative exclusiveness, the centrality of the concept of faith, and the deep way in which it is analysed, the struggle over the relation of faith and works and of synergism or monergism in the work of salvation (the ape and the cat school), which characterize this type of Indian religiosity are very conspicuous in the history of Reformation theology. Ramanuja, just as Pascal, was not satisfied with the God of the philosophers ; with passionate religiousness he vindicated a really living God, not merely a theistic conception of God.

We will return later on to this impressive similarity with Christianity, which is also a soteriological religion, when we discuss the problem of adaptation. Here it is our task to penetrate into the inner structure and tendency of the *bhakti*-faith against the background of the entire Hindu view of life.

Ramanuja and his successors represent in India the theological side of this remarkable religious movement, and the popular mystical singers, before him, the emotional ecstatic side. Ramanuja breaks in a radical way with the classic Hindu ideas about God, the soul and the world. The world is real, not *maya* ; the soul and human consciousness consequently are so also. The eternal, personal God, Ishvara, is the sole and personal God and Saviour, not merely a god-representation necessary for man in a certain stage in his quest for the *summum bonum*.

The fascinating thing in Ramanuja is that his deep religious aspiration to vindicate Ishvara as the sole and

Eternal Saviour urges him to distinguish clearly between God, man and the world. With him the essential identity of Brahman and Atman—thou art that (*tat twam asi*)—becomes the dwelling of God in the soul, in uninterrupted communion of life. To acquire the conscious enjoyment of this reality is the great thing in life. This elemental soteriological drive in Ramanuja's quest is the reason why the theological and psychological similarities, the interests and forms of expression in Christianity and this *bhakti*-religion are so baffling. The wretchedness of sin, the deep longing for the divine grace, the intense feeling of trust and faith in Ishvara's all-conquering love, the experience of being divinely elected and of being called to a life of sanctification and praise of Ishvara, the deep experience of deliverance through faith and absolute surrender to God : all these things are expressed in striking ways in prose and poetry.

Nevertheless, the remarkable thing is that, despite all these theological and psychological similarities, the spiritual climate and the really dominant urge in this deeply sincere and fervid religion of deliverance are radically different from the prophetic religion of Biblical realism. Some chief points may be mentioned. Ramanuja announces his system and religious message as the interpretation of the Hindu Holy Scriptures, mainly the Sutras of Badarayana and the *Bhagavadgita*. The all-pervading naturalistic-monistic spirit with which these authorities are imbued keeps his conception of God, *notwithstanding his religious intention to the contrary*, in principle monistic. The world is not God's creation but evolves out of Him. There is between the different forms of philosophical theism which are current in the world one deep line of division, that runs along this line of the question whether the personal God is exclusively the " efficient cause " (*causa efficiens*) of the world or whether he is the " efficient and material cause " (*causa efficiens and materialis*) at the same time. Ramanuja adopts the second conception and must do so, because only if God the Creator is the religious *starting-point* and not the expression of an effort, however sincere, to construe a satisfying relation between the world and a personal God—which is a philosophical question and not primarily a religious one—can one confidently call God exclusively the *causa efficiens*.

The reality the world acquires in Ramanuja's system is startling if it is seen against the background of the radical acosmism of Shankara, which Ramanuja combated so fiercely. Against the background of Biblical realism, however, it becomes shadowy and unreal. Again, this must be so. As Ramanuja continues to move in the monistic Indian atmosphere, God does not really become the Creator in the radical sense of the word. Therefore the world does not become the real place where man, by divine ordinance, is set to live and to work. The world remains accessory, not one of the great items in God's purpose with man and history. The relative independence and reality of the world is in Ramanuja's thinking necessary because it is needed for the sake of the primitive soteriological drive in his thinking. The same is the case with the conception of a real, personal God. The religious demand of the heart for a real deliverance makes a real, personal God necessary, and in order to emphasize the reality of this Saviour-God the world gets a relative independence and reality. The message of a new order of life as revealed in Jesus Christ and of the expectation of a new world order, in which a new earth, a new heaven and a new redeemed humanity will become manifest as the Reign of God—which is God's real design with man, the world and history—are entirely absent from the whole field of *bhakti*-theology and experience. This is inevitable, for *bhakti*-theology and *bhakti*-religion are, despite the moving praises of God who forgives and is the exclusive cause of salvation, not theocentric, but fundamentally anthropocentric, as all good monistic, mystic Hindu religion is. The whole range of *bhakti* experience and thinking is set in motion by the need of the soul for deliverance. Certainly, this deep religious question : " How can I be saved ? " has been uttered in Christianity also, from the days of the jailer at Philippi and of Luther, and is still uttered to-day. It is one of the few cardinal questions man always and everywhere has to put. This question can, however, occur in a deeply-theocentric and in a deeply-anthropocentric atmosphere.

The deeply-anthropocentric character of *bhakti*-religion derives from the fact that this soteriological disposition is the *exclusive* creator of all religious experience and thinking. The only relevant thing in all existence is this soteriological drama between God and the soul. Only in so far as a real existence of the world is indispensable for this sole relevance is it taken as real. For the rest it vanishes out of sight. All moral exertion and religious experience are therefore exclusively individualistic. God does not love or reconcile the *world*, but He loves the soul.

The anthropocentric character of *bhakti*-religion, which is the inevitable consequence of its exclusively soteriological inspiration, implies also that faith is a *means of salvation*. In Biblical realism faith is the existential apprehension by which man obediently and reverently *recognizes* what aspect all things, and especially his own fundamental condition and reality, do have in the light of Christ, in whom the holy God of love, judgment and reconciliation becomes revealed to the conscience of man. Faith in the *bhakti*-religion and faith in the New Testament cannot be compared. Grace, forgiveness, even Ishvara Himself, are in the *bhakti*-religion essentially means to satisfy the need of the soul for salvation. Sin in these religions is not the result of the self-centred and misdirected human will that opposes the will of the God of holiness and righteousness, but an impediment for the realization of that fellowship of the soul with Ishvara, in which salvation consists. In other words, because of its exclusively soteriological and anthropocentric inspiration, the ethics of *bhakti*-religion are exclusively individualistic and essentially eudæmonistic. The ethics of a radically theocentric religion are the only non-eudæmonistic ethics.

These few suggestions [1] may suffice to make clear that *bhakti*-religion, despite all indications that seem to point to the contrary, essentially remains under the sway of the

---

[1] The treatment of the radical difference between the world of *bhakti*-religion and that of Biblical realism, notwithstanding the numerous theological and psychological similarities, could be developed much more. Here, because of considerations of space, we must exercise rigorous restraint. The similarity, psychologically and theologically, is even very striking. However, in actual fact, there is only difference.

cardinal apprehensions and attitudes of Hinduism. It rebels against, but is not really emancipated from, the basic naturalistic monism of Hinduism, and therefore neither from the anthropocentric and eudæmonistic tendencies that are inherent in this monism. God is not proclaimed as the God of holy love, both words to be taken with equally strong emphasis, but as the God of compassion (*karuna*). Out of compassion God disregards sin, and man consciously or unconsciously (compare various poems of Manikka Vasagar, for example) claims to be entitled to fellowship with God. In the theocentric world of Biblical realism, so to speak, the rôles are changed. God is anthropocentrically interested from the soteriological point of view. Man, on the contrary, in the apprehension of faith, becomes theocentrically interested, recognizing that the saving element in the supreme divine love is rather the fact that the holy Will of God, the Sole Master of life, remains integrally maintained. Therefore the deepest word in the soteriology of Biblical realism is reconciliation, wrought by God Himself ; the deepest word of *bhakti* soteriology is divine favour (*prasada*).

.   .   .   .

BUDDHISM

Before turning to the forms of *bhakti*-religion in Chinese and Japanese Buddhism, Buddhism as a whole needs some characterization. After what has been said about the primitive apprehension of life and about Hinduism, this need not be very long.

Buddhism is the most radical system of self-deliverance that ever has been conceived in the world. As such, and also in its cardinal presuppositions (*karma, samsara, moksha*), it is thoroughly Hindu. Yet, curious to note, it is one of the few systems that have ever been excommunicated by Hinduism, otherwise so hospitable and all-digestive. The reason is very significant. Buddhism was expelled from the house of Hinduism and not recognized as a child, not because of its peculiar, deviating doctrines, but by virtue of its having a different *dharma*, which *excluded conformity*. Hinduism sensed that Buddhism discarded one of its two indispensable foundations—its social conception of religion as a common *dharma*.

Historically speaking, however, Buddhism is one of the most superb plants that have sprung from the fertile soil of Hinduism, one of the most magnificent examples of aristocratic soteriology. Its originality and force reside in the fact that it conceived the transience (*anitya* or *anitta*) of all existence and the supreme need to achieve escape from it with such extreme intensity as cannot be surpassed. Therefore the doctrine of the pure, imperishable Essence (Brahma) plays no rôle whatever in Buddha's gospel. The glad tidings is rather that the Ego, the soul (*atman*), is non-existent (*anatman, anatta*). Deliverance consists in apprehending this in all its consequences and so shattering at one stroke the fetters of *karma*, the sole producer of all so-called existence. The peculiar nature of the Buddhist conception of deliverance (*nirvana*) is that it is not something that can be defined as in the case of *tat twam asi*, but it is the bliss of deliverance pure and simple. This is quite logical, for if the supreme moment of deliverance is to enjoy the " enlightenment " (*bodhi*) that the soul, the Ego, is nothing, there is no definable goal to be formulated. The psychological experience of bliss, however, is not the less real, as may be inferred from the rapture with which it is sung by monks and nuns.

Original Buddhism was a religion of monks, because it taught the way to achieve salvation by a solitary and relentless process of moral self-conquest and intellectual emancipation from the slavery of ignorance, the root of all evil. To make possible this life of exclusive devotion to the goal of deliverance for the lonely, daring wanderers on the noble eightfold path, it appeared indispensable to incorporate laymen in this religion of lonely world-forsakers, and this important step forced Buddhism, against its dominant motive, to enter into relation with the world.

In original Buddhism the aristocratic soteriology of Hinduism draws out its last consequences. Here it becomes plain that the idea of the Divine Essence is essentially irrelevant to the inherently anthropocentric nature of naturalistic monism. Buddhism teaches with a kind of prophetic vigour that what really matters is man and his deliverance, and nothing else.

Another important thing that becomes plain in it is the point we have already touched upon, that under the deep Hindu conviction of transiency lies an unquenchable thirst for life. The thirst for life (*tṛshna, taṇha*) is in original Buddhism one of the cardinal shackles in the famous chain of the Causal Nexus of Existence.

A third point in which Buddhism reveals its strongly Hindu character is that its ethics are exclusively propædeutic, a means to an end ; or to repeat the term we have used already frequently, its ethics betray a strongly eudæmonistic character, because its soteriology is exclusively anthropocentric.

Mahayana-Buddhism, which has become the great missionary religion in Buddhism, derives its peculiar character from two facts. In it the monk-soteriology of Hinayana becomes a complicated and huge system of various lay-soteriologies. The way is open to everyone. All the devices of religious psychology, speculation and practice, and not less the whole arsenal of magic, are brought into action to procure the highest maximum of soteriological effect. The thirst for deliverance reaches out above the normal goal of deliverance from the dreary cycle of *samsara* ; it is, so to speak, a gigantic soteriological ambition that dominates the system, for the new goal, " the great Vehicle," is to become oneself a Bodhisattva, a Saviour and Deliverer of erring, miserable man. Here, as in so many cases, Buddhism manifests its tendency to develop the consequences that lie deeply hidden in all naturalistic religion. The Bodhisattva-ideal is *the* apotheosis of anthropocentric self-assertion in the guise of a religion of grace and divine deliverance.

The second fact is that in the Mahayana-system and in its many ramifications Buddhism resolutely takes up again the relation with naturalistic monism and the primitive " totalitarian " apprehension of existence, which were ignored in the rigorous and intense moralism of Buddha's teaching, but not vanquished and transcended. With great force of speculative philosophical thinking and psychological penetration the different schools of thought weave the monistic pattern of the relation of the absolute to the phenomenal, and do not even shrink back from the extremest illusionist and nihilist consequences, as, for example, in the school of Nagarjuna, who with daring consistency declares that of no thing or idea can one state its being or non-being, not even of the Buddha or of the way of deliverance. Here in this Mahayanist speculation naturalistic-monistic thinking unhesitatingly deduces its last consequences and ends in an absolute relativism. " All (the Ego, the world, *samsara*, the way of salvation, the Buddha) is void and illusory "—that is its creed, which is proudly called the " second turning of the Wheel of Dharma," placing it thereby on equal level with the momentous act of Buddha himself in the deer-park near Benares. In accordance with this it develops a massive theory to justify relativism by classifying the different theories of religious philosophy and the ways of soteriology as accommodated truths, each being in its own sphere the authoritative standard for a certain stage of human development and insight into the absolute truth.

There are many other systems, shading off in different degrees, that can be called examples of idealistic monism, as, e.g., the Tendai and Shingon schools in Japan. They move, however, in the realm of naturalistic monism and grow into huge syncretisms of speculative philosophy and popular religion in its most fantastic and bizarre forms. It is not to be marvelled at that the leaders in modern Buddhist philosophy in Japan, as, e.g., Nanji Bunyo and Inoue Enryo saw in Hegel's synthesis of Being and Non-being the affirmation of the cardinal tenet of Mahayanist philosophy.

The primitive " totalitarian " apprehension of existence and its classificatory systems become the framework and at the same time the inspiration of these complicated Mahayanist theories of life and existence. The groups of Dhyani- and Manusya-buddhas and of Bodhisattvas, in most cases with Vairocana or with the Adibuddha in the centre or at the top, follow the pattern of the sacred numbers of the primitive classificatory systems (centre, 5, 9). The dualistic classification of the primitive apprehension according to the masculine and feminine moieties in the universe break through in the Buddhist Shakti cults and Tantric systems, in Buddhism called the Vajrayana. Their root-idea and starting-point being sexual duality and the urge for the Oneness of the Totality, elaborate systems of erotic and orgiastic magic of all kinds became incorporated and sanctioned in these soteriologies, that have sprung—marvellous to relate—from Buddha's search for escape from existence. In this case of Shaktism and Tantrism the term eudæmonistic soteriology, which expresses the general character of Mahayanism, must have a strongly deprecatory significance, and not simply a descriptive one, as in most previous cases when we used the word to characterize the ethical systems of those religions that are founded on naturalistic monism.

Thus, the historical development of Buddhism is very instructive for one who wants information about the possibilities of naturalistic monism as one of the fundamental apprehensions of the totality of existence, about its infinite creative fertility in the fields of civilization and culture, and about its disastrous tendency to become the justifier of all, even the basest, things because of its lack of a real criterion and authority. Behind the screen of sublime philosophies and mystical and ethical " ways " to deliverance, or in the garb of fantastic textures of magic and occultism, man remains the measure of all things. Buddhism began as an heroic rigoristic moralism, exclusively inspired by the thirst for deliverance and therefore indifferent to all metaphysics ; it became by listening to the lure of unvanquished naturalistic monism and by the anthropocentric orientation of its soteriology the most consistent and unscrupulous exponent of this monism, and a huge syncretistic religion.

. . . .

The " Pure-Land " School, which represents *bhakti*-religion in Buddhism, has acquired its deepest and richest developments in Japan, and not in China. We may be allowed therefore to limit our observations to Japanese Amidism, as it is called in Japan, because they can be applied to Chinese Amidism as well. It is a deeply interesting variant and pendant of Indian *bhakti*-religion, with many characteristic features. Just as in India, there can be noticed in Japanese Amidism the same psychological and theological similarity with Christian Pietism in its various expressions and with Reformation theology.

Amidism or the Jodo-shu is one of the remarkable movements of reformation that arose in the twelfth and thirteenth centuries in Japan as a protest against the abstruse soteriological machinery of the scholastic systems, Tendai and Shingon. Their purpose was simplification and purification of the way to deliverance from *samsara* ; and their motive was to open the road for the laymen, who did not find their way in the jungle of syncretistic religious philosophy and magic offered to them. It is striking to see how many dominant personalities of religious and moral greatness, with the vigorous temperament of prophets and reformers, have been the leaders of these movements.

Jodo-shu was meant by its founder, Honen Shonin, to be the way of deliverance through faith for the laymen. He felt compassion for the multitudes. The background of the Gospel of Amida Butsu's all-sufficiency as a Saviour is the distinction between the way of *shodo* (holiness) or *ji-riki* (self-deliverance) and the way of Jodo (the Pure-Land) or *tariki* (deliverance by a Saviour). According to Honen Shonin Buddha taught both ways, because both have the same goal to achieve Buddhahood. Under the impression of his own sinfulness, Honen Shonin became an assiduous religious seeker, and the light he found was that the path of personal moral and intellectual achievement, the path of holiness, is too high and arduous for the masses and can be realized only by a few elect moral and intellectual athletes. His gospel was that the path of holiness and self-deliverance is arduous and impassable ; the path of deliverance through faith in and invocation of Amida Butsu (namu Amida Butsu) is easy and passable. Amida Butsu (in the Buddhist system the Dhyani Buddha Amitabha) opens in his endless mercy the way to everyone who calls on his name with sincere faith and desire for deliverance in his heart. After age-long practice of the way of holiness Amida Butsu himself had acquired Buddhahood, suffering for sinful humanity, and had created the Pure Land of Bliss for those who believe in him. The rock on which the certitude of the believers is built is the Primordial Covenant (*purva pranidhana* ; *hon-gwan*) of Amida, for one of the vows he made was : " When at my achieving Buddhahood any living being in the ten worlds, who desires to be reborn in my Paradise, invokes ten times my name, trusting to my Vow, if he does not become reborn there, I will not enter the state of perfect enlightenment."

The point that is constantly stressed is that everyone can be saved, even the greatest sinner, provided only that he has sincere faith in his heart when pronouncing the glorious name. As in all gospels of salvation, there rings through this one a note of deep exultant joy. It is indeed entirely intelligible that we should read of revival movements in virtue of this gospel of salvation.

A man of still greater religious and prophetic sincerity is Shinran, a pupil of Honen, who gave a puritan version of his master's gospel and became the founder of Shin-shu. He proclaimed a practically monotheistic religion of salvation with a strong ethical temperament. The certitude of salvation with him too comes from resting on Amida's Primordial Covenant or Vow. He accentuates strongly the principle of faith alone with exclusion of any effect of good works, for it is Amida alone who works salvation. This doctrine was a rejection of the faith in good works as a means of salvation that had sprung up in the original branch of Jodo-shu. Among the many remarkable similarities with Protestantism as it began with Luther may also be mentioned his discarding of asceticism, saint-worship and all sorts of popular religious practices. Specially noteworthy in the realm of the religious civilizations of Asia is his denunciation of magic. His religion is a religion exclusively of faith. To rely upon Amida's Vow is the central religious principle ; ethics are set under the light of living a life of gratitude because of Amida's mercy.

Here again we have a theological and psychological climate closely akin to that of Protestant Christianity. The many deviations towards a religion of good works and practices to acquire religious merit we do not touch upon because we are here only interested in the undiluted and dynamic principles of these remarkable movements.

H. Haas in his well-known book, *Amida Buddha unsre Zuflucht*, has pronounced the judgment that it is simply a duplicate of Christianity in Buddhist garb. This judgment is apparently too rash, because Haas sticks exclusively to the theological and psychological similarities. It would have been quite right if he had equated Amidism with a minimized form of New Testament Christianity such as is represented in a certain type of Pietism, that—it is worth while to note—also had and always has the same tendency of soteriological eudæmonism as these Buddhist forms of Pietism show. The prophetic religion of Biblical realism, however, moves in an entirely different sphere. Honen Shonin, in recognizing the two ways of salvation, that of rigorous moralism and gnosis and that of faith in the Saviour, remains thereby worlds apart from the core of Paul's justification by faith, which is rather the radical *démasqué* of all forms of moralism as man's means of self-assertion in the face of the holy, divine Judge. The emphasis on faith has in Honen's gospel a strongly opportunist colouring, for the constant emphasis on the fact that this way is an *easier* way is a symptom of spiritual opportunism, and stands in radical contrast to the sphere of Biblical realism, where there is no question about the easiness or arduousness of ways, but everything centres in the eternal validity of God's holy Will and God's sovereign opening of a way where there is no way at all. Here, as in Indian *bhakti*, the centre around which all moves is man and his salvation from *samsara*. Faith is a means to work salvation, and not the organ by which man apprehends and recognizes that God has in Christ restored the right relation between Himself and man. In reality the *ta-riki* remains a *ji-riki*. Amida is important in so far as by him man satisfies his need for salvation. The fundamental theocentric atmosphere of Biblical realism is entirely absent. Again, as in Indian *bhakti*, God is not the Creator, the God of holy love, who reconciles man unto Himself by His act of revelation in Christ ; but He is exclusively the compassionate Saviour, who exists for the succour of man's helplessness, the only thing such exclusively anthropocentric soteriology, as Amidism is, is really interested in.

Shinran with his deep religious sensitiveness conceives faith as a gift of Amida and not as the act of man that works salvation. His gospel is also exclusively concentrated at the soteriological point, where all emphasis falls on the utter impotence of man to save himself. God and His holy reality, in face of which sin and the sinner cannot abide, do not, however, enter his sphere of religious thinking. This is the reason why his *sola fide* has a radically different connotation from that in Biblical realism. The exclusively anthropocentric character of his soteriological gospel keeps it in the sphere of being the sole and ultimate psychological instrument to acquire salvation. His deep religious sensitivity, however, induced him to conceive faith as a gift of Amida.

A very marked and decisive difference between Biblical realism and the two Saviour-religions of Honen Shonin and Shinran is that in the first God's act of salvation in the incarnation of Jesus Christ is a real historical act, because God, the Creator, and the world, His creation, are objective realities. Amida and his Vow belong to the realm of mythology. It is really startling to state that a man of such deep religious sensitiveness as Shinran appears to be in his doctrine and in many religious and ethical observations in the works he wrote, entirely disregarded this cardinal point, because on account of this fact his whole soteriology remains, fundamentally speaking, a projection of human desire for salvation. In this disregard shines through the secret influence of the basic naturalistic monism in Mahayana-Buddhism, of which this disregard is a characteristic element. There are other indications of this secret influence of naturalistic monism in Shinran's world of thought, but we must confine our remarks to these.

CHAPTER VI

THE NON-CHRISTIAN SYSTEMS OF LIFE AND THOUGHT (*continued*)

CHINA

CHINA and Japan, through Buddhism, have been deeply influenced and moulded by Indian thought and religion. The amount of enrichment in philosophical thinking, in religious quest, in psychological penetration, in art, that these two great cultures have derived from their being impregnated by Buddhism and the cardinal Indian motives of life, is simply incalculable. Without this Indian impact the civilizations of China and Japan would probably never have known to such a high degree real metaphysical thinking, acute logical analysis, the lofty heights of radical mystical gnosis, the deep mellow tones of the longing piety of faith, and the great development of rigorous ethical systems of discipline which have become their possession. In short, the many-sided cultural stimulus that has gone out from India influencing these two civilizations is enormous, and demonstrates convincingly that the Indian type of apprehension of existence is one of the most cardinal and representative of the existing types in the world.

The civilization that is China's original creation, however, is also one of the truly remarkable expressions of the human mind. In its own very characteristic way, which is the outcome of aptitudes and geographical and historical circumstances different from those of India, it is an expression of the primitive apprehension of the totality of existence. Confucianism and Taoism, the typically Chinese spiritual creations, are so emphatically an expression of this apprehension that the comprehensive endeavour of the great Sinologist, J. M. de Groot, to evaluate Chinese culture as a whole has caused the enormous elasticity and fertility of the primitive apprehension of existence to become more widely understood. He has given it the name of " Universismus."

In the preceding chapter we indicated that the two outstanding tendencies—following from the primitive apprehension of existence—of the tribal religions and of the great religious civilizations of Asia are that they are strongly naturalist and strongly social in conception and outlook. China affords a very vivid illustration of these two inseparable strands in Eastern religion. The French scholar, M. Granet, whose works testify to great knowledge and great originality, has characterized Taoism as a " *naturisme magico-mystique* " and Confucianism as a " *sociocentrisme* " with ethical ends. This formulates the Chinese situation tersely, but aptly. The naturalist and social apprehension of religion have in China acquired an exceptionally high degree of interdependent unity, which in its turn has produced an adjustment and attunement to the universe that from the standpoint of cultural history must be called marvellous and unsurpassed. This exquisite spirit of harmony is China's characteristic and outstanding achievement ; and in it lies the explanation of the fact that this so-called practical people has manifested such extraordinary artistic ability and taste.

The interdependent unity of the naturalist and social apprehension of religion has been so peculiarly strong in China because in Confucianism the notion of religion as *dharma*, as a divinely-sanctioned social order to which everyone necessarily has to conform, was not linked—as in India—with the fissiparous conception of caste. Nor was it confined to the family and the clan—although in this respect also Confucianism is the classic expression of religion as a social notion—but it contracted a very intimate relation with the State and its symbol, the Emperor. Thus the grand idea of the interdependence of the primordial cosmic order and the social and political order is made the creative impulse of that aristocratic life-conception which we call by the name of Confucianism. This is also the reason why Chinese civilization has become the classic embodiment of conservatism with its vivifying and petrifying possibilities. The Chinese mind, because it served as the vehicle of the primitive, naturalist

apprehension of existence, can be as exuberant and grotesque
in its phantasies as India. But this strong concentration on
man as a social and political being, and on the discipline
needed to make him function harmoniously in the totality,
gives Chinese civilization that aspect of common sense and
aristocratic reserve and restraint which is lacking in India,
where social thinking has remained caught in the concept
of caste and the religiously-established superiority of one
priestly caste, the Brahmans. The enormous sweep and
width which this amalgamation of the naturalist concept of
the universe and its majestic order with the social concept of
the Empire and its august prestige has instilled into the
Chinese view of life is the background for its remarkable
creation of officialdom, open to everyone, from the highest
to the lowest strata of society, so radically in contrast to
caste-ridden India. One could go on drawing outlines,
for the study of Chinese civilization as a cultural achievement is a fascinating theme, but it would carry us too far.

The highest category of the Chinese apprehension of the
world and of life is Totality, or the Primeval and Eternal
Order (*Tao*), which is the moulding principle of the
universe. It manifests itself in a process of antithetic but
complementary rhythms, such as Yang and Yin, macrocosm
and microcosm, which correspond with and counter-
balance each other. To preserve the harmony of this
primeval rhythm is the meaning of the natural and the
human world. The law of nature and the law of human
social life, namely morality, are essentially one. Man and
the cosmos are one undivided unity of life. Primeval
Totality or Order (*Tao*) realizes itself in the ordered life of
man, and the reverse. Therefore the first commandment
of all Chinese ethics is to live in harmony with *Tao*, and
the second, which is like to it, is that the traditional rules and
etiquettes through which society and state function reflect—
or ought to—the behaviour of the cosmos. To keep this
harmony intact and to find herein the true life is the foundation of both Confucianism and *Taoism*. *Tao* and *Li* are the
appropriate terms to express these two cardinal aspects of the
Chinese apprehension of life and the world. It is a symbol

of the Chinese apprehension that Chu Hsih, the great systematizer of Neo-Confucianism under the Sung dynasty, knows in his system only cosmology and ethics.

Confucianism and Taoism have each elaborated this naturalistic monism and this cosmic-human monism in their characteristic way, virtually becoming radical contrasts, but essentially springing from the same life-impulses. Both coincide in the immanentist, anthropocentric and relativistic key-note which pervades the background of all their attitudes. Here again not the problem of truth but of realization of spiritual values is the guiding principle. The hyper-individualistic ethics of Taoist *wu-wei* and the aristocratic social ethics of Confucian conformity and etiquette, in which self-mastery is the way to world-mastery, are both thoroughly immanentist and anthropocentric. Not the Will of God, but the ideal of the " Perfect, Holy Man " whose inner being is one with *Tao*, and that of the "Noble Gentleman," is the norm of ethical striving and aspiration. A transcendent norm of ethics is impossible in this naturalistic apprehension. The command of Heaven is to be found in the heart. All ethics are a form of human wisdom, never the expression of a personal divine Will which is the Measure and Judge of all life and action. The whole spirit of Chinese civilization is that of humanism ; it is one of mankind's classic achievements in humanism. In this idealism of harmony good and evil are, of course, no real contrasts. Everything or every condition that breathes harmony is *eo ipso* good, for instance universal welfare. The same subtle or coarse eudæmonism, that is everywhere the child of a naturalistic-monistic apprehension of existence, permeates all Chinese ethics, for within this *harmonia præstabilita* of the natural order of the universe and the moral order of human life it is impossible to see the irreparable rent of sin that runs through it. The much-debated Chinese aversion to a personal conception of God has its deep roots in this same naturalistic monism. In its sphere the conception of transcendence and of so-called pure spirituality of God is, properly speaking, absurd. The conception of the Divine as something wholly independent of nature or man is simply impossible, for nature and man are *aspects* of Totality, while Totality expresses itself in man and nature. A real difference in substance or essence is unthinkable. The Chinese mind has therefore always abhorred the idea of a transcendent God-Creator, who again and again takes the initiative and acts in history. In religious speculation the Chinese mind turns naturally and inevitably to the conception of an impersonal, *super-divine* entity. We intentionally use the word super-divine, because the divine belongs to the sphere of the world, of nature and man. The ultimate is super-divine, ineffable, indefinable, immutable Essence, outside all activity. In other words, naturalistic monism leads always to some kind of ontological conception of the Divine or Ultimate Reality, in irreconcilable contrast to the voluntaristic conception of the God of history and in history embodied in Biblical realism.

Gods with personal traits in Chinese mythology are not the expression of a really personal conception of God, with what this implies in regard to the whole conception of God, man and the world. They are products of the natural anthropomorphic habit of human thinking. The real gods are the " holy " and the " noble " men, who according to the Taoist ideal or to the Confucian ideal have realized attunement to and identification with the natural and moral world order (*Tao*) by their complete harmony with it. To live in harmony with nature is the formula used to express the ideal life. Taoism has always shown its deep affinity with nature by its liking for quiet spots to practise its quietist activism of *wu-weio*. The Confucian literati, whose conventionalized etiquette was the standardized expression of the " Way " of the universe in the social sphere, protested in a more direct way the fundamental relation to nature which underlies their whole ideal of life by their habit of retiring in old age to nature, in the literal sense of the word, and enjoying it.

As was remarked already, in quoting Granet, Confucianism is a *sociocentrisme* with ethical ends. Confucius moved with his mind in the world of the cardinal ideas indicated above. His problem, however—and in this he had the characteristically Chinese preoccupation with man as a social and political being—was to rediscover, in a time of social and political crisis, stable foundations for corporate life. Not from disbelief—for he took the whole world of gods and demons and religious practices for granted as the matter-of-course attribute of corporate life—but on account of practical agnosticism he waived all metaphysical conceptions that were not to him self-evident tenets of the axiomatic harmony between the macrocosmos and the microcosmos. His concern was right sonship and right subject-ship, if it is permitted to coin this word, because citizenship would convey a wrong idea of the Chinese conception regarding the relation between political authority and the body of subjects. He wanted people to learn to live rightly with their fellow-men, and so he became the father of this remarkable synthesis of naturalistic-monistic universism and social ethics that aspired to turn out ideal sons and ideal subjects, but above all ideal emperors and officials. Ancestor-worship and a theocratic conception of the empire became the dominant motives in this universist philosophy of political reconstruction and stabilization. The term theocracy must be understood here in an entirely immanent sense. The Emperor is the *pontifex maximus*, the mediator between heaven and earth, by whose mediation and virtue (*teh*, that is his harmony with the world order) the natural and social process functions rightly. The officials, his representatives and minor duplicates, are ministrants to serve the same purpose in this immanentist and humanist theocracy of virtue. Loyalty to the Emperor and Mediator in the rhythmic inter-relation of macrocosm and microcosm has to be their cardinal virtue, just as filial piety is the cardinal virtue of everyone.

Confucius turned to history to strengthen his structure ; not to history in the sense of the working-place of God in His dealings with man, but in the sense of a venerable manuscript, illumined by illustrious examples of men, such as the great mythical emperors of antiquity who had realized this ideal and therefore needs must be the standard models for imitation. The deeply humanistic nature of Confucianism shines very brightly in the strong belief in education and the educability of man by which it is marked out among the many political philosophies that the world has produced. The famous thesis of man's natural goodness is quite intelligible in the humanistic sphere of the harmonistic apprehension of existence, and was at the same time a necessary pre-supposition for this educability of man.

Three mighty factors have thus co-operated to make Confucianism the climax of static conservatism. First, it was rooted in, and never emancipated itself from, the traditionalist view of primitive apprehension ; second, its naturalist and universist inspiration made the cyclic and rhythmic course of nature its secret pattern ; third, it was animated by the ideal of conformity to historically fixed ideals. On these foundations the social and political, and one may add the spiritual, life of China has been built for some millennia. For the first time in its history the dynamic forces of world history are trying now to demolish this colossus. The officials constituted in this theocracy a moral and intellectual aristocracy, being the guardians of tradition and decorum. The State-cult, of which the Emperor and they were the natural officiants, sought to preserve and strengthen the harmony of the different world-orders, and so to perpetuate and strengthen life ; for in China, as everywhere in the world, the natural human desire for life is the often secret but always dominant urge in religion. " A thousand years to live ! A life without end ! " is the favourite method of wishing in China.

Taoism represents the other side of naturalistic monism and universism, the naturalistic and vitalistic side. Taoism in its higher stages of contemplative and serene mysticism and in its many lower stages of occultism, of magic and sorcery, of systems to acquire immortality, of fantastic heavens and hells, is as chaotic as nature itself. In contrast to the rational, well-balanced mastery of life incorporated in Confucianism, it is unsocial and averse from conformity. The leading ideas of the primitive apprehension of existence, namely, the inter-correspondence of macrocosm and microcosm, the cosmic-mythological classificatory systems, the participation of man in the universal order, have in Taoism assumed the form of massive occult sciences, running to seed again and again, a truly tropical vegetation of sublime and ridiculous phantasies. Taoism is always considered as of small significance in the present life of China. Not knowing China by actual contact, we refrain from passing an opinion. It is proper, however, never to forget that Taoism is one of the most typical and characteristic products of Chinese universism, and that the " religion " of the people is mostly this inextricable mixture of ancestor-worship, vegetative agrarian cults, family- and clan-obligations, and—last but not least—the numberless crude ideas and practices that shoot up from the fertile soil of universistic apprehension of life.

Whosoever wants to conquer magic, sorcery and all the bizarreries in which the minds of millions are enslaved, and to destroy this kind of Taoism, must destroy naturalistic monism, the ever-bearing womb of all these strange children of human desire and fear. Confucianism, with its strong rationalistic tendency, has nevertheless not made any effort to break the chains of this bondage to magic and the like. It itself had its roots deeply sunk in the soil of naturalistic monism. In addition to that, the temper of proud aloofness from the common people which was implied in its aristocratic moralism and its social conception of religion, made it unfit to do that service for the great civilization of China. The literati, those masters of urbanity and those artists of life, are fascinating specimens of refined humanism, but they fostered that contempt of the multitude which is the attribute of all aristocratic moralists. The real concern for one's fellowmen, especially the less privileged, as a moral and inescapable obligation is only born in the prophetic religion of Biblical realism, where the love of man is derived from the love of God, and is at the same time the only valid and accepted proof of love for God, for " he who will not love his brother whom he has seen, cannot possibly love God, whom he has never seen " (1 John iv. 19).

Buddhism in general has already been dealt with. Here some remarks must be devoted to Buddhism in China. Buddhism was a " foreign " religion, bringing ideals and life-patterns to China radically opposed to the most ingrained ideals of that country. Its principles of world denial and denial of the family were an insult to the Chinese cultural self-consciousness. It never succeeded in supplanting or weakening the position of Taoism and Confucianism. It was often persecuted, but one can safely say that these persecutions, often very cruel and ruthless, had always political motives, the problem of religious truth being left alone. The relativism inherent in naturalistic monism is not very much interested in the problem of religious truth. All religions are, as regards the question of truth, equally to be recognized. Besides, the social conception of religion naturally tended to value every religion, especially such a religion as Buddhism which seeks to provide for individual religious wants, from the standpoint of its social and political value or danger. Accordingly Buddhism met not only with persecution but also with protection.

Buddhism has not become the one religion of China, but has acted as a very important ferment in the higher regions of Chinese culture and in the life of the people. It has pro-vided for the deeper, truly religious needs ; it has enriched enormously the capacity for speculative thinking, and has stimulated and deepened artistic expression. In the course of the ages Buddhism has insinuated itself in numberless ways into the life of China. This was made easier by the fact that Mahayana-Buddhism, which penetrated into China, repre-sented a new edition as well as an adulteration of original Buddhism, because Mahayanism is a recrudescence of the monistic naturalistic apprehension of existence. So, notwith-standing the fact that Buddhism as an institutional religion is monastic and in opposition to the strongly patriarchal ideals of China, this deep affinity with the pre - suppositions of Chinese universism paved a royal way for the šymbiosis of Buddhism and Chinese religious life. Such concrete things as the worship of Kwan-yin, the merciful Guide to Paradise and the Kind Helper in the many distresses of feminine life, the care Buddhism takes of such an important thing in human life as the funeral rites, and some other practices, have obtained for Buddhism a firmly established position in Chinese life.

M. Granet, whom we have already quoted, makes in his

La Religion des Chinois a remark that in substance could serve as a description of the practical religious attitude in all Asia and Africa, and of many forms of popular religion in " Christian " countries too. He says that to the Chinese in general religion is primarily an arsenal of gestures, formulas and obligations to strengthen life according to one's own wishes. From this point of view the hospitable nature of the naturalistic-monistic apprehension of existence, about which we have spoken in regard to Hinduism, manifests itself in China in respect to Buddhism so as to produce appreciation of the increase of effective rites and practices which Buddhism affords.

.   .   .   .

JAPAN

Japan is a country with an extremely interesting cultural and religious history. Because of the influence upon it of Confucianism and of Chinese Buddhism it is one of the great sectors of the Chinese region of civilization. Through their peculiar character and talents the Japanese people have welded the universist background of Chinese civilization, the political and social ethics of Confucianism, and the wealth of metaphysical and religious motives of Buddhism, into an original and extremely interesting whole, along with its basic native elements, which were enshrined in Shinto. The Japanese atmosphere has a very special and fascinating quality through the peculiar way in which this merging process has grown and has been achieved. It is particularly striking to note how many strong, domineering personalities the religious history of Japan has produced. There is perhaps no country in the region of the naturalist religions where the figure of the reformer, characterized by a *prophetic* temperament, is so relatively prominent. A prophet is a man who is driven by a force greater than himself. He must speak and act, whatever the consequences and the opposing forces may be. He is dominated by a sense of irresistible obligation towards a power which has absolute authority over him. In the wide area of the naturalist religions such figures hardly grow. The history of China and India, the two great civilizations, tells hardly anything about " prophets." The soil of naturalistic monism, so extraordinarily fertile in nearly every respect, is not far from complete sterility in this respect. In its atmosphere those men do not breathe who were driven by Amos' simple but mighty vision : " When the lion roars, who does not shudder ? When the Lord Eternal speaks, *who can but prophesy* ? " Now the peculiarity of Japan, which as a religious civilization wholly belongs to the sphere of naturalistic religion and the primitive apprehension of existence, is that it has produced a number of men full of prophetic vigour and the prophetic temperament. Their distinction from the Hebrew prophets is, nevertheless, very marked, and this is in accordance with their naturalistic background. The prophetic figures of Japan (Honen, Shinran, Nichiren, etc.) are always driven by an imperative urge for the salvation of men or for the glory of their country. One might say, the quality of their prophetic consciousness of inescapable obligation is always exclusively soteriological or nationalistic. The prophets in the sphere of Biblical realism—and there lies the difference—are absolutely theocentric. The holy, righteous Will of the Lord and His glory are the things that matter, in comparison with which everything else and everyone else is insignificant, but at the same time through which everything and everyone gets its due place and recognition.

Among the most fascinating creations of this blending of native Japanese culture and religion with the mighty impulses of the two great representative civilizations of India and China, are found the type of the Samurai and his code of Bushido, the spiritual heroes of Zen-Buddhism, the many scholars and officials, models of probity and rectitude, moulded by the various forces of Japanese virility and Confucian sincerity. Even the well-known tea-ceremony, that is also a curious fruit of the Samurai-spirit and of Zen spiritual discipline, should not be omitted. All these creations have some characteristic features in common, which go back on the original stock of the Japanese mind. However refined all these cultural and religious creations may have become they are dominated by a spirit of manly vigour and a leaning towards strong discipline, both intimately connected with the feudal spirit of loyalty of the vassal to his liege which permeates so deeply the whole outlook of Japanese life.

Shinto, the native religion of Japan, belongs to the well-known type of " primitive " tribal religions. Its component parts are cults of nature and its manifestations ; cults of the ancestors, in which clan-heads and the heads of the nation as a whole are included ; and a wealth of vegetative, cosmogonic and theogonic myths, which are striking instances of the classificatory and cosmic-mythological views and of the vitalistic and naturalistic tendencies which we indicated to be standing elements of the primitive apprehension of existence. How deep and innate is the naturalistic tendency in Japan's native religions appears from the just remark of a modern Japanese scholar, Anesaki, who says that the question of monotheism or polytheism in Japanese religious life is quite irrelevant, because one virtually worships in many forms the omni-present and ever-active Life, which manifests itself equally in nature, men and gods, one and at the same time many.

It is of crucial importance to note that in Shinto the spheres of nature-myth, of ancestor worship and of national history and destiny are from the beginning entirely intermingled. The division of the gods into terrestrial and celestial gods, of course originally deriving from the great dualistic division of earth and heaven which occurs universally in the primitive apprehension of existence, later on in Japan became modelled on the lines of political and dynastic history. The gods in Shinto-mythology that belong to the conquered tribes of Yamato are classified as terrestrial gods, and those that belong to the conquering nation of Kyushu as celestial gods. The two great sanctuaries of Izumo and Ise fall into the same categories.

Gundert in his *Japanische Religionsgeschichte* expresses the significance of Shinto in this striking way : " According to Shinto, Japan as a geographical and historical unity is at the same time a religious subject and a religious object. In the forms of mythology and cult Shinto is the expression of *the belief of the Japanese people in itself.*" The Emperor and his house, descending from the Sun-goddess Amatera-su of

Kyushu, is the natural head of all cults, because all cults are under his guardianship. The indissoluble unity of religion, nation and state in the person of the Emperor is suggested by the fact that his ruler-function is called *matsurigoto*, which signifies cult-observance. He is the Ceremonial High Priest of the nation. The central myth of Amatera-su, who resides in the holy insignia at Ise and thus literally dwells amongst her chosen people, contains the tale of the founding of the Japanese state and the formation of the Japanese people. The institution of the imperial dynasty is a divine act. With this theocratic background it is wholly intelligible that Shinto at the present time has such an enormous significance. Through the widening of the spiritual horizon and the accompanying intensification of national ambition, the national and tribal religion of Shinto even gets to-day a universalistic aspect. The creation of the Japanese nation and dynasty by divine act is conceived to have happened for the good of the whole world. The Japanese nation is a divinely-created people with Messianic significance for the world. Shinto has virtually become the mythological and metaphysical foundation of a fervent and ambitious patriotism and naturalism, deliberately used by the Government to foster *kokumin dotoku* (national morality). This whole modern development is a natural growth from the basic elements of primitive Shinto.

Again, just as it was important to note the remarkable appearance of prophetic figures on the Japanese stage, it is equally important to call attention to the peculiar quality of the Japanese theocratic idea. China, as has been mentioned, was a universist theocracy, in which the Emperor was the natural mediator between Earth and Heaven, cosmic and social *Tao*. This conception is wholly embedded in the naturalistic type of thinking. The Emperor's position is a product of the cyclic process and movement of the all-embracing universal order. In the Japanese conception there is a very special twist, attesting the virile, vigorous temperament of this combative people. The mythical act of the creation of the Japanese nation and dynasty is isolated from the great cyclic movement of nature, and conceived as the central and decisive act, because of which all others fade away. So the Japanese theocratic texture gets a peculiar woof. It has an aspect of very rigorous self-consciousness. By its resolutely anthropocentric nature, however, it constantly betrays its origin in the soil of naturalistic monism and the primitive apprehension of life. Shinto expresses in mythological forms the self-deification of the Japanese nation, not the sole Lordship and sovereignty of God the Eternal, as is the case in the theocracy conceived in Biblical realism. It is therefore highly advisable to remember that the term theocracy can only be applied to China and Japan in a very qualified sense, because undefiled theocracy is only possible in a radically theocentric apprehension of existence.

Just as with the community religions of antiquity, Shinto aims at procuring civic well-being. The end of all sacrifices and cults is to " procure happiness " and to create the conditions whereby it becomes possible for dynasty and nation to realize their divine destiny. Japan being mainly an agrarian country, a great number of the cults and *matsuris* (feasts) are connected with the hopes and fears of agricultural life. The ever-recurring object is welfare and harmony, or, to express it still more adequately, to heighten and perpetuate life.

Shinto is not a very important religion by reason of its depth or any other characteristic. It is an ordinary instance of " primitive " religion. Its exceptional importance derives not from its nature but from its historical fortune. Having become very early the standard expression of Japanese national self-consciousness, it is the only primitive religion that has maintained its independent existence as an institutional religion, notwithstanding the commanding presence of Buddhism, which is a world religion, and of Confucianism, which meant a vastly superior civilization. From this angle Shinto is a really unique phenomenon.

Confucianism and Buddhism were both the bearers of a higher and more refined civilization. Confucianism, which meant Chinese civilization, brought by its universism a deepening and multiplying of the naturalist apprehension of life, and an enormous enrichment of political-ethical thinking and practice. Buddhism meant to primitive Japan a special process of Sinification, and at the same time an inoculation with Indian religious metaphysics. It has been for Japan of far greater significance than for China. As B. C. Chamberlain has justly remarked, during many ages Buddhism was the paramount moulding influence in Japanese life in the fields of philosophy, religion, medical science and care, education, art, etc. In every field it can point to men of great stature. Perusing the history of Japan between the tenth and the sixteenth centuries one is struck by its similarity with the history of the European Middle Ages. As in Europe, the scene is rigorously dramatic. We read of great religious revivals and reformations with leaders of outstanding personality ; wild political conflicts ; virile culture and effeminate refinement ; holy and single-minded Gcd-seekers and virtuosi of the contemplative life ; rich and powerful monasteries, inhabited by strong-willed monks, burning for lust of power, riches and the gratification of the senses.

Buddhism came to Japan from China. In accordance with the political and social—and consequently the utilitarian—connotation that religion always has had in all climes and times, it was recommended by the Korean King, Syong Oang of Pàkcye, to the Japanese court as a valuable asset for a happy reign. In the literal sense of the word it was " tried " for some time as to its efficiency and at the end of the sixth century it was recognized. The Emperor entered the Buddhist fold, but this did not change his position as the head of all cults. Prince Shotoku Taishi, the Regent of Japan from 593–621, was a great exponent of Chinese civilization and the Chinese art of government and was at the same time a great promoter of Buddhism. In his famous Seventeen Articles addressed to the State officials, Buddhism is recommended as a means to strengthen loyalty to the Emperor and the State ; some years later, with the same end in view, he recommends the worship of ancestors and ancestral gods.

Buddhism, thus, has from the outset been intimately connected with the interests of the nation and the dynasty, and has itself, from the outset, accepted as a matter of course the position of being one of the many cults. Till the seventeenth century it maintained this intimate relation with the political and social life of the country. The religious policy in Japan has in principle been the same as that in all civilizations that have grown on the basis of naturalistic monism and the primitive apprehension of life, as, for example, China, India and the Roman Empire. The important side of a religion is not its doctrines and tenets or religious truth but the fact that it constitutes a peculiar " way of life," a *dharma*, a *nomos*. In so far as they are considered to serve the welfare of the community, which is conceived as the paramount end of every form of religious life, religions are tolerated and granted equal rights. So Shinto, Confucianism and Buddhism were three spiritual forces, recognized as equally serving the welfare of the community, which term in Japan has always been characteristically identified with the support of the dynasty.

In our short delineation of Buddhism in the preceding chapter we have touched already on some very important manifestations of Buddhist life in Japan. Therefore we add here only some supplementary remarks.

The Nara-period (eighth century) was a time of illustrious Buddhist cultural and religious activity. Magnificent temples were built ; even roads, bridges and ports were made under the guidance of Buddhist monks. The religio-philosophical thinking blossomed out in many schools. These were not separate churches but were different types of religious and philosophical thought. They agreed in the cardinal elements of Buddhist thought. These are the convictions that the Ego is merely a fleeting stream of psychic molecules ; the resultant conception that empirical reality is an illusionary product of this psychical stream, with its metaphysical counterpart, the conception of the immutable transcendental Reality ; and the call to walk the way of deliverance, consisting in the liberating insight that empirical reality is unreal. This problem of the relation between illusory phenomenal reality and absolute transcendent Reality has been through all the ages the procreative force in Japanese Buddhist thinking. The common people as such never have cared about these schools and their tenets, because it is religious philosophy and not religion which animates the differences of the schools. Japanese popular sentiment has, however, become thoroughly imbued by the Buddhist apprehension of transiency, of *karma*, of heavenly rewards and tortures of hell, of gentleness of mind towards all creation as a result of the teaching of *ahimsa*.

The two great schools of the ninth century which achieved a colossal amalgamation, mixing and combining the highest tenets of idealistic monism with baser and even the basest elements of popular religion, were the Tendai school of Dengyo Daishi and the Shingon school of Kobo Daishi, both men of extraordinary ability. The fundamental tenet of Tendai conceives the relation of the absolute and the phenomenal as that of water and wave, inseparable, indistinguishable, and yet not one. The phenomenal world is neither really real, nor unreal or void. It exists only in human consciousness, and because the phenomenal and the absolute are inseparable and indistinguishable, the identity of the absolute with the basic depth of consciousness is proclaimed. One psychic moment contains all the three thousand worlds. Gnosis aims at the attainment of Buddhahood, which means the realization of the identity of the Absolute with human consciousness.

Shingon is the Japanese representative of Tantric Buddhism and is conceived to be an esoteric doctrine. All reality, phenomenal and absolute, is united in Mahavairocana Tathagata or Dai Nichi Nyorai. Therefore, the illusory phenomenal world and the world of the absolute are identical. Everything becomes thus a mirror of reality. On this basis of idealistic monism a complicated system of religion, magic and nature-symbolism was erected.

The reason why these very bare indications are given is to call attention to the all-dominant significance of idealistic monism in Japanese Buddhism as a result of the naturalistic monistic bedrock on which Mahayanism rests, and also to make clear that all idealistic monism in the world, whether it is Vedanta, Neo-Platonism or Hegelianism, springs from the same primordial soil and evinces the same ingrained tendency of justifying every type of spiritual life and giving it its so-called due place.

The reaction against the complicated abstruseness of these systems and the cry for religious simplification that took shape in the revivalist movements of Nembutsu have been dealt with. Here is the place to point to two other movements of reaction, which are still of great importance in Japan.

The Zen movement is the most radical simplification of the way towards deliverance that can be imagined. Intellectual and philosophical speculation, study and ritual techniques, were all discarded. All authority of Sutras or masters is put aside. The only thing that remains is to reach through severely-disciplined contemplation (*dhyana*, *zen*) the serene rapture of enlightenment (*bodhi*, *satori*), which is described as realizing Buddhahood. It appears at once that the roots of Zen are hidden in the broad vitalistic soil of naturalist religion, when one knows that Buddhahood in Zen Buddhism is the essence of everything and is identical with universal life. Its anthropocentric nature, as in all idealistic and vitalistic monism, reveals itself by the fact that achieving Buddhahood [1] is realization of self.

The other movement of reaction and simplification was that of Nichiren (thirteenth century), and it followed a course quite opposite to the aristocratic Zen movement. Japan's diversity of religious personalities is amazingly great. Nichiren was a man with great prophetic passion. His problem in the confusion of the abstruse religious philosophies and the many popular soteriological sects was, What is truth? This quest of religious certitude was accompanied by another quest, expressed in his second problem, How can Japan get religious unity and so be a strong nation? His search was therefore also for simplification, which was found in sweeping aside all ritual and speculation, and achieving Buddhahood or absolute truth and deliverance by believing the great Lotossutra (Saddharma-pundarika or Myoho-renge-kyo) to be the purest embodiment of the eternal Buddha or the Cosmic Soul. Nichiren proclaimed his gospel with vehement

[1] In other parts of the world this is called theosis.

aggressiveness and intolerance, denouncing all other sects as false.

This prophetic thirst for the *only* absolute truth and the only true doctrine is a very remarkable and exceptional phenomenon in the sphere of naturalist religions. Yet, here again it seems that the similarity with the absolutist apprehension that is characteristic of prophetic religion as a result of its theocentric character, is merely external and psychological, not internal and essential. The source of Nichiren's passion appears to be his passionate patriotic longing for national unity and the greatness of Japan. For Nichiren already expressed the conviction, now so widespread, that Japan is the Messianic country by which the salvation of the world will be wrought. It is obvious that Nichiren's reform movement is virtually Japanese national self-consciousness in Buddhist garb, a Buddhist counterpart of Shinto in its nationalist aspect.

SYNCRETISM

In conversing on religious subjects with people in Java one almost inevitably has some such experience as the following. In more than ninety out of a hundred cases one hears the stereotyped remark : " All religions are ultimately one." It comes from the lips of the intellectuals as well as from those of the illiterate villager. This saying expresses a world-wide opinion, world-wide in place and in time. All the religions of antiquity and all the naturalist non-Christian religions to-day are deeply imbued with this conviction. The religions of revelation are the sole exception to this rule.

Everywhere in the world, in the religious world of the Roman Empire as well as in all the great naturalist non-Christian religions, the practice of a bewilderingly undiscriminative (as we might say) assimilation was and is the order of the day. In Syria every village-saint is the object of inter-confessional worship, for behind this cult-object stands the primordial Semitic God of their ancestors, who personified universal life and is still persistent in the minds of the people. In Japan the pilgrims and tourists sacrifice their homage-coin (*saisen*) alike at Buddhist temples, Shinto shrines and

Roman Catholic cathedrals. In India, Hindus and Muslims have been known to worship simultaneously at each other's shrines. It would be easy to multiply by the hundred instances of this truly universal phenomenon.

One of the best-known features of Chinese universism is that the three religions—Confucianism, Buddhism and Taoism—are virtually treated as one. The religious allegiance of the average man is not related to one of the three religions. He does not belong to a confession or creed. He participates, unconcerned as to any apparent lack of consistency, alternatively in Buddhist, Taoist or Confucian rites. He is by nature a religious pragmatist. Religiously speaking, we find him *prenant son bien où il le trouve* (taking his due where he can find it). It is very significant to note that Mohammedanism, which by its prophetic origin has a more rigid and clear conception of religious truth, has never been allowed to enter the Chinese League of Religions, although there is no objecton whatever to it from the standpoint of the three great religions, and Islam has been established for many centuries in China.

A really gigantic and systematic attempt towards religious syncretism is Ryobu-shinto (bi-lateral Shinto). In it Buddhism and Shinto have thoroughly amalgamated on the basis of naturalistic kinship. The great leader in this enterprise of religious amalgamation has been Kobo Daishi, the founder of Shingon. The procedure was an extraordinarily easy one. Hotoke (Buddhas, Bodhisattvas and Arhats) were identified with the Shinto Kami. Vairocana and Amatera-su became interchangeable. Buddhist-Shinto temples were built as places of worship. Even now every Japanese, if he is not a pure Shintoist or Buddhist (as is the case of Shinto sects and the Puritan Shinshu of Buddhism), is registered as a member of a Buddhist sect and worships in a Buddhist *tera* (temple) as well as in a Shinto *miya* (shrine). He participates in Shinto *matsuris*, but his funeral rites are performed by Buddhist monks. In his house he has a kami-altar (*kamidan*) and a Buddha-altar (*butsudan*) and he sacrifices and prays to both. In China one can meet many similar conditions. The pragmatist attitude in religion and the natural innate syncretistic apprehension dominate the religious scene in all naturalist religions, whether in the past or in the present. The religious philosophies of India, China and Japan find in the justification of these two dominant characteristics one of their two main themes, the other being the speculation about Absolute Pure Essence and Reality. Japan and China, however, force these characteristics upon the attention of the onlooker still more emphatically than India does, because the man- and clan-centred mind of the Chinese and the nation-centred mind of the Japanese bring it about that religion in its different forms is preponderantly conceived as a means to satisfy the welfare of the individual and of the community. India's attitude and apprehension are not less pragmatic and syncretistic. When compared with that of China and Japan, however, it might perhaps be said to be somewhat disguised, for two reasons. The numerous *dharmas* contained in the caste-system are all clear symbols of the pragmatist attitude, and in Indian religious philosophy they are explained and justified by the same relativism which animates all naturalist religions. In practice, however, each *dharma* gets an aspect of practical absoluteness by the rigid separation between the different castes. In the second place, India, through the peculiar nature of its religious history, instinctively emphasizes in the way it conceives religion the aspect of openness to a world of indestructible spiritual reality.

We are repeatedly told, especially of the Chinese and the Japanese (but one can safely extend it to all other peoples which adhere to one of the naturalist religions) that they have a deep-rooted indifference towards dogma and doctrinal differences. In the Roman Empire it was the same. Apuleius invokes in his well-known prayer in one breath Isis, Minerva, Venus, Diana, Proserpina, Juno and Kybele as one deity, calling them all *rerum naturæ parens* (parent of the nature of things) and *elementorum omnium domina* (mistress of all elements). Nock in his book on *Conversion* says : " It was commonly held that the gods of different nations were identifiable, that the Egyptians worshipped Athena and Zeus under other names." In a foreign country one paid homage to its gods as a matter of course. About the whole area of naturalist religions, including those of antiquity, the testimony is given again and again that they are exceedingly tolerant.

All these instances demonstrate in an impressive way the underlying inherent unity of all these religions. The reason for this inherent unity is the fact of their being products of the primitive apprehension of existence and their naturalistic monistic framework.

We are accustomed to call the phenomenon illustrated by the preceding instances by the name of syncretism. From all that has been said in this and the preceding chapter it will be clear as daylight that syncretism and religious pragmatism are necessary and normal traits in the religions that live on the primitive apprehension of existence. In view of the fundamental nature and structure of these religions it is nothing capricious or unprincipled ; it is consistency itself. It would be abnormal if this were not so. One can safely speak about a fundamental syncretistic and pragmatist predisposition of those religions. It is rather interesting to note that the term syncretism is, properly speaking, inadequate if we judge this phenomenon from the standpoint of the fundamental nature and structure of the religions in which it occurs, which, scientifically considered, is the only legitimate method to be followed. The term syncretism has always more or less the connotation of expressing the *illegitimate* mingling of different religious elements. This peculiar conception of syncretism could only grow in a Christian atmosphere—and has actually grown there, for the word and the concept are a result of theological controversies in seventeenth-century Protestant theology—where it is legitimate and obligatory to speak about illegitimate mingling, because an absolute standard of reference is implicitly assumed. From the standpoint of the naturalist religions, however, it is not correct to speak of syncretism as an illegitimate and unexpected proceeding, because it is just what one should expect to happen. A more adequate term, devoid of any value-judgment, would be amalgamation. Ryobu Shinto is in so far a special case that it is a deliberate attempt at the amalgamation and harmonization of two religions, whereas in most cases syncretistic attitudes are practised without deliberate purpose, because it is as natural as breathing.

This amalgamation, the universal pragmatic attitude, the typical tolerance, the aversion to doctrinal borderlines, the relativist and, ultimately, very subjectivist (despite all seeming indications to the contrary) conception of religion, are all the natural products of the naturalistic monism in these religions.

Every form of religion, every system of religious tenets and practices, is to the mind that consciously or unconsciously lives on the naturalistic-monistic apprehension of existence one of the many possible and available ways and methods for the *realization* of a purpose or end that man has set himself. That may be a base, a decent, or an exceedingly noble end, for example, one's wishes for a good life, consisting in riches, ease, and many children ; for rebirth in better conditions of life ; for the entrance into Amida's Paradise ; for communion with God and experience of His exquisite love ; for enlightenment and final deliverance. This is the reason why in this sphere of naturalist religions there are so many forms of religious life that are virtually huge hedonistic machineries, and others that are marvellous expressions of self-mastery and metaphysical serenity.

Religion, in its many positive forms, necessarily belongs in this sphere of naturalist religions to the domain of human *psychology*. It is sought primarily for its experience-value, not for its truth-value. It is exceedingly important to grasp the significance of this fact ; it is another way of expressing the fundamental relativism of naturalist religions. On account of this fact, it becomes at once clear why the quality and nature of religious experience are always taken as *the* standard to measure the value of a religion. The pragmatist question :—What value does it have, what results does it yield ?—is, as a matter of course, considered to be the decisive question, and not the question of truth and objective validity.[1]

---

[1] The Greeks expressed the pragmatist conception of religion they had by the unequivocal words : Χρῆσθαι τοις Θέοις. This is wholly appropriate to the religions we are discussing.

Why should one pose the question of truth? This whole world with all its forms of life belongs to the sphere of the relative, the unreal. Religion as manifest in different systems and ways, all belonging to the relative sphere of this phenomenal world, stands by the nature of the case outside the question of absolute truth. It is an endeavour of man to realize his ends, and as such altogether a social and psychological affair. A good illustration of this is that many *bhaktas*, although they are convinced and avow that real ultimate *moksha* is the supreme moment of *tat twam asi*, (thou art that) openly proclaim that they "value" the "experience" of *bhakti* much more than ultimate *moksha*, which is the only *moksha* that wholly deserves the name. Psychological pragmatism here quietly takes precedence over truth and ultimate reality.

The latitude towards doctrine or creed does not mean indifference to doctrine in the sense of having a doctrine-less religion. The three great religious civilizations of India, China and Japan have been profusively creative in the field of doctrine and metaphysical speculation. But in accordance with their fundamental nature as naturalist religions they envisage doctrines as expressions of relative truth which consequently can also only be relative. They are relative, intellectual realizations of man in the whole of his endeavour towards self-realization. Radhakrishnan in his *The Heart of Hindustan* praises Hinduism highly for this latitude towards doctrine and creed, which are all relative to the general character of the people who profess them. "That different people," says he, "should profess different faiths is not unnatural. It is all a question of taste and temperament." This doctrinal latitude and relativism could not be expressed more strongly. Gandhi, though he declares Truth to be God and though he is a man of deeply moral temperament, treats positive religion with the same easy-going relativism, as is demonstrated by his passionate *swadeshi*-ism in religion. And here we have the same remarkable phenomenon to state as in the pseudo-religious nationalisms of Europe. Gandhi stresses the relativist nature of all religions, for they are products of the country, and Truth Itself is unattainable.

Yet, in practice, this fundamental relativism behaves itself as a militant absolutism.

This applies not only to the religious doctrine, but also to moral doctrine. In this whole naturalistic monistic world-conception with its cardinal division into the phenomenal relative world of unreality and the absolute world of reality, all moral systems—even morality as such, because it pre-supposes activity—belong to the relative sphere. They are means—in noble or dubious forms—to an end. God or the Divine in the fully valid sense of the word—not in any way qualified or accommodated—does exclusively belong to the absolute sphere. God is above all morality, for what has the Pure Essence to do with good and evil, with choice and responsibility, with activity and purpose ? The deep-rooted universal conviction in the East, that the acceptance of the absolute antagonism of good and evil is a rather childish and narrow-minded idea and that the only conception which behoves him who really " knows " is the " *Jenseits von Gut und Böse* " (above good and evil), appears thus to be a quite natural and logical conviction.

For the same reason it is quite natural to the average Easterner, who has deeply drunk from the waters of natural-istic-monistic religion, to explain traits in his chief gods that are, according to common moral feeling, scandalous—for example, Krishna's well-known erotic adventures—as " divine condescensions." In this light the well-known tolerance of those religions becomes clear, and also the amiable, suave quality it always shows, which evokes so often enthusiastic admiration. The enthusiasm and the admiration are in many cases understandable against the background of harsh and detestable intolerance with its bickering and petty controversies, which is the result of the distorted intellect-ualist conception of truth that corrupts so many human minds. But this admiration is no contribution whatever to the comprehension of the real character of this kind of tolerance. Tolerance, real tolerance, is everywhere in the world equally rare, and intolerance is everywhere in the world equally common, whether in the West or in the East. We are receiving to-day in both respects the most drastic and unforgettable lessons. The proverbially "tolerant" area of the naturalist religions with its extreme "tolerant" temper in the realm of religious truth is extraordinarily intolerant in respect of the social aspect of religion. The law that rules all corporate religious life in the religions that spring from the primitive apprehension of existence, the "tribal" religions as well as the cults and religions that belong to the three great religious civilizations of India, China and Japan, is the absolutely obligatory observance of, and conformity to, the traditional religious behaviour of the group. To break away from this conformity, however strong the call of conscience or truth may be, is unpardonable sin and *défaitism*. Rigorous intolerance is then considered the most natural thing in the world and is unhesitatingly applied. The caste system and its rules are a clear illustration of this intolerance in a land "religiously" so tolerant as India. Religious persecutions have been as common in Japan and China as anywhere else in the world, because *everywhere* in the world, East and West, North and South, man in different forms is the same self-assertive being and therefore prone to intolerance. The "religious" intolerance of these persecutions, however, had little to do with religious doctrine or truth (for there the usual doctrinal latitude obtained), but sprang from political or social motives.

The universality and intensity of intolerance in the realm of the naturalist religions suggest strongly that the not less marked phenomenon of tolerance needs some qualification. This tolerance in the realm of religious truth has to be interpreted in connection with that basic religious relativism, pragmatism and subjectivism which are a necessary consequence of the nature of the naturalist religions. It follows from the secret religious agnosticism that lies at the bottom of the naturalistic monistic life-apprehension. For the sake of clarity it would be advisable not to speak of religious tolerance for this phenomenon, but of truth-equalitarianism. In many cases truth-indifferentism might even be more appropriate.

The amiable suavity which often sweetens this pseudo-tolerance so agreeably ought not to blind our eyes to the fact that it is dearly bought at the price of a radical relativism. In the same way the repellant impression that detestable intolerance makes must not make us forget that it at least, though in a very perverted way, evinces awareness of one of mankind's most precious gifts, the persistent demand for absolute truth as a matter of life or death, for *everyone* and not only for the elect. Where in the sphere of the naturalist religions in some form the problem of truth becomes paramount, the fierce struggle for it easily and deplorably takes on an aspect of intolerance, because the art of real tolerance belongs to the highest arts of life, in all climes and times rarely achieved. A very illuminating instance of this easy sliding off to intolerant bitterness is the way in which Ramanuja vehemently refutes in his *Shribhashya* Shankara's acosmist monism. Why was this noble seeker for the precious pearl of loving *bhakti* to the God of infinite mercy such a vigorous and mordant fighter in the field of religious dialectics? Because he had the sincere conviction that he had to defend religious values of supreme value, for himself and for others.

Real tolerance is an arduous lesson to be learnt. It presupposes the combination of unswerving obedience to, and vindication of, the authority of absolute and evident truth with acceptance of the liberty of others to reject it or to adhere to other convictions, even though they be considered erroneous. The breeder of all doctrinal intolerance is an intellectualist conception of truth. Real tolerance can only grow when it is fully recognized that truth can only be really obeyed in perfect spiritual freedom, because anything else or anything less is disobedience to and misunderstanding of the real character of truth. The possibility of achieving the most dynamic form of real tolerance is to be found in the purely apostolic attitude of being an obedient and joyful *witness* and not a *possessor* of the truth that God has mercifully revealed, and entreating man to join in accepting and obeying it.

The spirit of syncretism, relativism, pragmatism and subjectivism that runs through the veins of the naturalist religions, has of course various and different incarnations.

Primarily there are its practical forms in the life and practice of the millions. Secondly, however, there are various rationalized forms in the shape of the many religious philosophies, which all contain a justification of the many types of religious life and purpose. The philosophical or epistemological background of these rationalized forms is the juxtaposition of the illusory world of relative, empirical existence and the real world of pure, absolute Essence, to which we have alluded already. All religions and what they tell about God, man, the world, deliverance, etc., belong, in these rationalized forms, to the sphere of illusory relative existence. Truth pertains exclusively to the sphere of absolute pure Essence. All religions therefore at their best can only be accommodated truths. All differences and contrasts have already a sameness, and therefore are at the bottom irrelevant. There is in this abstract ontological conception of Ultimate Reality or Truth no relation whatever between the Divine and empirical man, because man in his essence is one with relationless Essence. Its counterpart is the doctrine of the unreal character of the phenomenal world and of the positive forms of religion. Through this theory the syncretistic and relativistic attitude, which is implied in naturalistic-monistic apprehension, is rationalized. From the standpoint of Pure Essence all is sameness ; from the standpoint of accommodated truth all is difference. Monism and pluralism, polytheism and monotheism can equally be true, while equally false, and they have therefore the right to co-exist.

In India this " tolerant " justification and sanctioning of the religious *status quo*—for that is what it comes to—uses still more persuasive arguments. In the sphere of relative empirical existence all religions and confessions have their significance and value. For every individual the religion and confession in which he is born is, so to speak, the religious place assigned to him by *samsara* and *karma*. For the same reason *mukti*, or deliverance, is only possible for him in this religion and this confession, for the law of *karma*, which determined all the physical, social and other circumstances of his birth, is the supreme disposer. Although of relative value, to him this religion and this confession are his pre-destined stage of apprehension of religion and truth. As always, naturalistic monism or the ontological apprehension of existence appears here, notwithstanding the seeming capriciousness of its variegated forms, to be extremely logical. It does not even shrink in its ontological absolutism and its empirical relativism from declaring that the obtaining *status quo* of conditions and standpoints is the normal and inevitable state of things in every given period of history. It does not account for any real change, and thereby makes the world meaningless. In the last instance this follows logically from the axis on which this monism turns. The Sole and Ultimate Reality is motionless, actionless Pure Essence. The ever-recurring cyclic process of nature, which is in non-speculative naive naturalistic monism the world-process as it is enacted, becomes in its rationalized speculative form a mirage.

What has been said shows clearly how abysmal is the difference between the ontological apprehension of Ultimate Reality in the naturalist religions and the voluntarist apprehension in Biblical realism. In the first the Ultimate is relationless, actionless, blissful, Pure Essence ; in the second it is the " God and Father of our Lord Jesus Christ," who yearns for the relation with his prodigal sons and who constantly acts and creates anew. In the first the world is a gorgeous and yet nauseating pageant, an endless series of variegated and fascinating but at the same time disgusting processes of life, all ultimately unreal and meaningless ; in the second the world is the creation of God, enigmatically perverted by sin, but yet God's working place, led by Him to its consummation, desperately real, and the place of responsible decisions between God and man.

It is not to be marvelled at that the prophetic religion of Biblical realism does not show this syncretistic, pragmatist, relativist and subjectivist trend of the naturalist religions. It contrasts entirely with the endless assimilative and adaptative elasticity of naturalistic monism. It is disturbing by its " exclusivist " attitude, that is not lessened in the least by the fact that the Bible radiates with the lustre of love and freedom of the Spirit, and with the personality of Christ who sovereignly breaks through all limitations and proclaims the truth that " sets free." This enigmatic " exclusivism " brought it about that amidst the tolerant and conforming mystery-cults Christianity stood alone " intolerant " and nonconformist. At present the International Buddhist Society, founded in 1934 by Inoue Tetsujiro, has defined as one of its objects the absorption of Christianity. From the standpoint of Mahayanist Buddhism, whose monistic all-embracing tendency has been made clear in our discussion, this is a very reasonable object. Radhakrishnan in the book just quoted is of opinion that there is not much serious difference between Hinduism and Christianity on the question and the nature and means of salvation. This is certainly a mistaken opinion, for Christianity proclaims salvation from sin by forgiveness of sins, which implies a religious world totally different from Hinduism, which preaches salvation from transiency and ignorance.

More significant for our present discussion are, however, the sequel of Tetsujiro's and Radhakrishnan's arguments. The Buddhist Society, while disclaiming any objection to the Christian Message of salvation, emphatically rejects the Christian apprehension of God, the Creator and Judge of the world, and the Christian claim to proclaim the exclusive truth. Soteriological Mahayanism thus claims agreement with Christian soteriology, but not with its theocentric core. Radhakrishnan, although in his opinion the Cross is not an offence or a stumbling-block to the Hindu as showing how love is rooted in self-sacrifice, strongly rejects, however, atonement and reconciliation. Evidently he is not aware that in the theocentric religion of Biblical realism salvation has its real meaning in atonement and reconciliation, because in it is expressed the fact that God solely and really creates a way where there is no way.

SOME DEBATED QUESTIONS

Before closing this fundamental outline of the naturalist religions, a few remarks have to be devoted to some much-debated questions that are of some consequence to the Christian mission in the non-Christian world.

In the first place let us take the current habit of speaking of the spirituality of the East in contrast to the materialism of the West. In the second chapter we quoted Hu Shih's protest against this superficial and misleading judgment, which he calls an " old myth." His protest originates from his enthusiastic gratitude for the forces of science and humanism as liberating man from age-long bondage in ignorance, fear and submission, all sanctioned by religion. This is entirely right, yet it seems to us that only in the light of our discussion of the primitive apprehension of existence and its possibilities, are we able to treat this question in a way wholly devoid of any controversy.

The overwhelming place of " religion " in the life of the East always nourishes the opinion that the East is " spiritual." It will have become clear from our discussion that " religion " as such is no sign of spirituality, especially not in the areas where the primitive apprehension and its undifferentiated conception of life rule supreme. The naturalist and vitalistic basis of the naturalist religions is the reason why, as we explained, religion is both the organ by which man's sublimest achievements in the religious and moral quest are expressed and also the garb in which the unbridled, materialistic instincts of life try to obtain satisfaction. A great deal of the religious life of mankind therefore is merely very crass materialism and a massive natural secularism, related to objects known as religious. To express it still more adequately, the objects of religious worship and the worship itself are in this case means exploited to satisfy man's coarse and materialist hunger for life ; what goes by the name of " religion " in the world is to a great extent unbridled human self-assertion in religious disguise. The whole world of magic and a great deal of religion are the expression of this human exploitation of the so-called " divine " world. This dominant but concealed materialistic vitalism in religion is not a specific characteristic of the East, but of man all over the world, and therefore in all the religious areas of the world in the West and in the East one can notice it in different forms. The naturalistic core, however, in the religions that spring from the primitive apprehension of

existence, does not counteract this religious materialism ;
it continuously generates and preserves it, while the " higher "
systems of mysticism and religious philosophy, by virtue of
their relativistic conception of religious life, condescendingly
justify and sanction it.

It will never be possible to vanquish this religious
materialism on the basis of naturalistic monism, because this
does not mean merely a combat against magic and superstition.   In the last analysis it means a combat against
human self-assertion in coarse materialist or in highly
refined spiritualist forms.   Naturalistic monism is never able
to be a convinced fighter in this combat, because by virtue
of its nature it recognizes the " relative value " and accommodated truth of each of these phenomena.   The theocentric
prophetic religion of Biblical realism lays bare the real
purport of these " religious " and " spiritual " tendencies,
and indicates where the right directives and strength to
vanquish them are to be found.

The anti-religious movement in China that started in
1922, and the anti-religious campaigns that begin to arise
now everywhere in the Orient, must be viewed from the
angle of a more realistic conception of the spirituality of the
East.   These movements are certainly wholly blind to the
significance of religion in its real sense, and their efforts,
great as the external results may become, will not less
certainly ultimately end in disappointment.   It is one thing
to drive magic and superstition temporarily underground,
and quite another thing to vanquish the *entente cordiale* of
self-asserting human vitalism and basic naturalism.   Yet it
ought to be said that in the actual situation these anti-
religious movements, notwithstanding their blindness, are
far more realistic and useful than the many Western and
Eastern sentimentalists who thoughtlessly identify " religion "
and " spirituality."

This point needed some clarification because it suggests
that our so-called enemies are often unwittingly on our side,
and that our analysis of situations in mission countries
greatly needs to be deepened.

There is still another question that needs some discussion.

In descriptions of the Japanese and Chinese peoples there is always a division of opinion on the question whether the Japanese and the Chinese—especially the Chinese—are religiously-minded or not. Many writers consider the Japanese deeply religious, many others hardly at all. The opinion about the Chinese almost without exception tends to the negative. They are supposed to be too practical-minded and hard-headed, too temperamentally averse from all speculative and doctrinal approach to life, too naturally humanistic, to have a religious bent of mind. In outlining Chinese religion some hints on this subject have been given already. Now this much may be added.

The pragmatist, conformist attitude towards religion which is the rule in China (and which is apparent all over the world, though not always so unveiled as in China) certainly does not testify to a deeply religious mood. India, where the pragmatist and conformist conception of religion is also very common indeed, is, when compared with China, a country whose inhabitants have a distinct capacity for deep religiosity in their nature, an intuitive attitude of receptivity to the realm of the eternal.

In stating these differences we remain, however, on the surface. Surveying mankind in time as well as in space, one is driven to the conclusion that man, everywhere and always, can be called a religious, and with the same right an irreligious, animal. He is religious because he is created for God ; yet he is irreligious because he has fallen away from God through his self-assertion. By virtue of this " dialectical " condition man protests in his religious life at the same time his religious and his a-religious attitude, his " divine " and his self-assertive nature. In this respect all peoples and men of the world are similar, because they are in the same " dialectical " condition. There are, however, important differences of nuance. Speaking fundamentally, there is hardly any difference between the massive pragmatist religiosity of the East, in which the natural secularism of the human heart is wrapped up in a religious garb, and the outspoken a-religious secularism of modern man. The essential similarity between them is their prime secularism.

Their difference—and this is practically speaking, of course, overwhelmingly important—is that in the Eastern case a weird system of religion and magic serves to satisfy this prime secularism ; in the Western case religion has become irrelevant because man has learnt other ways towards satisfaction and can easily dispense with " religion." Deep as this difference may be in practice, yet this whole " dialectical " situation, *in the setting of the present destruction and reconstruction of life- and thought-systems*, might suggest that the leap from the state of a superstitious, religion-ridden Eastern villager to that of a de-religionized, modernized and secularized one is perhaps not so great as is usually supposed, because under the thick veneer of religion he often is already an outright secularist.

In all times and in all places man's cardinal and elemen· tary need is not to be religious, but to be *sincerely* religious. In our present period of catastrophic transition this is specially urgent. Sincerely religious means that, apart from its efficaciousness and its satisfying powers according to our human desires and standards, religion is always and everywhere the most relevant thing to man, because it embodies the prime human necessity of being in the right relation to God, his Creator and his Lord. This *radical* religious sincerity is the only means to overcome the religious irreligion of the many massive religiosities of mankind, and the a-religious irreligion of modern man. This radical sincerity is only born from the prophetic theocentric religion of Biblical realism.

.   .   .   .

ISLAM

Islam is a religion that is indeed a branch from the prophetic stock of Judaism and Christianity. In its entirety, however, it has become, like Roman Catholicism in Christendom, a great syncretistic body wherein are welded in one system theocratic and legalistic Islam, mysticism and various sorts of popular religion, in which the naturalistic vein of the primitive apprehension of existence shines through. Its genuine and original elements and structure are the result of the prophetic message of Muhammad, who proclaimed this message in the name of God the Compassionate, the Merciful, as the direct revelation of God. This distinguishes Islam clearly from the stock of naturalist religions ; besides, this religion is unthinkable without the background of empirical Christianity and Judaism. To a great extent it is legitimate to understand Islam as a modified reflex of, and reaction upon, these two religions. Since its coming in the world till the present day different people have been inclined, therefore, to conceive it as a Christian heresy. There is much to be said in favour of this judgment ; though in our opinion it misses the mark, because it ignores too much the independent self-consciousness which Islam has had from the outset.

In its main, genuine structure Islam is a simple religion. Its students are never weary of extolling its simplicity, pointing to the concise *lapidary shahada* (creed) : There is no God but Allah, and Muhammad is His Apostle. Gibbon, the sceptic, in his *Decline and Fall of the Roman Empire*, describes Islam with subdued admiration, just because of this simplicity which contrasted so favourably with the intricate subtleties of the christological dogmas he had dealt with in previous sections of his work, and which seemed to agree admirably with the simplicity of the favourite religion of his age, natural religion. Gibbon calls the first " word " of the *shahada* about the uniqueness of God an eternal truth, and the second " word," as a good son of his century, he describes as a necessary fiction. His admiration bursts out in the sentence : " A philosophic atheist might subscribe to the popular creed of the Mahometans, a creed too sublime for our present faculties."

The truly remarkable and puzzling thing in Islam, however, is that it is, notwithstanding its undeniable simplicity, a manifold riddle. Why ? Some reasons for this statement, which in our opinion is fundamental to a real understanding of Islam as a religion and to the missionary approach to it, may be mentioned.

Islam in its constituent elements and apprehensions must be called a superficial religion. The grand simplicity of its conception of God cannot efface this fact and retrieve its patent superficiality in regard to the most essential problems of religious life. Islam might be called a religion that has almost no questions and no answers. In a certain respect its greatness lies there, because this question-less and answer-less condition is a consistent exemplification of its deepest spirit, expressed in its name : Islam, that is, absolute surrender to God, the Almighty Lord.

On the other side, however, it is also the result of its superficiality. This superficiality appears from the deeply unsatisfactory way in which Islam deals with the crucial problems of religious and moral life, and this becomes the more evident because it arose in the shadow of Biblical realism.

In the most emphatic sense of the word Islam is a religion of revelation. *Wahj*, revelation, is the pivot on which it turns, and one of the central themes of its theological thinking. Muhammad, with true modesty, declared in the troublesome years of his courageous ministry in Mecca that the particularity of his person and his mission consisted exclusively in the fact of his being the conveyer of God's words made known to him, and in nothing else. The *Quran*, the collection of God's words made known to Muhammad, is thus the immutable word of God. Islam has rightly sensed and still senses that this book is the sole foundation for its claim to be an independent, to be *the* universal, God-given and ultimate, religion. The unassailable infallibility of this book has consequently been one of the deepest concerns in Islam, and has given rise to an enormous amount of stubborn, ingenious theological thinking. The Islamic idea of revelation is widely different from revelation in Biblical realism. The idea of revelation is there, even in a very rigid form, but in comparison with revelation in Biblical realism it has become externalized, fossilized as it were. Revelation in Biblical realism means, God constantly acting in holy sovereign freedom, conclusively embodied in the man Jesus Christ. In Islam it is a set of immutable divine words that take the place of God's movable acts and His speaking and doing through the living man Jesus Christ. The foundation of Islam is not, The Word became flesh. It is, The Word became book.[1] It is quite logical and intelligible that Islam should have developed its own species of Logos speculation in the well-known dogma of the uncreated, pre-existent and celestial *Quran*.

This externalization and fossilization of revelation in Islam seems to us to be one of the great marks of its religious superficiality. By its starting-point Islam is condemned to feed on a mechanical idea of revelation. The religious advantage, however, of the idea of divine revelation as the basis of life in Islam is that it has fostered in its adherents a deep sense of the value and existence of absolute truth.

As a second instance of superficiality in crucial religious problems one might adduce the clumsy, external conception which Islam has of sin and salvation. Again, this is the more striking because Islam is of prophetic origin and has intimate relations with the sphere of Biblical realism. It satisfies itself with fragmentary and superficial opinions about these central problems in prophetic religion, speaking in an exceedingly facile and unconvincing way about the *tabula rasa* of the human mind at birth and about God's grace. It is significant to note that in Moslem theology there is hardly anything that could be reasonably called anthropology. There is hardly any surmise, either in the *Quran* or in its standard theologies, about the stirring problems of God and man that are involved in the terms sin and salvation. The whole drama of salvation between God and the world, so vivid in Biblical realism, from which Islam, historically speaking, is an offshoot, is entirely absent. Obedience in surrender to the God of Omnipotence is the core of Islam. This accounts for the strangely eventless relation between

---

[1] How near this conception is to the human mind appears from the fact that in Christianity it has always been the fatal inclination to interpret persistently the dynamic prophetic conception of revelation, as evident in Biblical realism, in the terms of this mechanical conception. The human mind, in Islam as well as in Christianity or elsewhere, expresses its desire for a sure guarantee of religious certitude in the clumsy form of the literal inerrancy of the document in which God's revelation is told. In Islam this mode of expression is in accordance with the basic conception of revelation in the *Quran* ; in Christianity, however, it signifies a radical distortion of the basic conception in Biblical realism, because there the subject of revelation is not the Bible (as in Islam it is the *Quran*) but the living God of holy love as incarnated in Jesus Christ.

God and man that characterizes Islam. Obedience in fellowship with the God of Holy Love is the core of Biblical realism and accounts for the peculiarly eventful relation between God and man that characterizes Biblical revelation.

A third instance is the conflict about the relation of faith and works which has played a conspicuous part in the history of dogma in Islam. In the *Quran* the germs are present already of the two conceptions of faith that arise in every religion which has a set of central religious tenets. The first is the intellectualistic conception, which considers faith to be intellectual submission to authoritative tenets ; and the second the deeper dynamic conception of faith as an inner conviction or, as it was formulated in Islam, to hold something as truth by the heart and confess it by the tongue. Ghazali, who reconciled orthodox Islam to mysticism, is, as so often, one of the deepest voices of Islam in this field. Yet in dogmatic controversy this important religious and moral problem of faith and works took the aspect of the relation between inward and outward conformity to Islam as a religious, social and political community, and lost its touch with the deeper religious question of which it is a part, namely, what is, respectively, the significance of faith and works in the problem of salvation ?

Now we come to the riddle. This, religiously speaking, rather shallow and superficial religion has a grip on its adherents greater than any other religion has. Everyone who knows the Moslem world by personal experience will bear witness to the truly remarkable fact that a Moslem, whether he is a fervid and convinced or a lukewarm believer or even a secret disbeliever and agnostic, as a rule becomes beside himself with anger if a man turns Christian or changes his religious allegiance. All over the Moslem world we know the curious and disquieting (disquieting because it affects one so strangely) phenomenon that the average Moslem, though he may be extremely lax as to the observance of his religious duties and even dissolute in his behaviour, is ready to die for the sake of Islam, or to kill a man whom he considers to be a defiler of Islam. Europeans call this " Moslem fanaticism " and feel extraordinarily uneasy about this enigmatical enthusiasm for a faith whose rules are constantly neglected and transgressed. In Christianity one is accustomed to consider " martyrdom " for the faith only possible and reasonable in men who are devoted believers in word and deed. A very noteworthy fact in the Moslem world is that Islam as such, the religion of Islam apart from its content, is the object of fierce loyalty and absolute surrender. " The glory of Islam," " Islam in danger " are concepts able to evoke paroxysms of devotion.

The second reason why it appears legitimate to call Islam a riddle is that this religion, so lacking in depth, is also, when one considers its origin and material, an unoriginal religion, and yet notwithstanding that it excels all other religions in creating in its adherents a feeling of absolute religious superiority. From this superiority-feeling and from this fantastic self-consciousness of Islam is born that stubborn refusal to open the mind towards another spiritual world, as a result of which Islam is such an enigmatic missionary object.

Is there any explanation for solving this riddle of incompatibles ? We might venture one by trying to find out where the core of Islam lies. Muhammad was possessed by two great religious aims—to proclaim God as the sole, almighty God, the Creator and the King of the Day of Judgment ; to found a community, in Arabic called *umma*, ruled by the Law of God and His Apostle. These two objects constitute the core of Islam, its strength and its weakness.

Islam is radically theocentric, and thereby proclaims in the clearest possible way its prophetic origin. It takes God as God with awful seriousness. God's unity and soleness, His austere sovereignty and towering omnipotence, are burning in white heat within Islam. Whosoever has listened with his innermost being to the passionate awe that vibrates through the well-known sentences : *Allahu akbar* (God is great) and : *La sharika lahu* (He has no associate), knows that Islam has religious tones of elemental power and quality. The apprehension of the naked majesty of God in Islam is simply unsurpassed. Even in the dry books of *kalam* (the science of dogma) the theocentric character of

Islam is overwhelmingly demonstrated by the fact that their main content is the doctrine of God, His Essence and His attributes. The Moslem who in sermons or in dogmatic controversies sincerely protests against *shirk*, that is the unpardonable sin of giving God an associate (in more arid terms, the sin of polytheism), is always a telling figure. This intense awe in the presence of God is the reason why the so-called Moslem prayer, the joint worship of the community, is always a deeply impressive ceremony, even when under the cloak of outward reverence and discipline the heart of the matter is gone. It is very significant to realize that in Islam the object of the meeting of believers for common worship is not to attend or participate in sacramental rites or in liturgical acts, dramatizing various relations between God and man, or to hear the Word, but simply to join in an act of reverent adoration and worship of God. In this light Moslem prayer is one of the most pertinent expressions of the religious spirit of Islam.

It is a very curious thing to note that in the really religious conceptions of Islam one can point to what might be called a process of super-heating. The conception of revelation in its ruthless consequence is super-heated. The same can be said about the conception of God. Islam is theocentric, but in a super-heated state. Allah in Islam becomes white-hot Majesty, white-hot Omnipotence, white-hot Uniqueness. His personality evaporates and vanishes in the burning heat of His aspects. These de-personalized aspects, although of course not devoid of the personal connotation connected with Allah, are the real objects of religious devotion. The surrender to Allah, the fundamental religious attitude in Islam, has that same quality of absolute ruthlessness. The ideal believer, the *abd* (or servant, as Islam says), is, so to speak, personified surrender and nothing else. God's Will becomes virtually august divine arbitrariness. To speak of a voluntarist conception of God in Islam is, properly speaking, inexact ; one ought to call it a " potentist " conception, if such a word existed.

This hyperbolic theocentricity, which is accompanied by a hyperbolic over-intensification of all central religious apprehension in Islam, derives from the fact that man has no real place in the relation of God and man. One of the favourite expressions about God, which testifies to an intense religious feeling is, He whom everyone needs and who does not stand in need of anybody or anything. Man is entirely absorbed in the greatness and majesty of God and vanishes away. Fellowship does not exist between God and man. God is too exalted for that, and the relation of Father-child between God and man is not primarily abhorrent to the Moslem because of the association of parenthood and sexual life, but because it suggests a sacrilegious lack of reverence towards the Divine. The hyperbolic over-intensification of the purely religious element in the relation of God and man destroys that intrinsic unity of the religious and the ethical that is implied in a real relation between the divine and the human, for relation means fellowship and obligation. Man is so evanescent in the hyperbolically theocentric atmosphere of Islam that problems of theodicy, of the cry for a God of *righteousness*, etc., are entirely absent.

This hyperbolic religiousness may explain somewhat the intense grip that Islam has on the minds of its adherents.

The second element in the core of Islam, namely the conception of the Moslem community as an *'umma* ruled by the Law of God and His Apostle is, however, still more helpful to explain the tenacious grip of Islam on its adherents. Islam is a theocracy, a community, that is at the same time a religious, political and a social unit. In Medina this *'umma* and this conception were born, not in Mecca, because there the community was only a handful of believers, expecting God and His Day of Judgment. Because of this theocratic character the *shari'a* (religious law) is so absolutely central in Islam, and the theological discipline par excellence is the *fiqh* (religious jurisprudence) ; whilst the recognized religious leaders are the *'ulama'*, that is, those who know the *shari'a*. The problem of modernizing Islam means therefore to come to terms with this *shari'a*, for the *shari'a* is virtually the regulation and sanctioning of a mediæval society on the basis of the revelation.

The deepest, the most crucial problem of Islam is that

its theocracy from the very first moment, when the '*umma* was born in Medina, has been a thoroughly secularized theocracy. By this expression we intend to suggest that the primary inspiration of this theocracy was not the vision of the Will of God as the sole valid law of life (although it is there too), but the necessity and desire in Muhammad to achieve by organization of his '*umma* a more powerful position. So Islam in its cradle was already a specimen of religious imperialism, which is another name for secularized theocracy. It has expressed this in theory (in its canonical public law) and in practice (in its history) by its claim to be the sole power divinely entitled to rule the world both in the religious and the secular spheres. The well-known division to be found in the *shari'a* of the world in a *dar-al islam* (the House of Islam) and a *dar-al-harb* (the House of War) expresses this in a very terse way. The fact that the only dogmatic differences that gave rise to real schism, such as the Kharijites and the Shi'a, were political [1] controversies, is very instructive.

It seems to us that a problem, still deeper than this deep problem, is that never in the whole history of Islam has this inherent and initial secularization of its conception of theocracy become a vexing religious problem for Moslem thinkers. Even Ghazali, unquestionably the man of the greatest religious and theological depth and sincerity that Islam has ever produced, does not touch it. Because the fact of its being a secularized theocracy from the outset is the backbone of theoretical and empirical Islam. Again and again one gets the impression that Islam is the religion of "natural man" notwithstanding its strong religious elements. In Pascal's short reflections on Islam in his *Pensées* he lays his finger with great religious intuition on the sore spot. He says : "*Mahomet a pris la voie de réussir humainement, Jésus Christ celle de périr humainement*" (Muhammad chose the way of human success, Jesus Christ that of human defeat).

The preceding picture is not at all complete in regard to

[1] The question was, Who has the right to be the head (*Chalifa*) of the theocracy ?

empirical Islam as a whole, but it gives the whole *essence* of Islam. Islam being a civilization and being also, as every religion is, an historical growth, comprises many other elements. To mention two only, it comprises a system of ethics and especially a many-coloured body of mystical religion. As the last has such a great significance in nearly all Moslem countries, it is indispensable to say something more about it.

Original Islam has no connection whatever with mysticism. To discover in the *Quran* the first seeds of Moslem mysticism, from which the whole garden has supposedly grown up, is erroneous. The core of Islam is thoroughly anti-mystical and unmystical. The current method of construing developments in mysticism, beginning in the *Quran* and ending in Ghazali or Ibn-al-Arabi, demonstrates only the evolutionary passion that still animates thinking in the field of the history of religions, and nothing more. Islam as a civilization is the continuator of the Hellenic-Eastern civilization in its Christianized form. The Christian populations that were Moslemized naturally took their religious propensities and tendencies with them into the " House of Islam " and learned to express them in Muhammadan moulds, terms and outlooks. Margaret Smith's book, *Studies in Early Mysticism in the Near and Middle East,* and her books on al-Muhasibi and Rabi'a give an insight into this remarkable process. It is very interesting to note that the great and moving mystic literature of Islam, where the " way " of the " traveller " (*salik*) to God is described in its various stages, is born, like Eastern Christian mysticism, from the Terror of " the Day of the Lord." Just as in the Eastern Christian mysticism of those centuries, to abstain from the world, to conquer sensual desire, and to purify the heart are the stages on the way to God. The peculiar atmosphere of Christian mysticism betrays itself by its emphasis on joy and adoration ; the peculiar atmosphere of Moslem mysticism by its emphasis on the awe of God. This pertains only to what may be called emotional mysticism. The so-called heterodox mysticism of Islam is a plant of a quite different soil ; it belongs to the category of speculative developments of the ontological implications of naturalistic monism.

Ghazali has made mysticism in Islam from being a very important element in Moslem religious life into a recognized part of the great orthodox system. He did this by assigning to the *shari'a*, the *kalam* (dogmatical theology) and mysticism each its proper place. The religious law (*shari'a*) is the daily food ; dogmatical theology provides with weapons necessary to defend the faith against unbelief and scepticism ; mysticism is religion as an affair of the heart and vivifies the two other aspects of religious life with its warm breath. Since Ghazali no development of really decisive importance has taken place in the religious life of Islam. He saved Islam from petrification by his great synthesis, embodied in his famous work, *Ihya ulum al-din* ; but at the same time he sanctioned the legalist and scholastic fetters in which Islam as a system was and is chained.

Ghazali is one of the deepest apologists of religion that have ever lived. He criticized, with amazing depth, Aristotelian rationalism and Neo-Platonic monism from the standpoint of real religious faith. He could do this because he was driven by two great, really religious urges, that so often create great religious men : the personal need of religious certitude, and his deep concern for the spiritual needs of the common man. His severe and fateful limitation was his conception of revelation. He remained bound to the conception inherent in Islam, namely, that revelation is constituted by the immutable words of God, contained in the *Quran*. This means actually that tradition (*naql*), not the living Reality of God, is the source and criterion of religious life. By virtue of this traditionalism and also by his patriarchal, emphatically non-prophetic vision of the masses, he justified and sanctioned, despite his " religion of the heart," the huge block of legalistic religion that is enshrined in the *shari'a*. Islam is still in this (religiously speaking) desolate condition. The process of conflict with and penetration by Western civilization in many respects plays havoc with Islam. This conflict has not yet released a really religious awakening, because the many modernist reactions to it are, on the whole, vindications of Islam in the face of modern life. The deeper issues of the essential nature of revelation and of its being a secularized theocracy are still evaded. Its defensive attitude rather strengthens than diminishes its (religiously speaking) unjustified feeling of superiority.

.   .   .   .

JUDAISM

This section will be very short, although Judaism falls also within the wide dimensions of the title of this book. *The Christian Message in a non-Christian World* implies naturally Judaism, for Judaism is an exceedingly important reality in the non-Christian world of to-day, and the validity as well as the obligation of the Christian mission prevails equally in relation to Judaism as in relation to the rest of the non-Christian world. Thus there is no theoretical reason whatever why we should not treat Judaism and the problems of missionary work among the Jews at the same length as those of the other non-Christian religions and the missionary task amongst them. The sole reason why this section is very short, and why discussion of the problems of fundamental apprehension, of contact, adaptation and the building up a Christian Church from converts from Judaism will be omitted, is a practical one. The writer has never had personal experience in the field of Jewish missions, nor did he have time to study them, and he is therefore not entitled to write about their problems. The few observations he tenders are such as every Christian can and must make, who is aware of the responsibility which is implied in his relation to the Christian mission in the non-Christian world.

Historically speaking, Christianity is a child of the religion of Israel, the religion of Moses and of the prophets. Jesus stood deeply rooted in this ancestral heritage and breathed in this atmosphere of God's revelation through His dealings with, and His spiritual gifts to, the people of Israel. The religion of Israel is an important part of the world of Biblical realism, and Jesus Christ, in whom God revealed Himself decisively, is in His human thinking and feeling altogether a child of Israel.

The history of Israel and the fate of Judaism are an important indication of a too-rarely-understood fact. Revelation, the self-disclosure of God, is not a simple process of the divine mind communicating exceptional truth and insight to the human mind, but is the profound and long-drawn-out struggle of God, who in His revelation is ignored and rejected by man. The whole Old Testament from Genesis to Malachi is the record of God's revelational working on the people of Israel. It is a stubborn and moving fight, in which the most stirring episodes are often those when the people of Israel appear blind at the moments when God reveals most persistently His real character and heart. In that respect the Jews are simply the representatives of the human race. The climax of this struggle between God and man, which is implied in the event of revelation, is reached in Jesus Christ and the way His human destiny under the Jews worked out. The Jew, Jesus, was rejected by this people because He proclaimed himself the Messiah, *the* ultimate and final fulfilment of what God's revelation through the prophets really meant. The moment of moments in God's revelational dealing with mankind was the moment of man's most radical misapprehension and rejection.

The grand and pure monotheism, the lofty and virile ethics and other precious elements of Judaism, which already in the Roman Empire attracted attention and admiration, are all fruits grown on the soil of the prophetic revelation of Biblical realism. The pith of the Biblical revelation, however, is contained in the triumphant and concise confession of the first Christians : *Christos Kurios,* Christ is Lord. This gave Paul the strength to recognize on the one hand the Old Testament as the document of God's revelation, and, on the other hand, to abolish the law by the new life of faith in Him, who fulfils and at the same time supersedes the law and the prophets.

The obligation of the Christian Church to carry out its apostolic privilege and duty towards Judaism is therefore as stringent as it is towards the rest of the non-Christian world. Even more stringent, for several reasons. In the first place, because the Jewish people and its history is more intimately related to the divine economy of revelation in Christ than any other people. In the second place, because the Jews are living in millions in the area of the Christian Church, and are therefore the most obvious objects of its apostolic calling. In the third place, the empirical Christian Church owes to the Jews, especially in the present time, a clear demonstration of what Christianity really means. There are reasons which make anti-semitic movements intelligible in this complicated world, with its conflicting interests and ideals and with the tendency towards self-isolation that is founded in the " national " and " communal " conception of religion in Judaism. But no reason whatever could and can ever justify the Christian Church for having adopted or adopting a policy of hate or indifference, or exempt it from its obligation to obey God's will of love and service, of hating iniquity and loving righteousness, in relation to the Jews.

CHAPTER VII

The Present Religious Situation in the Non-Christian World

TO review in a satisfactory way in one chapter the present religious situation of the various non-Christian religions is clearly impossible. A whole volume would be hardly sufficient. Yet for the development of our argument we cannot avoid giving a sketch in some short strokes. A few introductory remarks may be made regarding the general background.

It is necessary to remind ourselves with great insistence that this whole vast world is a world in transition and revolution, in disintegration and in reconstruction. Change, adjustment, adaptation, reform, reaction, revival, and cognate concepts and terms are all applicable to the situation of these religions. A deep feeling of malaise and thrills of new hope invade alternately the minds of their adherents when they think about the future prospects of their religious heritage. The attentive observer distinguishes melancholy deterioration or decline as well as increasing vigour and progress. In short, the picture is full of conflicting and confusing elements. All religions, without any exception, are in a time of great crisis. Political and economic elements, for two reasons, play not a small part in this religious crisis. First, all these religions are virtually civilizations and to a great extent undifferentiated unities of life, in which the religious motive permeates and governs all the spheres of life. Great changes or modifications in the political, economic and social structures of life thus necessarily react severely on the religious apprehension and attitude. This is reinforced by the second reason, namely, that in various cases (Turkey, Persia, China, to mention the most important) the new political order and outlook and the economic changes mean a direct challenge to the fundamental principles of these ancient religions. For the very first time during their whole long historic career, under the colossal pressure of the world situation, questions that would have been in the past absurdly inconceivable are thrown as devastating bombs into the midst of these religions ; such as, Is religion worth while ? Is religion relevant ? Is not religion an oppressive dream or enervating opium ?

The chaotic and kaleidoscopic state of these huge unwieldy religious bodies, moreover, does not spring from inward causes, but is a response to external causes, namely, the multifarious impact of the Western world. This means, in a succinct phrase, that the great world of primitive apprehensions of existence is assailed by another world that represents the rational apprehension and endeavour to master existence, and which is leavened more or less by the religious and moral impulses of Christianity which derive from the prophetic religion of Biblical realism. To estimate in due fashion and with the right emphases such a chaotic and kaleidoscopic situation is impossible. There is no historical distance, and therefore the observer is constantly in danger of over-emphasizing the importance of the aspect of change and transition and of forgetting the deep furrows that these religious systems have made in the mind of the millions of their adherents, and the tenacity and resiliency which such deep-rooted structures have, as history witnesses, in the life of mankind. But who is able to evaluate these last-mentioned factors since one cannot see or control, but can only surmise, them ? Throughout our short description we keep in mind this enormous difficulty, How are we to find the right balance in the evaluation of the manifest changes and the latent invariables ?

THE WORLD OF " PRIMITIVE " PEOPLES

The " primitive " religions of all those greater or smaller groups of men who live in some sort of tribal organization in Africa and in the Islands of the Seas, in the South and East of Asia and around Australia, are all destined to perish and disappear as *institutional and organized* bodies of religious life.   In this sense one can speak unhesitatingly of the passing of the " primitive " religions and of the " primitive." This type of religion cannot survive in its organized form, because it can only function either in a world of kindred religions and civilizations, that is to say, in a world of cultures and religions that have grown in the same primitive apprehension of existence ; or, if that is not possible, it needs in order to survive a rather high degree of isolation. It has become the fate of these religions, however, to be dragged forcibly within the sphere of Western civilization and its political and economic framework.   This lives by motives and for ends radically different from those that issue from the primitive apprehension of existence.   Instead of being granted isolation they are invaded by new influences such as they never had imagined to be possible.   There are still in Central Africa and in Australia tribes that are comparatively untouched, but ultimately they will not escape their fate, for their doom is approaching.   What this means in terms of misery as well as of liberation, of annihilation as well as of new horizons, cannot be expressed in a few sentences.

All the characteristics we have described as peculiar to the tribal pattern of life are disappearing or are in a process of incalculable modification and transition.   The life- and behaviour-patterns, without which no corporate group of men can duly function, are in a condition of disintegration and of adjustment to totally new conditions, and some generations will pass before a new elastic stability of life is reached.   In this situation these peoples have to work out their destiny, and governments and missions have to formulate their own tasks and obligations.

These tribal peoples were or still are in a modified sense closely interdependent structures of material and spiritual life.   This interdependence has been shattered or severely shaken by the repercussions of modern history.   They were or still are partly governed by the mighty law of tradition, but for the reasons just mentioned this law is abrogated or is in a process of acute devaluation.   The structures of social cohesion in relationships, in clan organization, in the hierarchies of sex and age-stages, which were the vessels of their moral conceptions and the occasions for religious rites and manifestations, are very severely damaged, and the moral and religious certitudes of the past are left floating in the air. Groups of men having a corporate life become more and more congeries of loose atoms. Such is the dangerous road to a new and unfamiliar conception of individuality. The harmony and equilibrium of life, which was the object of their desires in the past, has fled from their life. This uprooting of all their political and social institutions and the many profound changes that are taking place in their economic life are destroying the intimate connection with the ancestors, who always formed an integral part of the community and whose worship was one of the pillars of their religious life. This worship becomes meaningless and in many cases impossible, because the necessary conditions cannot be fulfilled in the radically changed situation. The cosmic-mythological view of life, with its system of rites and practices and sacrifices, becomes childish and meaningless in the merciless light of the modern rationalization of life. Neither magic nor witchcraft nor superstition, nor genuine religious belief, find any more the right soil in which to strike their roots. Paganism is intellectually shattered, although this does not mean in the least that it is shattered in men's hearts.

Such in broad outline is the condition of the " primitive " world of tribal religions and civilizations, although it must be kept in mind that the stages in this process are numerous and various. Every people and every region has its own type, its special aspects, and requires a special approach. So the phases of readjustment are also very different. Many new possibilities and even many new realities of great value have entered their lives. For the well-ordered but narrow and stereotyped circle of their life in the past has been substituted a more dynamic attitude, an active turning to the future and not a constant repetition of the past. New and more differentiated capacities and abilities are developed, a wider conception of the world and of life enters their horizon. Also previously unknown unrest, bitterness and competition shape their sentiments and actions, and new aspirations and visions fill their minds.

The preceding refers exclusively to those peoples who gave their religious allegiance to their own tribal religions. There are still many millions who—in the tendencies and practices of their religious life, manifesting itself in ancestor worship, propitiatory rites, worship of demons, spirits and gods, observance of sacred times and sacred places, etc.—are hardly different from them. Notwithstanding that, they are in a different condition, because they are incorporated in a system of " higher " religion (Islam, Hinduism, Buddhism) and have been penetrated by elements of these religions. The curious result is that, although they do not have that un-broken, institutional self-consciousness of the tribal religions but are more diffused in their aspect, they derive on the other hand a greater tenacity from the fact that they live in the shadow and with the connivance of these " higher " religions, even borrowing a glimmering of their prestige. This is a type of " primitive " religion in itself, and ought to be mentioned in order to avoid misunderstanding, as if " primi-tive " religious life melts away before the scorching rays of the sun of modern civilization.

This is far from being the case. The problem before which the tribal civilizations are standing, and the whole world with them, may be stated in the following way. The intellectual and social vessels of paganism are shattered or cracked. Sentimental respect for paganism, however, is still very strong, though diffused and disorientated. A new foundation and pattern of life must be built up. The elements that seem to be at hand for this task are parts of their old heritage, new instruments put at their disposal by the modern world, and new attitudes that are the necessary adjustments and adapta-tions to the new rhythm of life, to which they willingly or unwillingly are driven. Well-considered, this is a rather poor equipment for such a colossal problem. Modern civilization, despite its strength, has no soul to transmit because it is soul-less ; it has lost its metaphysical background. Pure and undefiled religion is always and everywhere the foremost need of man, if he recognizes his real condition in the light of the fact that his relation to God is the prime and all-determining relation in human life. This must be said in a very emphatic sense of this primitive world of transition. Religious regeneration through allegiance to the Gospel of Jesus Christ could afford the foundation on which to build a new life and a new destiny in a new period of their, until now, inconspicuous history.

. . . .

INDIA

For the sake of the right balance, which is easily disturbed by looking too exclusively at the many important events and movements in modern Hinduism which catch easily the eye of the observer, it is perhaps rewarding to devote first some attention to the position of the religion of the masses. This, of course, in a country of so many cults and backgrounds and religious traditions as India, is a very multiform phenomenon. These cults and backgrounds and religious traditions, despite the dissolving effects of sundry influences, are at present still fully alive. They will, prospectively, still for a long time exercise a great domination over the life of those millions. Life in India is for those masses so desperately poor and difficult, their desire is so pathetically great to avail themselves of all means at their disposal, whether suitable or not, to alleviate their hardships, and these cults and traditions have such deep and strong roots, that the thraldom of superstition and weird forms of religion and magic will not easily be broken. Aldous Huxley's exclamation in his *Jesting Pilate*, when he describes what he saw along the borders of the Ganges at Benares, expresses this in a vigorous way : " If I were an Indian millionaire I would leave all my money for the endowment of an Atheist Mission." We do not mean to say that this religious life of the masses has not its redeeming and touching features. Of course it has. The deeper yearnings of the human mind, the greatness of man even in his abject helplessness, shine through. But on the whole we must speak, with all possible emphasis, of thraldom and bondage. In a country like India, where religion in the good and the bad sense of the word has developed into a sort of monomania, this is even more true than anywhere else. This congeries of cults and beliefs, of religious idiosyncrasies and aspirations, confused as it may be, is fortified and strengthened by its being enshrined in Hinduism. From this fact it derives a heightened self-consciousness and also a quickened sense of dignity, because the suggestive authority of Hinduism lifts it above the stage of a tribal religion ; and a dim knowledge of sacred scriptures, of divine helpers of universal dimensions (Ram, Krishna, etc.), of holy and wise men, of unfailingly saving gnosis, etc., foster a vague but strong conviction that one is somehow in touch with the realm of truth and wisdom. On a smaller scale the same situation is to be noticed in the small island of Bali, where the same sort of symbiosis between popular religion and Hinduism has taken place.

In the fortifying shadow of the tree of Hinduism popular religion in India to-day is the blending of crass religious materialism and pathetic piety which all over the world is characteristic of popular religion. In India, moreover, the enormous authority of the Brahman as the disposer by birth-right of salutary and dangerous religious forces must especially be noted, and not less the central place of the " guru." The guru (often represented in the sadhu) has become in the popular soteriological cults and religions the absolute guide of life. He is not only unconditionally obeyed and believed ; he is worshipped as a god, because in him is personified the longing for salvation that stirs in the masses. Independently of his moral or religious integrity or depravity he is regarded as the embodiment of sacred saving-power. This enormous sway of the mystagogue, with its crude deification of man, is of great and in most cases disastrous significance in the religion of the Indian masses.

By keeping this reality before us, the effects of the economic, political and social crisis that scourges the country can perhaps be estimated in more due measure. This crisis is very severe and, like real " acid," bites very deep. Being in the midst of the process, however, it is impossible to determine exactly its effect and future consequences. One can offer surmises only. The more so because the modern development of all Eastern peoples is mainly due to the external cause of the impact of Western civilization and is therefore prone to a convulsive reaction. The fervent extolment of Hinduism in all its forms that was common with intellectual Hindus thirty years ago, and the anti-religious spirit that is at present increasingly pervading their minds, is a very good illustration of what is meant by this convulsive reaction.

The political changes are enormous. The Government of India Act, that came on the Statute Book in August 1935, has raised the number of voters to thirty-five millions, in which number six million women voters are comprised. Under the leadership of Pandit Jawaharlal Nehru, Indian nationalism grows more and more out of its romantic phase. Nationalism has always had and still has two faces, although of course in different periods each of the two was of different significance. It has been and still is a secularizing emancipating force, making eager attempts to imitate, or to adapt itself to, new ideals and ends subversive of the old world-order. It has also often been, and still is, a strong affirmation of values and ideals that are peculiarly Indian. So it combines a revolutionary and a conservative tendency. The classic example of this combination is Mahatma Gandhi. Nationalism has therefore long been the substitute-religion and the idealism of the cultured intellectual. Jawaharlal Nehru's attitude tends to strip nationalism of its romantic trappings, of its self-centred self-glorification, and make it realistic. The political and social emancipation of the masses as a demand of justice and humanity is his battle-cry.

This programme is full of dynamite. Communism with its intolerant and fiercely dogmatic atheism and its crusade against all religion may exercise here an influence of decisive importance, although Jawaharlal Nehru himself evinces in religious matters more a mood of sad and mild agnosticism. However, there is nothing so difficult as to gauge the real purport and concrete effect of communism amongst the Eastern intellectuals and masses. The positiveness with which this subject is always presented is no guarantee that it represents actuality. Many factors work for change, dissolution, reconstruction. Among these are the campaigns for social and economic uplift and reconstruction, which, of course, all turn on issues of moral and religious purification and simplification, as is particularly clear in the movements and legislations against child marriage and devadasi ; the movements for combating harmful customs, superstitions, wasteful feasts and ceremonies, untouchability ; the hopeful women's movement with its enormous possibilities for good ; the communistic agents that sow their hatred of all religion and all established morality, and other authorities all over the country ; the disintegration of old bonds through the new possibilities of communication or industrialization ; the silent intellectual emancipation that is a consequence of the widening of outlook, and the equally silent fading out of old practices, because modern life and its equipments put many gods and spirits on the list of the unemployed ; the political organization of the masses and its attendant programme of intellectual emancipation ; and the great process of conflict, reaction and adaptation by which the religious and philosophical Hindu outlook of life is adjusted to the Western outlook. Who, however, is able to appraise the weight of each of these factors and their significance for the future of the religious life of India ? We are on a wide and restless ocean and do not yet see land. The outcome of all these seething movements and motives may be very conflicting. We have some indications that point in this direction.

A movement, pregnant of enormous possibilities for good and demonstrating how effectively the ferment of the political, economic, social and spiritual crisis is working, is the outcaste movement, especially since it came to full Pan-Indian self-consciousness under the leadership of Dr. Ambedkar. The outcaste movement, when judged on the whole, is essentially a movement for social equality in a country that lives by a religiously-sanctioned system of inequality. Dr. Ambedkar expressed it in October 1935 at the Conference at Yeola by saying that to remain in Hinduism meant to remain chained to caste-inequality. Therefore in India with its preponderantly social notion of religion this issue must become a " religious " issue, to be defined in this way—Which institutional religion is a suitable spiritual and social home for us, because Hinduism patently is not ? The real cry that is behind it is the cry for freedom to become man. The impact of the West, with conceptions of man as a social, political and moral being that are so different from the Indian, has in the long run released in those outcaste millions the impatient and indignant demand for human dignity. It is one of the grandest things in modern history, and those to whom has fallen the task of leading these masses have an enormous responsibility.

This outcaste movement is certainly highly revolutionary in its character. On the other hand, however, one of the most disastrous and anti-emancipatory features of the modern political development is the constitutional justification of the country's political organization along communal lines. Modern democracy will now be abused on a gigantic scale, because the social connotation of religion, so deeply ingrained in these religions and still magnified by the natural tendency towards self-assertion which all human organisms have, will be fanned into white-hot passion by the principle of organized conflict implied in the conception of democratic government. For the benefit of India's political and cultural development this decision ought to be rescinded as soon as possible, and even still more from the standpoint of pure religion. For this political legalization of communalism will perpetuate and even intensify the social conception of religion (already strong) with all its attendant intolerance, bitterness and fettering of the spirit ; and it will vitiate all really religious issues by the poison of passionate political rivalry and obstinate social self-assertiveness. The way in which the discussion and conflicts about the issue of the religious allegiance of the outcastes threaten to develop is an illustration of a very dismal kind. Gandhi's stubborn resistance to and lamentable misunderstanding of " conversion " and " proselytism " is, in a man morally and religiously so great and courageous as he, a still more dismal illustration of the stupendous religious confusion. The challenge towards truth in the face of God, which is the only permissible religious challenge and issue, is entirely submerged in the clamour of claims about social, political and cultural identity and their integral perpetuation. And Gandhi, the man who made and wrote *Experiments in Truth*, becomes the mouthpiece of that social and biological conception of religion which implies the benumbing of the search for truth. This surely is one of the saddest signs of the decomposition of the religious and moral judgment that has invaded the world. Undefiled religion and truth threaten to become lonely and deserted in India, one of the classic countries of the seekers for religious truth, as everywhere in the world.

This may suffice to suggest the difficulty of foretelling with any certitude the religious developments of the near future. Modern secularism, in all its forms, whether noble humanism, outspoken materialism, or communism, has both dissolving and liberating effects, but it is impossible to tell which of these two will preponderate.

The intellectuals, under the influence of the modern trends of thought and life, for the most part show little interest in organized religion, although family and other considerations induce many of them to conform to the customary religious practices. Their dominant interest is in most cases in India as country and nation, and for that reason we have called nationalism a temporary substitute-religion. They often participate, therefore, in anti-religious campaigns, and the mood of many of them is akin to that of Hu Shih, who considers religion, as it has manifested itself in the life of the millions, a baneful enemy of human happiness and progress. Religion largely passes for superstition and an antiquated view of life and the world. There are people who enjoy their newly-won liberty through an attitude of defiant atheism. Julian Huxley and Bertrand Russell are their favourite authors. However, although many show no actual interest in the higher elements of Hinduism, this does not justify the conclusion that their minds are emancipated from the dominant Hindu conceptions and have become thoroughly modernized. These conceptions are so pervasive and permeate so strongly the Indian atmosphere that it would be strange if this were true. The great distance that so often separates the reasoning and the emotional realm in the human mind causes all over the world the well-known phenomenon of the harbouring of two incompatible worlds in one mind. This phenomenon is at present very common throughout the East and also in India.

Dr. Macnicol, in his *Living Religions of the Indian People*, points to the fact that hardly anyone in India escapes the subtle, pervasive influence of the spiritual climate of *advaita*. Throughout all Indian religious history up to the present day it remains the steadfast rule that, even in the most fervently theistic speculations and conceptions, the doctrine of divine immanence, founded on the essential identity of the human Atman and the Paramatman which is the Pure Essence, is implicitly or explicitly conceived as the *esoteric* doctrine. Theism, emphatically as it may be extolled for a special reason, is considered *exoteric* as a matter of course. The *Bhagavadgita* illustrates this clearly and nourishes it in the present day. Although there are some voices raised aganst the doctrine of *karma*, it is nearly universally accepted by the religious agnostics and indifferentists as the best explanation for the problem of suffering in the world. The *avatar*-idea preserves its prestige, as it is considered a good mythological expression for the sound idea that the helpers of mankind are those great souls who by their purity and spiritual and moral attainment have raised humanity. There is no real rejection of idolatry, for an idol is conceived as a psychological aid for the human mind to concentrate upon the divine. These few examples may suffice to indicate that the anthropocentric conception of religion reigns unbroken in these re-interpretations, and that all over the world in the sphere of the naturalist religions, in ancient Greece and in modern India, intellectuals who have lost vital touch with the religious life of their environment, maintain a certain relation to it by rationalizing it according to similar methods of procedure.

In recent descriptions of Indian religious life the expression resurgence of Hinduism is frequently used, and it is considered the most important angle from which to judge the situation. This resurgence has two aspects. The first aspect is that of reaction to the meeting and clash with the Western mind and its creations. From another point of view one might call this also the permeation of Indian life with " Christian " ideas and ideals and of adaptation to them in theory and practice. The second aspect is that of active response, expressed in movements of aggressive self-assertion, of renewal of self-consciousness, and of strong propagandist instincts. Most movements that belong to the category of resurgence participate in both aspects, although in very different proportions. This two-sided resurgence is not new, for more than half a century ago it appeared in two movements—in the Brahmo Samaj, which represents a chastened, rationalized and severely-reduced Hinduism, a kind of dignified Unitarianism with a Hindu atmosphere, and in the reforming, but highly aggressive and propagandist, Arya Samaj. Then as now we have to note the same phenomenon, that the rationalizing movements of intellectuals have always had an exceedingly small number of adherents, while the agressive ones have a much greater number. The Arya Samaj has more than half a million followers and they develop an amazing activity. This would suggest, in the first place, that missionaries and European scholars have always very unduly exaggerated the objective significance of the rationalizing movements, probably because they discovered in them many ideas and ideals cognate to their own, and laboured under the evolutionary illusion that these " highest " forms of adjustment to the present time set the goal for the whole " natural " development of Indian religious life. In the second place, it suggests that in India, too, religiously coloured nationalism most easily sets the chords of the human heart vibrating.

The great significance of Western and " Christian " influences is very conspicuous in the strong emphasis on social service in many movements. Social service has become in India the highest note of idealism, and the eager response of many Indians to it is an indication of the high degree to which the religious and moral past of India has prepared Indians for a life of devotion and service. Gandhi's many movements, those issuing from the Indian National Congress, the Ramakrishna Mission, the Hindu Mission—which combines missionary zeal for Hinduism with uplift work, etc.— have all of them social service at their centre. The real inspiration comes from an elevated nationalism that makes for national reconstruction, and which draws strength from the noble and pure elements in the Indian religious and ethical heritage.

The more exclusively self-assertive resurgence manifests itself to-day in the revival of cults and feasts, in the rebuilding and repairing of temples, and, above all, in such movements as Shuddhi, the Mahasabha, the Hindu Mission, the Arya Samaj, the activity of the Hindu University at Benares, etc. In these cases the deepest motive is often a defiant religious nationalism, inspired by self-defence and an aggressive propagandist spirit. They are also connected with the rival militant communalism that has been released through the political development. " Hindustan for the Hindus " is the slogan of the Mahasabha ; the Sanatana Dharma, Hinduism, is the cause to which people are summoned. Military training and eating of beef are recommended as invigorating instruments, fostering activity. Hinduism, as Sanatana Dharma, has become a cause to call people to with a passionate fervour as never before. The prestige and the power of the community, the dominion over the souls and bodies of the greatest number, are consciously sought for as the immediate and laudable objects of religious striving.

It is very hard to discern a hopeful religious prospect in this rising orgy of religious nationalism, with its stunning of the deeper and purer religious motives and questions. India seems to have become caught in the clutches of the same spiritual and moral dementia that rages in all quarters of the globe. The great danger of India in the religious aspect seems to be at present that religion in the pure sense of the word is more and more strangled because it is sacrificed to the claim for political and social power. At the same time the essential sameness and unity of all religions is theoretically maintained. This is only a seeming contradiction. This sameness is maintained by virtue of inherited religious relativism, reinforced by modern religious indifferentism,

This last point enables them to fight for the power and prestige of the " religious " community with less moral scruple, for the prime object of interest to-day is the consolidation of the group, of which the basis is " religion " bequeathed by the past. In the past the prime object was to find a satisfactory way of religious experience and realization ; in the present it is not. This illustrates vividly how deeply secularized India has already become, and that secularization does not necessarily mean the repudiation of religion in the social sense.

The fact that the Hindu religious resurgence is essentially a resurgence of religious nationalism [1] accounts for the fierce character it shows on many sides. There is no real religious and moral sense of direction in it, because there is no norm of judgment. In this modern situation the secret and deepest difficulty of naturalist monism, namely, its ultimate normlessness, comes again to the surface.

This note of fervent activity, which manifests itself in a splendid spirit of devotion and sacrifice in the movements of social service, and in more contrasting ways in those of the more aggressive type, is a startling phenomenon. The Hindu apprehension of life, expressed in the doctrines of *samsara, karma, maya* and the sole Reality of Atman, is still virtually unbroken and cannot afford a real basis for any activism whatever, except that of the individual struggle to escape *samsara*. It is easily understood that in this situation of spiritual incompatibles the *Bhagavadgita* acquires a still higher prestige than it already had through being a much beloved sacred book. The type of religion represented in the *Gita* is that of manly faith and trust ; the mellow tones of the *bhakti* poets of South India are absent from it. Such is its central problem. In order to reach the goal of salvation, which consists in the cessation of *karma* and *samsara*, the wheel of activity should be stopped ; yet to strive for it means to keep the wheel turning. How is it possible under these circumstances to reach salvation ? The famous answer is, by detached, desireless (*nishkama*) acting, which consequently

---

[1] An impressive symbol is the temple in Benares, founded by Gandhi's efforts, where the map of Mother India is the sole object of worship.

will be *nirphala* (without *karma*). So in the *Gita* there is taught a kind of qualified affirmation of the world and of acting, although essentially speaking the world is really void. This qualified activism of the *Gita*, which is only concerned about personal salvation, serves to-day as the basis for the modern activism, which aims at social, political and cultural reassertion.

The modern philosopher of Hinduism, who tries to weave all the new activistic, self-assertive elements into the ancient texture of quietistic Hinduism, is Radhakrishnan. His starting-point, in good Hindu style, is the transitoriness of the world, behind which the imperishable Absolute Brahman is the Sole Reality. The moulding influence of European philosophy and Christianity on his thinking is evident in every term and explanation that he uses. He speaks by preference in terms of personal *bhakti*-theism, such as " the redemptive purpose of God," " the love of God," " the heart of the world," which betray Christian influences, but in the last instance conceives them to be only manners of speech. Yet he declares that " the difference between God as absolute Spirit and the Supreme as the personal God is one of standpoint and not of essence. It is a difference between God as He is and as He seems to us." *Karma* and rebirth he accepts as self-evident, and the caste system he explains in a modern way as a harmonizing of opposites, namely of the claims of the individual and of society. He commends Hinduism for its latitude and tolerance, yet he requires Hinduism to learn from Islam a more uncompromising denunciation of imperfect conceptions of God and crude forms of worship. He speaks about God as the Absolute, the self-existent ultimate Reality, and about God as the loving Creator, responsible for this changing world. The world and history he takes as real although it remains obscure whether this affirmation points to an objective reality, and if so, how this can be justified in the whole of his system.

One cannot get rid of the feeling that this realism is more an assertion than that it is motivated. The desire to emphasize it is noteworthy, however, against the background of Indian philosophy. In the sphere of this un-Indian realism he speaks about religion as combative, as meaning profound dissatisfaction with the existing state of humanity, and an active preparation for a new life. Yet, *sattva, rajas* and *tamas* [1] are aspects of the world and of *God* ; *moksha* is reached if one performs faithfully the law of *dharma*, automatically by development, not by grace ; and *avatars* are to be considered to be revelations of God or realizations of the potentialities of man. This equalization of revelation of God and the realization of human potentialities is very instructive as to the radical monism that animates the system, despite the use of such terms as Creator, purpose of God, and so on.

We give these few hints about Radhakrishnan because his eclectic unorganic way of combining Hindu, European and Christian elements in a delusive synthesis affords probably the best symbol of the chaotic and confused state of religious thinking and life in India, as is to be expected in a period " between the times."

CHINA

China presents a similar, but differently-drawn, picture of a restless chaos. Similar, because the impact of the West has put in motion the same welter of old and new as in India. Different, because Chinese mentality and attitude towards life are widely divergent from the Indian. Decline and revival, rejection and rejuvenation of religious life jostle each other here, too, but on a different earth and under a different heaven.

China's contact with the West is a story full of disturbance and illumination. The adaptation and adjustment of China to the new situation created by Western aggression was very haphazard, as Hu Shih says. The reason is that China's solid cultural self-consciousness made it underestimate seriously the significance of those red-haired barbarians of the West in the first half of the nineteenth century. In the

---

[1] According to Indian philosophy matter has three constituent qualities (*gunas*), namely, the quality of goodness and purity predominant in gods (*sattva*) ; that of passion, predominant in man (*rajas*) ; that of darkness or ignorance, predominant in demons (*tamas*).

beginning of the second half such a man as Li Hung Chang began to realize that Western military equipment and methods of economic exploitation were useful and indispensable. The movement for Westernization was still so weak, however, that it collapsed in the unsuccessful reform of 1898. In the beginning of the twentieth century, when the horrors of the Boxer insurrection and the utter inefficiency of the Court had revealed the bankruptcy of the superb Chinese state-system and civilization, which had lasted longer than any other in the world, the time of self-reproach and of appreciation of Western virtues and qualities dawned. In 1905 the famous system of examinations was abolished. Since the Han dynasty this had been one of the pillars of the Confucian world-order and of the State. In 1912 the Imperial House was expelled, and so the second pillar of the Confucian structure was destroyed.

The ideal of modern democracy, which worked as dynamite in this static world, fired the imagination and impelled to new experiments in state-building, which were full of vicissitudes and disappointments. Sun Yat-sen, with his three principles of Nationalism, Democracy and Livelihood, was the driving and organizing spirit. Apart from his tenacious and resolute revolutionary purposefulness, his greatness consists in the fact that for the first time in Chinese history the people, its interests and life became the direct object of concern. It is a marvel that this tottering colossus in such a short period should be finding solid ground again.[1] When we remember that China, by its haughty misinterpretation of the new situation, had become in the nineteenth century a prey to Western and Japanese aggressiveness and was bleeding from many wounds ; further, that in the beginning of the twentieth century it demolished by its own hands the foundations of its great political and social system, and that it was thrown into the turmoil of an unprecedented cultural and moral crisis, it is, indeed, a marvel. The National Government under the leadership of Chiang Kai-shek has become the centre of consolidation and upbuilding in the "national crisis," as it is called. The work of genuine

[1] For footnote, see p. 283.

adjustment, which does not consist only in outward organizational measures but in a definite change in inner attitude towards life and its problems, has still largely to be done.

In this laborious and painful process of the re-orientation of a rich and old civilization in a world radically different from that to which it was the accomplished attunement, the New Culture or New Thought Movement arising about 1917 has played an important rôle. This movement courageously and steadfastly pursued emancipation from the intellectual bondage to the past and from the fetters of tradition. Inspired by the liberating force of modern scientific outlook and invention, it assumed an attitude of free criticism and creative re-evaluation towards the cultural heritage of China. One of its most important features has been the use of the spoken language (*pei hua*) for literary purposes. A new and rich literary life has grown up as a result of this great act of emancipation, made possible by Hu Shih's clear-sightedness.

The words " national crisis " ought to be taken with all possible emphasis in regard to China. The National Government in Nanking is the symbol of the first steps on the long way towards new consolidation and upbuilding, but this does not include a unity of purpose and of tendencies. In the political realm fascist and communist tendencies are constantly at war across the middle-path that more or less is steered by the National Government. Twenty years ago the best minds were captured by the problem of political reconstruction, but at present their deepest concern is that of economic and social reconstruction. The desperate condition of the millions, the glaring evils of corruption and banditry—a legacy of the past and aggravated by the chaotic conditions of the present—press upon the minds of thoughtful and serious Chinese the prime necessity of creating a tolerable social and economic order. Endeavours for reconstruction and extreme revolutionary economic and social theories are therefore occupying the attention of many young men. Social sciences, social reconstruction, the works of Lenin and Marx now catch the attention of young intellectual people ; while ten years ago Dewey, Russell and Shaw, and the problems of sex, family and marriage, occupied the thoughts of this same class. The work of Dr Y. C. James Yen with his helpers in Hopei for social reconstruction is an indication that the problem of the millions, who always endured, more and more agitates the minds of thoughtful people. The necessity for honest and efficient Government and for common justice is increasingly felt as one of the life or death matters for China. A left and right wing are clearly discernible. The right wing is moving strongly in the direction of State-totalitarianism, though with liberal reminiscences on account of the Anglo-Saxon inspiration of Chinese nationalism. The left wing comprises various groups, including people of liberal tendencies who defend the democratic rights, such as Hu Shih and his Crescent Moon, the Proletarian Culture Movement, the Liberty League and the Federation of Leftist writers, who see the great enemy in capitalism and imperialism, all of them thoroughly anti-religious.

The changes in the social system and outlook of China are simply stupendous. The vocations of merchants and soldiers were despised in the old order with its patriarchal-aristocratic cultural judgment ; now, by virtue of the great economic adjustment to the conditions of the modern world and as a result of the endeavour to build up a strong, self-respecting and respected nation, they are acquiring an honoured position in the new system. The family system, the ancient bedrock of Chinese civilization, ethics, and political and social life, is thrown into the melting-pot. Apart from the ferment of new individualistic ideas, urbanization and industrialization expose the family system and the time-honoured conceptions of sex relations and relations of the age-grades to a severe process of dissolution. This thoroughly family-minded people is learning the hard lesson of becoming social-minded. Filial piety, one of the great basic and creative ideas of ancient Chinese civilization and the typical attribute of a static society, is breaking under the strain of forces in the new dynamic society of to-day.

These remarks on the great process of cultural, political, social and economic adjustment ought to be made, because without due recognition of these factors no intelligent judgement of the modern religious situation in China is possible.

It lies in the nature of the case. Old China was primarily
a great civilization and a system of social ethics. Therefore
its consciousness was primarily cultural and social and not
religious. In passing general judgments on possibilities of
religious developments and tendencies one should in the case
of China never lose sight of its natural, pragmatic temperament in religious matters. The present religious developments and tendencies are necessarily all more or less attended
by a flavour of fickleness. Sympathy or antipathy to
Confucianism, Buddhism or Christianity, for instance, is
dependent to a high degree on sympathy or antipathy
towards definite political social theories that are supposed to
be in agreement with or hostile to these religions. Therefore,
within the range of only a few years one can report both
a sympathetic and an inimical attitude towards religion.
Religious problems are thus, generally speaking, not conceived in the really religious realm, but in the cultural or
political realm. A vivid illustration of this utilitarian attitude towards the religious problem is what is told about
some of Yuan Shi-Kai's generals, who considered whether
Christianity should be introduced into China, because this
would " increase the power of the country." The colossal
economic distress, the political unrest, the uncertainty of life
have in some cases stimulating effect on demonstrations of
popular religious life ; in other cases they have a deadening
influence. The necessity to conquer the world anew by
industry, science, techniques and political reconstruction
naturally tends to turn away the minds of the intellectuals
from religious problems as commonly conceived, namely,
as solely concerned about the salvation of the individual soul.
The humanist and moralist temperament which is the
inheritance of the past reinforces this general tendency to take
the religious problem not really seriously, but to treat it in a
pragmatic and positivist way as a social or political expedient.

Faith in science and in modern humanism, which are
rightly felt by their inherent relativism and pragmatism to be
akin to Chinese mind-patterns, is therefore in the present
Chinese scene a phenomenon of more than semi-religious
quality. Science is felt as the most efficient means available

to deal with the problems of life. Western rationalism and humanism not only appeal by virtue of their proven effectiveness in the immense struggle against ignorance, superstition and tradition, but also by their fundamental secularist outlook, which makes man feel completely at home in this world. Confucianism, with its man-centred conception of the universe, is easily converted into a cognate secularism if it is stripped from its cosmic naturalism, as has been done by many who have been nurtured in the Confucian atmosphere. In 1923 there arose a very interesting controversy in which more than fifty prominent Chinese took part on the problem of science and metaphysics, which accentuates again the shifting character of the Chinese spiritual scene in this time of revolutionary transition. Liang Chi Chao proclaimed the bankruptcy of science. A pupil of Eucken and Bergson, Chang Chin Ma, conceived science to be objective, the mastery of problems by logic and analytical thinking. Life seeks, however, he said, to be subjective, intuitive and synthetic. Therefore science cannot help to solve the problems of life. A third defended science as pertinent to life, while connected with metaphysics through its interest in truth. Hu Shih wrote then his " naturalist creed," which expressed strongly his anti-supernaturalist bias and his wholly immanent interpretation of life, because man has acquired in the different sciences the means to master the problems of life and to exercise his creative intelligence and moral power. Religion is to live for the species, striving for social salvation, not for the ego and individual salvation.

This may serve to illustrate the contention that China is and must be in this period of its life in a state of constantly shifting conflict of opinion.

In this connection the vicissitudes in the modern career of Confucianism must be considered. After the abolition of the examinations in 1905, which virtually meant a definite break with Confucianism, endeavours were made to maintain it as a philosophical and ethical system. What never had happened during its long career happened in 1906 after the virtual repudiation of Confucianism as China's life-basis. Confucius was raised to the status of deity, and the same sacrifices that were due to Heaven and Earth were prescribed as his prerogative. His words were declared direct divine revelation. The Chinese mind, emotionally still deeply bound to Confucianism, sought in this pathetic gesture and this imitation of Western religious " habits " a compensation for the fact of its rejection as the basis of political life. The trend of events revealed the emptiness of the gesture. The revolutionary leaders after 1912 repudiated Confucianism more emphatically than ever, because to them it was the symbol of feudal, patriarchal, anti-democratic absolutism. They were believers in modern principles and, consequently, idol-breakers. Efforts were made in 1916 to introduce Confucianism into the Constitution as the religion of the State ; but this plan was frustrated through the great volume of resistance which it evoked from the progressive groups and from the other religions in China—Buddhism, Christianity and Islam. Confucianism remained " disestablished." Yet, whether confessed or not, Confucianism as an ethical life-pattern, as a habit and attitude of mind, as a distinct species of life-apprehension, is of course still deeply rooted in the life of China. As such it is still fully alive, whatever its official position as a life-system and world-view may be. This is demonstrated by the various movements of Confucian revival that regularly emerge and disappear, and that are prompted by motives germane to the present chaotic situation. The Heart Cleansing Society in Shansi, for instance, has as its aim to build up a fellowship of Confucianists. It modelled its organization on Protestant lines, having religious services with preaching and silent meditation. There are movements which motivate a revival because of the necessity for a moral bulwark ; others recommend it because the ethical principles of Confucianism are considered to be of universal significance ; others, again, discard the cosmic and universist elements of Confucianism, but interpret it as essentially a philosophy of self-reliance and human welfare.

This prevailing aspect of a China feverishly trying to find new ground for its spiritual feet to stand upon is also indicated by the many eclectic societies that appear and disappear in restless succession. Syncretistic organizations and clubs with a Taoist colouring, inorganically combining Confucian, Taoist and Christian elements (to mention some, Tao Yuan, Wu Shan She, Tung Shan She, the World Redemption New Religion, the Ethical Awakening Society) in which the claim for divine revelation, the practice of geomancy, the craving for healing of illness and the note of social service are specially prominent, accentuate by their mushroom growth the unrest that dominates the situation. The predominance of such features as revelation, geomancy, healing, point in a pathetic way to the longing for certitude and for deliverance from helpless distress.

The New Life Movement, inaugurated in 1934 by Generalissimo Chiang Kai-shek, is one of the clearest indications that China is desperately trying to rediscover new stability, now that its ship of life has become cut off from its moorings. It is an endeavour to build new foundations in the great and painful experiment of adjustment to a radically new world situation. It is born from the insight that political and social regeneration and consolidation are dependent on a moral and physical regeneration ; especially on the first, for Chiang Kai-shek has defined the weak side of China as " its lack of sincerity and enthusiasm." The Movement intends to help the people to become modern and rational beings, and to restore the widely lost sense of direction. China's chaotic transitional condition, as everywhere in the world to-day, cries out in this New Life Movement for discipline. This desperate need for discipline in life, by the way, is one of the chief reasons of the wide appeal in the Orient, as elsewhere, of the Oxford Group Movement. The New Life Movement is founded on the four ancient Chinese virtues : *li* (regulated attitude), *i* (right conduct), *lien* (clear discrimination and honesty) and *chih* (true self-consciousness). Its purpose, of course, is national regeneration in every sphere of life.

It is difficult to see whether this Movement will turn out to be ephemeral like many others. The official protection and guidance it enjoys can be its strength but also its weakness. But whatever may be its fate in the future, its greatest significance lies in the fact that it is a symptom of the pathetic effort of the greatest people and the oldest civilization of the world to recover a sense of direction and stability of life.

Against the background of the picture given in the preceding pages we can deal briefly with Buddhism. There the same two-sided picture of decline and revival and the same kaleidoscopic incalculability of the many shifting movements are to be noticed. It has suffered many blows through the impact of Western civilization and the new political and social situation. Temples have been destroyed or confiscated for other purposes. The monks have gone through hard times, and Buddhism has always had in China an organization too loose to be able to recover quickly from such blows. Religiously speaking, however, it ought not to be forgotten that Buddhism is a real religion with an enormous philosophical tradition, with a definite religious way of life and a gospel of salvation, and with an ecclesiastical organization, although in China this is rather loosely knit, as has been said already. Confucianism, on the other hand, is primarily a culture, and as a humanistic apprehension of life will also in the future colour deeply the Chinese mind. Many estimates are given about the significance of Buddhism in China. Most critics do not value highly its importance for modern China. It is generally regarded as a decaying religion, gaining little good repute from the type of the majority of the monks. It is difficult for one who has never lived in the country to say whether this estimate is right or wrong, although one may be permitted to have some doubts. It may be that the pervasive, intangible influence of Buddhism is much greater than is often surmised.

The revival movement in Buddhism touches only the upper social classes. Indeed the unstable conditions of the time impresses upon the lives and minds of man the stamp of the transitoriness of existence, and is one of the reasons why a considerable number of intellectual and well-to-do laymen join the Associations for the study and cultivation of Buddhism, the Vegetarian Halls and the various Brotherhoods and Sisterhoods. Fortitude and light in the distress and complexities of life are sought in these associations.

At the same time they are signs of a new feeling of responsibility to rehabilitate Buddhism for the forum of modern life and to demonstrate its social value. The note of social service is therefore very clear in these movements, although the means seem to be very inadequate. The members of these movements are mostly intelligent laymen, who are far more active than the monks, most of whom remain caught in the old sluggish temple routine.

The two figures around which the conscious revival and reinterpretation of Buddhism turn are In Kuang and T'ai Hsü, who are for thousands of people the Guide of Life and the Dispenser of revealing mysteries, because they themselves attained the goal and have " broken through." In Kuang belongs to the Ching-tu school, the Chinese example of *bhakti* or soteriological pietism, centering around Amitabha and his Western Paradise. He has aroused great evangelizing activity in preaching halls, recommending the Pure-Land doctrine fervently on the well-known ground that it is the safer and quicker way to salvation for the common layman, and he exercises a great influence as a pastor of souls.

T'ai Hsü is a quite different type of man. He is a religious philosopher and organizer, full of missionary zeal and developing great literary and teaching activity. He preaches, teaches, lectures, gathers inquirers, evidently borrowing these methods from the great evangelistic campaigns customary in Protestant missions. His life-purpose is to reinterpret the essence of Mahayana Buddhism in the light of modern conditions and interpretations of life. His magazine *Hai Ch'ao Yui* (the Voice of the Tide) is one of the outstanding religious magazines. The theological colleges in Nanking and Wuchang are centres of the study of Buddhism, comparative religion, ethics, philosophy, sociology and psychology. T'ai Hsü gives a dynamic interpretation of Buddhism, conceiving it as an idealistic cosmism which interprets the nature of the universe as constituted " by a conjunction of inherent and affinitive elements," all mutually related, in which the naturalistic underground clearly emerges. On this mutual relation and on the Buddhist doctrine of *karma* and self-deliverance he builds an activist ethic of self-reliance and responsibility for the bettering of the world and a happier social order. In this way a positive relation to the world is construed. On this basis he proclaims a radical humanism of self-reliance, in the sense of man's sufficiency and sole responsibility for creating a better world. Saviours (also Buddhas) are only forerunners and teachers who " broke through " to the attainment of unsurpassable, perfect and universal enlightenment. The Buddhism of " priests and monasteries " he repudiates as an embodiment of passive negativism and of degeneration.

He revives the fundamental atheism of ancient Buddhism, and he declares that the Buddhist illusionist conception of all sentient, phenomenal life is supported by the modern schools of European philosophy. His religious philosophy is essentially an idealistic and vitalistic monism, in which universal Consciousness is the only objective reality in the whole subjective process of events. To Christianity he and his followers evince a determined opposition. The exclusiveness of Christianity and its conception of God as a Person and as the Creator offend him, while he considers its supposedly naive supernaturalism a religion for the weak and superstitious. Mahayanist religious philosophy is the sole philosophy which agrees with science. He strives to revive in Buddhism a new consciousness of its world mission and does not leave Europe and America outside the scope of his missionary dreams. He is the leader of the young, progressive lay-Buddhists and the younger monks, and is opposed to the hierarchical position of the monks, vindicating the view that laymen can as well " break through " as monks.

T'ai Hsü's action is an important symptom of the possibilities of revival in Buddhism and its permeation with new ideas and ideals. The most remarkable feature in it is a resolute this-worldly concern on the incongruous basis of Mahayanist illusionism and of a religion of radical concentration on the goal of individual salvation, which consists in the cessation of the meaningless process of life. This alone is an indication that this dexterous but too-cerebral reinterpretation of Buddhism can only be a passing stage in a more arduous journey. The stern realities of to-day and the vehement life-rhythm of our modern age require a more stable and more genuine foundation than the intellectual synthesis of elements that have no genuine relation to each other. The indispensable condition for genuine social ethics is a profound belief in the reality of the world and of history. This problem of the reality of the world and of history, and of the foundation on which alone it can be solidly maintained, is one of the crucial problems for the great naturalist religions, which all tend by nature to a more or less unqualified illusionism.

These more fundamental reflections lead also to a cautious attitude regarding the question whether the present movements in Chinese Buddhism are real revivals or not.

The masses go on as in other countries, secretly affected in their crude spiritual life by the influences going out from the great political and social changes. With fits of eagerness or lassitude they practise their feasts, their pilgrimages and rites. What their mental and religious attitude will become in the future is difficult to foretell, because the factors which determine this are largely latent.

JAPAN

To a similar degree as India and China Japan is in a state of spiritual fermentation, and has all the attributes that attend a condition of spiritual unrest and instability. Yet the framework in which this is happening is very largely different. The crucial experience of adaptation and adjustment to the new situation introduced by the impact of the West has taken place in India under the leadership of a foreign power ; in China it happened in a haphazard way, until the beginning of the twentieth century, by means of revolutionary and disastrous collisions, because the gaze of China remained obstinately fixed on the past. Japan, however, has faced this cardinal turning-point in the recent history of all Eastern peoples in an entirely different way. It met it fully conscious of the great adventure it was entering upon. It meant to Japan a break with a long-standing policy of determined isolation from the outside world. This policy of isolation under the Tokugawa regime was pursued on account of the strong will of Japan to preserve its national integrity and independence. This deep urge for national integrity, which is such a dominating feature of the Japanese psyche and Japanese history, was also the motive for abandoning the policy of isolation and following the irresistible call of the trend of world history. The leading men of Japan understood how necessary and inevitable it was that they should steer the new course of entering the life of the world, and they deliberately assumed the lead in the adventurous process of disintegration, amalgamation, adaptation and reassertion that was set in motion thereby. As a result of its isolated past, Japan, moreover, entered this scene as a strong unified state, and saw in the preservation and strengthening of this unified state its chief concern and the main object of its programme of adaptation to the modern situation. To become increasingly strong and increasingly unified was its great ambition. The government of Japan has been from the beginning the leader in the process of adaptation and amalgamation with the West. This distinguishes Japan from all other countries that have become subject to the same experience of adjustment.

The whole modern development has to be viewed in the light of this strong nationalist urge and this determined and clear-headed leadership. They afford their peculiar aspect of development to the many forces that have arisen in the clash and mingling of ancient and modern. To the many uncontrollable forces which help to mould the religious situation in Japan belong, of course, also the rapid increase of the population, the effects of industrialization and urbanization, the tensions that arise from the adjustment to modern capitalism and to liberal ideals, and the communistic and socialistic leanings. These latter tendencies are not at all exclusively foreign importations, but can feed on autochthonous elements in the agrarian and feudal structure of Japanese society, as is demonstrated by the mingling of fascist and socialist ideals about the structure of society in the imperialist and passionately nationalistic officers of the Army who emerged in the revolt of the 26th February 1937. Japan is a thoroughly agitated country, desperately trying to master the mysterious and volcanic forces that have been released by the huge experiment of fitting the inherited structure of life into the new exigencies, and of evolving a modified structure in which sundry new elements have been inserted. As described in Chapter VI, Shinto, which is the creation of Japan's peculiar religious genius, has developed into a religion of which the core is a magnified tribalism, the glorification and deification of the collective Japanese self. In accordance with this deep-set urge the direction in which Japan's spiritual development seems to tend is that of preserving its self-identity throughout the moulding and modifying process of the Western ordeal. The final outcome is still a hidden mystery, but we must reckon in Japan, as in the other great civilizations of the East, with the reassertive power of the forces and tendencies that have created and shaped these civilizations.

What was the spiritual condition of Japan when it stood at the threshold of the new period in its history?

The masses lived then, as nowadays, by a sort of vulgar religion, a mixture of Buddhist and Shinto elements, a blend of Shinbutsu. The object of religious worship was (and is) mainly to satisfy the lower or higher needs and wants of life. Buddhism was in a rather decadent condition, as its priests were mainly of a degraded type. The Samurai nourished their spirits on the ethical discipline of Confucianism, which to-day still appeals to many minds. Shinto comprised on the one hand the various religious sects that in most cases started as revival and salvationist movements, and on the other hand the aggressive wing of self-conscious pure Shinto with a national and dynastic emphasis.

To characterize the modern religious situation in Japan some discussion of Shinto in its various manifestations is necessary, for the opening of the Meji-era meant at the same time the restoration of Shinto as an independent entity. The varying religious policy which the government has followed since 1868 is always some sort of interpretation of Shinto and has been unceasingly animated by the desire to preserve and strengthen cohesion under the heavy strain of the Western impact. The reassertion of Shinto as an independent and highly self-conscious entity is no recent growth. In the fifteenth century there are already the first signs of Shinto recovery in the efforts of Kanetomo to purify Shinto from Buddhist elements. This movement was also stimulated by the centre, founded in the eighteenth century by the Tokugawa, for the study of ancient Japanese history and mythology. Mabuchi, its mouthpiece, reached back to original Shinto and disentangled it entirely from its alliance with Buddhism. Fukko Shinto (pure Shinto) was focused on the theocratic idea of ancient Japanese mythology, but shows in its ethical outlook many Confucian influences. Motoöri Norinaga became the herald of this Pure Shinto, and in the first half of the nineteenth century, under the leadership of Hirata Atsutane, it assumed an aggressive turn by its strong dynastic tendency. In the agitation that preceded the Meji-era it played a great part by its slogan : " Honour the Emperor, expel the barbarians." The restoration of the Emperor to his central position after a thousand years of shadowy existence under the Shogunate was chiefly a result of this Pure Shinto. It preached the Kodo, the way of the Emperor. The two pivots on which it turns is the person of the Emperor and the Kokutai (the Japanese State-idea in its ideal realization). The Emperor is the high priest of the people and fulfils this function by worshipping his divine ancestors. The kami-cult of the people is the accompaniment of this worship. Properly speaking, in this whole act of worship the collective self of Japan is the true object, because the divinity of the Emperor is in reality the expression of the divine creation of the people of Japan and its destiny. In recent years especially this becomes more and more evident. All kinds of fascism find their common centre in the conception of " sacred Japan." Kakehi Katsuhiko, one of the leading thinkers in this doctrine of theocratic Shinto, proclaims it a world religion. With ever more passion and emphasis voices are raised that testify to Japan's Manifest Destiny as being a consequence of the divine order of *nature*, to the divinity of the Emperor and to the sacredness of Japan, which has a mission to create universal peace by drawing all men and all peoples into the

Kodo, the way of the Emperor. So Shinto has become a militant theocratic imperialism, in which the religious glorification of the Japanese people stirs the passions of political megalomania to fantastic extremes. It is very important to note that the name Kodo is not wholly adequate, because, on close observation, the Emperor has only the place of a symbol in this imperialistic philosophy. The kernel is the deification of the collective self of Japan, and nothing would have to be altered if the Emperor fell back into the same shadowy position as during the Shogunate. It would not impair or weaken this religious nationalism of Kokutai.

Since 1870 the religious policy of Japan has been balancing between two poles : the desire to use Kodo as the means for national cohesion, and the principle of religious liberty, borrowed from the West. In the very beginning the determined adherents of Pure Shinto succeeded in virtually making it the religion of the State. The Religious Department was the first in rank. Preachers of Kodo were appointed. In 1871 Buddhism and the cult of the Kami were declared separate religions by Imperial Decree, thereby undoing, at least officially, the syncretistic system of Ryobu-Shinto. There was a certain amount of persecution of Buddhism ; Buddhist temples were burnt. Buddhism, so deeply woven into the texture of Japanese life for more than a thousand years, was pronounced a " foreign " religion that vitiated the morale of the people.[1] The feverishness of the process of adaptation and the fierce clash of the different tendencies are revealed by the fact that already in 1872 this persecution of Buddhism was stopped and this experiment in making Pure Shinto the religion of the State was abandoned. The more clear-headed leaders of Japan saw that it was self-contradictory to begin a new period by seeking alliance with the West and at the same time live by the principle of " anti-barbarian " isolation. They contended for the principle of religious liberty, which triumphed in 1875.

This year dates the beginning of the policy of distinguish-

[1] Compare the interesting parallel in Germany now in respect to Christianity.

ing between an official State-Shinto (Jinja Shinto), that is declared to be no religion but a means to foster the patriotic spirit by systematically inculcating reverence for the ancestors, and the purely religious Shinto of the " sects " (Kyoha Shinto), that are conceived as free churches, living just like the Buddhist sects and the Christian Churches (the preaching of Christianity was allowed in 1873) under Article 18 of the Japanese constitution, which reads : " There is freedom of religious belief within the limits of the land if not prejudicial to peace and order and not antagonistic to duties as subjects." It is not necessary to relate here the many shifts in the policy of the government in this matter. The root of the matter remains always up to the present moment that this Jinja Shinto is the domesticated government edition of Pure Shinto, emphatically declared to be no religion, but only an instrument to promote and strengthen national unification. Everyone is allowed to think about it what he likes, but the government considers it non-religious, pointing as an evidence of this to the fact that no credal assent is asked. The instruction in the schools in this State-Shinto with all its temples and feasts and methods of worshipping is considered to be neutral instruction in national ethics. The chief cult-objects in this " patriotic " cult are the Imperial Rescript of Education of 1889—which is virtually treated as a Holy Scripture and in which the Throne is declared to be " cœval with heaven and earth "—and the portrait of the Emperor. The difficulty, however, is that the strongly religious nature of this product of artificial bureaucratic domestication constantly breaks through, confusing many minds and making the principle of religious liberty very nebulous.

Repeatedly the attention of the Government has been drawn to the fact that the ritual of the State-Shinto shrines is full of the old nature mythology, that amulets are sold and sacrifices and prayers are offered, and that the people regard the shrines undoubtedly as places of religious worship. The government, however, persists in its view of them as non-religious institutions for developing patriotism through honouring the Emperor and Kokutai, which are the two central tenets of Kodo. To justify its position the spokesmen of the government always explain that religion is characterized by a founder, dogmas, the concern for individual salvation of the soul, preaching and sacraments. Dr Genchi Kato, the present authority on Shinto, brushes these distinctions aside and openly declares it to be a full-fledged religion.

In the last ten years the discussion on the question whether Jinja Shinto is a religion or not has greatly agitated the minds of people in Japan. In 1929 a Commission was appointed to investigate the system of State-Shinto and to study and report on the Shrine situation. No tangible results have yet come from these labours, because this is evidently not desired.[1] The tension between the principle of religious liberty and a disguised State-religion becomes greater and greater, as is shown by the Minobe incident, by the establishment in Korea and in Manchuria of a prescribed cult of State-Shinto and of Confucian ceremonies, and by the increasing frenzies of religious nationalism and patriotic terrorism in late years. The atmosphere of ambiguity in which this whole problem is always consciously kept is a symbol of the fact that Japan has been standing already for nearly ten years at the cross-roads. It has postponed its decision whether it will walk the way of religious liberty and of the natural clash of spiritual forces which it observes in the liberal democratic West ; or whether it will make an artificial religious nationalism the authoritative rule of life and reassert its innate tendencies. The anti-liberal anti-democratic current in the West of to-day is a strong inducement in the last direction. The decision will be a fateful one if it is taken, full of consequences for Japan, for the world, and especially for the Christian Church.

[1] Dr Minobe, Emeritus Professor of Tokyo Imperial University, who in recognition of his legal scholarship (!) was appointed a member of the House of Peers, was the well-known exponent of the organ-theory, namely the theory that the status of the Emperor under the Constitution is described in legal terms as the head of a juridical person. In 1935 this " Western " and " secular " conception of government was denounced by one of the peers, as this peer held Japan to be created and not founded, and the Emperor to be sacred and inviolable. Dr Minobe had to withdraw " voluntarily " his writings so offensive to Kokutai, but refused to recant. There was hardly anybody who dared to defend him.

"Religious" Shinto numbers thirteen "sects" or churches. In this case we find the same situation as is found in the case of Pure Shinto. These Shinto -sects are no recent growth. Since the sixteenth century such movements, all with revivalist features, sporadically appear in the form of pilgrim-clubs. They have been especially frequent, however, in the last hundred years and testify to the great fermentation within Japanese life as a consequence of economic distress and disruptive cultural conflicts. They are popular religious movements that are of great significance in the religious life of Japan, and provide for the religious needs of the masses by their strong emotional appeal. The total number of their followers is more than sixteen millions, and some sects have a membership exceeding half a million or even attaining two millions. Tenrikyo and Omotokyo are the most numerous ; but the second was suppressed in the beginning of 1937, probably because its tenets and propaganda, although a hyperbolic form of the common religious nationalism, assumed chiliastic features, disturbing peace and order and therefore alarming the authorities.

All these popular movements have a number of characteristics in common which in their frequency are typical for Japan and suggestive of the religious needs of the people. Their founders are all prophets who are " called " and who bring divine revelation, codified in a book. Some of them are ignorant women and peasants, but remarkable personalities. Their cults and rites and practices (*hoben*, outward performances), to the people the essential elements of religion, are manifold. Pilgrimages belong regularly to their equipment. Exorcism, methods of healing and healing prayer are common features. Some of them evince a deep consciousness of sin and of the need of deliverance, or develop a great moral energy (for example, Tenrikyo). Their doctrinal tenets tend all in the same direction of identifying the divine in man and in the universe, expressed in different mythological forms, and of inciting to a life of purity.

These movements, which clearly show the eclectic effects of the modern age with its commingling of spiritual spheres, are important indications of the trends of Japanese religious life.

The position of Buddhism, although it was only persecuted for a short time during the modern era, is considerably weaker than in preceding ages. It has lost its intimate contact with the court, and the lavish State-subsidies which it formerly received for its temples have been withdrawn ; many privileges which it had have been abolished. It has become a disestablished religion. This shock was followed by the impact of Western influences. Both these shocks have acted as incitements to introspection and reform, because they forced its followers to muster its latent as well as its manifest resources. Besides, the appearance of Christianity on the religious scene drove Buddhism into an attitude of partly inimical, partly friendly, competition, borrowing many of its methods and means in order to strengthen its own prestige and influence.[1] Buddhism is now, like Christian missions, equipped with Young Men's Associations, Sunday Schools, a Salvation Army, a Federation of Sects, Street and Radio Preachings. A Kingdom of God Movement was planned in 1934 ; it develops an amazing literary and publicity activity ; social service is continuously stressed, and Buddhism is recommended as a religion working for social happiness and betterment.

According to the Year-book of the Buddhist Federation of Sects of 1930, there were then 56 sects and 72,000 temples, and the number of people more or less closely connected with Buddhism was given as amounting to forty millions. It does not seem, however, that these figures are the right standard by which to judge the significance of Buddhism in modern Japan. By reason of its quite different history and its strong hierarchical organization, which even has aspects suggesting military discipline and organization, Buddhism is much more deeply entrenched in Japan than it is in China. The long-lasting alliance between Buddhism and the national religion in Ryobu Shinto has permeated the Japanese mind

---

[1] A picturesque piece of evidence of the large-scale imitation of Christian methods and ideas is the following verse, taught in a Buddhist Sunday school : *Buddha loves me, this I know ; For the Sutras tell me so.*

with Buddhist elements and made it familiar with Buddhist figures and expressions, just as the age-long silent but persistent occupation with Confucian ethics has left a deep imprint on the Japanese outlook. The fact that life for the masses in Japan is full of distress and hardships predisposes the mind to some degree for the penetrating pessimism of which Buddhism is the messenger. Many people belonging to the higher classes of society find in Buddhism discipline and guidance for their life because of its great store of psychological and spiritual wisdom. The fervent piety of the Jodo-shu affords to many men and women deep satisfaction, and one can cite instances (cf. those given in Reischauer's *Studies in Japanese Buddhism*) in which the expression given to this piety is exactly similar to heartfelt expressions of Christian Pietism. At present Japanese Buddhism is unquestionably the most alert part, intellectually, of the whole Buddhist world. Valuable historical and philosophical contributions are made by leading Japanese scholars to the study of Buddhism. A great and laudable activity in the field of editing Buddhist sources is going on. Much zeal and ability are spent on the modern reinterpretation of Buddhism and the demonstration that no religion can so easily and naturally be harmonized with the leading European systems of philosophy (such as Kant, Hegel, Spencer) as Buddhism, because Mahayanist philosophy, which really is a symposium of all possible philosophical apprehensions, harbours all sorts of idealism and philosophical illusionism as well as agnosticism.

Yet, despite all its activity and all those great assets which it has by virtue of its historical position and its resurgence in the face of modern conditions and challenges, it is very difficult to form a definite opinion on the question whether we have the right to speak of a Buddhist revival and of a strengthening of its position. There is much to justify a negative answer. In the first place, the grip of religious nationalism on the minds of the people has supplanted Buddhism's former dominant position. In the second place, the many " free " Shinto cults for the time being seem to satisfy the religious and other cravings of common people more than the elaborate temple observances, cults and feasts of popular Buddhism. For the rest, the alternately rising and declining tide in the zeal for the frequentation and upkeep of these temples shows how hazardous it is to speak confidently in these restless times about revival and decline. In the third place the basic pessimistic world-denying attitude remains the core of Buddhism, notwithstanding the Protean versatility which Mahayanist religious philosophy, on account of its basic monism, has developed and which has enabled Buddhism to develop even such world- and life-affirming vitalist philosophies as Zen-Buddhism. This world-denying pessimism will not easily find a vital relation to the modern temperament of taking this world and this life as stark and all-important realities. In the fourth place, Buddhism is in the same plight to-day as all great religions. It is passing through a crisis, because of the wave of secularism that goes over the world and because religion as such is universally questioned and tested. It is very noteworthy that the number of people who begin to get weary of the fascinating and enervating fallaciousness of the theory of accommodated truths seems to be growing, because this facile theory begins to offend the sense of sound realism that the contact with the world in all its fullness has brought.

Not less remarkable is it that one reads about people who suffer under the knowledge that the glorified love of Amida is founded only on a subjective mythological basis, and who begin to clamour for objective validity and to protest against the delusion, fostered systematically in the whole area of naturalist religions, that the value of spiritual experiences and realization is the best standard of reference for truth. In the fifth place, it is not unfair to say that a considerable part of Buddhism's aggressive activism of to-day has its roots in its confrontation and competition with Christianity, and is, therefore, a defensive reaction. This fact determines its lines of action, and causes also a permeation with modernized Christian ideas. A look at the able sermons of the Shinshu preacher, Todakanae, with their elevated sincerity and their positive evaluation of the world, is sufficient to convince one to what a high degree Christian apprehensions leaven the outlook of many Buddhists in Japan.

All these considerations, and many more, justify serious doubt as to whether the resurgence of Buddhism is issuing from an urge from within or, perhaps, is more adequately interpreted by calling it a galvanization mainly through external causes.

The " revival " of Japanese Buddhism is richer in aspiration than in real activity. Probably it is too rash and superficial to expect and demand under the existing circumstances a reform coming from an inner urge. The tumult of life is so great, the pull to immediate action and the need for rehabilitation in the turmoil of the many distracting influences of the modern crisis are so irresistible that bustling self-assertion is for the time being a more natural phenomenon than a resort to those depths where genuine regenerative reforms originate. This does not apply to Buddhism only, but to all the great non-Christian religions in the present crisis. The clash with Western civilization was met by them at first with an attitude of haughty declinatory reserve ; then with confused indecision, manifest in the efforts to vindicate their self-confidence by protesting their essential equality with or superiority over the dominant ideas of the West and at the same time seeking some kind of adaptation to them. Rehabilitation is the general note of this period. The present period is one in which the dominant feature is the endeavour to reassert and consolidate their position as bodies possessing social and mental power. In other words, the great non-Christian religions, as is intelligible from the nature of the case, are in the storm of modern life so deeply absorbed in a struggle for the maintenance of their *position* as centres of spiritual power and prestige that hardly any energy is left for the cardinal problems that pertain to the genuine religious quest.

Japanese Buddhism, in fighting its own internal problems, will perhaps be led to deeper religious issues. These internal problems revolve around the struggle for the recovery of a purer Buddhism, free from the shackles of the complicated scholasticisms that are so common in Mahayana Buddhism.

Historical, exegetical and dogmatic research take a prominent place in this process, and are a Buddhist replica of what has happened to Christian theology since the eighteenth century. The Buddhist Church in Japan, moreover, has deep cleavages. The cleavage between the *ta-riki* (self-power sects) and the *ji-riki* (the Pure-Land sects) seems unbridgeable. The choice that is before serious-minded people, now that revived historical research has increased the ability to discover differences, is that between original agnostic soteriological Buddhism and the peculiar Japanese inter-pretations of Buddhism as a religion of the efficiency of faith (Honen, Shinran) or as a religious philosophy of some kind of idealistic monism.

The bulk of the people and the monks who provide for the temples and the many paraphernalia of the daily religious routine stand outside these struggles. This, added to the social and political crisis which causes the curve of events in all spheres of life to take such an irregular and convulsive course, demonstrates sufficiently that it is not possible to hazard very definite opinions about the present strength of Buddhism. However, it is always opportune to consider that a religion, which has for centuries dominated the life of a country and permeated men's minds, has many hidden resources, either of a passive or an active quality.

Nobody can tell what will be the effect of the present conflict between China and Japan on the religious situation in these two important countries.[1] This uncertainty must make one entertain a very modest estimate of all appraisals of the contemporary religious situations in this present world of feverish changes.

ISLAM

Islam is the sole non-Christian religion which, like Christianity, witnesses a great extension of its territorial and spiritual dominion amongst the " primitive " peoples. The characteristic feature of this fact is that with some small exceptions to the rule, it happens without any systematically

[1] This is written in the first days of October 1937.

organized missionary activity. The opening up of the world by Western penetration paved the way for Islam in Africa and in many parts of pagan Asia, because there the two vigorously missionary religions among the world religions, Islam and Christianity, appeared on the scene. In the very near future Africa and those parts of Asia (especially the Dutch East Indies), which were formerly occupied by the various tribal religions, will be wholly ruled by the two great religions, Christianity and Islam, if, at any rate, the possibility of the rise of an irreligious region of the world is excluded. The crumbling of the " primitive " tribal religions has become for Islam the great occasion of its extension. In the Middle Ages and thereafter the above-mentioned regions experienced already on their fringes a process of Moslemization. Islam came then with the prestige of political power, of being a comprehensive and inclusive civilization and a higher religion, easily assimilating itself to the new pagan environments. The process was essentially one of imperceptible transference of culture, in which purely religious factors rarely played a decisive rôle. This is one of the many instances demonstrating the universal fact that political, social and cultural factors are in most cases the determining causes in large-scale extensions of world religions.

The extension of Islam in the modern age results from three main reasons. In the first place, the need of the tribes which became religiously homeless by the Western impact for a new spiritual home of universalist dimensions ; in the second place, the unobtrusive but very self-assertive mission-ary attitude of the average Moslem, who comes among those pagan peoples in the capacity of a merchant or a lower government agent ; in the third place, the very moderate religious and moral demands that Islam makes of those who want to enter its fold. To-day the extension of Islam does not mean, as in the past, the incorporation of extended territories and numberless people within a higher religious civilization, but within the stagnant and sterile religious community that Islam has become in the last centuries. It constitutes therefore a very important problem, not only from the standpoint of Christian missions, but also from the standpoint of the world at large.

.   .   .   .

Islam is a theological system and at the same time a complete civilization in the mediæval sense of a *Corpus Islamicum*, and also an intensely political religion because of its theocratic inspiration. There is no religion in the world that has fostered in its adherents all over the world such a unity of theological attitude, cultural solidarity and theocratic-political sentiment as Islam has. The existence of distinct regional types of Islam does not considerably weaken this threefold unity. This must constantly be in the back of our minds in order to be able to understand the reaction of Islam to the modern situation in which it finds itself. The two elements that dominate the modern situation of Islam are therefore its clash as a unified body of civilization with modern civilization, and its political predicament. After its consolidation in a theological and legal system of civilization Islam became very rigid, and after its decline as a political power it became extremely sensitive in political response. It became very rigid, because its system claimed to be the embodiment of divine commandments, and so a new historical situation such as the modern one, which imperiously calls for adaptation and change, has been met with a great lack of elasticity. To part with the divinely-sanctioned mediæval *Corpus Islamicum* (for this it is what the adaptation and adjustment to the modern world involves for Islam) meant for Islam not so much reform as revolution. It became extremely sensitive, because its theocratic consciousness of being not only the sole legitimate aspirant for religious world dominion but also for political supremacy made its reactions on the victorious impact of the Western world in political, economic and cultural respects quite different from, and more bitter than, those of any other religion. It was an exceedingly hard lesson for Islam, which is superiority-feeling incarnated, to recognize its inferiority, and in its innermost heart it refuses to accept this lesson till the present moment.

Before the World War the fate of the Moslem world in

its political aspect was very melancholy. Year by year the process of its political disintegration and of the loss of its independence assumed an increasing momentum. This more than anything else released a sentiment of religious decay and crisis in Islam. The great " Rouser " of Islam in the nineteenth century, as he was called, Sayyid Jamal al-din al-Afghani, indicated as the great problem for the Moslem world the restoration of its power. In cultural matters Islam reacted along two lines, each of which has a very interesting history. The conservatives rejected European culture altogether, defending " the House of the Lord," because they instinctively felt that to accept the new age meant to face the crumbling of the whole system, which was their life-breath. Those who had felt the movement of the new tide and perceived in it an alluring liberty and widening of horizons, reacted in a different way. They pleaded for reform and adaptation and protested that the leading ideas of Europe corresponded with the essence of Islam, if understood in the right way and cleansed from the rubbish of many retrograde traditions. This was and is still in the main the attitude of the many apologists of Islam, such as Muhammed Abduh, Sir Muhammed Iqbal, Khuda Buksh, divergent as their approach may be. This double reaction of rejection and partial acceptance began in the eighteenth century in a very realistic way. As with China and Japan, so with Turkey, the first motive to assimilate reluctantly some elements of the progressive and powerful West was due to the need for military strengthening with modern Western weapons in order to maintain the country's political integrity. Turkey started on this course after the humiliating Peace Treaty of Küchük Kaniardja with Russia in 1774. Mehemet Ali had the same motive for his first experiments in westernizing Egypt. This need for military and technical training, coupled with the ever-increasing pressure of the irresistible Western penetration, led unexpectedly to Westernization and to the clash between the *Corpus Islamicum* and modern civilization and its dynamic principles.

Since the World War the situation has undergone a radical change. Instead of a politically disintegrating

Islam, the Near and Middle East, which is the central Moslem area of the world and which had virtually become the chess-board on which the Great European Powers played their game for concessions and protectorates, now offers the spectacle of increasingly vigorous and independent Moslem States. This recovery of political independence with the ensuing cultural activity in the Arabic-speaking Moslem world is one of the most amazing and unexpected outcomes of the World War. Even more startling is the renaissance of Turkey and Iran under the leadership of Kamal Ataturk and Riza Pasha Pehlevi. Turkey was at the end of the War almost reduced to nothing, the powerless object of many clashing interests. Iran was virtually divided up between England and Russia. The iron determination of two strong-willed men, who knew how to rouse the spirit of national self-respect and self-sacrifice, and who profited by the enormous changes in the political constellation resulting from the appearance of Russian communism and its wise and astute policy of fair dealing with the Eastern suppressed nations, forced Europe within a few years to adjust itself to the fact of new rising nations determining their own destiny. Not only in these two countries, but also in Arabia (Ibn Sa'ud) and in Afghanistan, dictators supplanted the old-time rulers with their policies of conciliatory acquiescence and of ignoring the crucial problems of adjustment, and inaugurated a clearly-defined policy of reconstruction on a nationalist basis. The Anglo-Egyptian Treaty of Friendship of 1936 fits in with this entirely new development.

These startling political changes have set the whole problem of Islam as a religion on a new basis, and that this is the case is the best evidence for the eminently political character of Islam as a religion. The main conclusions that derive from these changes are the following. First, European political supremacy in the central block of the Moslem world has definitely come to an end. Second, the pressure of Western civilization and all it stands for has now become more irresistible than ever. Their future now lying in their own hands, these countries, though with differing degrees of intensity and along different ways, avail themselves voluntarily of all the intellectual and technical instruments that must necessarily belong to the equipment of a community that will play an active part in the modern world. Resignation and passivity have been supplemented by determination and activity. Their dominant aim is to acquire full political maturity and economic self-determination, and to achieve this a radical modernization is inevitable. This involves, of course, that the problem of Islam as a religious system and its relation to modern culture must become more acute. The prospect is, however, very confusing and conflicting. In Turkey it has become very acute indeed and has led for the time being to the virtual suppression and emasculation of Islam. In Iran a middle way is steered in this conflict. The other new Moslem States (Egypt, Irak, Arabia, Afghanistan), however, with renewed emphasis, find in Islam their spiritual cohesion and unity and the guarantee for a much-needed stability in the midst of the turmoil of the great transition.

Apart from the question of its religious truth or the depth of its social and cultural adequacy to this modern age, one has to reckon with the fact that by its long historical influence and the strong sentimental attachments Islam has built in the minds of these peoples, Islam will become in the near future in a new active sense their rallying centre, the fortress behind which they will try to protect their self-identity in the whirlpool of modern dissolution, their basis of moral cohesion, for the simple reason that no other is immediately available at a time when such a basis is so badly needed. The Muslim Congresses of 1924, of 1926 and of 1931 (this last being one in which the Grand Mufti of Jerusalem took such an important part) are groping efforts to assert Muslim solidarity. In this context the exceptional character of Turkey's method of dealing with the problem of Islam becomes still more prominent.

In the third place, this drastic change that has taken place has been effected in the case of Turkey and Iran (the leading countries in this respect, for the changed situation in the other countries is more dependent on external factors) by a radical nationalism and secularism which everywhere, especially in Turkey, have demonstrated enormous powers of reconstruction and destruction alike. The powers of reconstruction are manifest in every field of life. The powers of destruction have been especially evident in the method of dealing with the minority problem. Massacres and deportations have been the methods whereby modern nationalism in its desire to realize national unity has " solved " this problem, which ancient Islam solved by its system of *millets*.[1] The Armenian massacres in 1915 were born of nationalist fanaticism, not of religious. Nevertheless this minority problem is also very important from the religious point of view, because in the Near and Middle East, as a legacy of the past, " nation " and " religion " are still largely synonymous. It is likely therefore that the unity and spiritual cohesion which Islam affords as a cultural sentiment and life-pattern will make it at the present time a precious asset for nationalist ends, and so corroborate the value placed upon Islam as a social asset. In other words, it is highly probable that the strenuous occupation with national, political and economic problems will strengthen in the Moslem world the pragmatist valuation of Islam as a religion. This implies on the one hand a stiffening and hardening of Islam and on the other hand a deviation from genuine religious questioning.

The various situations in those Moslem countries that are under foreign governments, as Algiers, Morocco, Tunis, India, the Dutch Indies, show very different aspects. They have at the same time some striking traits of similarity. Although, of course, in all these countries there are many signs of modernism, many tendencies of reform and adaptation to the modern world and many silent processes of secularization, yet their general attitude in religious matters is considerably more conservative than in the politically independent Moslem countries. The Moslem populations of the countries subject to foreign rule are all more or less vehemently nationalist, their nationalism by the nature of the case being one of protest and vindication of rights and

---

[1] *Millet* is the name of the non-Moslem religious communities that had their own heads and laws.

liberty. Indian Islam, by the exceptional fact that Islam is in India a numerical minority (of more than seventy millions) in the midst of an overwhelming Hindu majority (nearly five times stronger), is very lukewarm in regard to nationalism. In their minority position Indian Moslems are acutely conscious of the prime claim of Islam on their loyalty, and clearly put Islam first and India (because that, for the most part, means Hindu India) second. But apart from this exception it may be safely said of all Moslem countries under foreign governments that their nationalism is easily allied with a markedly conservative attitude in religious matters. The principal reason for this phenomenon is political, as is so natural in the case of Islam. The presence of a foreign government naturally accentuates the inclination to consider Islam as the protective shell behind which one can more easily maintain a certain measure of independence. The nationalism of protest and vindication of rights to which they are condemned cannot possibly have the creative quality of the more healthy nationalism of self-determination and the shaping of a self-defined future, as is the case in the independent countries, and therefore Islam in this case easily becomes rather an instrument (and by its political character a very explosive instrument) in the movement of protest than an object of really religious and moral concern or reform. This is the reason why *tabshir* (Christian missions) in these countries is always identified with *isti'mar* (colonization, or foreign rule) ; and in the last decade this occurs with increasing vehemence. In the independent countries, quite in accordance with the wholly different quality of their nationalism, missions are judged from quite another angle, namely, whether and how far their activities are considered conducive to or compatible with the supreme aim of national consolidation and reconstruction as conceived by the respective governments. The fate of Christian missions in these countries is dependent on the affirmative or negative answer given to these questions, and is therefore at present and in the near future uncertain.

It is in keeping with this whole situation that reports on the spiritual climate of such countries as Syria, Palestine,

Transjordania, Tunis, Morocco, India, etc., without exception tell of prevailingly orthodox trends, partly issuing from a less drastic experience of modernization but mainly from the peculiar political situation. For only this last factor can explain how it is that a great many of the intellectuals in those countries are as private persons indifferent to all religion, but in their public life are staunch and passionate defenders of Islam as the symbol of group-solidarity. Among the gods of the world of to-day there is none that has such a great number of devoted worshippers all over the world as group-solidarity in its various avatars. It is the Allah of the modern world, beating all other gods as to popularity, and nationalism is its prophet.

Some special attention must be devoted to Egypt, Turkey and Iran, because in these three countries the cardinal problem of Islam and the modern world is treated in three markedly different ways.

Egypt can already boast of a rather long and deeply interesting history of conflict between the Westernizers and the conservatives. The first group stresses adaptation to the modern world, and as men of modern culture and taste are only mildly interested in Islam. In their ranks there are, of course, many shades of opinion and attitude, dependent on their more fervent or more tepid appreciation of Islam. These different appreciations derive in the case of some from primarily political motives ; in the case of others from primarily social considerations ; in the case of others still from primarily religious preference. Sheich Ali Abd al Raziq, his brother Mustafa, and Taha Hussein are examples of these different types. The Wafdist party belongs to this Westernizing side. The second group has not at all closed its mind towards the benefits of European thought or implements, because that has become impossible, but their emotional emphasis rests on the restoration of Islam to its religious and cultural supremacy. In this case, too, the emphases are different and even lead to conflicts. Sheich al-Maraghi, the present Rector of al-Azhar, is in this group the representative of enlightened progressiveness, but often meets with strong criticism and resistance. The Azhar is the most important centre of this group. Conservative politicians have many connections with it. Their principles naturally appeal to the masses in the provinces, and their influence has increased in late years because the energetic policy of founding many schools created a great need for teachers and the government had to take what it could get. So most of the teachers are Azharites, who make these schools a sort of modernized *maktab*.[1]

Both groups unite in their desire to modernize the country in the economic, social, educational and hygienic respects towards which the aim of the present government is directed, but differ according to the secularist or Moslem stamp that marks their acts. A very noteworthy feature of the Egyptian situation is that in Egypt the ambition to become the centre of Moslem consolidation for the whole Moslem world is very strong. It is therefore highly probable that national reconstruction in Egypt will follow the prudent line of consolidating Islam as much as possible and of preserving its social structure. In this context must be placed the fact that at the Montreux conference freedom for foreign institutions (educational, medical, scientific) is granted under the jurisdiction of the Mixed Tribunals and Egyptian Law, but that Egypt at its entry into the League of Nations refused to guarantee religious freedom, that is to say, freedom for other religions than the State-religion. The unpredictable religious future of Egypt is best illustrated by this equivocal attitude of neither denying nor granting religious freedom.

As a Moslem problem Turkey is in many respects a riddle. There the unthinkable thing has happened that, within the course of a few years, Islam has been reduced from the status of a religiously-sanctioned cultural, social and political system that dominates life in all its spheres, to the miserable position of a private and unfavoured religious opinion, the very position that Islam according to its intrinsic theocratic character can never accept. The most enigmatic thing about the whole story is that this has been perpetrated without any considerable outburst of dreaded Moslem fanaticism. Martyrs there have been only a few. Is the

---

[1] *Maktab* is the Moslem parish school.

explanation of this remarkable fact to be sought (if we leave out of account the quick and merciless suppression of all resistance) in that curious blend of the feudal quietism of the East, which instinctively rejects the idea of rebellion against the prince, with the natural quietism of the suppressed masses ? These take the turning of the political wheel with fatalistic resignation and with the religious quietism so natural in the hyperbolic theocentrism of Islam, which feels no responsibility for a personal protest but leaves " the vengeance to the Lord Almighty." There certainly is much protest in Turkey against the religious policy of the Nationalist Government, but it is buried in the heart.

The new Turkey that has been hammered out by Kamal Ataturk from the miserable fragments of the Ottoman Empire has become within a decade a strong Mediterranean State, which will have one of the leading positions in the Near and the Middle East. The instruments to achieve this have been a radical nationalism and secularism. This radical determined nationalism and secularism are by their nature the antitheses of Islam. The Moslem Shari'a presupposes a theocracy, in which this Shari'a is the real Head and the Caliph is the executive organ of this theocratic law. A separation of spiritual and secular is inconceivable in Islam and therefore the abolishment of the Caliphate in 1924 was inevitable, because it had become null and void. Islam has become radically bereft of its political nature. The aims of the the nationalist state are purely secular : power and prosperity. Religion, which was in the Islamic state the pivot, becomes wholly irrelevant. Being, however, a historical and social reality, the clearly prescribed line of policy is to make it subservient to the purely secular ends of the national state.

In these few lines the religious policy of Turkey is defined. Although since the introduction of the Civil Code in 1926 all religious distinctions have been abrogated as regards their bearing on civil rights, and in 1928 Islam as the religion of the state was definitely abolished, in one respect one might say that Islam is still the religion of the state. It is entirely in the hands and the control of the government as regards its finances and its organization. Islam has become the tool of the state, used or not used at its bidding ; and this bidding is controlled by purely political and secular inspiration. The genuine desire for a vigorous, fruitful and powerful national existence, which includes a comprehensive programme of economic, social, intellectual and moral reconstruction, lends to this secularist subjugation of Islam a more or less irritated note, because Islam is the symbol of decay, of cultural retardation and of the emasculation of the Turkish spirit.

Against this background the whole process of new legislation, included in the new codes and pertaining to dress, script, education, religious instruction, emancipation of women, etc., is one succession of deliberate blows to demolish the political, social and cultural hegemony of Islam. Constitutionally speaking, Turkey is now a parliamentary, democratic state, since for historical reasons Turkish secularism has always been orientated towards France, but in reality it is a despotic oligarchy. This oligarchy tries by its Diyanat Ichleri (Ministry of Religion) to exploit serviceable elements of Moslem ethics for its combat against Eastern passivity.

There is indeed a subtle twist in this Turkish policy towards Islam. It has shattered Islam in its aspect of the *Corpus Islamicum*, because this mediæval theocratic structure is incompatible with a secularist state. The leading men, for the time being, are even indifferent to Islam as a private religious opinion. However, Islam being on historical grounds the symbol of spiritual unity and solidarity, the government utilizes Islam from social considerations as an important cement of unity. The well-known incident with the women teachers at the mission school at Brussa is a very apt illustration of this nursing of Islam as the symbol of unity. According to the Lausanne Treaty, Christian Greeks, who were Turkish subjects and spoke Turkish, were gladly exchanged against Moslems who spoke no Turkish. So the policy towards Islam is two-sided. On the one hand, Islam is starved in every possible way ; on the other hand, on account of its unitary value for the secularist state, it is distinctly privileged above Christianity, and to insult Islam or the Prophet is severely punished. Everyone, so to speak, is permitted to revere Islam as an abstract *sacrum*, and certainly even many thoroughly secularized people do so.

Our consideration of the Turkish situation leads to the following, partly tentative, conclusion.

As H. E. Allen has said in his illuminating book, *The Turkish Transformation*, the secularization of Turkey is one of the most startling experiments in the world to rebuild a nation on a purely irreligious humanist basis. For the time being the results are amazing. Turkey as it has become since the eventful battle at the Saqariah river in August 1921 is the best evidence of this. One of the most amazing results of the experiment certainly is that it has annihilated in an incredibly short time the unwieldy theocratic *Corpus Islamicum*. It has also forced Islam to make an experiment it never would have dreamed of on its own account, namely, to *start its career as a religion pure and simple*. Nobody can penetrate the future or tell what the outcome of these two great experiments will be. Knowledge of human nature and of history teaches unequivocally that the secularist experiment must end in moral breakdown and spiritual nostalgia. In what way Islam will survive is unpredictable. There are many signs that point to its gradually dying away, even among the simple people of the villages. There is hardly any training of leaders, because the government applies here its policy of starvation. One vainly asks where Islam is still manifesting itself in Turkey as a living flame. Yet, to ring the death-knell over it would certainly be too rash in this present world of startling revolutions.

Iran, again, offers a different picture. Here also was a country on the verge of ruin and already with a chequered history regarding the conflict between Islam and modern civilization. In this case too, the orientation of the Westernizing elements had always been towards France and its famous revolution of 1789. Iran, like Turkey, has taken a new road in its history by means of resolute self-willed reform and reconstruction under the leadership of one man, Riza Shah Pehlevi, the impelling forces being nationalism and secularism. While the religious policy of Turkey has been plainly spectacular, that of Iran is more gradual, but the nationalist and secularist determination in the leader is not less strong. Riza Khan's *coup d'état* had, on account of the Iranian circumstances, not the same excess of heroic appeal that Mustafa Kamal's exploit of national regeneration had. The clergy in Iran held a far stronger hierarchical position and had a much greater command over the minds of the people than the Turkish clergy had. Mustafa Kamal's task was to smash the Shari'a to pieces; Riza Khan's more arduous task was to undermine cunningly the seemingly impregnable position of the powerful religious caste of the *mujtahids*. In 1925 they prevented Riza's plan to make Iran a republic by denouncing it as anti-Islamic. Yet it is amazing that he has succeeded to a very great extent in the crushing of the power of the *mujtahids* within the small compass of one decade. To think about it is to realize once more how full of extraordinary revolutions the world has been in the last fifteen years.

This difference of background explains the gradualness of the Iranian religious policy. The integral reorganization of the country in all departments of life and administration goes hand in hand with a legislation that marks step by step the emancipation from the ancient Islamic system. Religious freedom is not among the liberties guaranteed by the constitution. Islam is still the state religion, and a Committee of Moslem *ulemas* has still an official position in the administration of the legislation of the country. However, by his new legislation in different Codes, by his far-reaching measures as to dress, emancipation of woman, prohibition of the veil, introduction of sports and gymnastics for girls, altering of the marriage law, imposition of military service on theological students, and many other measures, Riza Shah Pehlevi has weakened Islam considerably as the ruling force of all life-spheres. In other words, in Iran, too, the *Corpus Islamicum* has been curtailed. In 1935 Riza Shah went even so far as to forbid what is the bulwark of religious tradition and frenzy, namely the flagellations and the *taziyehs* (dramatic representations at the tenth day of the Muharram). In the same year the Id-al-Qurban was prohibited. All these measures and many more have been accompanied by a systematic glorification of the brilliant pre-Moslem past of Iran. Yet it is interesting to note again the difference between the outspoken secularism of Turkey and the veiled secularism of Iran. In Turkey all new measures are and were motivated by the argument of self-reliance; in Iran they are all justified by quotation from the *Quran* and the Traditions. The continuity with Islam is not broken. For the time being, however, the powerful position of the *mujtahids* is broken. As H. Filmer tells us in *The Pageant of Persia*, the Shah demonstrated this unequivocally at the opening of the tenth session of the Majlis on 6th June 1936. He wore a European military cap and took it off, contrary to all Eastern custom. During his speech the principal *Mujtahid* did not, as usual, stand beside him, and no Moslem dignitaries were present.

Again we have to repeat that the future of Islam and of religion in Iran is unpredictable. The moral emptiness of secularism must in the long run, when the nationalist elation and tension have diminished, become manifest and reveal its devastating aspect. Islam has been tamed and clipped, but not eliminated. Dictatorial rules are by the nature of the case full of quick and startling results, but they are uncertain because they depend on incalculable personal elements. These are reasons enough why it is impossible to see the future clearly.

. . . .

While these momentous changes are going on all over the Moslem world, men and women continue to satisfy their needs with the ordinary religious means of saint-worship, pilgrimages, visits at shrines and tombs, participation in the exercises of the mystical orders, which have still an enormous sway over the minds of simple people and intellectuals alike. Just as in Hinduism the *guru* or *pir* or *mullah* or *sheich* is the director of the souls and minds of untold thousands. It is extraordinarily instructive to read in this respect the youth reminiscences of Taha Hussein, the brilliant Egyptian scholar.

In the intellectual realm the usual explanation of Islam as the religion of fraternity, of reason, of reconciliation between faith and science is offered in many books and pamphlets. Reacting on the problems of to-day, Islam is also recommended as the ideal middle course, the *via aurea*, between selfishness and charity, the religion of aristocratic democracy, of common sense and adaptability to man's needs and propensities. Most of these courses of argument are covertly or openly offered as providing a means of comparison with Christianity, and are often combined with attacks on that religion. The most active agent in the broadcasting of this apologetic and polemical literature are the Ahmadyya, and it must be said that they make, generally speaking, a real impression on the mind of the Moslem public with this line of argument. The feeling of superiority is still stirring in nearly every Moslem mind and it feels satisfied by this kind of literature. This is not surprising, because the Moslem tenets can easily be rationalized (as the predilection for Islam on the part of the eighteenth century Deists and adherents of " natural religion " teaches), and the spiritual confusion in the world of to-day largely prevents quieter investigation.

Footnote to page 246.

This and the following is, of course, written in order to evaluate the situation as it was before the outbreak of the present war between Japan and China.

CHAPTER VIII

THE MISSIONARY APPROACH

IN the preceding chapters we have seen in what kind of world Christianity is confronting the great non-Christian religions, and what are the different moods in which the missionary spirit of the Christian Church is trying to express itself. Further, the essential nature of Christianity, according to what we have called the prophetic religion of Biblical realism, has been outlined ; and a sketch of the elementary forces and factors which condition the past and the present of the non-Christian religions has been given. Now we have reached the point where the proper subject of this book has to be discussed. As the satisfactory treatment of a problem is always dependent on the place and rank it occupies in the complex whole of problems to which it belongs, some stocktaking and drawing of conclusions is advisable in order to know where we stand.

The experience, then, of a hundred and fifty years of modern missions and of modern history in general, and of a hundred and fifty years of assiduous investigation into the huge complexes of spiritual life that are represented in the living non-Christian religions, has taught us some precious lessons which the missionary enterprise cannot afford to forget if it will be up-to-date in the deepest sense of this word.

The first lesson is this. The impression with which modern missions started their career, namely, that this universe of living non-Christian religions was adequately conceived by taking it to be a vast, degrading and decaying section of the spiritual life of mankind, steeped in darkness and error, has turned out to be utterly erroneous. The annals of modern missions testify to the natural vitality and tenacious strength as well as the inertia of these religions.

They are the product of man's great efforts in the field of religion, and it must be affirmed with all possible clearness that the primitive apprehension of existence, from which the great naturalist religions sprang, has proved to be particularly creative both for good and ill in the matter of religion.

A very chastening and salutary lesson has also been that it is no longer possible to identify a so-called " Christian " civilization with Christianity. Empirical, historical Christianity, although its fundamental position is very different, has also to be viewed largely as a specimen of human effort in the field of religion, and therefore to be brought into line with the other religions as expressions of human spiritual life. The many striking similarities between historical Christianity and the other religions, evident in the startling correspondences in psychological experience and theological expression, are therefore not at all disquieting facts which need to be explained away, but the best evidences by which the unity of man as a religious being is demonstrated. Or to put it in other words, all the types of religion in the world and their variegated manifestations—the naturalist, the mystical, the moralist, etc.—have found their sublime and their more degraded expression in all religions, empirical Christianity included.

The significant difference between historical Christianity and the other religions lies in another direction than that of grade or richness of religious experience. Within the other religions the naturalist, the mystical, the moralist and other types and variations of religion are, to take only their most lofty embodiments, the development of apprehensions inherent in and fundamental to these religions ; in historical Christianity they are always somehow misapprehensions of the prophetic religion of Biblical realism. The high and pure quality of religious and moral life that occurs in other religions as well as in historical Christianity is, we have now learnt, quite natural. It is evidence of the high capacity man has shown in the course of history in every branch of life, and consequently also in that of religion. The many appalling and abject phenomena in the non-Christian religions and also in historical Christianity are also quite natural, not, of course, in the sense of praiseworthy and un-objectionable, but in that of being the expression of the other side of man's double nature.

In this light it becomes clear that the two opposite attitudes customary in missionary circles are equally wrong and unrealistic. Some speak grudgingly or fault-findingly about the heights of the non-Christian religions and are inclined to lay all stress on their horrible depths. Others assiduously emphasize the heights of these religions but remain largely silent about the dark sides. Both, therefore, have a distorted view of these religions, not so much because they unduly vituperate or unduly praise them (although they certainly do so), but because they have a distorted view of man, whose nature is angelic and satanic. We must honestly recognize the angel as well as the demon in man, wherever we find him, in Christendom, in Hinduism, in China or anywhere else. All superiority-feeling is ridiculous from the standpoint of cultural history ; and from the special religious standpoint implied in the Gospel which gives to a real believer in Christ the status of a forgiven sinner, it is in direct antagonism to the rudiments of essential Christianity.

Another lesson that modern missions must take very seriously in order not to foster misguided expectations or illusions, is the solid but never duly realized fact that these great non-Christian religions are to be understood in the first place as complex civilizations and social structures. This has enormous consequences for the way in which the modern missionary enterprise has to estimate the human possibilities and limitations of its peculiar modes of activity and appeal. All rash prophesying (such as has been so profusely practised in missionary publications) about the approaching destruction of such religions is naive.

In the first place social structures are often unusually tenacious, and, in the second place, the decline or the survival of such religions is, just because they are civilizations and social structures, more dependent on other (political, social, cultural) than purely religious factors. The term " religious " in connection with these religions is nearly always used in the specially " religious " sense of a life of conscious fellowship with God or of direct religious experience. It cannot be too often said that, when speaking in terms of life-systems, religion is a complex cultural, political and social entity, and the word " religious " therefore has primarily a social connotation. Modern missions, by principle and by necessity, work only through moral and religious persuasion and therefore they cannot and will not bring to bear upon the situation other influences than those that are strictly religious. The political, the social and the cultural factors, which stand largely outside the scope of missionary activity (although it is, of course, not without influence upon them), are therefore of greater significance for the negative or positive development of these religions as social institutions than the various instruments of missionary impact.

This alone is sufficient to demonstrate that the problem of the secularization of the East cannot, from the missionary point of view, be handled in the simple categories of rejection or approval. *If* the non-Christian religions are to be overthrown, as the phrase has it, it is not likely to happen as the result of the direct efforts of missions to replace these religions by Christianity, but as the outcome of a definite concatenation of these indirect factors, which is not in human hands. The highly important conclusion to which this leads is that Christianity's eventually becoming the dominant religion instead of the other religions cannot be represented as the simple result of the contest between truth and error, as was done so floridly in the militarist missionary rhetoric of the past, for the history of the disappearance of religions and their substitution by others teaches unambiguously that many political and cultural factors are of decisive importance in bringing this result about.

Further, the aim of all missionary work has therefore to be the clear and persevering witness in words and acts to Christian truth and life and the building up of living Christian communities, trustfully leaving to God what He will do with the work of His servants. This aim brings with it an enormous liberation of the mind from all agitated thinking and acting, and a purely religious attitude of lifting the eyes to the mountains whence help comes. Modern missions strive for a purely religious revolution through moral and religious persuasion. The modern world-situation which divorces religion from the other spheres of life expresses itself also in the principles of religious neutrality. This is a typically Christian product, because the peculiar sensitiveness that attaches to it derives from the fact that religion is assumed to be an inner conviction and not conformity to a standardized mode of group-life. Thus, Christianity will not find itself in the situation in which it was after Constantine and in the Middle Ages, when the overthrow of Roman-Greek paganism and the annihilation of the different forms of West European heathenism were mainly the result of political and cultural measures and revolutions, which aimed at the victory of Christianity as a *social* phenomenon. Modern missions can never aim at this, because the concrete situation as well as the purely religious tenor of its activity excludes it. The modern missionary enterprise may therefore be compared to David, who in his combat with Goliath put aside the armour, the helmet and the sword of Saul, because he could " not move with these," and trusted to the " sling in his hand " (1 Sam. xvii. 39). The sling in its hand is the clear and persevering witness in words and acts to Christian truth and life and the building up of living Christian communities.

Still another lesson, far-reaching in its effect on the whole character and temperament of our missionary thinking, planning and expectation, is connected with the well-known fact that, through the witness and the activities of missions, the religious, moral and social outlook in the non-Christian world has to a considerable degree become permeated and leavened by " Christian " ideas, ideals and standards. In our description of the present condition of the non-Christian religions we have often had occasion to allude to this fact. Many ideas and motives that can historically be proved to be fruits from the tree of Christianity are incorporated in the modern expressions of the ancient religions. Christian modes of worship, or religious education, nurture and propaganda are freely used and assimilated. It is not exaggeration, or Christian self-complacency, but simply stating a fact to say that the process of purification and revivification which within the last hundred years has come over all great non-Christian religions is to a great extent due to the invigorating example of Christianity as represented by the missionary enterprise. The homage that in the modernization of the non-Christian religions is paid to the ethical and social note in religious life has been learnt from Christianity, rooted as it is in the prophetic religion of the Kingdom of holiness and righteousness, in the Kingdom of God. This *indirect* influence of Christian missions on the religious and on the whole social and cultural, and by virtue of that, even on the political, evolution of the modern East is really enormous. Latourette uses the term " mass modification " for this permeative process. Many people, inside and outside missionary circles, see in this indirect influence the greatest and most important result of the missionary enterprise. Even many friends of missions conceive this permeation to be either the kind of result with which missions ought gladly to be satisfied (only, if possible, in a still more accentuated form) or take it as an embryonic form of Christianity that will in the long run develop into a well-made, living body of functioning Christian life and conviction.

This appreciation of the process of permeation is, it seems, erroneous, because from the standpoint of theology and from that of daily experience with the non-Christian religions it is naive. It takes dreams, created by a noble type of humanistic idealism, as realities. Theologically speaking it is naive, because it tacitly assumes that conscious and exclusive loyalty to Christ and to what His life, His words and His work mean, is the natural outgrowth of idealistic attitudes and ideas. This tacit assumption is in glaring contradiction with the prophetic religion of Biblical realism which is (as has been shown) the " crisis " of all religions, philosophies, idealisms and world-views, none excepted. It is in no less glaring contrast with the actual facts as daily experience with the non-Christian religions presents them to us. Everyone who is familiar with conditions in the East knows that many non-Christian peoples have no objection whatever to recognizing Christ as one of the highest religious figures humanity has produced. To give Him an honourable place in the different pantheons does not meet with serious opposition. But to recognize Him and what He represents as the Lord of life, to whom supreme loyalty is due, is resolutely refused and rejected even by those who revere Him. Gandhi is a very clear example of this.

And what other reason than the inner conviction that He is *the* Truth and the sole One who is entitled to claim supreme loyalty from everyone, will induce anyone to risk the painful experiment of abandoning his ancestral religion with its many precious social and emotional bonds? This is especially true in the sphere of the naturalist religions that are by their syncretistic nature entirely bent on absorption, annexation and assimilation. By their relativism they have taught their adherents to give every religion and form of worship its " due " place, and have inculcated in them an aversion from making a definite, irrevocable choice. Moreover, a little sociological insight makes it evident that permeation, however valuable it may be culturally (and it certainly is), never can make this permeating religion the dominant moulder of religious and moral life. That is possible only when this religion is, *socially* speaking, the officially recognized and dominant spiritual force, or when it is, not a disembodied set of ideas and ideals that lend a definite colouring to the already existing apprehensions, but a clear-cut, self-conscious religious entity. Willoughby in his *The Soul of the Bantu* justly remarks that, despite all legitimate criticism of institutional Christianity, it is impossible to keep the essence of our religion alive unless it works through some human institution. Only if one of the alternatives mentioned above is realized in a civilization or in a people can one reasonably say that this religion is an established religion that has a really determinative influence in such a culture. In all other cases one can only speak of it as a more or less influential factor within a people and a civilization where a different religion or life-apprehension is the tacitly recognized spiritual authority.

On theological, on religious and on sociological grounds it is therefore vain and illegitimate to expect that the remarkable permeation of the East with ideals and ideas that are, historically speaking, derived from Christianity will naturally grow in the long run into a self-conscious Christian Church, for it is a mistake to conceive this permeative reality as an embryonic Christianity. One might even go further and state that it has, to a great extent, as experience teaches, rather the effect of stiffening the mind against religious change than of predisposing the mind in its favour. The great non-Christian religions have utilized the permeation of Christian ideas and ideals for their own internal and external strengthening. Movements such as the Brahmo Samaj have not proved stepping-stones to Christianity, as was originally expected. This stiffening reassertion in the process of assimilative change is quite natural. Religions all over the world are not pondering philosophers, who try disinterestedly to make out where truth lies ; they are huge social bodies (comprising life-patterns, ideas, attitudes, volitions and strong emotions), that, as in the case of all social bodies, instinctively strive for self-assertion and self-perpetuation. Men like Gandhi, Tagore and Radhakrishnan, who evince each in his own peculiar way a strong permeation with ideals and ideas deriving from Christianity, are no " unbaptized Christians," as F. Heiler terms the two first-mentioned on account of the Christian elements in their thought-world, but have rather become invigorated Hindus by the process, with an unmistakable element of irritation in their attitude towards Christianity. There are elements in the concrete situations which make much of this curious blend of assimilation and irritation intelligible, but even if these elements did not exist, this blend is not at all strange when the peculiar character of Christianity, in the sense of Biblical realism, is kept in mind.

To *decide* for Christ and the world He stands for implies a break with one's religious past, whether this past is " Christian " in the qualified sense of the word or non-Christian. This break is something radically different from taking a sympathetic attitude towards His personality and teaching. It is even unfair and contradictory to call men like Gandhi and Tagore " unbaptized Christians " as Heiler does, because this interpretation of these two men by Heiler is given in order to accentuate the superb qualifications which Hinduism (in his opinion) possesses for forming a religious synthesis with Christianity. It suggests, however, the inferiority of Hinduism and the superiority of Christianity, and demonstrates that Heiler is still unconsciously haunted by the idea of superiority and inferiority in the relation of Christianity to the other religions. As a matter of fact, in the case of Gandhi and Tagore, however drastically their activist attitude towards life may differ from Hinduism as we know it, and however emancipated many of their leading ideas may be from dominant Hindu conceptions, the crucial fact is that they consciously keep to Hinduism as their recognized spiritual home, and even announce their new interpretation as being *for the sake of Hinduism*.

These few remarks about the mass-modification as caused by permeation are given in order to provide a warning against vain expectations and wrong missionary directives. They are not given to minimize the great importance of this cultural permeative process and the share missions had and have in it. This permeative process will go on in the future, probably to an even greater extent, and it is highly desirable that missions and the Christian Churches should continue to partake in it, not for the sake of permeation, but for the sake of revealing the true nature of the Christian Church as a body that releases refreshing forces of light and life because of obedience to Christ and His Spirit.[1]

This discussion, as to how far the value of permeation goes, leads us on to another important conclusion from all that has been said in the preceding chapters. This conclusion is the more important because it furnishes the fundamental background for all thinking on adaptation and indigenization.

The conclusion we have in view is that the only valid motive and purpose of missions is and alone can be to call men and peoples to confront themselves with God's acts of revelation and salvation for man and the world as presented in Biblical realism, and to build up a community of those who have surrendered themselves to faith in and loving service of Jesus Christ. Why is this the only valid motive and

[1] In Chapter X. we will return to this subject.

purpose ? Because only on the basis of this apostolic attitude and consciousness is the missionary enterprise really lastingly tenable and reasonable. All other motives and purposes may, according to circumstances, be of greater or less secondary importance and value, but if they take the place of this primary motive and purpose, mission work as such is no really tenable activity and must in the long run die from its lack of valid foundation.

All these other motives and purposes labour under an overt or covert relativistic subjectivism. To infuse Christian ideals and ideas into another people or religion or civilization and to do that in a sympathetic, generous spirit ; to instil into the emerging world culture the blessings of an enlightened, free and reverent spirit ; to seek with men everywhere a more adequate fulfilment of the " divine possibilities " of personal and social life ; to strive after the spiritual unity of mankind—these are all very noble, altruistic and humane ideals, which have their own peculiar value and necessity, *provided they are kept in their place.* If they usurp the place of the apostolic motive, which is the alone valid and tenable one, they transform the Christian Church into a goodwill agency for the diffusion of refined and cultured idealism, which has lost all intrinsic relation with the central apostolic consciousness that we are to be witnesses to God and His revelational dealing with man and the world.

This, however, is not the only weak side of this standpoint. Another of its fatal weaknesses, though not always apparent on the surface, is that this subjectivist idealism can claim no right whatever to insist upon the value of its exertions in the face of other religions and civilizations. What will it answer if this foreign religious civilization says : I do not want your help and your permeations, despite all the nobility and charitableness of spirit in which you offer that help, for I have my own spiritual resources to draw upon and want to become saved according to my own fashion ? There is, from the standpoint of secondary motives and purposes that have been falsely converted into primary ones, no valid answer to this argument.

There is no valid answer possible, not even if one takes

the line that Jesus Christ is the only way by which men can reach a *satisfying* experience of God, or if one starts from the idea that the central concern of Christian missions is to be found in " the highest spiritual interests of mankind." Why not ? Because—it is rather paradoxical to state this—these standpoints, that are born out of abhorrence of absolutist views and that seek the test of a religion not in an *a priori* certainty of its truth, but in the pragmatic demonstration of its worth, are themselves absolutisms. For, as *in their opinion* Jesus Christ provides men with the most satisfying experience of God, and missions are concerned with the good of " humanity," they think that they have the right to intrude upon the religious civilizations of the East. What will they answer if these civilizations and peoples say : " Our experience of God is as satisfying as yours. How do you know that yours is more satisfying ? We have our own ideas about our highest spiritual interests." There is no answer from this standpoint because, although it is born of a deep and honest loyalty to Christ, it remains too subjectivistic.

The only valid and indestructible foundation of missions is the apostolic consciousness of joyful obedience to God's Will as manifested in the revelation in Christ, and our gratitude for this divine gift. All questions of superiority in the field of cultural achievement or psychological religious experience are irrelevant in this context. No pretensions whatever, derived from presumably superior ethical or religious or cultural elements, have anything to do with the apostolic claim and obligation of Christianity. Its only foundation is the objective and plain reality of God's revelation in Christ, and therefore, speaking fundamentally, it is quite immaterial whether the world asks for it or not. The only way to become wholly purged from all kinds of superiority-feeling is not the direct pursuit of a sympathetic or generous spirit towards other cultural experiences, however praiseworthy and valuable this may be, but the radically apostolic attitude ; for this presupposes the not less radical humility that issues from the fact that all men of all civilizations (the " Christian " included) are, in the light of God's revelation, forlorn sinners and rebellious children of God.

" Orthodox " as well as " liberal " Christianity must therefore cease to try to effect the purification of the missionary atmosphere by quarrelling about the invalidity or validity of non-Christian religious experience and achievement ; for the great significance of this experience and achievement is a solid fact. Orthodox and liberal Christians must both enter the purifying flames of the apostolic vision which confronts all civilizations and religions with God's revelation in Christ, and then discovers their common solidarity in forlornness and their being equally called to deliverance. In other words, in this case as in all other cases, our starting-point must be the dynamic theocentric world of Biblical realism, which is the direct antithesis to the static intellectualist conception of revelation so widely current, and also to the naive evolutionary conception of Christianity as a movement of growing truth. The only thing that being a Christian can mean is to make continuously renewed discoveries in the dynamic world of God's revelation and so grow gradually to the stature of full-grown men in Christ (cf. Eph. iv. 13).

In this light it is undeniable that the widely prevalent aversion to evangelization, to proselytism, to conversion, and the recommendation of " sharing religious experience " or of social service as the only valid missionary methods, are the offspring of a fundamental religious confusion. It is clear as daylight that once the cardinal fact is grasped that the apostolic theocentric apprehension is the only valid Christian apprehension, the Christian Church has not only the right but also the duty to take conversion and evangelization as prime necessities for mankind. To regard proselytizing, evangelization and conversion as " invading and violating the sacredness of personality " is built on a misinterpretation of religion as primarily the purveyor of psychological experience, which misinterpretation has lost all consciousness of the prophetic character of the Christian revelation. Nock in his *Conversion* explains very lucidly that the pagan religions in the Roman Empire did not really know the concept " conversion," because naturalist religions cannot conceive conversion in its real sense. The concept " conversion " occurs only in its intense and essential meaning in the realm of the prophetic religions. Jesus started His public career with the call to conversion, for the Kingdom cannot be grasped except through conversion. The concept of conversion in its essential meaning can only grow in the prophetic religion of the Christian revelation, because this is the sole religion that knows the absolute difference between good and evil. The inherent relativism of naturalist religions prevents them from having a radical conception of conversion.

The emphasis laid lately on " sharing religious experience " and on social service in substitution for evangelization as the most valid missionary approach, issues from the same religious confusion. " Sharing " labours under a conception of religion that takes it primarily as a psychological, cultural and immanent value. Making social service the main and most legitimate missionary approach is the direct fruit of a pragmatist evaluation of religion. In both cases the real basis of missions and the prophetic and apostolic character of Christianity are destroyed, although in reality this destruction will remain concealed for a certain period. Or to put it in other words, in both cases the revelational basis of Christianity is implicitly, though often unconsciously, denied. The very urgent necessity that religion must find expression in the right quality of life—the thesis on which social service as the main missionary motive and approach is based, and which is in itself a right and indispensable proposition—never can wipe out the fact that in the field of religion we have only this alternative : either the paramount thing in a religion is that it conveys objective truth without which life has no real meaning, or its truth-quality is of secondary or minor importance and we remain for ever caught in the chains of relativism, golden as they sometimes appear to be.

Evangelization, proselytism and conversion, then, belong to the core of the missionary enterprise. The real difficulties that exist in regard to these three concepts and attitudes in relation to the missionary approach are of quite a different order, and even apart from the fundamentally religious confusion we have treated already, make it intelligible why so much confusion and so much opposition have arisen around them. In the first place, the concrete forms in which the emphasis on and the occupation with evangelization, proselytism and conversion often exhibit themselves, in many cases make the impression of crude propaganda and intrusion upon the inner life of a fellow-man. A deal of what goes by the name of evangelization or proselytism or conversion is not to be identified with apostolic and prophetic obedience and witness, but often looks more like the mishandling of another man's spiritual life, although it springs from the conviction of missionary obligation. The protest of " liberal " Christians against this is often justified, for its attitude is often too oblivious of the radical humility and sensitivity that are included in the prophetic and apostolic consciousness of being pointers to God's revelation, just as the dread of evangelization felt by " liberal " Christians is often born of a complete, though unintentional, sacrifice of the revelational character of Christianity. A great deal of the " orthodox " missionary attitude needs as much purification and regeneration in the cleansing waters of Biblical realism as the " liberal " attitude does.

In the second place, another important reason why the problem of conversion and proselytism is so vehemently discussed at the present time is not at all religious in the strict sense of the word. It is a result of the fact that all over the world the great non-Christian religious systems, like many States, are in a stage of re-assertive consolidation that reveals itself in a hyperbolic sentiment of group-solidarity. We explained in the preceding chapter that Islam as a religion is this group-solidarity incarnate, and that this is the reason why it offers such a stubborn resistance to all missionary effort. With the great naturalist non-Christian religions the situation is somewhat different, but essentially the same. They also, as was pointed out in the fifth chapter, are religiously sanctioned group-solidarities.[1] Because of their naturalist character they do not understand the radical sense in which conversion is meant in Christianity. Moreover,

[1] It ought to be said that the Christian Churches are always prone to succumb to the same danger.

in the modern deluge they are in a state of defensive consolidation and self-assertion, which intensifies the inherent tendency towards stressing the necessity of religious conformity as an expression of group-loyalty. This is the real background of the protest against conversion and proselytism which is so specially strong in India. That it is led by a man of such deep moral and religious sensitivity as Gandhi is one of the puzzling features of the situation in this puzzling country. Knowing this background the missionary enterprise need not be perturbed by it, but must strike its roots deeper in the apostolic prophetic soil of Biblical realism.

" Sharing religious experience " and " social service " are wrong and misleading as definitions of the real missionary motive and purpose ; but as methods of approach and expression of the Christian mind they are valid and very valuable. Apart from the fundamental religious confusion that has been treated already there are other reasons which can account for the particular emphasis at present laid on these two attitudes. There is the haunting dread of all superiority-feeling ; the delicate and justified desire to have real human contact on the footing of spiritual give and take ; the partly-intelligible aversion from " dogmatic " religion and many forms of too one-sided stress on preaching, which is often in reality mere annoying interference. Another reason is the noble insistence on the necessity to demonstrate in practice that to be a Christian means a new quality of life, strengthened by the contemporary situation in which Christianity is tested as to its practical moral and social value. All these elements have co-operated in making the emphasis on sharing of religious experience and social service intelligible and partly justified. Every good missionary who knows something of the apostolic and prophetic temperament of Biblical realism knows about sharing religious experience, and even loves it ; likewise he sees the great necessity of social service and will be devoted to it. To raise these methods of approach and expression of the Christian and missionary mind to the status of essential motive and purpose is a different matter. When to this is added the rejection of the validity of its apostolic and prophetic inspiration we have, fundamentally speaking, nothing else than the suicide of missions, though in practice they may continue for a certain period of time and even accomplish much work of noble quality.

.   .   .   .

GENERAL REMARKS ON APPROACH

The object we had in view in our stocktaking and drawing of conclusions was to emphasize the fact that the essential meaning of Christianity is to witness to the world of divine and human realities as revealed in Jesus Christ. We cannot make of it what we like. As T. C. Chao remarked in 1929 in Jerusalem : " It is very important to express Christianity in Chinese forms, but it is still more important first to understand and to live it." Without this fundamental clearness about what Christianity is in the sense of the prophetic religion of Biblical realism, and what it is after, all approach to the non-Christian religions results in confusion of ends and methods. In our sketch of the Christian faith and the Christian ethic we have tried to effect this fundamental clarification. This statement of Christian truth, in accordance with the character of Biblical realism as being the tale of God's self-disclosure and of the disclosure of the genuine condition of man and the world in the light of the divine Self-disclosure, is the standard of reference for the religious life of all mankind.

In its searching light we know how to define our position towards the non-Christian religions, and we become clear-sighted about the problem of the point of contact. It delivers us from delusive endeavours as, for instance, that it is possible to find in " higher " and seemingly kindred elements of other religions, taken as fragments detached from the total reality, the starting-point of the road that leads to Christ and to Christian truth. The practical monotheism and theism of the *bhakti*-religions, for example, is in the proper sense of the word no real point of contact for Christian theism. In the first place, because this practical monotheistic theism in the *bhakti*-religions is in its total religious apprehension a secondary and inorganic growth. Now the determining factor in every religion is its total religious apprehension. In the *bhakti*-religion this total apprehension is anthropocentric and soteriocentric and not theocentric. In the second place, because Christianity is no religious philosophy with a theistic God-idea, but a religion that proclaims the God and Father of Jesus Christ as the sole and absolutely trustworthy Lord of life, to whom alone allegiance is due. God is proclaimed as the Eternal and not recommended as the most satisfying conception of God, which is the end of religious philosophy.

Notwithstanding the close theological and psychological similarities between Christianity and the *bhakti*-religions in India and the Far East concerning faith and grace, this is not a point of contact in the sense that it is a stem on which the Biblical conception of faith and grace can naturally be grafted, for faith and grace in Christianity and in the *bhakti*-religions are embedded in a totality of religious apprehension entirely different from each other. For the rest, it is very noteworthy that the *bhaktas* do not show any more inclination to accept so-called kindred Christianity than others do. Rather the contrary is the case. The fictitious similarity acts more as a barrier than as a bridge. This reveals the great gulf there is, religiously speaking. Also it is very noteworthy that Pandita Ramabai, who had grown up in the splendid atmosphere of the *bhakti*-religion of Western India, after her conversion to Christianity deprecated all adaptation and assimilation and exclusively stressed the contrast, by virtue of her deep religious sense.

Yet, although fundamentally speaking there is no point of contact, in practice the religious needs and aspirations that are embedded in these great religious systems often offer, of course, splendid opportunities of practical, *human* contact.

To sum up. When the word "approach" is taken in the sense of Christianity as a total religious system approaching the non-Christian religions as total religious systems, there is only difference and antithesis, and this must be so because they are radically different. To minimize this results in a weakening and blurring of the true character of Christianity.

Wilamowitz in his already-quoted book on *The Faith of the Greeks* mentions as one of the principal reasons of the victory of Christianity in the ancient world the fact that it rejected all other gods and proclaimed the absolute monarchy of the One Living God ; in other words, that it remained true to its essential nature. To remain true to its essential character is also to-day the unbreakable law for Christianity.

In former days the modern missionary enterprise manifested its obedience to this exclusive character in its wellknown aggressive, controversial attitude towards the nonChristian religions. This was a wrong intellectualist expression of a right intuition. It was deservedly met by irritation and counter-aggression, and inevitably interpreted as offensive pride, so creating the least favourable atmosphere for a deep and humane religious encounter. This aggressive, controversial attitude has therefore to be entirely abandoned on religious and psychological grounds. On the religious ground it is contradictory to the radical humility which is, as has been explained, implied in the fact that the apostolic nature of missions means gratefully and persuasively to entreat men to surrender to God's revelation in Christ, which is not our religious achievement or possession, but God's free gift. On the psychological ground it is unwise and unfair, and therefore arouses opposition on the part of deep-seated loyalties.

The reaction in missionary circles against this aggressive controversial approach has led to the so-called sympathetic approach of tracing similarities and trying to build bridges on the assumption that Christianity is the crown of the best in the non-Christian religions. In different places we have tried to show already that this mode of approaching the non-Christian religions as systems of religion in their totality, proves, on closer investigation, to be fictitious. It makes the religious mistake of overlooking the radical difference between the Christian revelation and the other religions. It makes also a great psychological mistake. Although it honestly starts from the very laudable and (for a missionary) indispensable desire to show open-mindedness and genuine sympathy for the best in the other religions, it starts from the assumption that Christianity is the crown of these religions, and so it evinces a hidden feeling of superiority, that is rightly sensed as condescension. This, in its turn, arouses also sentiments of opposition on the part of deep-seated loyalties. These sentiments are strengthened by the fact that non-Christians, even if the judgment of a Christian about their religion were fair and right, naturally think his judgment unfair, and so the exact opposite of what this mode of approach aims at is achieved.

Evidently there must be another mode of approach. Past missionary experience teaches that the aggressive and controversial assertion of the Christian claim of paramount exclusive religious truth is a wrong and utterly inadequate translation of the apostolic and prophetic nature of the revelation in Christ, and that the " sympathetic " approach of Christianity as crown and fulfilment neglects too much this translation and is beside the mark. A deeper knowledge of the religious life of mankind has taught us to recognize our own image in the way in which, through the fusion of high aspirations and far aberrations in the religions of mankind, the greatness and misery of man are inextricably inter-related. Their true character is revealed in man's inherent relatedness to God as a creature of God, called to do His Will. Is there a modern mode of approach that is true to the apostolic urge in its double-sided character ? This involves the announcement of the Message of God which is not adaptable to any religion or philosophy, and which yet has to be presented in a persuasive and winning manner so as to evince the real Christian spirit of service to God and to man. About the first enough has been said. Now we must turn to the second.

We propose to call this mode of approach the evangelistic, and distinguish three aspects in it : evangelism, adaptation and service. We bring these three aspects under the heading of evangelistic approach in order to emphasize that all activity of the Church in words and deeds, in preaching, in life, in forms of expression and in social service has to spring from its prime apostolic nature. With adaptation we will deal later in this chapter ; with service in the tenth chapter.

Here we confine ourselves to the evangelistic approach in particular.

The evangelistic approach means to have constantly in mind that a missionary is a living human being among other living human beings, whose minds are soaked in the atmosphere of their own religions. This being so, it goes without saying that it is impossible and not permissible to approach them without a thorough knowledge of their religious and general human background.[1] This includes some important consequences.

In the first place, there is the obligation to strive for the presentation of the Christian truth in terms and modes of expression that make its challenge intelligible and related to the peculiar quality of reality in which they live. For the missionary or evangelist this means a constant process of self-denying training, for the love of Christ and the love of souls, to find the ways in which to tune this presentation to the peculiar sound-waves of these peculiar human hearts. We take it too easily for granted that we really present the Message, where, as is often the case, we speak in a quite mysterious language. It is possible to interpret the Christian truth, say, in Chinese to Chinese and in Tamil to Tamils and yet to speak in mysteries, because through the lack of this self-denying training one might as well have spoken in Latin. The preaching of the Gospel in a foreign world with a different spiritual climate and background is a translation of meanings and not of detached words. Openness and truthfulness and not antagonism are the natural implication of this attitude, because to win men for Christ is the dominant inspiration in this activity.

In the second place, it includes the presentation of the Christian truth against the background of the universal human problems of aspiration, frustration, misery and sin, because these men and women must be for us in the first place human beings, fellow-men, and not non-Christians. This is of fundamental importance for a real approach. Connected with this thoroughly human approach, it is

[1] We refer to the end of Chapter IV. where the missionary himself is discussed as the most important point of contact in the practical aspect.

necessary to emphasize constantly that the Gospel is not in a departmentalized way exclusively concerned with some " religious interests," but that it penetrates all human life.

One of the fundamental laws of all presentation of the Christian truth everywhere in the world is that this truth is vitally related to all spheres and problems of life, the most common and trivial as well as the most elevated. The millions of the East are, by their circumstances, deeply absorbed in what is called common and trivial. The simple artless way in which in the Lord's Prayer the coming of the Kingdom, the necessity of our daily bread and the concern for the temptation of sin are combined, is a splendid specimen of this thorough humanity of the Gospel. The radically religious view of life as embodied in Biblical realism is of the same vital significance to man's relation to his friend or fellow-villager, or to the way in which he spends his money or works his fields or accepts his material successes or adversities, as to the nurture of his spiritual life or to his religious needs and experiences in the more restricted sense of the word.

Controversy as a method of approach is in the present day generally abandoned, and rightly so. Yet, although it has to be abandoned as a method of approach, it cannot be altogether avoided in daily practice. The Eastern mind liked and likes religious discussion. In the past this was quite natural, just as it was the case in the past in Europe. All these civilizations had in religion their unifying factor. The higher activities of the mind were naturally expressed in theological and religious terms in the great civilizations of mediæval type, because the dominant and only available apprehension of existence was the religious one. It is therefore misleading to declare an Easterner in general more of a religious *animal disputax* than a Westerner. In the East the period in which the human mind expresses its searchings and exercises its wits in religious and theological terms has lasted longer than in the West (and still largely continues to exist there). In the West man is just as much an *animal disputax*, because he is certainly not less inquisitive of mind. The excessive differentiation of life and the consequent disappearance of religion as the unifying factor have diverted the larger part of the inquisitive and controversial spirit to the fields of philosophy, politics, and economics. The greater emotional value of religion easily produces in religious discussions and controversies a character fuller of possibilities of passion and irritation than is the case in other fields.

So the two cardinal objections to controversy in religion are the intellectualist and hence irreligious character it so easily assumes, and the bitterness and estrangement it causes thereby. Nevertheless controversy in a higher sense than the well-known kind of contest in theological and religious acumen cannot, and even should not, always be avoided. It cannot always be avoided, for it obviously follows from the fact that numberless people in the East, especially those who are steeped in their ancestral religious atmosphere, find a controversial religious conversation the most natural thing in the world. Even if the representative of Christianity systematically tries to avoid it on religious and psychological grounds, they certainly will try to force him into it again and again.

Often in such a case, by the way in which this unsought controversial situation is met, religiously and intellectually, the spiritual prestige of Christianity and the Gospel comes to be at stake. Taught by past experience and by a surer grasp of the non-intellectualist and superrational character of religion, it is of vital importance that one should be alert to avoid the two principal weak spots of all controversy—the religious and the psychological—and turn them to advantage. This requires real grace, a thorough contact with the atmosphere of the Bible, especially with the tender and yet forceful way in which Jesus dealt with people, a good knowledge of the religious situation and a clear insight, springing from sympathy and love, into the psychology of the people. This side of the approach thus points again to the central importance of combining a vigorously religious conception of Christian truth with real knowledge of, and sympathy with, the people among whom one works.

This higher form of controversy as a mode of approach should not be avoided, for the sake of the moral, religious and intellectual prestige of Christianity. In countries where grand and imposing religio-philosophical systems have been developed, and where at present all specimens of modern thinking exercise thousands of minds, yielding their contribution to the moulding of the spiritual outlook, Christian truth in its fundamental nature and characteristic structure needs to be developed against the background of the concrete spiritual scene. Then these systems and spiritual currents can be laid bare as to their fundamental tenets, aspirations and aberrations in the light of the revelation in Christ. If this is done in a spirit of deep religious sincerity and moral dignity this higher kind of controversy may be a very precious thing.

Professor Hocking expresses in his pamphlet on *Evangelism* the opinion that there are wanted in the mission field what he calls " watch-towers of thought." This suggestion is very valuable, for indeed the missionary enterprise and the Younger Churches need such men in the colossal confusion of our present transitional period. To find them and *systematically* use them we must not only look to the ranks of the Christians in the Younger Churches or of the missionaries, but also to the Christian thinkers and scholars all over the world. A more deliberately thought-out marshalling and using of its forces in this respect on an ecumenical scale is an important concern for the world Christian community to-day.

Another observation that must be made is that a study of Jesus' unbiased use of the terminology and ideas of the people He spoke to, of His entrance into their joys and sorrows, of His higher opportunism which takes hold of any dominant note or need, of His method of controversy that penetrates to the depth of things, is also very rewarding and stimulating.

In closing these general remarks on approach, there is still one aspect that needs to be stressed with all possible seriousness. In our argument we have duly urged the necessity of a clear consciousness of what the Christian Message is, and of real knowledge, springing from love and sympathy, of men and their environment. Just as at the end of Chapter IV, so here we must turn to the vital significance of missionary ethics. The exquisite purity of the Message and a great compass of knowledge and insight on the part of the messenger remain largely impotent if the missionary or evangelist by what he really *is* as a man does not awaken that personal, human element of trust and confidence in himself as a man, without which all approach will remain barren. The best missionaries always stress the importance of this point. It is worth while to note that the Japanese, K. Kato, in his *The Psychology of Oriental Religious Experience*, again and again brings to the fore that often, apart from other causes, such as personal religious crisis or deliverance from the confusion of polytheism, the determining human factor in cases of conversion to Christianity has been "the respect for the Christian character of the missionary, a conduct which shows a wealth of affection, kindheartedness and manliness." The well-known utterances of Gandhi and Tagore about what they expect a missionary to be, although the way in which they express it indicates a very confused conception of Christ and of the Christian life, point in the same direction.[1]

This vital importance of the Christian personality of the missionary in its relation to the necessity of having a clear consciousness of Christian truth and a real knowledge of the world to which the approach has to be made, reminds us of St Paul's reasoning in 1 Corinthians xiii. We may speak with the tongues of men and of angels, we may have such absolute faith that we can move mountains from their place, but if we have no love, we have *nothing*. Paul with his characteristic religious radicalness does not shun the word "nothing," which word we incurably intellectual people would surround with all sorts of qualifications.

ADAPTATION

Surrender to Christ, belief in Him and allegiance to the prophetic religion of Biblical realism mean in the first place

---

[1] Gandhi said once : "Missionaries and Christians must begin to live as Christ." Tagore in a letter to a young missionary expressed it as follows : "You cannot do something good before you are yourself good. You cannot preach Christ before you have become as Christ."

a revolution, a total rupture with one's religious past, because it presupposes conversion in the deepest sense of the word. In Chapter IV we alluded to the Apostle Paul, who expresses this rupture and revolution by the well-known words that he has counted his religious past and everything else " a loss compared to the supreme value of knowing Christ Jesus my Lord " (Phil. iii. 8). This is fundamental.

However, this does not imply that Paul despises his religious past. He speaks with great reverence about it in the same passage, for although " for Christ's sake " and in comparison to the supreme knowledge of Christ it is " veriest refuse," in itself it is the world of human moral and religious endeavour, in which it becomes manifest that man, though fallen, is still related to God and has still the Law of God written in his heart. In other words, Paul and John in their day expressed and formulated the essential meaning and content of the revelation in Christ against the background of, and in conflict with, the moralistic and legalistic conception of religion in Judaism, and with the naturalistic and gnostic mysticism of the paganism of that time. So it is obvious and legitimate that Christian truth must be at present expressed against the background of, and in conflict with, the moral and religious content of the non-Christian religions.

Here we touch the problem of adaptation at its deepest point. Adaptation in the deepest sense does not mean to assimilate the cardinal facts of the revelation in Christ as much as possible to fundamental religious ideas and tastes of the pre-Christian past, but to *express* these facts by wrestling with them concretely, and so to present the Christian truth and reveal at the same time the intrinsic inadequacy of man's religious efforts for the solution of his crucial religious and moral problems. The New Testament, especially in the Synoptists and in the writings of Paul and John, is the unsurpassed document of this deep adaptation and so is our indispensable model. The more so, because there in a classic way all the central religious problems that crop up in all civilizations, religions and periods of history have been put in their right place under the light of the revelation in

Christ. These problems can be summed up under the headings of those apprehensions of the totality of existence which we have repeatedly discussed : the primitive or naturalist apprehension, the rationalist and idealist one (which is virtually a variation of the first with a strong independent character) and the prophetic one. Under the naturalist religious apprehension fall the universal religions of traditional and social cohesion and of mysticism, for all real mysticism is a child of the naturalist apprehension of life ; under the rationalist apprehension fall all forms of idealism in the shape of ethical or religious monisms. Under the prophetic apprehension fall all forms of moralism and legalism. The common human denominator is that they are all somehow conceived as a way of salvation.

In the New Testament the content of the revelation in Christ is expressed in terms coined in the process of wrestling with these universal and perennial religious motives. Paul and John lived fully in the world of their day, moved in its thought-forms and ideas, used their wording and imagery, and shared with the men of that time the way in which the world pictured itself in their minds with all its celestial and sublunary spheres. They probably did not bother much about adaptation as a special problem, *but about expression of the revelation of Christ and what it meant.* They dealt without bias with the elements of expression that were put at their disposal by the Old Testament, by Judaism, by Greek philosophy, by Oriental Gnosis and the mystery-religions, but in doing so (and this is of vital importance) their minds were neither bent on assimilation to these elements, nor on intentional refutation of them, but on presenting and formulating vigorously the revelation. So the Logos-idea, the offspring of monistic religio-philosophical thinking, was used to express the Incarnation, the scandal of all monistic religious philosophy. In his exposition of justification by faith Paul unveils the greatness and the bankruptcy of all human moralism, whose deepest kernel is the endeavour of man to achieve by his own heroic or petty efforts perfect holiness and holy perfection, springing from the smothered or poignant longing for perfection that haunts the human mind on account of its relatedness to God. Yet this universal and perennial problem Paul expresses in his great theme of the Law and the Gospel in Judaistic terms, reducing it to the terse formula that this moralism of self-perfection, self-deliverance and self-realization stands over against the revelation in Christ as the " righteousness of my own " against the " divine righteousness that rests on faith " (Phil. iii. 9). The doctrine of justification by faith is therefore not only the deepest and most radical way to unveil the inadequacy of the legalistic and moralistic solution of the problem of man as it is expressed in austere Judaism and its conception of the Law. It also shows the inadequacy of the solution presented in Kant's idealistic moralism of the categorical imperative, in Buddha's ascetic heroism of the Eightfold Path, in the aristocratic self-mastery of Zen-Buddhism, and in the masterful mental technique of Yoga.

All ways of salvation (in India called *marga*, in Muslim mysticism *tariqa* or *martaba*), usually so intimately connected with different types of mystical religion, whose intrinsic object is oneness with the divine Essence, get their real perspective in the light of the Christian revelation. In the presence of the holy righteous God and Father of Jesus Christ, there is in all ways of salvation a disregard of man's deepest problem, which is that God alone can solve it and that the only adequate way is the wayless way of man's recognition and apprehension of this divine solution by faith. All moral and religious virtues in the New Testament are hence logically set in the light of *charismata*, divine graces, and not of *yoga*, results of exertion, although often admirable and heroic.

We have seen that all the great non-Christian religions, except Islam and Judaism, are naturalistic religions. Without consciously aiming at determining the position of the revelation in Christ towards naturalistic religions, Paul has done this very thing by the way in which he calmly uses the terminology of the naturalist and sacramental mysticisms of the mystery-religions and *thereby forcefully expresses the opposite character of the prophetic religion of revelation.* He does not bother about making contrasts or building bridges, but *he is entirely absorbed in expressing the truth* and so reveals gulfs and bridges at the same time.

To take some instances. In 2 Corinthians iii. 18, believers are spoken of as reflecting the glory of the Lord with unveiled faces and being transformed by the action of the Holy Spirit into the same likeness as Himself from one glory to another. P. Wendland in his exegesis of the Epistles to the Corinthians [1] remarks that it is quite legitimate to suppose here the use of terms borrowed from the sacramental rites and mystical experiences in the mystery-cults, for these rites produced in the initiate a vision of the mystery-god and caused him to become one with the god through this vision (*henosis, theothènai*, to become one with the mystery-god, to become god, was the object of all the mystery-cults). Paul is far away from that. Although he uses the terms, he expresses the opposite, for the believers in Christ do not become God or Christ. They remain entirely distinct, but they receive and partake in the glory that shines forth from Him. Moreover this " grace " is a gift to all believers, and not, as in all mystical religion, the achievment of religious virtuosi, a conception that is radically antagonistic to the theocentric and prophetic religion of the revelation.

In Romans vi. the terms of death and resurrection that are used in connection with baptism remind one strongly of ideas and practices in the mystery-religions. Again Paul uses these terms and ideas freely to express forcefully the revelation in Christ, the exact opposite of what these mystery-religions were seeking after. According to their naturalistic character, in the mystery-religions it is the rites that effect automatically and repeatedly, just as in nature, the deification of the initiate ; it is a magical transmutation into a higher kind of nature. Paul does not shun the use of terms and ideas so near to these mystery-religions, but he uses them here also to express in a clear way that to believe in Christ is to become a quite new moral and religious being as the old self has died, free from slavery

[1] *Das Neue Testament Deutsch*, Neues Göttinger Bibelwerk.

to sin, and the new self has arisen, alive to God in Jesus Christ.[1]

.   .   .   .

The conclusion that we derive from the New Testament, the book that contains the expression of the revelation in its concrete conflict and intermingling with the Jewish and Hellenistic world of religion and civilization, is that the religion of revelation stands in revolutionary contrast to this concrete Jewish and Hellenistic world, but at the same time freely uses its ideas and thought-forms to express itself, and so Christian truth experiences its first incarnation. Pandita Ramabai's aversion to the use of the Indian religious vocabulary for her Bible translation was, it must be said with all due reverence for this great Christian personality, unnatural and mistaken. The New Testament is our example, because this incarnation of Christian truth is at the same time a vigorous assertion of its true character. In the course of history Christian truth has taken upon itself various incarnations. It did this in the historical development of the first centuries, in Augustine's philosophy of history, in the mediæval synthesis of Christian, Greek and Germanic elements, and in the various national expressions of Christianity in Protestantism. And this does not only apply to its theological formulation and emphases, but also to its expression in various forms after the pattern of social or other institutions, and through the assimilation of customs that gave to the many regional types of Christianity their peculiar flavour. History teaches that the commingling of a prophetic religion (Christianity, Islam, Judaism) with other cultural and religious spheres evokes two tendencies, namely, a self-conscious fencing-off of its nature from this alien historical and psychological atmosphere and a process of mutual interpenetration.

In many respects it would be easy to write a vigorous criticism of these many incarnations, because without any

---

[1] One could write much more extensively about the sovereign way in which in the New Testament the religious terminology of the world in its day is used to express the content of the revelation, but this much must suffice to suggest how important this is for our missionary thinking.

exception they fall short of the example set by the incarnation of Christian truth in the New Testament. They often represent more a dimming and suppression of the true character of the religion of revelation by the alien forms and instruments than an expression of it. However, the point that needs now to be made is that, in principle and for reasons of history, new incarnations and adaptations of Christianity in the concrete Asiatic and African settings are natural and legitimate. Christianity never fell and never can fall into a religious, cultural and social vacuum, and therefore must find in its various environments an intellectual, emotional and institutional expression that in its psychological and social aspects can reasonably be called an expression and not an impediment or inhibition. Barth, who so strongly emphasizes the problem of truth, considers this also as a matter of course. In the present situation, as missions have been till recently largely in the hands of Europeans, these Europeans can proffer no reasonable objection to adaptation in the sense of various, characteristically Asiatic or African, expressions, because their own national and regional Christianities, which they often cherish highly, are all adaptations.

Why, then, is this problem of adaptation and of indigenization of Christianity in modern missions such a burning problem? Why is it that in reading and in hearing discussions about it, one gets the impression of artificiality and sterility? It is, indeed, no exaggeration to use the words artificiality and sterility. In the Fact-finders' Report of the Laymen's Missionary Enquiry [1] one finds the result of a very valuable investigation about the question of how far Christianity has been adapted to Chinese genius and culture, and the results are very meagre. We have pointed already to the fact that adaptation was no conscious problem to Jesus, nor to John or Paul. This need not be ascribed to the eschatological outlook, which is so often unnecessarily adduced to declare the New Testament situation to be irrelevant to ours, or the reverse. In the first place it was by virtue of their prophetic and religious radicalness that they bent all things into tools for their witness and message.

[1] Tome v., Supplementary Series, Part II.

In the second place it was, of course, because Christianity was entirely new, and this consideration leads us to one of the main reasons why adaptation and indigenization cannot but be an arduous problem for modern missions.

Christianity is preached and established in Asia and Africa by the Christian Churches of the West, who have a long, rich and multi-coloured development behind them in their religious, theological and institutional aspects. At the same time they have grown up, religiously and theologically, in a cultural environment that is entirely different from the environments of the various non-Christian religions, and this cultural environment is in divers ways allied with Christianity, as it has been brought and interpreted by the Western Christian Churches. So, as to its content as well as to its form, it is utterly foreign. This foreignness is still further accentuated by the circumstance that the non-Christian religions identify community and religion, and therefore inevitably regard as foreign every religion that is no product of the soil and of its own history.

This foreignness, for the reasons mentioned and because of the fact that the Europeans who are the bearers of Christianity belong to the politically, economically and culturally dominant race of foreigners, is what makes the problem of adaptation a very urgent one for modern missions. Even in former missionary periods, when the cultural, mental and social gulf between the bearers of Christianity and the peoples to whom it was brought was not so wide as at present, adaptation was an important missionary problem, simply because Christianity then also had already a history. We may refer, for example, to the famous missionary instruction of Pope Gregory the Great in 601 regarding the Christianization of England.

If one realizes adequately this foreignness, which attaches inevitably to Christianity for all these reasons, independently of the will or the working of modern missions, one becomes vividly aware of the vital importance of the problem of adaptation. It is no exaggeration to say that it is a crucial problem for the Christian Churches in Africa and Asia and for the missionary enterprise in those continents.

At this point, then, enters the queer and disquieting element in regard to it, because of which we used the words artificiality and sterility. Besides the reasons which are independent of the will or the working of missions and which make it already such a huge problem, there are evidently other reasons too. The many discussions about indigenization and adaptation in missionary literature, and the note of impatience and disappointment that more and more pervades these discussions, are indications that the importance of the problem is really felt and recognized. We have a host of definitions explaining what an indigenous Church adapted to its environment ought to be. During the Conference at Jerusalem in 1928 it was said, for example, that by an indigenous Church was meant a Christian Church that was best adapted to meet the religious needs of these Eastern peoples, most congenial to Eastern life and culture, and most effective in arousing in the Eastern Christians the sense of responsibility. Similarly in China there have been voices saying that a church which is the natural outgrowth and expression of the corporate religious experience of Chinese Christians, and which brings out the best in the life, culture and environment of the Chinese people, is a really indigenous Church. We leave aside the question whether these definitions are right or have perhaps a rather artificial and academic flavour. What interests us here is that what has been achieved is very little. Real creativity in this field is rare ; a rather high degree of impotence is everywhere evident. How is this to be explained ?

Apparently the explanations have to be sought as much amongst the Western missionary agencies as among the Eastern Christians. To begin with the Western missionary agencies—the first reason is, leaving exceptions for the moment out of consideration, a great lack of imagination and of flexibility of mind. In most cases Christianity is preached and transplanted in the historical, theological and institutional forms that have been developed in the West, and in the case of Protestant Missions this is still further aggravated by the fact that the various and often separatist-minded denominational, theological and institutional expressions are the models on which various types of Christianity in Africa and Asia are moulded. Most Western missionaries, like the majority of ordinary human beings, are unable to emancipate themselves from the cultural, mental, emotional and social frame in which they are accustomed to live and to express their religious life. They consider their own theological approach, their own forms of ecclesiastical life and of worship, etc., in the main those that are *normal* for the African or Asiatic Christians as well.

This is a serious failure. Whosoever pronounces the criticism, however, must remind himself that the mental conquest of self and the imaginative capacity and self-denial needed to transpose oneself *creatively* into the spiritual and social reality of another cultural background are comparatively rare faculties all over the world. For a sober and realistic view of the situation this, so to speak, biological reality must not be lost sight of.

However, the problem of adaptation becomes still more complicated and success in solving it still escapes us, because the missionary world can be divided into two camps in connection with it,[1] namely, the adaptationists and the anti-adaptationists. The second group is composed of those who hold that the unique and final character of Christianity precludes all modifications to fit or please another cultural and social situation. After our previous remarks on the need of imagination and remembering what has been said in the preceding pages about the prophetic character of Biblical realism, eternally stable and eternally flexible at the same time, it requires no long argument to indicate the disastrous error contained in this position. If it is analysed, it simply means to identify one's own peculiar theological and ecclesiastical rigidity and lack of cultural and mental imagination with the eternal validity of the Gospel, and to overlook the solid fact that all our Western Christianities, theologies and ecclesiastical forms are adaptations and consequently relative, and often not very successful, expressions of the Biblical religion of revelation. It is a truly remarkable and pathetic

[1] For the moment we exclude the creative achievements in the field of adaptation from the discussion.

fact that those who are the champions of the eternal and absolute validity of the Gospel perpetrate so easily the fatal mistake of raising the relative, historical expression, the earthen vessel, to the status of the absolute divine act and gift. It is one of the most subtle forms of idolatry.

The only reason that to a small extent exculpates this fatal standpoint is the peculiar way in which many adaptationists proclaim their enthusiasm for adaptation and indigenization. Many of them overlook too much the theological, pyschological and sociological problems that are involved in it. Their idea of adaptation, although they intend the opposite, inevitably leads to the weakening of Christianity, for in practice it is not the endeavour to bring Christian truth to its most vigorous and clear expression by indigenous ways, but to recast Christianity into an indigenous philosophy of life, in which the dominant elements are the pre-Christian apprehension of existence, coloured and sanctioned by supposedly kindred Christian elements. Moreover, they have often a quite unrealistic conception of psychological and sociological possibilities. By virtue of their aversion to institutional and dogmatic Christianity they talk too lightly of the disembodied spiritual and ethical realities of the Gospel and of Christian ideals and ideas, of which missions ought to give the spiritual content and then challenge the indigenous Christians to do creative thinking according to their own racial spirit.

Willoughby in *The Soul of the Bantu* has a more realistic view of the matter when he speaks about the disappointment that comes from spreading the spirit of Christ and Christian ideals and ideas, for, as he wisely remarks : " The pure essence of our religion is never found without some sort of container," and he ends by saying about institutionalism : " But for it we should never have had the same essence of our religion to steer us, nor even the books that tell us the story of Jesus." And as to the creative thinking of the indigenous Christians we refer to what was said above about the rare gift of creativity. It is simply superhuman what the adaptationists expect from the indigenous Christians, and it runs counter to what the knowledge of human nature teaches. The creativity that is hoped for in these theories should be (if it were really to achieve what is claimed for it in noble optimism) of such stupendous strength and dimensions as never occurs in human history. Moreover, leaving this point of creativity alone, there is another very important consideration that cannot be left out of account in discussing this whole problem of adaptation. We emphasized already as a basic fact that Christianity in Africa and Asia does not enter a social and cultural vacuum, and that this fact alone is sufficient to demonstrate the inescapability of the problem of adaptation. It is equally true, however, that Christianity does not begin its course there as though it then for the first time entered the world and had no history at all. This history cannot be neglected, whether we like it or not.

Hence, the contributions that are at the present juncture to be primarily demanded from the Western missionary agencies for the solution of the problem of adaptation are a radical self-delivery from our orthodox and liberal limitations, and a not less radical concentration on the only vital problem. This problem is how to help in paving the way for the expression of the religion of revelation in indigenous forms so as to be a true and vigorous expression of its real character. The surest way to this is a deeper conception of what is implied in obedience to and ambassadorship for Christ, for wherever the Spirit of the Lord is, there is freedom (2 Cor. iii. 17), freedom not to do what one likes, but what He likes.

Turning now to the Christians of the Younger Churches we discover still other aspects of the problem of adaptation. The more thoughtful amongst them are grievously troubled by the foreignness of Christianity and feel much in it to be unnecessarily foreign and antagonistic to the atmosphere of their own cultural background. Their souls are aspiring after an indigenous expression of Christianity that will deliver their religion from the blighting curse of foreignness, although, generally speaking, their aspiration is rarely translated into definite shape. Many of them are more absorbed in the complaint of foreignness than occupied with the expression of the essential Christian religion, the more so because the rigidly unimaginative way in which Western missionaries often prefer to present Christianity drives them to exasperation. In cases where they try their own way of expression they often mistake cardinal and essential elements of the Christian revelation for cultural idiosyncrasies of the West or for mythological crudities, deeming it an unnecessary difficulty that to become a Christian should mean to repudiate one's own native religion, or considering incarnation or reconciliation (to take only some examples) superfluous metaphysics. This confusion is partly a result of their religious past, which rebels against the prophetic character of the Christian religion, and partly a result of insufficient religious and theological guidance.

The impetuous younger elements are carried away by their absorption in the great vision of the reconstruction and regeneration of their country and nation after a long period of humiliation and impotence. This sympathetic and wholly intelligible nationalism, however, seriously threatens to vitiate the problem of adaptation. The cultural and religious heritage of their beloved country becomes so dear to them that adaptation virtually means amalgamation of indigenous and Christian elements, and in such a way that in this amalgamation the cardinal life-apprehensions of their cultural and religious heritage tend to remain the dominant tendencies, undergoing only a more or less important modification through Christian influences. Because of their deep national enthusiasm they are unconsciously more occupied with being good Hindus or Chinese or Japanese or Africans than being good Christians. Their efforts, involuntarily, tend more in the direction of saving and rehabilitating their higher cultural and religious heritage than in that of trying to find the way for a vigorous translation of essential Christianity through indigenous means. This syncretistic amalgamation of the different heritages with Christian elements, manifest in so many publications, is one of the results of the general religious confusion. In view of the urgent need for the sound development and strengthening of Christianity in the Younger Churches, this is a great danger.

Among the thoughtful Eastern Christians there is also a group who are more cautious in their attitude towards programmes of adaptation or assimilation. This group of people is mostly to be found in China and in Japan, but their caution springs from different causes. In China, the country of revolutionary transition, the question naturally arises ; Adaptation to what ? To ancient or to modern China ? There are people who in the midst of the crash of ancient China and the emergence of new China come to the position that Chinese culture has lost all integrating and directive principle and has nothing essential left to which Christianity can be adapted. This, certainly, is a great underestimation of the significance which the cardinal tenets and attitudes that have been created in the religious and cultural development of some millennia still have and will have for China in the future. Yet, this hesitating, cautious attitude is a reminder how easy it is in this time of transition and feverish seeking for new forms of life to approach the problem of adaptation in a too-theoretical spirit and to produce phantoms instead of building realities.

In Japan the caution has a different cause. The problem of adaptation and indigenization cannot be said to awaken a vital interest there, because the Christian Churches are composed to an overwhelming extent of urban, intellectual and Westernized people. Moreover, the number of Japanese Christians is, when compared with the total population, very small, though their influence and prestige in Japan far exceeds their numbers. The urban character of Japanese Christianity lessens the pressure of the problem of adaptation very greatly ; by their small number Japanese Christians have become deeply alive to the necessity of having a clear-cut, well-defined conception of Christianity as the most effective means for preserving them from succumbing to the subtle influence of the overwhelmingly non-Christian religious atmosphere, and for maintaining their Christian self-consciousness.

The bulk of the indigenous Christians throughout Asia

and Africa do not really trouble about the problem of adaptation and of the foreignness of Christianity. If we consider the matter objectively, they suffer severely from this foreignness, because, on account of their being obliged to move in the awkward and uncongenial framework of Western modes, their indigenous and spontaneous faculties of religious expression are continuously being hindered and inhibited. If, however, we consider the matter in its subjective aspect, we find that they do not trouble much about it, because in most cases they already cherish the forms in which they received Christianity from the Western missionaries as a precious tradition and a symbol of social prestige. These two apprehensions are the result of universal human inclinations and legacies of their pagan past, as tradition and social prestige were then important elements in " religion." At any rate, the foreignness of Christianity is not so poignantly felt that it rouses to much action, although there is much discussion.

How much clarification the thinking of Eastern Christians still needs on the problem of adaptation is vividly illustrated by a passage in the Fact-finders' Report of the Laymen's Missionary Enquiry about China. It declares that to many " liberal " missionaries, who have much sympathy with adaptation, it has come as a shock that many leading Chinese Christians, now that the Churches have become more independent, are inclined to reduce the whole problem to that of the control of the Church's machinery and its material resources, and are only slightly interested in the problem of " relating Christian faith and practice to cultural heritage."

Our incomplete picture of the situation as to the problem of adaptation would be wholly incomplete if we failed to deal with two other features which have been hitherto omitted. We did this on purpose in order to bring into relief the state of confusion in which, for objective and subjective reasons, this problem still remains amongst the mission agencies and the indigenous Churches. The two features that have been till now suppressed in our discussion are the following :

All over the world there are going on many sincere endeavours in evangelistic approach, in forms of worship, in architecture, in institutional forms, in theological formulation, to adapt the expression of Christianity to the environmental conditions. To mention some instances, there are Dr Reischelt's efforts in evangelization amongst Chinese Buddhist monks ; the many experiments in indigenous forms of worship as described, for example, in *Worship in Other Lands* by H. P. Thompson, and others ; the examples of indigenous Church architecture in Fleming's *Heritage of Beauty* ; the efforts in Africa to incorporate and christianize tribal forms of social organization and ancient institutions, such as initiation, etc. It is not unfair to say that, generally speaking, Western missionaries are more creative in initiative and action in these fields of adaptation than indigenous Christians are.

The other feature is of a quite different nature. The Fact-finders on China state at the end of their investigation into the indigenization of Christianity in China that the amount of unintentional adaptation that is going on in Chinese Christianity is much more than the intentional. This is a very important point, which is excellently formulated in a remark of Professor Westmann, when reviewing Rosenkranz's book *Der Nomos Chinas und das Evangelium.*[1] He says : " The main developments with regard to the stupendous meeting of the Gospel with the spirit of China are of course going on less in conferences in Shanghai or in theoretical discussions at home than in the ordinary life of missions and churches up and down that great country. He who wants to study the matter earnestly will have to go into the life of individual Chinese Christians, pastors and laymen, men and women, the group life of congregations in prayer, discussions of synods and councils, sermons, etc. etc." Every missionary who is observant by nature would be able to adduce a host of extremely interesting examples to illustrate this side of the problem, and these examples would, of course, show that this unintentional adaptation is both praiseworthy and deplorable. One of the most creative

[1] See *International Review of Missions*, 1937.

means to further adaptation as a vigorous expression of the true character of the Christian revelation in indigenous terms of thought and life would be to gather this material in every missionary area and expose it to the light of Biblical realism.

. . . .

The problem of adaptation is that of the genuine translation of Christianity into indigenous terms so that its relevancy to their concrete situations becomes evident. Genuine translation presupposes a thorough grasp of what Christian truth is and of the material in which it must be expressed. Both are equally vital, the first in order to get rid of the religious confusion in which missionary thinking is ensnared and take hold of the only valid orientation point ; the second to free us from our timidity and enslavement to our traditional ways, and to teach us to utilize the many instruments that lie ready at hand in the religious, social and cultural traditions of the non-Christian world. The deep concern of the Christian Church in the non-Christian world should be the clear expression of the Christian revelation ; consequently its no less deep concern should be to find the best available form and the most creative pedagogical and psychological approaches. Only along this line can the needed combination of Christian self-consciousness and flexibility of mind and approach be guaranteed.

The question whether one has to be mainly bent on bridge-building or on making contrasts takes on then a quite new aspect. It is not a matter of partisanship in bridge-building or contrast-making, but, by concentration on the living Christian truth of Biblical realism and on its living expression, of finding out where to build bridges and where to emphasize contrasts. This is also the only way to avoid the danger, now so often apparent, that the experiments in adaptation are, virtually, intentional experiments in cultural or intellectual synthesis, and hence are artificial. A fundamental principle in all adaptation and indigenization must be that its inspiration should be thoroughly religious, new religious insights and attitudes seeking for characteristic expression. *Intellectual* syntheses are rarely lasting if they are thought out without being related to an actual development of the spiritual life. Similarly, *right* cultural syntheses are always the result of a long and living development, not of a premeditated intellectual construction. Heiler's programme for a creative synthesis of New Testament Christianity, stripped of all European wrappings and petrifications, with all the great and sacred elements that ever existed in India, is a striking example of this artificiality and unreality.

It is an illusory programme for three reasons. In the first place, the great and the sacred elements in Indian religion, because of the radically different religious apprehensions they represent, are not material for any real synthesis with Biblical realism. In the second place, the Western expressions of Christianity that occurred in Church History are not exhaustively characterized as the obscuration and petrification of New Testament Christianity ; it is something different as well, and although New Testament Christianity is the only valid orientation point for all Christianities, present, past and future, the Younger Churches cannot live and grow as if Church History had never occurred. In the third place, if a synthesis of Christianity and Indian or other elements will ever come about (and it certainly will) such a synthesis will grow slowly out of the stress and need of life, but never can be the result of a premeditated effort, apart from living and continuous contact with the actual situations. The words in which Heiler formulates his programme show that they issue from a too theoretical and academical approach.

In the problem of adaptation, therefore, as it emerges in the stress of concrete life, the crucial point is the same as in the case of the point of contact.[1] No catalogue or vademecum can be made, but the great pathfinder is the apostolic urge to pave the way for Christ and stimulate the growth of communities consisting of Christian men and women, who in the way they express Christianity are not clumsy imitations of Western Christianities, but have the flavour of their own environment. In our description of the non-Christian religions we have repeatedly stressed how rich and varied

[1] See Chapter IV.

are the ways in which man there has tried to give expression
to his religious needs and aspirations, in theology, in worship,
in art, in forms of organization, in different ways of presentation. To mention only some instances, meditation, asceticism
and retreats from the world ; or, amongst the tribal religions,
the natural need for a corporate expression of the religious
life. These are all deeply ingrained habits of the Eastern
mind and have at least as much right to exist as our European
lack of them has. It is not at all important that they do not
fit in with our Protestant traditions and natural reactions,
but it is very important to ask in the light of Biblical realism
how they can function so as to foster a pure and vigorous
Christian life.

It is all-important also to keep constantly in mind that
these peoples, though now plunged in the more rationalized
Western habits of thinking, are by the deep and long-standing
training of their minds in the primitive apprehension of
existence exceedingly different from Westerners in the ways
in which they feel and express things. What Lin Yu Tang
in *My Country and My People* remarks about the feminine turn
of the Chinese mind, being synthetic and not analytic,
concrete and not abstract, and hence fond of expressing
things in metaphorical language, in proverbs and parables,
etc., is wholly applicable to the whole of Africa and Asia. This
trait is of fundamental importance for the right approach ;
therefore its use should be infinitely much more encouraged
than is the case now, for it is as legitimate a way as the
more abstract European way for the expression of Christian
truth. Moreover, it gives a real homely flavour to things.

An instance from a different area of human life is the
use of the philosophical and theological terminologies and
thought-patterns in which the non-Christian religions and
civilizations have expressed themselves for centuries. Here,
too, we will have to conquer our timidity and enslavement
to our own traditional ways. In the course of its history
Christian theology has always freely employed the different
thought-patterns that were available, such as Platonic and
Aristotelian and Neo-Platonic-coloured Aristotelian philosophy. This was natural, because all speaking to man

must be done in his language and in the terminologies and thought-patterns he understands. It issued from a given reality that these patterns and ideas were in such a period the self-evident ones (compare Origen and Augustine), just as many modern conceptions are tacitly assumed by us as self-evident, from the spontaneous need to establish contacts and from the necessity to talk intelligible language. To witness to and express the revelation in Christ means practically always to do it in a language that has a radically different religious background and tendency, because this is in every concrete instance the language that is available. It is impossible to formulate the divine revelation in or through a linguistic vacuum, or to create out of a linguistic vacuum a quite new and adequate expression of it.

There is, hence, no valid objection to the deliberate use of the rich religious and philosophical terminology of the great non-Christian religious civilizations, whether the Hindu, the Buddhist or the Confucian. The real problem is not their use, for that is a matter of course, but *how* to use them. All fear is here misleading and evil. To avoid expressing the Christian message courageously (as the New Testament did) in the terminology developed in the different religious heritages of the concrete world in which one lives, is to despise the natural medium. It also ignores the fundamental rule in spiritual life, that if the Christians are really converted their minds will bend these inadequate and often uncongenial terminologies into tolerable tools, for all terminologies in the world need conversion and filling with new content if they are really to serve as an expression for the revelation of Biblical realism. This conversion and filling with new content, however, can only issue from the converted mind of the *indigenous employers* of the terminology.

The deprecation of all fear does not mean the denial of all danger. There are great dangers, and there have always been. These, however, are inherent in the nature of the case. Christian truth as embodied in the revelation in Christ is incommensurable. It is in its deepest content a stumbling-block to the Jews and sheer folly to the Greek, the " mysterious Wisdom of God," which " the Powers of this world did not understand " (1 Cor. ii. 7, 8). All human speaking about it is speaking in " foreign tongues." Hence the real problem is how we use the foreign tongues. The religious and philosophical foreign tongues which have been used in the past by the Christian Churches have served as much to distort and falsify the revelation in Christ as to express it. For example, the Apologists in the first centuries were fervent Christians and intended seriously to defend and justify Christianity in the face and through the medium of the Greek-Roman culture. They produced, however, not a tolerable and characteristic expression of Christianity, but a religious philosophy with monotheism in the centre,[1] because they were more bent on justifying the Christian truth before the judgment-seat of Greek thought than on using this thought as a medium to express the revelation as pithily as possible. Their efforts were directed towards demonstrating that Christianity was in agreement with the best in pagan thought, which is not an unimportant but a secondary thing.

Origen was a great Christian who preferred martyrdom to coming to terms with paganism, but in his Christian philosophy he involuntarily succeeded better in obscuring the true character and the cardinal content of the Christian revelation than in elucidating it, because the mythological and mystic trend of Platonic thinking predominated in him by far over the trend of Biblical realism. Emotionally he was a Christian, intellectually he was more than half a pagan. We see the same thing happen to-day. The whole history of Christian dogma is so to speak the story of the perennial tension and war between " the mysterious Wisdom of God " in His acts of revelation and the various foreign tongues. The entering of Christianity into the non-Christian world means and must mean a new chapter in the history of this experiment. For Christian missions and for the Younger Churches this experiment is an obligation that

---

[1] For the sake of justice it ought to be said that, although the Apologies were mainly tame religious philosophies when compared with the real content of the Christian revelation, the vigorous stress on monotheism was a very significant thing and a healthy purifying note in the religious situation of their day.

cannot and may not be evaded. But it is at the same time a very urgent call to see clearly and to steer clearly.

As we explained in the preceding chapters, the great naturalist apprehensions of life have all evolved huge and magnificent *religious philosophies*. The use of their terminologies and thought-patterns thus involves (just as the use of Neo-Platonic or Aristotelian thought-patterns did) a strong pull towards presenting the Christian truth as a religious philosophy, e.g. a theistic or an ethical one. The prophetic religion of Biblical realism rebels against such a process. The great need in this necessary and inevitable venture of adaptation is to be constantly alive to the necessity that the religious and philosophical heritage should be used to " tell " what Christian truth really is, and not to amalgamate elements of it as harmoniously as possible with this heritage. The tendency to do the latter is always very strong. The real programme is not to *relate* the thought of Christianity to the thought of India or China or another civilization, but to *express* it through these different heritages, and then see whether this in various cases may be called relating or not. This attitude alone guarantees a vital contact and wrestling both with Christian truth and also with the religious and philosophical heritage.

. . . .

There are still two points to be treated, that are of great significance to the clarification of thinking as to the problem of adaptation. These are the places which the Old Testament has to occupy, and the value and authority of current Christian thought as formulated since the first centuries until now.

The place of the Old Testament, or rather the substitution for the Old Testament of the sacred books of the various " higher " non-Christian religions as the preparation for the New Testament, has been widely discussed in recent years. The psychological and theological reasons for this phenomenon are obvious after all that has been said in the preceding chapters. The naturalist-monistic apprehension of the " higher " non-Christian religions stands in marked contrast to the prophetic apprehension embodied in the Old

Testament. The mind of educated and sensitive people
who are bred in the atmosphere of this naturalist apprehension naturally finds the Old Testament in many respects
repugnant. Modern research in the Old Testament along
the lines of historical criticism, by its evolutionist bias and
its ignoring of the peculiar prophetic character of the Old
Testament, intensifies this repugnance. The sympathetic
appreciation of the religious and cultural heritage, which
resulted from a deeper knowledge issuing in a fairer judgment,
grew as a consequence of the nationalistic spirit into reverent
and loving attachment to it.

The necessity to state clearly the relation of Christianity
to the ancestral religions, and to see one's way in the problem
of what the Christian attitude has to be towards the non-
Christian cultural and religious environment, helped towards
moving the emphasis from the Old Testament to the non-
Christian sacred Scriptures as preparations for the Gospel.
Hence the most sympathetic appeal to many minds was the
idea of fulfilment. Of vital significance to this whole situation was the fact that, although being emotionally fervent
and convinced Christians, intellectually many missionaries
and indigenous Christian intellectuals had a more or less
relativist conception of Christianity, springing from the
environmental naturalistic apprehension of religion and
from modern humanism and pragmatism. So, the doctrine
that the " sacred oracles " of the great non-Christian
religions are the Old Testaments of China, India, etc., and
validly take the place of the Jewish Old Testament as the
document of the *præparatio evangelica*, easily found support.

Whosoever has followed our argument up to the present
point will concede that this conclusion, however intelligible
it may be in the existing circumstances, is born of a deep-
seated religious and theological confusion. It is for ever
impossible to discard the Jewish Old Testament as an integral
part of the Christian revelation, and also to consider the
great documents of the non-Christian religions as its sub-
stitutes. This has nothing to do with a lack of appreciation
of the religious quality of these great documents. Even if
this quality were ten or a hundred times greater than is at

present claimed by those who rightly emphasize it, this opinion would stand unimpaired.

Neither does this mean that the Old Testament, as a document of religious development, is immaculate. In discussing this problem of the Old Testament Dr K. Hartenstein quotes very appositely a word of Luther about the Old Testament : " Hier wirst du die Krippe und die Windeln finden da Christus liegt, dahin auch die Engel die Hirten weisen. Schlechte und geringe Windeln sind es. Aber teuer ist der Schatz Christus, der darin liegt." (Here you will find the cradle and the swaddling clothes in which Christ is lying and to which the angels point the shepherds. These swaddling clothes are mean and trifling, but Christ, the treasure that is lying in it, is precious.) The crucial point is that, religiously speaking, the Jewish Old Testament is not primarily the document of Jewish religious experience, but of God's revelational dealings with the people of Israel and through them with the world, as an introduction to His decisive revelational dealing with Israel and the world in Jesus Christ, of which the New Testament is the document.

Jesus is rooted in the Old Testament or, as He Himself says, in the Law and the Prophets. He constantly refers to them and calls Himself the fulfilment of the Law and the Prophets. He meant by this that in Him the deepest problems and suggestions hidden in the Law and the Prophets became fully manifest, and found at the same time their solution. His attitude is therefore twofold. His person, life and work are unthinkable without the background of the Law and the Prophets, and so He constantly summons men to investigate " the Scriptures " and discover Him there. In the second place, however, by the divine authority of His " But I say unto you " (His *exousia*) He sovereignly disposes of the Law and the Prophets. Jesus at once maintains and transcends the Old Testament.

Paul does the same, although of course not on account of an authority inherent in his own person, but through the judgment acquired by faith in Christ. He maintains the relatedness of God's revelational dealing in the Law and the Prophets with that in Christ, and at the same time he transcends it, not hesitating, in his masterly criticism of Judaism, to contrast the Law of Moses, so deeply venerated by him, as the " administration of death " with the Christian apostolic obligation as the " administration of the Spirit " (2 Cor. iii.).[1] The primitive Church never hesitated in pursuing the line of Jesus and Paul and of all the Apostles and the New Testament writers, sensing that to exclude the Old Testament from the documents of God's revelational dealing and its culmination in Christ would mean to ignore arbitrarily God's revelational dealing and thereby to lose the historical foundation on which God placed it. Harnack in his book *Marcion* says that it would have been a mistake to reject the Old Testament as Marcion required the Church to do.[2]

Apart from the reasons we have mentioned, which hold that the Old and the New Testaments will remain for ever indissolubly connected, it is important to consider that the New Testament and the cardinal elements of the Christian faith (the Kingdom of God, God's personal acting in *history*, the Church as the true Israel, the prophetic character of the Christian ethic, etc.) would become, humanly and historically speaking, wholly unintelligible and without any basis, were it not for the Old Testament.

To treat the sacred Oracles of the non-Christian religions as the introductory, preparatory part of the integral Christian revelation, instead of the Old Testament, is, even from the standpoint of sound historical and psychological thinking, a very bad specimen of a marriage of incompatibles. Even if this marriage took place a divorce would be the only natural solution, because as in all marriages of incompatibles both

---

[1] For lack of space we pass by in silence the important Epistle to the Hebrews and shut out from the discussion the remarkable fact that the peoples who adhere to tribal religions, and the masses in the great cultural religions that practically belong to the sphere of so-called primitive religion, are more impressed by the Old than by the New Testament. The Old Testament is in the real sense of the word to them the door to Christ.

[2] He adds that it is a sign of religious and ecclesiastical paralysis when the Church in the nineteenth century still maintains this canonical recognition of the Old Testament. This restriction of Harnack's for modern Protestantism is, it seems, rather a sign of the religious paralysis that results from relativist historical thinking.

parties would become stunted personalities. Not because
these documents of the non-Christian religions are inferior as
documents of human religious experience—they are in many
respects splendid—but because it is simply an adulteration of
feeling and thinking to treat the documents of radically
naturalist, unprophetic religions, which, because of their
cyclic conception of life, lack all sense of the vital relation of
God to history, as the introduction to the basic elements of
the prophetic religion of Biblical realism. Omitting all other
considerations, merely for the sake of clear thinking, it is
necessary to abandon the idea of making the sacred oracles
of the non-Christian religions the Old Testaments of the
Younger Churches.

Despite their veneration for Plato and other authors of
sublime thoughts in the non-Christian religions of their day,
the Apologists rightly never dreamed of substituting these
documents for the Old Testament. A practical argument
of no mean importance is also the question where the unity
of the Christian Church would remain if all religious and
cultural heritages became the special Old Testaments of the
various Christian Churches.

The " foreignness " of Christianity, which makes the
problem of adaptation so important, is not only a consequence
of its having been brought by Westerners who transplanted
their Western approaches, institutions and patterns with
the peculiar flavour which results from their peculiar
historical evolution, but also of the fact that the presentation
of Christianity took and takes places along the dogmatical
lines that have resulted from the trend of theological development peculiar to the West. Oscar Buck in his *Christianity
Tested* even argues that the chief barriers to and the chief
cause of the failure and slow progress of Christianity in the
Eastern world is the incomprehensible way in which the
Gospel has been presented by dressing it up in the garb of
Hebrew-Greek vision and dogma. He asks whether we are
obliged to make the culmination of Greek Christian thinking (namely, Christian dogma) the entrance to Christianity
for Hindus, Chinese, etc. In his opinion we block the
entrance to Christianity by this incomprehensible formula-

tion of the comprehensible Gospel. He then urges in a very able and sympathetic way that, instead of spreading " the garments of Judæa, Greece and Rome before the universal Christ can ride into Asia," we must present the universal and essential content of Christianity to Asia under the aspect of God's eternal parental attitude towards the world, as the Gospel of the perfect social God and the perfect social man, of the Perfect Father and the Perfect Home, all embodied in the life of Christ, for—so Buck argues—this will universally appeal to the instinct of Asia that has always reverenced parenthood.

In our opinion Buck, although many restrictions ought to be made to his thesis about the appeal of parenthood and the supporting arguments, suggests here a splendid avenue of evangelistic approach which deserves close attention. Planting the Christian Church in other parts of the world is, however, not alone a problem of evangelistic approach, important as this may be, but also of continuing and building a historic Christian community. Losing sight of this side of the problem, Buck uses arguments that are in the light of Biblical realism and of Christian thinking not acceptable. In the name of history and the historical sense he sacrifices too much his historical judgment and circumspection.

To take some instances, the Sonship of Christ, His Redeemership, His Godhead and Incarnation, the Trinity, the doctrine of the Fall, etc., cannot be treated as truth and at the same time as merely Hebrew vision and Greek dogma, as Buck virtually treats them. They are not ideas and conceptions that are mainly historical products, not really relevant to the heart and body of Christian truth, but they are expressions of the essential structure of reality as seen in the light of revelation. It is a deplorable fact that they are often presented in an intellectualist way. Almost all sense of their intrinsic relatedness to the dynamic character of God's revelation may thus be lost. But this does not obliterate their importance. They belong either explicitly or implicitly to the core of Biblical realism and are the heritage of the Christian Church. To dispense with them means to dispense with the Bible and with the cardinal and vital elements of the

Christian revelation, and entails the danger of a severely curtailed Christianity.

Apart from this fundamental argument and many more that could be suggested, the arising Younger Churches can never live and develop as if the Christian Church had no history and had not coined a rich treasure of universally-used and respected religious terminology. Moreover it is fair to ask, Why be so deeply concerned about the religious heritage of the civilizations in which the Younger Churches grow up, but wholly unconcerned about the religious heritage of their own Christian religion and of that body, the Church, which rightly claims their prime loyalty? Buck's confounding of the evangelistic and other issues of still wider magnitude, which have to do with the future and not only with the momentary necessities of the evangelistic approach, is apparently another consequence of the present religious and theological confusion that we have repeatedly touched upon.

Nevertheless, Buck's argument draws attention to a serious drawback in the Christian approach and the problem of adaptation. Resolutely as the Younger Churches must lay hands on the religious heritage of the Christian Church, Christianity is far too much presented (it were better to say, concealed) through the unimaginative use of standard dogmatic terminology that is largely unintelligible to those who listen to it. Doctrinal rigidity and lack of missionary and apostolic flexibility are the causes of this widespread and lamentable condition. To be a missionary, to be a messenger of the Gospel means everywhere and always and in all kinds of work (not least in the case of spoken and written presentation) to *interpret*, to *translate*, that is to say, to impart the content of the Christian revelation to those concerned, not in a way we find correct according to our doctrinal standards, but in a way that can convey *meaning* to their minds and consciences, and that expresses intelligibly the contents of the revelation. From this angle Buck's complaint and protest have a right to claim very serious attention. The Christian approach to the non-Christian religions includes an equally firm grasp of the vital elements in the Christian revelation and of the necessity to speak and interpret it to the hearer in a way that stirs his living response, whether it is an affirmative or a negative one ; not in a way that pleases our particular orthodox or liberal doctrinal appetites, right as they may sometimes be.

This important instance of the problem of adaptation has a still wider compass. It includes the fact that it is more than time to become very serious about the terrible way in which the missionary agencies of the West hamper Christianity in the East by transplanting their denominational differences. We complain much of this. The situation, however, demands acts and not mere complaints. The authority and value of the universal Christian heritage for the Younger Christian Churches, as it has grown in the course of Church History, are incontestable. To afflict them, however, with our denominational accents and differences and make our Presbyterian, Anglican, Lutheran or other Catechisms the standard manuals for their religious imagery and vocabulary is a religious injustice, a missionary mistake, and an intellectual and psychological error. The root of the problem of adaptation is for missions to see that the precious obligation and privilege to interpret the Gospel and to transplant the Christian Church into new environments implies that every missionary problem must be primarily approached from the angle of the problems as they are for the Christian Churches and communities in their own environment. Western missionary agencies, in approaching the Younger Churches to-day, stand in need of an attitude like Ruth's towards Naomi, which can be expressed in the words : Your problems are my problems.

CHAPTER IX

THE MISSIONARY APPROACH (continued)

TO deal in a very limited space concretely with the Christian approach for the different great areas of the activity in the Christian Church in the non-Christian world is an exceedingly hazardous undertaking, because inevitably nobody will be satisfied, as nobody will find that full justice has been done to his special situation and problems. The more one studies the past and contemporary history of missions or of religious change in general, the more one becomes aware that, although very valuable generalizations can be made, they all need, in order to represent life-pictures, the concrete qualifications of their specific historical situations, and that is impossible in a limited space.[1] Yet, although assured of inevitable and legitimate criticism, an effort to deal concretely with the various areas must be made, on the basis of their peculiar backgrounds and of the problems that are at present most actual to them.

AFRICA

The world of tribal and " primitive " religions is much wider than Africa. All through the continent of Asia, in the island-world of the Dutch East Indies and in Australia, we encounter them in various types and grades. However, for the sake of brevity and conciseness, we shall focus our attention on the huge black continent, because of its great importance in the present period of world transition, of the

---

[1] A comparison of our contemporary missionary problems and situations with the Christianization of Western Europe in the Middle Ages would be extraordinarily instructive and fascinating, as well for its similarities as its differences. Lack of space prohibits us from doing this as originally intended. Following Professor Addison's book, *The Mediæval Missionary* (published by the International Missionary Council), with its valuable material, we need a book that draws comparisons and illuminating conclusions for the clarification of our missionary thinking.

very varied missionary activity in Africa and of the tense character which all problems, such as usually arise from the clash of Western civilization with the primitive worlds and from the missionary activity under peoples with tribal religions, assume in Africa. Hence it is justified to take Africa as the paradigm. By its enormous diversity of races, of types of tribal religion, of social, political and economic structure, of languages and cultural traditions, Africa is peculiarly suitable to serve as such. Moreover, the stupendous change that is coming over the non-Western world to-day through the impact of the West with all spheres and structures of its life, has in Africa a particularly vehement and complicated aspect. In this process of revolutionary change the Christian Church plays a highly important rôle, and the process itself to a very large extent colours and determines the modes of the present Christian approach.[1] All these features of the African scene are in different degrees of intensity valid for the entire world of tribal and " primitive " paganism.

The approach has to do in the case of tribal and " primitive " paganism with two great areas of life : with paganism as a system of religious belief and emotion, and as a system of social structure and institutions. The question is now, What should be the leading ideas in our approach ? In Africa the clash between Western civilization and the ancestral structure of life is very severe. The contrast of the economic and political interests of black and white people is particularly glaring, and hence the race problem has in Africa more bitter aspects than anywhere else. Christianity, which is largely identified by the African with Western civilization, bears in consequence very distinctly the stamp of being the white man's religion, a foreign religion. The eyes of thoughtful and imaginative missionary people have been opened in the last decades to the many precious values inherent in the ancestral African structure of life.

This, in broad outline, is the background for what might

---

[1] In the next chapters this theme will be developed in relation to education and other pedagogical or stimulating and constructive activities of missions.

be called progressive missionary thinking in relation to Africa, of which the recommendations of the conference at le Zoute (1926) can be taken as the formulation into a programme. All missionary problems were discussed there under the aspect of the new forces that are at work in Africa. The necessity was deeply felt to make it clear that Christianity is not a white man's religion, but the religion of the African, and to free the missionary mind from its too sterile attitude towards the African and what he represents as to religious, moral and social values. Against this background we find that the recommendation of le Zoute may be expressed as follows. The Gospel is the fulfilment of that towards which the Africans groped in the past, for the Divine Logos who lighteth every man has shone in the souls of Africans ; hence, no destruction but a systematic use of the African heritage is demanded. The life of the African being essentially social, while based on tribal conditions and apprehensions, everything good in the African's heritage should be conserved, enriched and ennobled by contact with the spirit of Christ.

It is clear from the whole trend of our argument in the preceding part of this book that our standpoint is radically different in its fundamental attitude, while it cordially agrees with the desire to adopt a constructive and creative relation towards the reality of indigenous life as the material in which Christianity needs must become incarnated. To see primitive and tribal religion *chiefly* in the light of a school in which the African has become gradually prepared for the Gospel, to take it *primarily* as a *præparatio evangelica*, issues from a radical misconception of the true nature of the Christian revelation as well as of the nature of paganism. Paganism and the prophetic revelation of Biblical realism are not continuous with each other. To combine the conception that Christian truth is founded on revelation, that is to say, on God's initiative and acts, with the idea that it is the outcome of human cultural development, is combining incompatibles and destroying the whole idea of revelation.

The same has to be said about the ideas of Dr Gutmann, whose fundamental thesis is that the " primordial social ties " of the Africans (*urtümliche Bindungen*) are the natural, God-given " creational orders " of life for them. In the feeling of solidarity, which is the moral cement of the community (*Gliedschaft*), he sees a prototype of the child-relation of man to God as this is effected by Christ. Gutmann betrays his continental theological background by his rejection of the idea, current in Anglo-Saxon missionary circles, that if the Christian approach would take place through the medium of the Christlike personality of the missionary, the results of our missionary activity would be amazing, and by the stress that he more frequently places upon the view that the transition from paganism to Christianity comes through conversion. Essentially, however, his attitude towards the pagan structure and apprehension of life is the same, although it is expressed in other terms than those used by Anglo-Saxon missionary theory. Anglo-Saxon missionary literature is more genially humanistic, as Christianity with them is chiefly characterized as representing the spirit of Christ as an attitude, a temper and a character permeated and inspired by this spirit—in brief, a lofty ethic ; while the religion of God's revelational acts in Christ as depicted in Biblical realism, though not at all absent from the mind, is hardly mentioned and seldom taken as the fundamental starting-point.

As Africa is such an important mission field and many highly important new and imaginative missionary initiatives are going on there (for example, in Masasi Bishop Lucas's handling of the problem of initiation, the Church Missionary Society's experiments with circumcision camps, the " Children of the Chief " School of Miss Mabel Shaw in Mbereshi, Dr Gutmann's stimulating ideas about the central and creative position which the Christian congregation, and not the missions, must have in all problems of the expression of Christian life in indigenous forms, etc.), it is at least very important to see clearly what the fundamental stand is that one has to take. What is needed in the approach to the two areas of pagan life (the mental and the social) is to get rid of all romanticism and become passionately matter-of-fact or, as the German expression goes, *sachlich*.

From the standpoint of fundamental thinking it seems to us that the background of le Zoute or of those who think on the lines of Dr Gutmann is unwittingly a kind of romanticism. The deep emotional vein that runs through it comes from having fallen in love with " primitive " institutions, attitudes and capacities. After the period of narrow-minded blindness to the value and significance of primitive life-apprehensions and life-patterns this is psychologically quite intelligible as a reaction. Romantic love-making, however, is no good and lasting foundation to build strong and lasting Christian Churches upon, though naturally this is what everybody aims at achieving. Dr Gutmann, in our opinion, errs in another direction, by conceiving the tribal life-structures and patterns as " creational orders," that is to say, as divinely sanctioned structures. Clan, tribe, people, nation, etc., are forms and spheres of life that are direct consequences of God's will. This is romanticism fortified by the weight of metaphysical reasoning. The different forms and structures in which corporate life amongst men is expressed in the world (clan, tribe, nation, people, state) belong to the relative historical sphere of existence, and as such are as ambivalent, as demonic, as full of angelic and satanic powers as all human creations are, man being such a demonic creature, double in his nature. In these forms man realizes and organizes his relations to his fellow-men. They belong to the domain of sociology and not directly to that of theology. They must be considered human efforts to master and organize corporate life, whether they are embodied in the more " primitive " forms of tribe or clan or in that of powerful nations and states. They are subject to the common historical law of rise and decay, and are simultaneously instruments of good and evil, just as man is the fertile producer of good and evil alike. To construe out of these sociological, relative forms of life entities hallowed by a poetical or metaphysical glamour is romanticism, which in many respects affects us as sympathetic, but is no sure guide for lasting work.

No poetical or metaphysical romanticism, but a realistic and penetrating knowledge of the " primitive " life-apprehensions and life-patterns is a crying need for the missionary approach, especially in this period of tremendous change, in which no mortal man can exactly tell what will survive and what will not. We termed this matter-of-fact or *sachlich* for two reasons. In the first place, the dominating motive in the whole Christian approach has to be, How can we translate and transpose Christianity into living language and into living forms in this particular environment, *for the sake* of Jesus Christ and *for the sake* of what is implied in His person, His life and His work? In the second place, in order to do that well we need an eagerness to know and to use the religious, moral, social and psychological reality for this translation, for this is the " language " in which these peoples are accustomed to express themselves.

In missionary circles it is an undisputed axiom (although not always adhered to) and a matter of course that the language of those to whom the Gospel is brought is used as the vehicle of Christianity. So, on the same grounds, it must become an undisputed axiom that the religious terminology and means of expression, the social structures and institutions, if they are not in a state of decay or on the verge of disappearing or clearly unsuitable for expressing Christian faith or life, are the natural vehicles of Christianity. Knowledge of language is a great and indispensable thing. There is, however, in missionary literature and missionary circles the delusive tendency to consider the stress on the great significance of the knowledge and study of indigenous languages as one of the greatest glories of Protestant missions. Despite the fact that this stress can indeed never be exaggerated, one is too much apt to forget that a real grasp of the structure of " primitive " life and an intelligent application of this knowledge in the work of building the Church, is as indispensable as good linguistic attainments. Here comes in the great value of the results of anthropological research for the Christian mission. In this respect a large part of the missionary body has still to learn open-mindedness, not for the sake of anthropology, but *for the sake of doing the missionary task well and making the Christian approach an intelligent, constructive one.* On the other hand, the missionary enterprise, though it can do no wiser thing than exploit the results of anthropological research to the utmost, must always remain aware of the fact that the anthropologist has a deeply different attitude and approach from his own. The anthropologist, apart from his purely scientific and indispensable concern to determine as exactly as possible the nature and function of the life-apprehensions and life-patterns of " primitive " societies, is prone to evince a strongly appreciative and often a conservative attitude, because to him a tribe is a cultural unit and he treats the object of his study in the spirit of a cultural biologist. Amongst them there are not a few intellectual romanticists, whom R. Thurnwald in his book, *Black and White in East Africa*, criticizes so deservedly ; they want to keep the people of tribal religions as much as possible in their ancestral conceptions and patterns of life, because these affect them more sympathetically and are therefore preferred by them to the stress and storm of the·modern transition. They forget what Julian Huxley in his *Africa View* remarks in relation to Indirect Rule that, in the present period of colossal and inevitable transition, existing native institutions should never be fetishes, but ought to be made, if possible, stepping-stones.

The missionary is a revolutionary and he has to be so, for to preach and plant Christianity means to make a frontal attack on the beliefs, the customs, the apprehensions of life and the world, and by implication (because tribal religions are primarily social realities) on the social structures and bases of primitive society. The missionary enterprise need not be ashamed of this, because colonial administrations, planters, merchants, Western penetration, etc., perform a much more severe and destructive attack. Missions, however, imply the well-considered appeal to all peoples to transplant and transfer their life-foundations into a totally different spiritual soil, and so they must be revolutionary. To the Christian Church the peoples and societies and religions are not primarily or solely cultural entities, viewed with an air of indifferent or sympathetic detachedness, but they are all human groupings, spheres of life, whose fundamental and decisive relation is their relatedness to God and what He plans for them in His revelation through Christ.

We would, however, be very unjust towards many present trends in anthropology, and very unrealistic about conditions that often obtain in missionary circles, if we let the matter rest there. Especially in Africa a band of able anthropologists, inspired by Malinowski's anthropology of change, are making very penetrating investigations into the structure of African life, and concentrate their attention on the problem of the right adjustment of the Africans to the colossal changes that have come over them through the Western impact. Thurnwald's book, just quoted, is a very noteworthy example of this attitude, and the work that is done through the efforts of the International Institute of African Languages and Cultures (to mention only a few examples) are of great value to missionary work. To make an energetic use of the results of anthropological research is an obligation incumbent on every missionary in order to do his work of effecting religious change, moral reforms and social revolutions or adaptations with more intelligence and clear-sightedness, and consequently better and more effectively. Many missionaries are not good revolutionaries, but blind ones, because their minds are closed to the inestimable advantage they can derive from the labours of the anthropologists, and to the grievous damage they cause by their blindness to the healthy development of those peoples. At the present time one of the great needs of the missionary task is that the missionary agencies demand from their missionaries a serious and intelligent appreciation of the significance of anthropological insight for the right execution of the missionary task.

The Christian approach should combine three things : First, the fervent apostolic attitude that knows its commission to be to confront all peoples, societies and religions with the revelation in Christ as contained in Biblical realism, and to entreat them to surrender in obedience to it. Secondly, this entreaty includes the great self-denying effort to recognize the relativity of our own accustomed religious, cultural and ecclesiastical apprehensions and patterns, and, on account of that, their frequent inapplicability to the peoples with whom we have to deal. Thirdly, the entreaty includes also the obligatory attempt to employ in a creative and imaginative way the mental and social means of indigenous expression that in the course of history have become their congenial modes of expression, or eventually to reject them. The decision to employ or reject must always be founded on the deep desire to find the best means for a vital expression of Christianity in accordance with the gifts and means that God has given to those peoples, not on the ground that we like or dislike it for some reason *extraneous to this particular situation.*

In the mental area of religious beliefs and conceptions there is to be found much wisdom about God, man and life that testifies to man's groping for Him and the realization of the true end of human life. D. Westermann in *Africa and Christianity* gives valuable information about this religious heritage. It is impossible without having special experience in a certain field to develop a system of approach in this matter. Moreover it ought then to be dealt with in detail. Three principal lines, however, can be laid down. In the first place, if the apostolic concern really becomes the prime motive of action, it makes one on the one hand eager to unveil Christ and His significance, and on the other hand as eager to seek in the beliefs and expressions of the people the elements that can serve as a human starting-point. In the second place, to employ the vague " higher " notions about God and the fate of man as the *foundation* on which to build the whole structure of Christian truth is false and in the long run disappointing. To employ these notions eagerly in the practical evangelistic approach is a missionary necessity of the first rank ; to employ them as the *basis* of a more systematic explanation of Christian truth to the leading group of Christians diverts the mind from its only legitimate point of orientation, the prophetic religion of Biblical realism. Also we must remind the reader of what has been said in the fourth chapter about the totalitarian approach to other religions, and about the sterile result of taking fragmentary elements from a religion without asking what real function and value they represent in the whole of this religion, thus trying to build Christian structures on an inadequate basis. In the case of the so-called high gods in the tribal religions, the subsidiary place they occupy in the total religious life is evident from the fact that these gods have no cult whatever.

In the third place, the evangelistic urgency to seek for human approaches and contacts and to demonstrate that the Gospel aims at the Bantu or at the Papuan in his actual needs, aspirations and frustrations as well as at the white man, because it aims at the human heart, must not make us forget that the most-needed approach is always a vivid presentation of God's dealings with man and the world as depicted in the Bible. Besides, there is an unerring instinct in man that the most important thing in a new religion is not that it is a further development or a more distinct affirmation of what he knew already, but that it is really something new. The really new has recruiting power. A good instance of the significance of presenting in a vivid and applied way the story of God's dealings with man and the world in the Bible is the story of the creation. Without exaggeration it may be said that, according to wide missionary experience, this majestic story of God the One, who created the world and man, causing all races to spring from one forefather, really works as a revolutionary revelation on the minds of tribal people, who live by their regional views of the world. At the same time the experience with this story teaches how important it is for the Christian approach not to ask : " What do I find necessary to tell," but " What must I tell in order that the hearer can get hold of God's revelation," for it is also a universal missionary experience that the first avenue (generally speaking, of course) to the understanding of the relevancy of Christianity is the dawning upon their minds of this unity of mankind through the One Creator, and not, for example, consciousness of sin, or the personality of Jesus. Consciousness of sin, and by virtue of that a deeper penetration into the background of the Christian revelation, is rarely the result of preaching, but most frequently that of a longer contact with the world of the Bible. Not the consciousness of sin brings men to Christ, but the continued contact with Christ brings them to consciousness of sin.

The approach to the area of social structures and institutions is of a different nature. The conception which tribal people have of religion and morality is that it means correct ritual and social behaviour, customs and laws, a moral and religious code of which the ancestors are the guardians. The tribe and the ancestors are a community of the living and the dead. This communal conception of life has the same dual character in relation to the Christian approach as all forms of human life have. It opens up many avenues for interpreting the Gospel in a way that appeals to deep-rooted needs and aspirations ; it offers also many stumbling-blocks. The Church and the sacraments, for example, represent apprehensions that have much affinity with these communal attitudes. The Christian Church as meant in Biblical realism is the true fellowship of the believers in Christ, their Head, in which fellowship the members are responsible to God, to each other, and to the world outside the Church. The sacraments are expressions of this fellowship in the form of symbolisms (water, bread) that have a universal appeal. To confront the current communal notions with these new Christian conceptions of fellowship is to discover a rich mine of possibilities of presenting the Christian truth in congenial patterns, and at the same time of uncovering the unregenerated, troubled character of the inherited conceptions and practices in relation to the idea of community. One of the most precious means therefore by which to incarnate the Gospel and to plant a living Christian Church is to devote great attention to the building up of Christian congregations and a Christian Church that represent a real fellowship under the authority of Christ. In these last words " a real fellowship under Christ's authority " the crucial point is contained. During the process of rearing the Christian Church, missionaries, Church councils and Synods or other functioning bodies cannot too often be reminded of the fact that not they, but Christ is the direct and sole Head and Authority of the Christian fellowship.

The complicated situation in the world of primitive religions to-day is that tribal life is disintegrating more or less quickly because of the new political, economic and cultural situation effected by the Western impact. Yet this need for fellowship and community is so thoroughly human and so ingrained in the mind of these peoples that this disintegration does not at all discredit this approach, but rather makes it more necessary.

The stumbling-blocks that on the other hand are implied in the pagan communal conception of life can be summed up in one term. The pagan idea of religious and moral life is thoroughly legalistic. Sin therefore is only understood in a very external way. This is the direct consequence of the social idea of religion. Here a great amount of missionary wisdom is needed. Legalism stands in radical contrast to the real meaning of the Christian faith and ethic. Yet these peoples expect from the new religion a clear and definite moral code, because that is their instinctive need. In the present destruction of all customary moral sanctions and foundations it is a matter of life or death for them, for one of the incontestable results of anthropological research is that for these peoples, still more than for peoples at other cultural stages, social behaviour-patterns are the indispensable vehicles of moral sense and moral conduct.

The need to solve the many problems in relation to their ancestral customs and modes of life that crop up for a group of pagans who have become Christians inevitably leads to a moralistic and legalistic attitude in the Christians as well as in the missionary body. The age-old problem of repressing, ignoring, or of destroying these customs and institutions presses itself upon our attention. From the pedagogical and psychological standpoint there are some attitudes worth recommending. As Willoughby in *The Soul of the Bantu* has said : " Repression and ignoring is driving to the background, not destroying. To put something better in its place is the best way of destroying." So, for example, the problem of re-creation and of feasts is one of the most urgent. It is one of the best instances to illustrate how a fundamental law of the Christian approach is never to oppose an institution or a custom that provides for a natural and vital need (even if it manifests itself in an objectionable way) without finding a substitute for it. It is essential to perform this search in very active co-operation with indigenous opinion, and to use it as a means to educate the conscience of the congregation or the Church. They should be confronted in all these problems with the fundamental elements of the Christian faith and ethic, according to which a prescription or a decision is never a law ; it is always a concrete religious answer to the question as to what, in a concrete situation, God's Will demands from us.

Another attitude is to employ existing institutions and customs that supplied a real need as the vehicle for new ends and contents. The attempt of Bishop Lucas of Masasi to use the time-honoured and deep-rooted African institution of initiation for the purposes of sexual, moral and religious instruction is a very good example of this attitude.

With all these inevitable pedagogical measures we are (it cannot be denied) head over ears in the legalistic and moralistic sphere. It is easy to lose sight of this important point in the heat of the day's work. A way to wrestle incessantly with it is to act by the principle that all these religious and moral decisions must be the outcome of the serious consideration of the Christian congregations themselves, in the light of their Christian understanding. Only if these decisions embody the voice of their Christian consciences *as they are and as they react to their confrontation with the Christian revelation* can they become factors of real spiritual growth. If they are experiments of missionary agencies while the indigenous Christians as a corporate unity stand largely passively aside, they lack this dynamic power. Gutmann justly speaks of this connection of the *Selbstbewegung der Gemeinde* (the initiative of the congregation).

Viewed from the purely religious side, in this whole complex of problems that are connected with the social expression of Christianity in customary or in new forms, lies a splendid opportunity of using it as an eye-opener to the thoughtful and leading minds of the congregation and of the Church, seeing that in these practical problems they are constantly confronted with the great and perennial problem of " the Law and the Gospel," and so are naturally led to the very core of the Christian revelation.

In missionary quarters opinions have been always divided as to whether the aim of missionary work should be the gathering of flocks of converted individuals or the Christianization of the people (*Einzelbekehrung* or *Volkschristianisierung* as the German terms are). The individualistic type of Pietistic and Methodist piety that were the originators of modern missions, and an absolute lack of insight into the communal conception of life and religion in the non-European world, led to the first standpoint. When through the results of missionary work achieved in different parts of the world of tribal religions (for example, the conversion of the Batak in Sumatra), missions had to face the fact that their work was not only evangelization and conversion but a many-sided task of nurture and education, the conception of *Volkschristianisierung* naturally won the day in theoretical discussion and in practical work. It is, however, safe to say that the trend of missionary thinking remained and remains individualistic, because conscious European thinking was and still is individualistic.

In pursuing the missionary task in a certain country or people it has been in the past extremely rare to start in a well-considered and methodical way from the solid fact of the communal conception and functioning of life and religion in the non-Christian world, and from the utter foreignness of our individualistic conception to its mind. Within recent years, however, this has become a topic of very lively discussion and investigation. Two examples of its sporadic occurrence in the past ought to be mentioned here. One is the way in which missionary work since 1890 has been carried on amongst the Toraja tribes in Central Celebes (Dutch East Indies) under the leadership of Dr A. C. Kruyt and Dr N. Adriani, and the other is the work of the Neuendettelsauer Mission amongst the inland Papua tribes in the part of New Guinea that formerly belonged to Germany and is now the mandated Territory of New Guinea under Australia. Kruyt and Adriani from the outset took full account of the fact that such a primitive tribe lives wholly in a communal and collective apprehension of life, and that it is therefore unnatural to them and detrimental to sound Christianization to proceed along the line of separating isolated individuals from the tribe and making them Christians in isolation from their given and inescapable basis of communal life. They and their fellow-missionaries worked many years patiently in order to gain a thorough knowledge of country and people so as to afford opportunity to the people to become acquainted with the missionaries and to learn to trust them as friends, and thus to sow the Message of the Gospel widely in ways adapted to their modes of apprehension and expression. After seventeen years of work the baptism of some groups of people, among them some leading men, took place, and since then the process of Christianizing these tribes is steadily going on, continuously inspired by two main principles. The first of these is that the decisive factor in this confrontation of the community with God in Christ is the work of God's Spirit and upon that our real trust must rest, and the second, that missions have to do this work on the basis of intelligent insight into the structure and functioning of the group life with which they have to do.

The prominent figure of the Neuendettelsauer Mission is Dr Chr. Keysser. He saw that primitive religion is primarily religiously-sanctioned group solidarity, founded on the biological fact of blood relation. Hence, the resistance against Christianity amongst such peoples is not primarily religious, but social. Recognizing the awkwardness and inapplicability of the individualistic approach to such undifferentiated unities of secular and religious life (at least when viewed from the standpoint of the European accustomed to a differentiated view of life), he approached the total community with the Message of the Gospel and the challenge of beginning *as a community* a new life under the leadership of Christ. After struggles of dramatic dimensions the community decision was reached that the roots of their group life should be transplanted. The group decided that its foundation and orientation point should be no longer their relatedness to the ancestors and their unchangeable customs, but their relatedness to the living God of Biblical realism with His ever-creative and stimulating Will. These depraved Papua tribes, along this way of group decision for Christianity and of building and developing their Christian life by group decisions also, on the basis of their gradually increasing understanding of it, have become vigorous Christian communities (of course with their ups and downs), with an astounding missionary zeal.[1]

In recent years the gigantic problem of the outcaste masses and Christianity, and Bishop Pickett's very valuable investigation in *Christian Mass Movements in India* have focused attention on the problem of group- or mass-conversion. In *The International Review of Missions* of 1937 Dr Warnshuis urges in a lucid article the great necessity of facing this issue very seriously, and Professor Latourette demonstrates with a wealth of material on pre-nineteenth-century evangelism how widespread in time and place the communal conception of religion and mass-conversion has always been.

When discussing the approach of Christianity to the non-Christian religions, especially to the tribal religions and the popular religions of the primitive type as practised by the masses of India, China, Japan and other parts of the world where these religions are mixed with elements from the higher religious civilizations in which they are enshrined, this group approach is of fundamental importance. The amount of missionary experience we have now achieved and the amount of intelligent insight which anthropology has put at our disposal, do not permit us any longer to neglect the basic importance of the group approach in missionary work. In pleading for it, no lowering of standards is recommended (as often is erroneously supposed or feared) but, on the contrary, its urge is to do more solid missionary work and to plant Christianity more firmly than is possible by conglomerations of isolated individuals, because it honestly

---

[1] Dr W. Freytag, one of the leading missionary thinkers in Germany, will shortly publish a book on this important mission field, which he studied carefully on the spot.

recognizes the impregnable fact that families, clans and tribes by their natural cohesiveness grow best into Christianity along the line of communal response. As Pickett's report and the literature on Central Celebes and New Guinea teach, in this group approach individual conversions continue to play a highly important and fruitful rôle. This is natural, because Christianity is essentially the religion of individual decisions, and there never can be a communal response that is really conscious of having decided for God and a new life until the individual consciences have been awakened and by virtue of this awakening *have appealed to their community.*

Of course, all over the world this communal conception and functioning of life is at different stages, and therefore the group approach has to be, accordingly, various. It would be very important if, besides Pickett's illuminating book, the writings of Kruyt, Adriani and Keysser became available to the whole missionary world, because they are extraordinarily stimulating.

However, what has happened in those corners of the world can, naturally, not be simply imitated. To mention only one instance to illustrate the necessity of judicious and selective borrowing, in Central Celebes as well as in New Guinea the decisive part of the work was done at a time when these tribes had as yet undergone no outside European influence. Nevertheless, the bedrock fact of the community apprehension and the necessity of group approach remain everywhere of the greatest significance.

There are in this group approach two main principles that apply everywhere. First, as it is a missionary approach, it must always be made in the spirit of a radically religious approach, the confrontation of the community with God in Christ, and not in the spirit of a sociological experiment. In the second place, the paternal attitude of missionary agencies must be entirely converted into an attitude of co-operation and guidance, for group approach implies working on the basis of group response, and group response means that this group, constantly confronting itself with the new world of religious and moral gifts and standards as contained in

Biblical realism, step by step takes its own responsible decisions and finds out its own way.

. . . .

ISLAM

Through all the ages Islam has been, in relation to the missionary efforts of the Christian Church, the teacher of patience. Its great function has been, and will probably continue to be for the present and for the immediate future, to remind the Christian Church that Christian missions, if they will be really Christian, that is to say if they spring from the apostolic obligation towards a divine commission, are not primarily driven by motives of spiritual conquest or success, but by the urge towards faithful and grateful witness to Christ. The confrontation of the Christian Church with the difficult missionary problem that Islam embodies means in the first place for the Christian Church to remind itself of what obedient faith is.

The exceptional stubbornness of Islam towards the efforts of Christian missions has two reasons, and it is well to look them straight in the face when the Christian approach is being discussed. In the first place, the secret of the iron rigidity of Islam is that its real " holy " and its real " god " is group solidarity, conceived with passionate religious directness. The " religion of Islam " is a sanctity apart; the unbroken unity of Islam the sacred treasure of the Moslem community and the Moslem individual. We children of the present time, who behold the enormous forces of fanaticism and devotion that are inherent in the creed of group solidarity, are probably in a more favourable condition to understand Islam than ever before has been the case. A very pertinent way to define Islam would be to call it a mediæval and radically religious form of that national-socialism which we know at present in Europe in its pseudo-religious form. As with all militant creeds of group solidarity Islam evinces therefore a bitter and stubborn resistance to any effort that might involve change of religion, or, to put it more adequately, to any break in the group solidarity.

In its relation to Christianity there enters, however, another factor of importance. The meeting of Christianity with the other great non-Christian religions is, properly speaking, a meeting of strangers, since they have been born in different geographical and spiritual hemispheres without any historical connection. With Islam the case is very different. Christianity and Islam are acquaintances from the very beginning. The first stood at the cradle of the latter and made no mean contribution to its birth. This might, however, be of slight significance, but there is another point that makes all the difference. In the years of its genesis Islam, having originally taken a friendly attitude towards Christianity as the valid religion of revelation for the " nation " of the Christians, became antagonistic towards it by the mouth of its prophet, that is virtually by the mouth of divine revelation. This antagonism to and indignant rejection of some cardinal elements of Christianity (Jesus' Sonship, His death on the Cross and consequently such doctrines as the Trinity and Reconciliation or Atonement) are incorporated in the *Quran*, the basis of the Moslem faith, and so belong to the system of Islam. To reject Christianity is with Islam not merely the natural and intelligible reaction of every religion or world conception that has sufficient vigour in it to want to maintain itself ; with Islam it belongs to its religious creed. To accept Christianity implies the explicit recognition of the error of Islam. This creedal antagonism towards Christianity is strengthened and still more embittered by the kind of political relations which Moslem and Christian peoples have had in the course of history.

This whole background one must constantly have in mind when thinking about the Christian missionary approach to Islam. If we do this, it is at once clear why the prime condition of the approach to Islam is faith, hope, love and endurance that never wear out, and of which love is " the greatest of all " (1 Cor. xiii.). By its stubborn rigidity and pride, implied in its being the deification of group solidarity, Islam is a trying religion to converse with. The missionary, however, who has fallen a victim to the attitude of fear or

disgust or hatred of Islam, does better to go immediately
home and never come back. Nobody has a right to throw
a stone at him, but it is certain that he can only do harm.
Only if faith, hope, love and endurance, however much
tempted, ever and again break through triumphantly,
will he perform his missionary obligation well. As this is
the prime condition of all missionary approach to Islam,
there follows from it the conclusion that the Christian Church
must stand behind her ambassadors in this difficult field with
prayer and loving remembrance to a degree quite different
from what is practised now.

Those two elementary conditions in the Christian
approach towards Islam are not mentioned here as mere
pious, edifying talk, but as hard, matter-of-fact conditions.
Whosoever nods impatiently, thinking, let us go on to more
concrete and practical subjects, never has understood the
root of the Moslem missionary problem and probably never
will. Detailed proposals of avenues to Islam will not yield
their full fruitage before these elementary conditions are
fulfilled. The Christian Church and its missionary agencies
should harbour no illusions about that. Whosoever has
become bruised and bleeding in the struggle with Islam can
testify to it.

Another important conclusion that in relation to the
approach can be drawn from the general Moslem background is that the entrance to this impregnable religious
citadel cannot be opened by presenting Christianity to the
Moslem mind as the enrichment of its half-truths as to its
belief in God, its veneration for Jesus, its logos speculation,
its conception of fraternity, etc., or developing into full
growth what is to be found, for instance, in the *Quran* about
the Holy Spirit (*Ruh*) and the need for an intercessor. As
the axis of Islam is wholly turning on the idea of group
solidarity under the ægis of Allah and the Apostle, all the
elements in the *Quran* or in the creedal evolution of Islam
that have some connection with Christianity (and there are
many because Islam is, culturally speaking, the continuation
of the Hellenistic-Christian civilization of the Near and
Middle East) have a wholly different character and tendency.

Hence this fragmentary method [1] leads to nothing, for these elements are not half-truths in relation to Christianity ; they simply belong to another plane of religious apprehension. The one thing that every missionary and Christian who preaches the Gospel in the " house of Islam " has to do with unwearying perseverance in regard to these elements borrowed from historical Christianity is to explain patiently what, according to Biblical realism, these elements really mean, and wait for the results. Generally speaking, the Moslem, however touchy he may be in religious matters, will listen attentively to a positive and restrained religious witness.

A significant item in the directly religious [2] approach to Islam is also that the best method undoubtedly is direct personal contact and study of the Bible in a spirit of human sympathy and openness, the Moslem being treated not as a non-Christian but as a fellow-man with the same fundamental needs, aspirations and frustrations, whose religious experience and insight are as worth while as the missionary's, simply because he is a living human being. The personal contact itself must show how one has to open the world of the Bible in every concrete instance, by beginning at the centre or at the periphery of Christian truth or somewhere between.

One point may probably be stated with great emphasis, namely, that especially in the world of Islam to present Christianity as a set of doctrines is the most awkward way conceivable. The following reasons may be mentioned to substantiate this dictum. Islam itself is creedal and doctrinal to the core. To present Christianity as a set of doctrines is to rouse the militantly intellectualist spirit of Islam (and of all creedalism), and to move entirely outside the religious sphere. Its wilful rejection of Christianity is directed against some definite Christian doctrines and is crystallized in some of its own doctrines. Moreover, even if the missionary avoids presenting Christianity in a doctrinal way, the Moslem will often force him by his attacks to pronounce upon

[1] Compare Chapter IV.
[2] For the moment the approach through schools, etc., is not discussed.

doctrinal matters. Further, in the course of the ages Islam
has lived together with the Eastern Churches, which are all
the most appalling instances of petrified doctrinalism and
ritualism. In consequence, the Moslem world has been
robbed of any opportunity to get an idea of the dynamic
forces of Christianity. A radical purging of the idea that
doctrinalism is the genuine aspect of religion in the higher
sense is badly needed in the Moslem world and in the
Eastern Churches. The missionary approach, in so far as it is
dependent on its own initiative, must abjure all doctrinal
approach and invite the Moslem to penetrate into the living
world of Biblical realism.

The presupposition on which these fundamental elements
of the approach to Islam are built are, of course, a direct
and vital contact with Biblical realism and a real knowledge
of the Moslem ways of thinking and living and of the religious
vocabulary of Islam. As long as the missionary societies
accept such a low grade of this knowledge in most missionaries, even in countries where life is steeped in Islam and
Arabic, it is self-deception to expect appreciable results.

In the discussion on the approach to Islam mysticism
and the quality of religious life as found in the mystic orders
(*tariqa*) have been very prominent. Very recently Dr Wilson
Cash in his book, *Christendom and Islam*, devoted much
attention to this side of Islam as one of the chief ways of
finding new approaches and building bridges by personal
contact with those Moslems who through mysticism search
for God. This tendency is very intelligible, for it is undoubtedly true that amongst the mystically-minded in this
religion the most sensitive spiritual people are to be found,
with whom true human and religious contact is possible.
Among these people one finds men and women of great
spiritual beauty. C. F. Andrews in his picture of Zaka Ullah
of Delhi has offered a very good model of this spiritual type
in Islam. It is the more intelligible because, as was pointed
out in our sketch of Islam,[1] for historical reasons Muslim and
Christian Eastern mysticism of the emotional and contemplative type have much in common. Many missionaries

[1] Chapter VI.

whose own religious experience runs along the lines of the devotional life and whose religious emphasis falls on the communion of the soul with God and the inner drama that ensues from it, recognize this with great gratitude.

Taking the problem of mysticism as an approach to Islam in its completeness we must again, it seems, make a very important distinction between the practical and the theoretical. From the standpoint of human, evangelistic approach it is undoubtedly true that among mystically-minded people it is possible to find the greatest number of individuals with whom genuine religious intercourse is possible on the basis of common humanity. As always, this is from the missionary standpoint of very great value, and in Islam it is of specially great value because the well-known barrier of self-conscious pride is then absent. The mystics with their concentration on " God and the soul " have removed the axis of religious life from group-solidarity to communion with God in the purely religious sense of the word.

Theoretically speaking, the situation is entirely different. The idea or expectation that mysticism or the mystic orders are probably the domains of religious life in Islam whence the road to Christianity will be paved is founded on a double error. The first is that, however widespread mysticism in Islam may be, it is wholly an alien growth in this religion. It is true that in the mystic quarters of the Moslem world one can often find a delicious rest from the impregnable rigidity of the genuine Islamic system of faith and law, but the real missionary problem is just this system and not the exception that is embodied in mysticism. At the same time this situation suggests very vividly that one of the best ways to soften this rigid system is to encourage in all kinds of ways personal religious life in Islam, in which all emphasis falls on a life of religious and moral fellowship with God. The second error is contained in the fact that mysticism is a very complicated phenomenon. This appears immediately from the simple facts that can be observed in all the non-Christian religions, namely, that mysticism is not only the most lofty form of religious life in them, but the most degraded form as well, and that one can notice (at present this tendency is very marked) so often the curious amalgamation of mysticism and anti-religious scepticism in one and the same person.

Mysticism is one of the great universal forms of religious life that are essentially the same in all ages and environments. The mysticisms of all religions are clearly akin to each other. The explanation of this well-known fact is that mysticism is one of the most sublime and most dangerous products of naturalistic monism. Hence, the oneness of God and the soul is its fundamental theme, in ways and accents that vary extraordinarily ; and the identity of the divine essence with the essence of man or the world is its fundamental pre-supposition. The grand theopanistic systems of India, of Far Eastern Buddhism, and of heterodox Moslem mysticism, in which man along the road of gnosis masters the rapturous certitude of his essential oneness with the Divine Essence and Ultimate Reality ; the graded ways of contemplative mysticism striving for the beatific vision of God, which we encounter in all religions ; the many variations of emotional mysticism, in which the soul pines and longs for the Eternal—these are all more or less offshoots from naturalistic monism. The first type of aristocratic theopanistic mysticism belongs wholly to it and is wholly antagonistic to the prophetic religion of Biblical realism. Contemplative mysticism has many affinities with naturalistic monism. It is easily prone, in its Christian forms, to live principally in a world of religious apprehension that is foreign to Biblical realism, but preserves the Christian colouring by Christian ideas and imagery. Emotional mysticism may be influenced by naturalistic monism, because hardly any form of mysticism escapes entirely the influence of this pull, but is often an independent growth in the positive religions of prophetic origin such as Islam, Judaism and Christianity. It is the need of the human soul for the imperishable and for the touch of fervour and immediate personal contact, entering upon a marriage with fundamental elements of, for example, Islam or Christianity. Mysticism in the typical sense of the word, either in its theopanistic, contemplative or emotional form, does not occur in the prophetic religion of Biblical realism. To call Paul or John mystics is to confound a tone of religious fervour and adoration with mysticism, which always has a tendency towards regarding *frui Deo* (to enjoy God) as the highest goal of the Christian life. To use other terms : the highest goal is to become absorbed in the contemplation and adoration of the pure Beauty of the Divine Essence, as, for example, can be learnt from Augustinian and mediæval Christian mysticism. In Biblical realism, however, in this dispensation the irremovable centre of religious life is the Divine Will. The mystical attitude, in the sense of longing for the eternal and for adoration in the realm of religious life, is, however, a universal phenomenon in the religious life of mankind, and will always create in any positive religion, Christianity included, various forms of religious expression.

Two cardinal points must be kept constantly in mind in relation to this universal situation. First, the sole standard of reference being the prophetic theocentric religion of Biblical realism, the mystical tendencies of religious life are as real as every other tendency (the legalist, the moralist, the dogmatic, the ecclesiastical, etc.), and have to obtain authoritative guidance from this theocentric religion. Secondly, in the problem of the relation of Christianity to the non-Christian religions, one must never explain the similarity of the universal mystical attitude, which is to be found in all religions, by a similarity between the fundamental religious apprehensions of the different religions (for example, Christianity and Islam ; Christianity and Hinduism or Buddhism). The first idea of similarity corresponds to a fact and hence can be a basis for universal religious contact ; the second idea is a fallacy and leads to confusion.

The preceding, it seems, is applicable always and under all circumstances. What is there to be said, however, about the approach in the concrete situation of Islam as it is to-day ?

The sketch of the present Moslem situation [1] has enlightened us as to the far-reaching effects of the cultural, political and economic revolution it is going through, and the typical differences between the politically dependent and

[1] Chapter VII.

independent Moslem countries. In surveying this whole scene it is very difficult to say whether, when compared with the past, the prospects of the Moslem missionary situation are at present brighter or gloomier. For both views substantial reasons can be adduced. In the past Christian missions had to do with a largely lethargic and stagnant Moslem world, in which missionary inroads were made along various lines. This work could, generally speaking, be done in the politically dependent as well as in the relatively independent countries by virtue of the protection of the great political powers. In the relatively independent countries (Turkey, Iran, for example) preaching to Moslems was practically forbidden and conversion to Christianity meant ostracism or death. A great and beneficent charitable and educational work was developed, and the evangelizing activity in the chief centres of Islam (Near and Middle East) was directed towards a revivification of the petrified Eastern Churches or (forced by the enmity of the bishops of these churches against the reformatory zeal kindled in their flock by the missionaries) the building up of Evangelical Churches composed of Eastern Christians. In the politically dependent countries, because this Christian legacy was absent and the principle of religious neutrality permitted a more direct witness to the Moslems, missionary activity had, according to the peculiar condition of Islam in these countries, a greater or less success in the gaining of converts. In India the results have been very meagre ; in Java it has been possible to an appreciable degree to build up from converts from Islam Christian Churches, which are at present steadily growing and adding to their number.

To-day we have a deeply agitated Moslem world, confused, but also defensive, defiant and aggressive at the same time. In the politically dependent countries there is a growing irritation against foreign supremacy, especially strong in North Africa and the Near East, which results in the strengthening of Moslem group-solidarity and in a growing resentment against missionary activity, which is interpreted as a tool of Western imperialism. In others (India, the Dutch East Indies) there develops more and more, along the lines of literary, propagandist, educational and charitable activity, a counter-move, aiming at defending and strengthening Islam and attacking Christianity.

In the politically independent countries the substitute-religion of nationalism, with national consolidation as the *summum bonum*, has taken the place of the religion of Moslem group-solidarity and has opened up a startling chapter in the religious policy of states that have been Moslem during long centuries. Islam is disestablished and purposely starved (Turkey, Iran) or, as in Egypt, Islam is definitely used as an instrument in the working out of the new national destiny, with a consequent recrudescence of its social prestige, which results in an ever stronger pressure on the members of the Coptic Church to become Moslem. In both cases the result for Christian missions is a severe hampering of the scope of its activity. An indication of the paradoxical character of the situation, however, is that although in such countries as Turkey and Iran religious " propaganda " of any kind is forbidden, on the other hand the opportunity of witnessing to the Gospel in personal religious contact with Turks and Iranians (which was formerly forbidden) is greater than ever before and, at least legally, one is free to choose his own religion. Moreover, in the future it may become of great significance that the radically nationalist line of policy has demolished the age-old *millet*-system, which marked Christians and Moslems off from each other as different " nations " and did so much to create a thick wall of mutual suspicion between Islam and Christianity. At present not only Moslems but also Jews and Christians are considered Turks, because the Turks are no longer a religious Moslem unity, but a people bound together by unity in language, culture and national ideals.

If the present Moslem missionary situation is considered rather gloomy, it is apparently not because it is less favourable than in the past, for the present great stir has unmistakable advantages, but because it is so extremely complicated and utterly uncertain. The continuance or the destruction of organized missionary activity in many Moslem lands depends entirely on the favour or disfavour of the moment.

It is impossible to discuss the many intricate problems that are connected with the various countries as to the concrete possibilities of approach, for example, the handling and the training of the convert, the condition of the Eastern Churches and the question as to how far they are fit for their apostolic obligation, because to discuss them satisfactorily would require more space and, above all, intimate practical acquaintance with the various fields. Only some main points can be touched upon.

A great stumbling-block to a right approach, especially in the present complicated situation with the severely restricted opportunities for evangelistic action, is the grievous lack of unity amongst the various missionary agencies and the rivalry between the quarrelling Eastern Churches. This discord undermines the forces that are already so pathetically exiguous over against the strong citadel of Islam, and, besides, evokes much justified criticism. It obscures to a lamentable extent the real character of Christianity. When one ponders on this situation one reminds oneself that especially in the Moslem mission field the aim of missions can only be the effort to unveil the content and meaning of Christianity in its purely religious aspects. It is utterly incomprehensible that the missionary agencies and Churches, always so eagerly on the look-out for new approaches to Islam, are so complacently inactive in relation to this situation. There is nothing in the conditions of the Moslem world that prevents them from setting to work at this matter. On the contrary, in view of the Moslem situation, literally everything urges towards the removal of this stumbling-block, which only waits for our determined will to be accomplished. In other words the practical demonstration of a deep and transforming ecumenical spirit in the missionary bodies and in the quarrelling Churches is one of the most needed and certainly most effective approaches to Islam.

A diligent cultivation of personal contacts on a high religious and moral plane of human openness and Christian humility, and the ministry to secular needs in a spirit of disinterested service are everywhere the roads that still lie open, although in view of the present situation these approaches will demand much ingenuity and tact.

The production of Christian literature, in periodicals or otherwise, aiming at the elucidation of what pure and undefiled religion is and wherein the essential religious and ethical character of Christianity consists, is in the present state of confused religious thinking and feeling not only a service to the cause of missions, but to the cause of humanity too. In this literary work one must also be always alive to the necessity of employing the religious terms and thought-forms of those to whom one appeals.

It seems that the time approaches more and more when the Christian Church will have to face a concrete meeting with Islam. Africa and the Dutch East Indies, the two great territories where Islam and Christianity are both spreading rapidly and where paganism as an established religion is on the brink of disappearing, will become in the near future the places where these two religions are the only official religions that occupy the field. Islam, especially in Africa, has many recommendations when the situation is viewed realistically. The Negro, by becoming Moslem, enters the religious, social, cultural and blood-community of Islam. Islam adapts itself very easily by its leniency to the current standard of Negro life. No long catechumenate is demanded ; magical practices and ideas, so dear to the native mind, are easily incorporated ; polygamy, that deep-rooted social institution in Africa, is even sanctioned and not at all combated as in Christianity. It is no self-complacency to say that Islam is in Africa at present stagnant and sterile, that it arrests real development because it does not afford such a real moral background as is to-day so badly needed in this continent, while on the other hand Christianity is progressive and does afford moral foundation. Yet there is no law that induces men to choose what is the best for them according to the thought of the best and most disinterested well-wishers of Africa. The way in which the white man handles the race problem subjects the Negro to revolting humiliation and teaches him daily the lesson that the godless " Christian " West does not know, as Islam does, about social, cultural and religious solidarity and unity with men of other races and cultures. This Christian-Moslem situation in Africa is for the missionary agencies and the Christian Churches a call to demonstrate real Christian unity and solidarity and to face race problems not as Europeans but as Christians who represent the community of Christ, in which everyone has his equal place irrespective of race.

How to educate the Churches in Africa and the Dutch East Indies to meet the Moslem problem in a way that does not fall far short of the spirit of Christ and the religious character of Christianity is a task that is looming up before us in the near future.

INDIA

Since the day in 1605 when de Nobili came into Madura and discovered that Christianity was a despised religion, because the Hindus identified becoming a Christian with following the customs of " the Prangui " (Europeans), up to the present moment, the foreignness of Christianity and the question how to adapt it to India's genius have been burning and much-contested problems. Possessing now, as we do, a better knowledge of the nature and temper of Protean Hinduism than was possible in the seventeenth century, and living in a time in which the religious and social system which Hinduism represents is undergoing such drastic changes as never before were dreamed possible, we are not at all astonished that becoming a Christian was (and is) conceived as following the customs of the Prangui. Nor will we so easily leap for the solution of the problem of the right approach to de Nobili's solution of excessive accommodation which he so valiantly defended and executed. For it must be constantly affirmed with great emphasis that we shut off the way to a realistic grasp of the problem if we forget that this identification of Christianity with following the customs of the Prangui is not only due to the unimaginative, rigid and dogmatically-bound mind of Western missions, but *at least as much* to the Hindu system itself. This is not said to exculpate Western missions, for the problems of the foreignness of

Christianity and of how to relate it to India, the most creative country on the earth in the realm of religious expression, are far too serious and burning to permit of spending energy on exculpations. It is said in order to effect an adequate estimate of the whole problem of approach. The dominant conception of religion in Hinduism is the social one, according to which religion is a set of attitudes and customs peculiar to India. Conformity with these attitudes and customs is the prime and self-evident religious obligation of everyone born a Hindu. This wholly collective and pragmatic conception of religion understands other religions in the same way. The modernization of Hinduism has not weakened this deep-rooted and instinctive conception, but has rather strengthened it. Gandhi's swadeshi-theory of Hinduism and religion in general is this ancient idea in modern dress, provided with an addition that is characteristically modern, namely, that because every country has its peculiar religion as it has its peculiar fauna or flora, Hinduism is sufficient for India's needs. In our sketch of the present condition of Hinduism we had to call attention to the fact that one of its characteristic features is the *militant* recrudescence of this pragmatist idea of religion. Many leading minds in Hinduism are at present not primarily concerned about *true* religion, but are wholly absorbed in the preservation of the Sana-tana Dharma (the " eternal " Hindu code of life) and the defence of traditional culture and religion, not because they are truth, but because they are the national heritage, which is a wholly a-religious idea. The article in *The International Review of Missions* (1937) on The Arya Samaj and Missions is very instructive on this point. It is in the real interest of India and of pure religion alike to announce the quest for truth, that is, interest in true religion.

Hence, when occupied with the problem of approach and adaptation the situation we have to face in India is formidable. Hinduism itself, being eminently a social religion of group-solidarity (though with an accent very different from Islam), stamps every religion as " foreign " that does not fit in with its whole socio-religious system. Although permitting its adherents to think what they like, it is very intolerant as to what they deliberately do or neglect in the realm of socio-religious customs and ceremonies. Christianity can never come to terms with this attitude, for two reasons. In the first place, because it belongs to its genius as a prophetic religion not to have a pragmatic or social conception of religion, but to conceive it primarily and emphatically in the terms of truth and in those of the objective reality of the objects of its faith. In the second place, although Hinduism permits one to think what he likes provided he does so without repudiating the socio-religious and ceremonial aspect that is demanded by the community, its customs and ceremonies presuppose and imply various religious apprehensions (idolatry, a polytheistic attitude, etc.) which are wholly compatible with the pragmatic and relativist temper of " naturalist " Hinduism, but are absolutely incompatible with " prophetic " Christianity. Whosoever soaks his mind for only a few hours in the radically religious and theocentric atmosphere of the prophets and the Gospels knows of this indelible distinction. With all due recognition of the great religious and moral sincerity that can be found in the practical manifestations of Hinduism, Christianity cannot but apprehend this fundamental " relativist " attitude of Hinduism as revoltingly insincere, and Hinduism cannot but apprehend the fundamental " absolutist " attitude of Christianity as offensively exclusive. Christianity never can give up its much-criticized exclusiveness, because if it did it would deny its prophetic core, that is to say, its life and essence.

Some very important conclusions follow from this elemental background. The problem of adaptive approach can never be solved in the direction of combining the spiritual allegiance to Christianity with that to Hinduism in some form or conception. Further, when we diligently seek for adaptive approaches our inspiration in doing so must not be the delusive expectation that the reproach of foreignness will then die out, for it lies in the nature of Hinduism to treat every non-Indian religion as foreign. This reproach will not die out before many, many millions of India's inhabitants have entered the Christian Church and so Chris-

tianity has in fact become an Indian religion. The diligent
search for adaptive approaches is an urgent programme for
other reasons. They have to be sought for the sake of the
right discharge of the missionary task, namely, in order to
get Christianity translated and interpreted in terms and
forms of expression that fit in with the Indian background,
or, to put it differently, in order to work for its Indian incarnation. They have to be sought, too, for the sake of
justice towards India, for this great country, like every other
country or people, has the elementary right not to be artifici-
ally pressed and choked in a foreign armour, but to wear its
natural religious dress. And at this point we see that it is
on account of their lack of imagination and of liberty of
religious spirit that the Western missionary agencies are prone
with fatal easiness to confound the " prophetic " exclusiveness as found in Biblical realism with their particular ecclesiastical and customary forms of expression, which, properly
speaking, means to identify unconsciously the historical and
relative embodiment of Christianity with the Christian
revelation itself.

The Hindu mind, by virtue of its historical background,
easily hears in the claim for truth and exclusive revelation
in Christ a contempt for other religions and a lack of modesty
in the face of the great mystery of Ultimate Truth. Christians
and missionaries almost as easily make the mistake of conveying the impression that they possess and dispense Ultimate
Truth, which in this Indian atmosphere suggests coarse
irreverence and vulgar mediocrity, and often is so. In
connection with this very important and subtle element in
the Indian background, it has to be laid down as a first
commandment that the claim for the exclusive character of
the Christian truth may only be made because the revelation in Christ is not a truth which the Christian Church
possesses in the sense of the philosopher's stone, but is the
truth and grace that God embodied in Jesus of Nazareth
and to which it reverently and gratefully points. Outside
this revelational act of God, which is not our doing or our
attainment, it remains true for all men, Christians and
Hindus alike, that Truth is a bigger thing than we can

grasp and that humility in the face of it is therefore the only adequate attitude.

. . . .

The religious heritage of India is so overwhelmingly rich that the approach of Christianity to it, starting from the background mentioned in the few preceding pages, can only be alluded to in some main outlines.

To begin with the approach towards the structure and the core of so-called " higher " Hinduism, the solution will not be found along the lines of a synthesis of Christianity and Vedanta or Bhakti. All intentional, intellectual efforts to weld these two worlds into a real synthesis are artificial and unnatural, because, as we have tried to show,[1] the prophetic and historical character of the religion of Biblical realism is incompatible with the naturalistic-monistic soul and sweep of these splendid achievements of Indian religious search and religio-philosophical thought. To walk this road would end in succumbing to the irresistible syncretistic spell of Hinduism. Nor, it seems, is the right approach to be found with F. Heiler in the direction of construing Christianity as made up of many splendid Indian truths, values and ideas, but these corrected and added to. To present it as a corrective would mean, for instance, to present Christ's incarnation as the improved and perfect edition of the Indian avatar-conception, or to present the Biblical conception of sin as a perfecting and purifying complement of the Indian idea that desire, passion and ultimately *avidya* (ignorance) are the root-evils of life. If we follow this same line of thought, additions to Hinduism would be the Resurrection, the idea of the Kingdom of God, the idea of the Church, etc. The objections to this approach are that, on closer investigation, it simply is not true that the ideas of incarnation, sin, faith, etc., as contained in Biblical realism, are corrections of similar ideas in Hinduism. This whole approach to the problem by construing additions and corrections is an artificial kind of religious and theological chemistry, since it ignores the fact that a living integrated religion cannot be treated in this mechanical way, which

[1] Cf. Chapters V–VIII.

smells of the study and not of life. Lastly it moves in the sphere of distinguishing superior and inferior religious elements and values, which will be rightly resented by Hinduism.

Hinduism in its " higher " forms being either contemplative or speculative acosmistic mysticism, and mysticism being generally considered the most sublime and religious specimen of religion, it is intelligible that endeavours are made by Dr Appasamy and others to interpret and present essential Christianity as the highest and most perfected specimen of mysticism. It manifests, according to them, its greater perfection in that it clearly teaches the communion of the human soul with the personal God and imparts great moral fervour, in consequence of which the deep Hindu conception of the indwelling of God (*antaryamin*) is purified and invigorated by the stimulus of prophetic transcendency in God. By this greater moral fervour, it is thought, the weak moral fibre of Hindu mysticism is strengthened, and the dangerous tendency towards identifying the human soul with the Divine is overcome.

It seems to us that the key to the problem of the right approach is not to be found here, for reasons lying both in Christianity and Hinduism. As we have argued already,[1] the prophetic religion of Biblical realism is no specimen of mysticism. It is unique by its revelational character and therefore as such transcends all types of religion, being their " crisis " and their fulfilment at the same time. Whosoever does not err in taking for mysticism the deep undertone of adoration running through the Gospel and the Epistles of John, and sees how markedly " prophetic " the spirit of these documents is, will not single them out as the classic documents of Christian mysticism. The adoring temper that pervades them has always offered many points of contact for those who in the course of Church History conceived Christianity along mystical lines. If John, however, were a thorough mystic (and he must be if he represents the standard specimen of mysticism) he never would have emphasized so strongly in his Gospel and his

[1] Cf. in this chapter under " Islam."

Epistles that " God became flesh," because the incarnation
in the historical person of Jesus of Nazareth is the greatest
stumbling-block to the mystical apprehension of religion.
Christian mystics respect it, because they want to be Christians, but they would never *create* a conception that is so
abhorrent as the incarnation is to the mystical view, in
which the historical has no real place. The avatar-idea
cannot be adduced to refute this, because an *avatar* is not
meant as an actual acceptance of flesh by God, but is the
mythological personification of a God conceived as a person
for practical reasons, while the real Divine is the attributeless
and actionless Pure Essence (nirguna Brahma).

The prophetic religion of Biblical realism is neither
mystical nor unmystical, it is supra-mystical, just as it is
supra-moral. Moreover, to present essential Christianity as
perfected mysticism and as the evenly-balanced proportion
of the sublimest religious elements in Hinduism, is to remain
in the sphere of a comparison and measurement of religious
values. This in itself is a very important and interesting
thing to do, but as an approach to truth it does not fit in
with the revelational character of essential Christianity.

Another reason why the presentation of Christianity in
comparison with Hinduism as the perfect form of mysticism
is not the key to the problem is that in doing so one commits
an injustice to Hinduism, which contains, from the standpoint of religious psychology, in *Vedanta* and *Bhakti* some of
the most perfect specimens of mysticism that are to be
found in the world. This is so by the nature of the case,
for Hinduism is one of the completest outgrowths of naturalistic monistic religion, and thorough, consistent mysticism
is the legitimate child of naturalistic monism. The inborn
trend of real mysticism, whether it is explicit or implicit,
is excellently expressed in *Enneads* I. ii. 6 : " the object is
not to be free from sin, but to be God." (ἡ σπουδὴ
οὐκ ἔξω ἁμαρτίας εἶναι ἀλλά θεόν εἶναι). To conceive
essential Christianity as mysticism is to disregard its real
nature and structure. The only approach that can be
fundamentally right in the Indian environment is to penetrate into the peculiar character of Biblical realism, to take

it unceasingly as the point of orientation and inspiration, and then to express it courageously by means of the great wealth of religious concepts and terms that are available in Hinduism. This wealth is simply stupendous. We refer, to mention only a few instances, to the deep and moving piety of the *bhakti*-poets, who rejoice in faith and grace and communion with God, and complain of sin and forlornness ; or to Ramanuja who fought with astounding philosophical and theological depth and acumen the religious battle for a personal God against absolute advaita-monism. It would be folly under these conditions to try to express essential Christianity in clumsy translations of Aristotelian or Platonic or modern philosophical terms and concepts (as has been done in the West) and to neglect these treasures. We repeat, however, emphatically what has been said in the preceding chapter : in the legitimate and necessary effort to use these Indian tools, soul and intellect must be bent on *expressing* essential Christianity, not on accommodating it, because if this is not done, there ensues a fatal confusion of points of orientation.

Nevertheless, although we cannot agree to the presentation of Christianity as the classic specimen of mysticism, the efforts of Dr Appasamy and others are extremely valuable. They spring from the deep and much-needed desire to have in India not an isolated, foreign, made-in-Europe Christianity. In his books[1] and those of his co-workers there is, despite the (in our opinion) often confused orientation and a too preponderatingly analytical approach from the angle of values and experiences, a great amount of penetrating Christian insight and feeling. Efforts like these are the natural and much-needed way for the Indian Christian mind to get hold of the Christian revelation in a peculiar Indian manner and to imbue its expression with genuinely Indian flavour. It is to be hoped that such efforts will not remain isolated phenomena.

The Christian approach as a practical problem (and not

[1] I refer to his books on *Christianity as Bhakti-marga, What is Moksha ?*, the series on *The Bhaktas of the World* ; V. Chakkarai's *Jesus the Avatar* and *The Cross and Indian Thought*, and C. S. Paul's *The Suffering God*.

only as a fundamental religious and theological problem) lies, so to speak, on the secondary plane of the Indian religious heritage. By the secondary plane we mean the host of important vehicles and patterns of religious expression that have originated in India apart from the elemental apprehensions and attitudes. These vehicles are *dhyana* (meditative prayer), *ahimsa, yoga, shanti, ashram, sannyasin* or *sadhu, kirtan,* the chanting of *purana's bhakti,* etc. If one analyses these concepts, practices and psychological states in vital relation to their true background, many of them certainly do not fit in with essential Christianity, for they are without exception refined outgrowths of spiritualized naturalist religions and have been created as means for a religion of self-realization and self-deliverance, which is quite the opposite of the prophetic religion of Biblical realism. Yet in themselves they are means of human expression. In the Indian case they have become deeply ingrained in the Indian mind, and are as legitimate as other means of expression of the human mind. In the sphere of Biblical religion there is no ground either for deprecating or for prescribing, for instance, meditative prayer (*dhyana*) or leading the life of a homeless wanderer (*sannyasin*) for Christ's and His Gospel's sake as Sadhu Sundar Singh did, or chanting the glad tidings of the Gospels in the India purana-style as Narayan Tilak in imitation of Tulsi Das planned in his Christayan. The sole rule is to live under the authority of Christ and to sharpen our consciences by faith in Him and obedience to His will and spirit. Hence, it is highly advisable to try to express Christianity in these typically Indian modes of expression, far better than to do it in the uncongenial European way, and to fill in the process all these modes, whose genuine Indian content and temper is different from the essentially Christian apprehension, with new Christian content.

The objection will be made that this is not without dangers. Of course it is not, because real life is always dangerous. To remain mainly paralysed by fear of dangers, or to imitate Western forms of expression that are in themselves valuable but come from an entirely different background, is still more dangerous. That on which the whole matter hinges is not that it is dangerous, but that it must be done for the sake of a vigorous Christianity. The only way to turn the inevitable dangers into stepping-stones is if the effort is made not out of sentimental love-making with indigenous forms, but out of the desire to live the Christian truth and life better, for, as Dr Stanley Jones once rightly said, " We must become more Christian and more Indian." If one stands with both feet firmly planted in the world of Biblical realism, the risk of becoming, in the close contact with Indian life, overwhelmed by the grandeur and profundity of Indian thought and religious experience, or by the subtly pervading polytheistic atmosphere in India, or by the deeply impregnated apprehensions of *karma*, *maya* and *samsara*, all entirely in contrast with the fundamentally Christian apprehension, will not merely be escaped, but will be met in the most fruitful way. Unless it faces these risks, Christianity in India will try to grow isolated from its living environment, in confronting which it has come to spiritual maturity. In the same way the Primitive Church by confronting, wrestling and commingling with the world of mystery-religions, Oriental Hellenistic philosophy and gnosticism in which it lived, got its peculiar grasp of the Christian revelation.

A splendid example is Sadhu Sundar Singh, who led the Indian sannyasi-life, practised *dhayna*, knew about *shanti*, stressed the indwelling of God in his heart through the Spirit (*antaryamin*), was a master in the Eastern art of figurative speech, and at the same time was thoroughly Christian, entirely freed from the Indian elemental opposites of transiency and eternity, *maya* and reality, *samsara* and *moksha* by self-deliverance, because his Christian life revolved around the " prophetic " opposites of sin and grace, rebellion and reconciliation, religious and moral self-assertion, and the concentration on the divine gift of salvation and renewal of life.

From the need for a related Christianity there have sprung two special modes of approach that require attention. In the first place there is that of the *ashram*. It aims at creating a thoroughly Indian atmosphere and mode of religious life, in order to bring Christians in contact with the genuine Indian background from which they often have become estranged, and to bring non-Christians in contact with Christianity in an atmosphere congenial to them. Such is the idea that lies at the basis of the Christa Seva Sangh in Poona. To mention a few others, the Christukula at Tiru-pattur (Arcot) grew more from the desire to transcend the boundaries of race and to demonstrate by service the spirit of a " Family of Christ " (Christukula=family of Christ). The Church Missionary Society has formed an *ashram* in the Nadia district in Bengal with the object of deepening the spiritual life and attracting young men to new channels of service in the Christian Church.

The *ashram* usually combines the Indian idea of retreat for the cultivation of spiritual life and religious study with the European idea of a settlement for service to the environ-ment in various ways. From the information available one receives the impression that this excellent idea does not make much headway. The idea is excellent, because the *ashram*, if led by the right kind of people, is full of great possibilities for creating a really Christian indigenous atmosphere, for practising different modes of Christian service in purely Indian ways, for becoming a meeting-place for Europeans and Indians where all that hampers truly human and Christian relations between them falls away, for thinking and working creatively in the interest of the indigenization of Christianity, and for creating a new kind of evangelistic centre. It is the more regrettable, therefore, that the number of Indian Christians who take to this more indi-genous kind of living and of expressing Christianity is exceedingly small and does not on the whole increase. The few *ashrams* that exist do good work, but they are not really growing, and nearly all the people who pass through them use them as temporary spiritual retreats. This is, of course, also of great value, but it does not alter the fact that as a very valuable mode of Christian approach the *ashram* has not yet struck deep roots.

P. Chenchiah says in an article in the *Student World* of

1929 that in India the problem of the relation of religions is not an intellectual or philosophical one as is the case in the West,[1] but a life problem. Other symptoms of this problem are such small movements as the International Fellowship and the discussions on inter-religious fellowship. Despite their smallness, these movements are in India, the country of many religions and religious atmospheres, important. They are an intelligible reaction against isolation and the narrow-minded superiority-feeling, but their weakness seems to be that they become easily the prey of a confused religious syncretism, in which the different faiths lose their distinctive character. This leads inevitably to unprincipled and sterile attempts at amalgamation of faiths, whereas fellowship of *men* of different faiths in order to achieve normal human contact would seem a healthier object to strive after.[2]

The huge world of popular Hinduism and of the outcastes is a problem in itself, because it is such an extraordinary mixture of weird primitive religious rites and taboos, dæmonism, polytheism, pilgrimages, austerities, dread of " holy " men and places, vague notions of " higher " Hinduism, all centering around the desire to avert dangers and obtain some happiness. It is impossible to write concretely about it when not knowing it by experience. In the evangelistic approach and in the building of their Christian life the same holds good there as for " primitive " peoples, namely, the value of using diligently their modes of expression. But the greatest need here certainly is to effect a close and personal relation to Christ, who is stronger than the demons and the sole Lord to be obeyed. This weird world of many lords and dreads and vain expectations and anxieties needs a drastic purification by centering it in Christ, who alone deserves to be believed and trusted.

Bishop Pickett's excellent book,[3] *Christian Mass Movements in India*, has done full justice to the pedagogical, social and

---

[1] At present this is no longer true of the West.

[2] Cf. the wise remarks made on this subject by Dr Macnicol in his book, *Is Christianity unique ?* p. 19.

[3] For this passage and the preceding passage on popular Hinduism the reader is referred to what has been said about group-conversion under *Africa*.

psychological problems that are connected with mass movements and with the raising of the outcaste to a new stage of spiritual, social and material life. The only contribution we would like to make to the subject of this book is that because of its sociological approach from the angle of uplift, which is in itself extremely valuable, the book does not bring out sufficiently that, however important and absolutely indispensable European or other guidance and education may be (especially in this case of the outcastes), the fundamental law of building Christian congregations is that from the very beginning the Christians must not be primarily treated as wards, but as a community that has to be trained to respond with its own moral and religious judgment to the newly-discovered world of standards and truths.

The problem of the most immediate interest and magnitude in the approach to India is at present the outcaste problem. The discussions that are going on in regard to it are very clear symptoms of the confusion in religious thinking that we have so frequently mentioned. The only attitude which the Christian Church, on account of its apostolic obligation, can take when masses of outcastes are lifting their eyes in its direction, is to do its utmost to bring them under the dominion of Christ.

CHINA

There is perhaps no country in our much-agitated world of to-day where the missionary enterprise stands in so great need of a steady course as China. The deeply humanistic trend in the Chinese mind, the absorption in national reconstruction in regard to political, social, economic and cultural life, the conflicting currents and deep sorrows that run through this people, the great antagonism between "liberal" and "conservative" missionary opinion, the desperate need for constructive forces and the disintegrating influence of many destructive forces—all these factors cooperate in making the problem of the Christian approach very intricate.

Christianity (Ya Chiao) is one of the five religions of

China, and according to the testimony of well-informed men it is the best-hated and the best-liked religion of the five. Since the day when Morrison posted himself at the gates of this empire, missions have gone through various stages. First it appeared to the mind of China, still wholly absorbed in its proud cultural self-consciousness, as a forerunner of Western imperialism. Then, gradually, it impressed China as one of the chief mediators of Western civilization and as a champion of progress and new liberty. The appeal of Christianity was mainly on the lines of its being the right tonic for national regeneration. Since the beginning of the twentieth century, however, China has more and more taken the steering of its fate into its own hands ; it has become acquainted with the West and its driving forces through many agencies, which are much more potent than missions with their restricted means can be. Science, the dominant un-Christian or anti-Christian philosophies of the West, and, after the World War, the revolutionary social theories of communism, have driven the Chinese mind hither and thither, have awakened in many directions an anti-religious spirit and dethroned Christianity and missions from their position of being the champions of progress. In the last decennia the voices are not rare which, instead of pronouncing Christianity the motor-force of the West, denounce it as a survival of its mediæval stage. Science, Marxism and the optimistic pragmatist philosophies, as, for instance, formulated by Dewey and Bertrand Russell, now for the time being have appropriated the prestige of being progressive, dynamic and revolutionary. Hence, it is no wonder that at the same time one finds reported about China an attitude of enmity, indifference or hunger in regard to religion.

This rapid survey, and this necessarily entangled aspect of China lying in the throes of a new age, suggest with sufficient clearness that the Christian approach, although it is naturally affected by these vehement oscillations, cannot build its hope and its work on these kaleidoscopic changes with their passing moods of favour and disfavour towards Christianity. It is worth while to state this explicitly, as too often one is prone to build too high expectations on, or to derive a too despondent outlook from, these rapid changes in regard to the Christianization of China as a whole. These alternating moods of favour and disfavour are, of course, very important from the standpoint of evangelism and from that of how to broadcast the Message, but the Christianization of China depends partly on factors outside the reach of any missionary agency, and partly on the building of a strong and living Church.

A symptom of the agitated character of the Chinese scene is to be found in the fact that Chinese Christianity in its popular constituency seems to be in danger of leaning too much on a certain routine of external Christian life, taking the Christian religion as a doctrine for granted. In its more intellectual membership it appears to be in danger of being confused about the real character and content of Christianity, demanding from it mainly the demonstration of its immediate social effectiveness. Frequently the question is put, What is Christianity ?

The prime condition for the Christian approach appears thus to be to furnish Chinese Christianity with a dynamic and radically religious apprehension of the Christian revelation, and to concentrate much prayer, energy and attention on the building of a Christian Church that demonstrates by its religious and moral life a strong and new quality of fellowship within its membership, and of concern for the world, which both belong to the fundamental elements of the Christian faith and ethics as manifest in Biblical realism. What is needed in China is not to adapt or assimilate the Christian revelation to Chinese ideas and ideals, because in its religious core it is inadaptable, but to penetrate into its real character and then express it in Chinese ways. This is the surest way to evolve a related and indigenized Christianity that stands fully and whole-heartedly both in Christianity and in the Chinese world.

These two points, namely, to penetrate into the real character and content of Christianity and then to express them in Chinese ways, needs some elaboration. It needs this for reasons that are to be found in Chinese Christianity as it is now, and in the conflicting tendencies amongst the missionary body.

When studying reports about the present condition of Chinese Christianity one is struck by the following features. There is in many respects great devotion to the cause of Christianity. In 1929 the Five Year Movement was started and awakened a more aggressive evangelistic attitude and a deeper sense of co-operative action in many churches. The severe test of persecution and hardship, through which the Chinese Churches went shortly before 1929 on account of the political and social troubles of the country, is certainly one of the causes of this awakening, although the idea of the Five Year Movement was a fruit of the Jerusalem Conference. Since 1931 various revival movements have made a great appeal to the minds of many Chinese Christians. The Apostolic Faith Mission with its method of healing, with its exorcism and speaking with tongues ; the Pentecostal Missions of the True Church of God, the Bethel Band, the Little Flock, the Spiritual Gifts Movement, etc., stir deeply the minds of people in various parts of the country. These revival movements have many features in common with the revivalist sects in Shintoism, while both are partly due to the deeply disturbed spiritual and social atmosphere. They are characterized by the desperate need for help in the distresses of common life (cf. the frequent emphasis on healing and exorcism), by vehement emotions (cf. speaking with tongues and the states of religious frenzy), by torrential confessions of sin and a passionate claim for " direct revelation," by a deep longing for absolute certainty and for reality in religious matters, which engenders a strong inclination towards so-called conservative theological positions. Some of the best leaders of these movements are highly cultured Chinese Christians who have had an academic training and draw upon a deep knowledge of the Bible, combined with a conservative theological outlook. The evangelistic tours of Dr Stanley Jones and Dr Sherwood Eddy aroused deep interest on the part of the students and had an inspiring influence on many Christian leaders.

As already mentioned, the common constituency of the

non-intellectual Christians in the village congregations evince a tendency to accept Christianity as a definite set of rules for life and of doctrinal tenets. They cannot really be called the expression of their faith and religious apprehension, but are understood by them to be the religious and moral code applying to the Christian religion.

The Chinese Christians of the intellectual class are in a very difficult position. Many of them are in the emotional aspect deeply attached to Christianity as the religion of God's revelational acts, culminating in Christ. The dominant humanist and ethical apprehension of life, which is the deep-rooted heritage of Confucianism, pervades, however, their whole outlook and their approach towards Christianity. The contributions in the *Chinese Recorder* of 1930 on Chinese conceptions about Jesus, and the booklet *The Jesus I know*, which contains similar testimonies, clearly demonstrate that Jesus is mainly conceived as the man who realized perfect goodness and perfect experience of God, and therefore is our perfect Guide and Model. This ethical conception of Christianity is a Christianized edition of the Chinese humanist doctrine of the mean, of the ideal " gentleman " who by his inner equilibrium and harmony, by the organization of his emotions and desires, and by his harmony with Tao, masters life.

The perennial Confucian tendency to accentuate the human relations, or, to express it in more modern terms, to emphasize social ethics, is the reason why Chinese Christians of the intellectual class, in this time of need for social reconstruction, mainly conceive Christianity as the most perfect social ethic, and insistently demand from the Christian Church the cogent evidence of its social effectiveness. On the other hand, the fact is repeatedly mentioned that Chinese Christians find fault with ecclesiastical organization of the Western type, because China itself knows only the family and the State as organized forms of life, and has always been disinclined towards systematic and corporate organization of religious life. This anti-ecclesiastical bias, according to the reports, holds many intellectuals back from becoming members of a Christian Church. Others, who were members, have left the Church, because their objections against the social ineffectiveness and the conservative trend of the Church in a time when courageous and radical dealing with social problems is necessary, became invincible.

Again and again it has been affirmed that one of the greatest obstacles to Christianity is that it demands that one should repudiate one's native religion in order to become a Christian. To recognize Jesus Christ as personal Lord and Saviour causes no peculiar difficulty, but to recognize Him as the *sole* Lord of life is considered exceedingly difficult. After all that has been said in this book about the pragmatist and relativist character of Chinese religion as a specimen of naturalist religion, this objection causes no astonishment. The fact, however, that the objection is often urged in a spirit of justified complaint, proves how extraordinarily strong still is the fascination of the inherited apprehension of life, while the peculiar and radically religious character of the Christian revelation is still very insufficiently realized.

In China's naturalistic monistic past with the mild indifference, inherent in it, towards the importance of doctrine lies also one of the chief reasons why one constantly hears in regard to Chinese Christianity of the strong aversion against theology, doctrine and theological distinctions. Lin Yu Tang in his *My Country and My People* certainly formulates a widespread opinion when he says that Chinese have no patience with doctrinaire theology and that Christianity must be altered beyond recognition or fail in China. In saying that it ought only to be presented as a way of life he undoubtedly voices a current opinion which derives from two sources, namely, the ethical bent of the Chinese mind and modern American schools of Christian thought.

There is, however, another chief reason for this widespread and undiscerning repudiation of theology and doctrinal expression of religious truth. It is to be sought in the Western missionaries, in the peculiar nature of their theological and denominational divisions, and especially in the dominantly doctrinal way in which Christianity often is presented to the Chinese. Fundamentalists and liberals are here equally guilty. The effect of the fundamentalist-liberal controversy in the minds of the Chinese Christians is very bewildering, and induces intellectual and non-intellectual Chinese Christians to ask in despair, What is Christianity? It is very significant to note that the ablest Christian leaders, as, for instance, Professor Chao, frequently express with all possible emphasis the opinion that the controversy between fundamentalists and liberals and the way it is fought out are meaningless to the Chinese in their situation, and exceedingly harmful to the healthy development of a genuine Chinese Christianity. As we have already more than once had occasion to remark, the liberals, with their often diluted conception of Christianity and their strong but very hazy sympathy for indigenous Christianity, mean to fight for a genuine form of Christianity but in reality are making the Chinese the victims of their liberal and generous idealisms. It is not so easy to cast out the domineering and patriarchal temperament of the Westerner! It appears even in the guise of generous enthusiasms, which are often another form of self-assertion and imposition. Many liberals forget that the Western contribution to the indigenization of Christianity can only be modest. It will never grow from the application of optimistic sociological and cultural speculations and experiments, but from a patient, realistic and self-denying search into the real needs of the Chinese and the exigencies of the Christian Faith.

The guilt of the fundamentalists is not less great. In their zeal for the truth of Christianity they identify their peculiar doctrinal and intellectualist expression of Christianity with the Christian revelation as contained in Biblical realism. This laudable zeal for Biblical truth does not exculpate them, however, from the great wrong of preventing many Chinese Christians and non-Chinese Christians from getting a right apprehension of the dynamic and supradoctrinal character of the prophetic religion of Biblical realism.

From this whole fundamentalist-liberal controversy the Chinese can hardly get another impression that that Christianity is either a set of tenets about the virgin birth, the

infallibility of the Bible, an external and juridical conception of atonement, etc., or the triumphant rejection of
" such myths." We do not deny in the least that it is,
theologically speaking, very important to have a clear
conception about these matters, but to make these theological
positions the *objects of faith*, as the fundamentalists do, is a
disastrous distortion of the Christian revelation. A tragic
proof of this distortion is the fact that such a fine Christian
and able man as Professor T. C. Chao sees only two ways
of trying to interpret Christ—either to believe in Him as the
ideal man, who by His moral excellence and achievement
is our Saviour and inspiration, or to believe in Him as the
second person of the Godhead. The divinity of Christ is
certainly an essential Christian *doctrine*, but to present
" Christ, the Son of the Living God " as the second person
of the Godhead is an intellectualist obscuration of the
Gospel, which necessarily has a revolting effect. If Christ
is introduced to China in the guise of arid and dogmatic
definitions, one cannot reasonably hope for an intelligent
grasp of the dynamic character of the Christian revelation.
When one remembers the aristocratic [1] temper of Chinese
civilization, the Chinese bias against metaphysical and
dogmatic thinking, and the modern conflict of ideas about
Christianity and its foundations, it is not to be marvelled at
that under such conditions Christianity presents itself to many
intellectual Chinese as " crude mythical and metaphysical
thinking." This is the more sad, because it is not at all
true that the Chinese in the past have been so averse to
metaphysical thinking as is so loudly proclaimed by Chinese
and Europeans alike. Their whole civilization is built on
and imbued with great metaphysical concepts, as has been
shown when dealing with the fundamental tenets of the
Chinese apprehension of life. To foster in Chinese minds,
by crudely intellectualist theology, an aversion to theological
thinking is not only highly detrimental to the healthy development of the Chinese Church, but is also in contradiction to the cultural past of China. Under the existing
conditions, however, it is wholly intelligible that so many

[1] Cp. page 162 *sq.*

Chinese Christian writers urgently clamour for " a simple Christianity not entangled in creeds and dogmas." Indeed, Chinese Christianity does not need in the first place to be confronted with our creeds and dogmas, but with the prophetic religion of Biblical realism.

The need for this latter confrontation is also evident in regard to another feature of the situation of Chinese Christianity. Much discussion is going on about the topic of the mutual relation of Chinese culture and Christianity. Generally speaking, the opinions tend in the direction of discovering a fundamental harmony between the " nobler elements of Confucianism and Christianity." Observers speak about two main attitudes that are discernible in Chinese Christianity, one leaning towards accepting revelation—the historic belief about incarnation, resurrection, the indwelling Christ, a transcendent God, etc., and one leaning towards Humanism, taking the experimental approach and using the inductive method. The first attitude, if it does not primarily mean the *doctrinal* acceptance of these items, certainly is what the Chinese Church needs if it will rise and grow in living contact with Biblical realism and in continuity with the historical, universal Church. However, it must be repeated, this will not be achieved by a nearly exclusive confrontation with our creeds and dogmas, but by a thorough and vivifying contact with Biblical realism.

In doing this, there is one point of crucial importance to be kept in mind in regard to China. Nobody will deny that China will be one of the classic places in the world where Christianity and Humanism will have their second eventful encounter (the first being that with Greek and Roman Humanism), because the deep Confucian influence will always leave its mark on the Chinese mind and its way of apprehending life. To disregard the inevitability and necessity of this encounter is a dangerous overlooking of Chinese reality and an injury to Christianity. The natural way for Christianity to become indigenous in China and remain at the same time truly Christian, is to relate itself to the fundamental apprehensions of Chinese culture by a process of mutual attraction and repulsion, just as the

Church went through a similar experience in the first
centuries of its existence in regard to its Greek-Roman-
Oriental environment. The way of avoiding or ignoring
this encounter leads to a petrified and isolated Christianity.

We must recognize that this whole process will proceed
with much stumbling and uncertainty. The confrontation
of Christianity with the Chinese heritage is at present in a
rather intellectual and artificial stage. The problem is
treated too much as one of the laboratory. Values on both
sides are defined as a result of cultural analysis, and then
an attempt is made to state how far they can be harmonized,
how far Chinese culture can make a contribution to Christianity or where Christianity can supply or compensate
what is lacking in Chinese culture. Instances of this way of
stating the problem are that the Chinese tendency towards
the " golden mean " needs to be supplemented by the
aggressiveness of the Christian temperament, or that Christianity and Chinese culture are in harmony as to their
conception of man's unity with Heaven.

The significance of these first conscious efforts is that they
can render service in developing a deeper insight into the
fundamental nature of the Chinese apprehension of life.
Their weakness and danger is that they deal too much with
the problem as one of spiritual chemistry, and are rather
tending towards a premature discovery of synthesis than
towards the clear delineation of the characteristics of Christian
truth. Moreover, one forgets too much that values, such as
moral discipline, patient cheerfulness, uncomplaining resignation,[1] etc., are no constant entities, because they are always
indissolubly connected with the relative factor of adaptation
to a given environment. It is in this context very instructive
to note the trenchant way in which Lin Yu Tang in *My
Country and my People* exposes the weakness of these values in
the environment of to-day, and India's passionate demand
for virility and heroic virtues, entirely in contrast to the
sublime *values* that are enshrined in the passive Hindu
qualities of the past. By its intellectual nature this syn-

[1] We enumerate some of those mentioned in the contribution to the Jerusalem
Report on values in Confucianism.

thesis is too artificial. At some time in the future there will inevitably arise some sort of synthesis of Christianity and the Chinese ways of life-apprehension and life-expression. However, such a synthesis is only natural when it is not the result of an intentional and intellectual synthesis of Chinese and Christian elements, but of the faithful reaction of the Chinese mind on the Christian revelation as the measure of all truth, value and life.

All the features of the present condition of Chinese Christianity which we have mentioned (the revival movements, the efforts for intellectual synthesis, the demand for social effectiveness in Christianity, the aversion to Church and theology, etc.), point, when we consider the fundamental needs of Chinese Christianity, in the direction we have already alluded to. The present need is in the first place that Chinese Christians and missionaries alike open their minds widely to the moulding influence of the radical theocentric apprehension in Biblical realism, with a view to reaching not synthesis or contrast, but a faithful if characteristically Chinese expression.[1] In the second place ought to be mentioned the urgent necessity to build strong, living churches that embody real Christian and human fellowship, and that in their functioning exhibit a sincere feeling of responsibility towards the world on account of obedience to Christ. That is the only way to produce social effectiveness in accordance with the available spiritual and material strength, and to learn that living Christianity is not at all interested in ecclesiastical organization as such, but is very deeply interested in a vital community life of the believers in Christ, " bearing one another's burdens " and so fulfilling " the law of Christ " (Gal. vi. 2).

Before ending this discussion of China three remarks must still be made.

[1] In the writer's opinion it is not feasible to give detailed hints of any value as to Chinese expression if one has not had the opportunity of intense personal contact. He may be allowed to give expression to a suggestion, made to him, during a conversation, by the Rev. E. R. Hughes, who pointed out that the conception of filial piety so deeply ingrained in China's mind and so hyperbolically glorified in its hagiographical literature, contains much material to express the meaning of Christ and His perfect sacrifice in a Chinese way.

In the first place, there is the attitude of the Christian Church and the missionary movement towards the New Life Movement. As was explained in preceding places [1] this Movement is a symptom of the turmoil of Chinese life. This great people is in search of a new direction of life, and the New Life Movement is an expression of this longing for direction and discipline. It goes without saying that the Christian forces in China cannot ignore this movement. The Chinese Christians are an integral part of their people and country. To show genuine sympathy and help in accordance with the strength available is a plain duty. Yet, it is very important to be aware of the fact that the ideal of the New Life Movement is a modernized and modified edition of the Confucian ideal of self-culture as the foundation of State and society, and that it is confusing, therefore, to recommend the support of this Movement by the Christian Church on the ground that it embodies practical Christianity. It is civic morality, widely different in inspiration from Christian ethics, but from the social standpoint very valuable.

Although on account of the present horrible conflict between China and Japan nobody can tell how China, which in the last years showed many propitious signs of consolidation, will fare in the future, there have been discernible in the last ten years some important trends in the policy of the Government to restrict religious liberty and bring as much as possible various religious movements and activities under State control. It is, therefore, not at all improbable that Chinese Christianity in the near future will have to face the problem of the relation of Christianity to the State, another evidence of the fact that the Christian Church all over the world is called to regain a new sense of true Christianity in the face of practically the same problems as, for instance, the State, humanism, secularism, etc.

As in every case, we have devoted almost all our attention to the Christian approach towards Chinese civilization in its fundamental aspects. It would, however, be a great mistake to forget that the life of the common people is still largely dominated by animism, shamanism, magic, astrology

[1] Cp. page 252.

and practices of divination, and that the actual work of the Christian Church and of missions has to deal with that situation. Virtually the same attitude and approach is in demand here as that delineated above. As, however, in this case religious life is largely a matter of customs and practices and not in the first place of conscious cultural attitudes and apprehensions, the task of planting Christianity sways still more noticeably between the two poles of a radical breach with the past by passing under the sway of an entirely new spiritual authority, and the duty to find ways of expression for Christianity that are congenial to these simple folk.

.   .   .   .

JAPAN

Japanese Christianity faces a situation very different from that of others. In numbers it is very small (not yet one-half per cent of the population), but its status and influence in the nation exceed by far its numerical significance. Although it is hazardous to evaluate the prestige which Christianity enjoys at the present moment, it may safely be said that since in 1873 the Edict by which Christianity was declared a forbidden religion was abolished, the moral and social prestige of Christianity has been exceptionally great. Gundert in his *Japanische Religionsgeschichte* enumerates the following elements as having gained a considerable influence on public opinion in Japan : familiarity with Christian monotheism, respect for Christ and the Bible, appreciation of the value of individual personality, a deeper sense of the significance of monogamy, of social justice and of labour.

The constituency of the Churches is mainly urban and bourgeois, which has many consequences for the character and outward manifestations of Japanese Christianity. It is one of the reasons why in Japan the problem of making Christianity indigenous and giving it a Japanese flavour does not attract the deep interest of Japanese Christians themselves. City life in Japan has outwardly a Western aspect, and therefore the Western aspect of the Churches does not contrast with the environment. Another and more important reason for the small amount of interest in the indigenization of Christianity is to be found in the fact that Japanese Christians are acutely aware of their living in small numbers in an overwhelmingly non-Christian environment. They feel deeply the lack of a clear consciousness of what Christianity is and stands for. The first Christian communities that were formed as a result of missionary work consisted mainly of young, vigorous, intellectual Samurai-people, the well-known bands of Kumamoto, Sapporo and Yokohama. Hence Japanese Christianity has produced a remarkably high percentage of very able and strong personalities.

Viewed within the framework of modern Japanese history, the spread of Christianity is a part of the absorption of Western civilization. This fact, added to the other of the high percentage of intellectuals, accounts for the assiduous contact which Japanese Christianity has had always with the various trends of European theology, and for the often-mentioned phenomenon that there is as yet hardly any peculiarly Japanese expression of Christianity. The great output of Christian and theological literature in Japanese is almost wholly, either in fact or in spirit, a translation of European and American books and thoughts. There is a strong tendency to attribute this to the imitative nature of the Japanese and their small aptitude for creative thinking in the field of religion. It may be doubted whether this explanation is the right one. The Japanese propensity to evaluate religion not as the supreme thing in life, but as to its ethical and social significance, and to be therefore more interested in values than in truth, is the natural outcome of the naturalistic-monistic apprehension of religion in Japan. The very characteristic and interesting forms of Buddhism that have developed in Japan are more than imitations ; they are original creations. It appears more plausible to ascribe the lack of genuine Japanese interpretation and expression of Christianity to the fact that its introduction is only of recent date, and that it penetrated into Japan in a period when all its energy was devoted to absorbing Western culture and adjusting the country to new political, social and economic conditions. Absorbing stages are rarely creative, especially in the realm of religious and philosophical thought. Evidences of genuine Japanese reaction to Christianity will be more easily found in sermons, in devotional and exegetical literature, which do not pass as recognized theological thinking, than in the systematic exposition of the Christian religion.

Notwithstanding the perturbed intellectual atmosphere in which Japanese Christianity has grown up, and the waves of theological liberalism and criticism coming from Europe and America that have exercised the minds of many, it is very markedly orthodox. This is the more noteworthy, because the rising tide of Christianity which took place in the period of universal openness to Western culture between 1873 and 1890 was not due to purely religious motives, but to the identification of Christianity with the new civilization, which was then welcomed as a means to strengthen the nation. The genuinely Japanese love of the soul, glory and destiny of Japan (Yamato-Damashii), and the not less genuinely Japanese devotion to the wellbeing of the kokutai (the idea of the State) aroused under the then existing circumstances a deep interest in Christianity in the hearts of young and ardent Samurai. Their conversion to Christianity was due to a great extent to their belief that this religion of the West with its strong moral fervour and religious purity and clarity had the power to save them and the nation. The preponderance of this intellectual and energetic type of man is probably the reason why the main tenets of Japanese Christianity are in accordance with the main tenets of historical Christianity. They were able to get a more intelligent grasp of the creeds and ecclesiastical institutions which the missionaries transplanted to Japan than a constituency mainly of villagers could have done. God, the Creator, revealed and incarnated in the God-man Jesus Christ, salvation through redemption on the Cross, the Resurrection, God's indwelling through the Holy Spirit, belong to the bedrock of Japanese Christian conviction.

It is worth while to compare this state of affairs in Japan

with China. In both countries the native religious atmosphere is thoroughly naturalistic and as thoroughly uncongenial to the characteristically Christian apprehensions. Anesaki, the Japanese Buddhist scholar, expressed this once in the following words : " The emphasis of Christianity lies just in what the Japanese fail to appreciate, monotheism, sin, redemption, humility." Yet the Japanese Christians cling, generally speaking, to a type of Christianity that clearly betrays its Biblical origin, while the more theological expression of Christianity in China centres around the " Perfect Man " (cf. the Confucian ideal) Jesus Christ, and prominent Chinese Christians openly avow that to conceive a personal God and a God incarnated in the man Jesus Christ causes many difficulties to their minds and intellects. The aristocratic, humanistic Chinese mind is long in discovering and digesting the theocentric religion of Biblical realism, fashioning it for the present according to its fundamental humanism. The virile temperament of the Japanese, though nursed in the same atmosphere of naturalistic and impersonalist religion, more easily adopts an attitude of fealty to the new religion and its fundamental tenets, while at the same time demonstrating the innate nationalism of the Japanese by relating the new faith to his love of Yamato-Damashii.

Not only the native Japanese temperament but also the circumstances lend a virile stamp to Japanese Christianity. Being a small minority in a richly variegated and strong pagan environment, the percentage of those who are Christian by strong conviction and special choice is high. A very remarkable example of all these traits is Uchimura. Christianity being in its initial stage in Japan, it is of slight significance to discuss the question whether Uchimura was an original Christian thinker. He was a typical Samurai, very independent, of extreme loyalty to his new-won faith, a man feeding on the Bible. The truly striking thing in him, by which he showed himself to be a Japanese Christian in the full sense of the word and not a mere absorber of Western theological conceptions, is his combination of a prophetic apprehension of religion with a fervent Japanese nationalism, the latter purified by the first. He (and other Christians with him) regarded his work for Christianity as a service to his country. This need to see these two, service to the faith and service to the country, as wholly one, is a genuine Japanese expression of Christianity. He died with the words : Banzai for the Gospel, Banzai for Nippon.

Another characteristic of Japanese Christianity is its strong denominationalism. The movement towards ecclesiastical unity is therefore progressing very slowly. This is probably partly due to the urban character of Christianity, partly to the tenacious clan-spirit of Japan. In the towns and cities the groups of Christians naturally tend to maintain their once-obtained communal unity and cohesion, the more so as the fact that they are Christians has loosened the religious and social bonds of the past. Perhaps in Japan the denominational divisions of the Christian Church do not attach such a damaging reproach to it as in other countries, because sectarian divisions are very numerous and conspicuous in Shinto and Buddhism. The non-Churchism of Uchimura and others is probably more a symptom of a strongly independent character than of a rejection of denominationalism on principle. Formerly it was due also to an aversion to European preponderance, but under the present circumstances this has changed enormously. The policy of devolution has taken away the resentment against missionary superiority, and the situation of danger in which the Christians as well as the missionaries constantly are by virtue of the religious policy of the Japanese Government, has engendered a more natural and fraternal relation.

Under the leadership and inspiration of Kagawa the aggressive evangelistic temper has been stimulated in individual Christians and in the Churches, which by their urban and bourgeois character always tend in the direction of respectability. The Kingdom of God Movement, which has been the result, and which aimed at bringing the number of Christians up to one million, has not obtained the amount of success that was hoped and expected from it. It will be continued, however, and carried on in closer co-operation with the Churches than has been the case hitherto. Kagawa's evangelistic appeal has also impressed the minds of many with the necessity for rural evangelism.

Other evidences of the evangelistic spirit and of the opportunities in Japan to sow the Message are (to mention some) the very remarkable experiment of Newspaper Evangelism, and the ardent activity of the Holiness Church (also called the Holy Teaching Church). The importance of this last movement is that it is a real piece of indigenous Christianity, that works along lines widely different from the concepts of many theorizers about indigenous Eastern Christianity. It is of the same revivalistic emotional type as many a Shinto sect and the revival movements in the Chinese Church, full of enthusiastic zeal with its customary beneficent and precarious results. Great self-sacrifice, entire self-support, aggressive evangelism, a great belief in prayer and the Bible, and the determination to make their Church a Church for all members, are some of the characteristics of this Holiness Church. If one would be inclined to call this " Western," a reference to the history of the Buddhist revivals in the Middle Ages is sufficient to remind one that it is more universal than our theories about the Eastern mind would suggest.

Individualistic piety has been and still is a keynote of Japanese Christianity, but since the beginning of this century the Japanese Christians, irrespective of theological views, became aware of the necessity of the social interpretation and application of Christianity. The stern suppression by Government of all forms of " dangerous social thought and action " and the difficulty of the social problem in Japan with its great economic distress, have driven the topic of the social application of Christianity into the background ; the more so, because the forces of the Churches are exceedingly small in comparison with the magnitude of the task. Barthian theology, which attracts great interest in Japan, has fixed attention more on purely theological problems, but the schisms in Europe in this movement cause much confusion in the minds of thinking Japanese Christians. Kagawa, who is in every respect a man of exceptional dimensions, remains steadfastly the apostle of the application of the love of God to all human relations and conditions, whether personal or collective. This modern Francis is a great evangelist, a man of great artistic gifts, a prolific author, a splendid organizer, a prophet of social justice, an apostle, a mystic and a great lover of men, who combats with heroic love all evil and suffering that come in his way. No disappointment or resistance can break his faith in the all-conquering force of unselfish love and sacrifice. His interpretation of the Sermon on the Mount as a social programme and his identification of the Co-operative Movement with the fundamental principles of the Kingdom of God is mistaken and its religious expectations certainly will end in disappointment, but it is the mistake of a great soul. He is one of the greatest, if not the greatest, gifts of Japanese Christianity to the universal Church and the world at large.

In the case of Japan, more than in any other, it is impossible to talk about the approach of Christianity in the abstract. This vigorous Japanese Christian minority lives in an extremely dangerous world, and therefore its attention has to be focussed on the religious fundamentals. Its position has much similarity to that of the Christians in Germany, with one important difference. In Germany the battle has to be fought in a secularized world with a long Christian past, while the Japanese Christians are living in a country, also scourged by the storm of secularism, but full of crudely primitive and highly refined forms of non-Christian religion, which display a feverish activity. The greatest adversary which this minority has to meet is the torrent of religious nationalism that dominates the country. The nearest analogy to the present situation of the Japanese Church is to be found in the Roman Empire in the first centuries. The same problems of Emperor-worship and socio-religious solidarity with the Empire arose then and now. One difference must be mentioned. On one hand the religious nationalism of present Japan pursues its totalitarian ideal with much greater relentlessness than was the case in the Roman Empire, and with means of organization and control perfected to a degree that the Roman authorities could not dream of; on the other hand, the problem in Japan is made more intricate because the Japanese Government as such declares all the ceremonies of reverence that are required to be non-religious patriotic acts.

Through all the ages religion has been in Japan the object of Government regulation. When Christianity entered Japan in the sixteenth century, it was political reasons that caused first its favourable reception and later its persecution and extinction. In 1873 the legal objection against the propagation of Christianity, during nearly three centuries considered a capital crime, was removed. The repugnance to Christianity that had resulted from the ban laid upon it by the Tokugawa, however, has never died out. At times it abated considerably, because of the enthusiasm for all things Western and the moral and spiritual prestige Christianity has won in the public opinion of Japan. In 1912 it was even fully recognized by Government as a national force, when its representatives were invited, along with those of Buddhism and Shinto, to support the Government in stemming the tide of materialism and moral disintegration. It may, however, be asked whether at present there is not a recrudescence of the deep-rooted repugnance. The Christians are sincere patriots. Uchimura, who was dismissed from a school years ago because he refused to join in the acts of reverence for the Emperor, ordered the following self-made epitaph to be chiselled on his tomb : " I for Japan, Japan for the world, The world for Christ, And all for God." Yet Christianity, the theocentric and prophetic religion, that knows of the Lord of all Lords and the King of all Kings, also does its work in the Japanese Christians. They are sincere and devoted patriots, but their supreme loyalty lies elsewhere, and the Church of Christ transcends with them also country and nation. Unconditioned patriotism accompanied by a constantly-increasing number of rites of pseudo-religious or purely religious character is more and more urgently demanded by the devotees of religious nationalism as the supreme obligation of every Japanese. Non-conformity, even in the sincerest patriot, is explained as lese-majesty or treason to the sacred cause of the nation. An unofficial inquisition, exercised by the zealots of religious nationalism, is forcing on every one a correct adherence to the creeds and the practices of this religious nationalism.

The Government authorities, however, although they enjoin shrine worship, etc., and tighten more and more their control of the activities and the message of the different religious bodies, Christianity included, take care not to repudiate the principle of religious liberty which is laid down in the Constitution, and continue to stress the merely patriotic character of all ceremonies.

To call this situation of the Japanese Christians delicate is a very weak description. To quibble in this stupendous situation about where religious worship and terminology begins that is only applicable to God and to nothing else, and whether we are in the sphere or on the borderline of purely human reverence or patriotic loyalty, would result in much justified and unjustified casuistry. It is undeniable that nationalist Shinto claims with intolerant vehemence absolute religious supremacy, and that this claim is materialized in an ever-increasing number of doctrines and ceremonies. The fact that all other loyalty is subordinated to that to the sanctities of religious nationalism is clearly demonstrated in this negative way, that it is forbidden to protest against the conception of the Emperor's Divinity and the sacredness of Japan, or to express, for instance, one's disbelief in the historicity of the myth of the Sun-goddess, Amaterasu. Merely to express a different opinion on these subjects from those of this dogmatism of religious nationalism is not allowed. In this atmosphere the Japanese Christians have to live out their Christian faith and their supreme obligation of obedience to God. The line followed by the Japanese Christians is to hold the Government to its word about the non-religious patriotic character of the whole affair, and to exercise all possible influence in order to achieve the removal of religious elements from the ceremonies ; or, to put it in other words, they prepare for persecution but try to avoid its precipitation by themselves. The interested outsider gets the impression that the Japanese Christians in their

explanation and handling of the intricacies of the problem
are going too far on the road of conformity and evasion, but
in expressing this opinion one ought not to forget that they
are weighed down by the feeling that the future of Christianity in Japan is at stake and depends upon their decisions.

What has to be the approach in this special case of
Japan? It is unnecessary to repeat what has been said in
the preceding pages about the attitude towards the indigenous
religions, or about the right and the necessity to express the
Christian faith and way of life in forms that are truly Japanese. This holds wholly true in regard to the religions
and the heritage of Japan. In the case of Japan this means
that Japanese Christianity, which in its whole bearing still
largely shows the marks of foreign importation, must learn
to state the problem of indigenization in more courageous
terms. The Japanese Christians are entirely right when
they reject the advice, given to them a couple of years ago,
to pursue a missionary policy which has virtually as its aim
to strive after religious synthesis and eclecticism. To be
open-minded, to recognize also man's religious creativity in
the good and the bad sense of the word in the religions of
Japan, to seek diligently for human contacts and modes of
approach in word or act that are congenial to the Japanese
background and enter into the universal and particular
problems of Japanese life, are simply implied in the right
conception of what a Christian missionary is. It does not,
however, in the least imply that the purpose of missions
and of the Church has to be sought in stimulating other
religions to grow toward the ultimate goal of unity in the
completest religious truth, while desiring that no variety
of religious experience should perish until it has yielded up
its own ingredient of truth. The facts prove that the meeting
of Christianity with other religions has in practice a purifying and stimulating effect on these other religions, but to
convert missions or the apostolic obligation of the Church
into an experiment for practical comparative religion is
in radical contrast to the revelational and apostolic character of Christianity. It starts from the assumption that we,
as gold-finders who shape all the grains of gold they have

found in many fields into one big lump of gold, in extracting every grain of truth from the religions of the world shape the lump of complete truth. It operates, moreover, with a very confused conception of truth. A Christian starts from the recognition that "truth and grace" are manifested in Jesus Christ, and that He is the standard of reference, and not an unknown final or complete truth.

Yet, although leading Japanese Christians rightly refuse to take this line, and although they see that the prime necessity is to become more and more grounded in the Christian faith as it is according to the fundamental Biblical data, their intelligible fear of becoming engulfed in the whirlpool of amalgamating syncretism makes them, apparently, resign themselves too easily to imported forms of religious and ecclesiastical expression, and makes them too indifferent towards the indispensability of an indigenous flavour in their religious life. As in all other cases previously treated, it has to be repeated here that the effort to express the Christian revelation in indigenous terms does not mean, as it is usually understood, to adapt its content to indigenous religious conceptions and thereby spoil it, but it does mean literally what the word says, namely, to *express* it, to interpret its real character and content in intelligible and familiar forms. This requires faith and courage, but the grasp of the Christian revelation is strengthened and deepened by it because of the necessity of constantly confronting oneself with it, and the indigenization of Christianity so becomes a natural and gradual process and not an artificial experiment, because the mind is directed toward interpretation in familiar forms.

In all times and under all circumstances it is a prime missionary duty to strive for building up a vigorous Church and a strong Christian community life. The claim that is made for the Holiness Church that it makes the Church a Church for *all* members, the body of united worship, action, service and testimony to the world, is an urgent need in all Christian countries, whether missionary or not. The situation of danger in which Japanese Christianity lives makes it still more imperative there.

To concentrate upon Christianity, not as a set of religious tenets, but as the prophetic religion of revelation in Christ and upon living a corporate life of Christian fellowship, is the way for Japanese Christianity to meet the storm of religious nationalism. As in so many places in the world of to-day, in Japan too, Christianity is in a position in which it can only recommend itself on its purely religious and ethical merits, as a message of God's revelational acts. The days have passed when the conditions of the European world and of the Eastern peoples were such that Christianity was conceived to be the pioneer of a new fervently-desired civilization, or the tonic that guaranteed the coming of a brilliant national future. This does not imply that missions and the Christian Church have to withdraw from their cultural and social task, or to weaken in their concern for the world and its conditions, for this task and this concern are an integral part of the prophetic religion of Christian revelation. It implies, however (and this very pertinently in Japan), that missions and the Church are aware of the fact that the purely religious appeal is their main and only strength.

In closing this section some words ought to be said about Buddhism. Nearly all that has been said about Hinduism, in its aspects as a popular religion, as a religion of fervent *bhakti*-piety and of contemplative mysticism, can be applied to Buddhism. At the Jerusalem Conference much attention was devoted to the "living forces" of Buddhism. These living forces are in Buddhism the same as in all religions, with the exception that they have in Buddhism, of course, a Buddhist flavour and background : to store up merits, to invoke the help and blessing of the Bodhisattvas in the needs of life, to acquire peace of soul or a happy re-birth, etc. It is indispensable for a missionary to know about these living forces and to recognize in them religious man in general and his own natural religious inclinations. There lies their value for contact, and there alone ; not in these living forces as such, because they need, in the light of Christ, regeneration and conversion.

To present Christianity in a Buddhist environment as an enrichment of values is misleading. Of course, the *result* of accepting Christianity is an enrichment of values, but at the same time its result is also (when speaking in this cultural and psychological line of thinking) a destruction of values, because there are " values " (for instance the high serenity of meditation, or the thorough psychological training in connection with its peculiar religious ideals) in Buddhism that can only be produced in *this* peculiar way by *this* religion. This result, however, can never be the *purpose* of missions, it is an important by-product. By virtue of its apostolic character Christianity is *primarily* interested in truth, which is " life eternal " (John xvii. 3 : " This is eternal life, that they know thee, the only real God, and him whom thou has sent, Jesus Christ "), and not in values. Besides, the way of " values " as a way of contact can be very illusory. To take only one instance in relation to Buddhism, if the Christian missionary considers an enriched personality the supreme value in human life, it is not at all certain that this will appeal to a good Buddhist, whose fundamental starting-point is the non-existence of person-ality and whose fundamental aim is to destroy the fiction of this personality idea.

Repeatedly (by Reischelt and Saunders, for example) there are endeavours to bring Christianity and Buddhism together by affirming an intrinsic affinity between the Mahayanist idea of the Godhead, its trinitarian conception, its Logos-speculation and Saviour-idea, etc., and the Christian idea. The Gospel of St John is then considered to be the deepest expression of Christianity, and " higher " Mahayan-ism the nearest approximation to this Gospel.

As a missionary and evangelistic approach it is, of course, of great importance to interpret Christianity to Buddhist monks, as Dr Reischelt does, in vital relation to the funda-mental apprehensions of " higher " Mahayanism. To present, however, essential Christianity as a more perfect and complete edition of essential Mahayanism is certainly erroneous. We refer to the chapters of this book in which was explained the naturalist character of Mahayanism, which precludes all possibility of comparison with prophetic Christianity except in regard to important mental and psychological similarities, and in which we tried to make clear why essential Christianity and the Gospel of St John are not specimens of mystical religion. In the sixteenth century when the Jesuits commenced to spread Christianity in Japan, the Buddhist priests in the beginning took it as a form of Mahayana. Their basic syncretism made this a natural thing for them to do. This estimate of theirs was a mistake. The International Buddhist Congress of 1925, which rejected the Christian conception of God as Creator as being antagonistic to Buddhism, evinced a far more realistic estimate of the basic difference between essential Christianity and essential Mahayanism.

In the realms of Buddhism as in those of other religions the missionary enterprise sorely needs men who live in that intimate and truly human contact with the representatives of other religions which a man like Dr Reischelt so admirably practises. However, to keep the missionary movement sound, it is absolutely necessary to keep in mind that the Gospel we preach does not represent a more perfected stage of religious development or production, but a quite new world of divine acts.

APPENDIX TO CHAPTER IX

A S the development of events in Japan demonstrates, the problem of religious nationalism becomes more and more acute. The claim for absolute surrender to it as the unique and sole standard of reference for truth and life more and more dominates the atmosphere in Japan. For Christianity no compromise with this claim is possible, just as there is no compromise possible with Rosenberg's Myth of the twentieth century. The policy which the Roman Catholic Church has followed since 1936 in regard to the Shinto problem is, therefore, deeply amazing and distressing.

For years Roman Catholic Missions took a very cautious attitude towards the religious policy of the Japanese Government, maintaining that, in spite of the declarations of the Government, the obeisance at the State-Shinto shrines was a religious ceremony. Voices were continually raised, however, that opposed this attitude; their argument was that the Roman Catholic Church had to demonstrate its loyalty to the Japanese State by holding the Government to its word about the non-religious, merely patriotic, significance of the rites, because the Government made the observance of these rites the touchstone of the indispensable patriotic spirit.

The controversy has now been brought to a close by instructions from the *Congregatio de Propaganda Fide* to the Papal Delegate in May 1936. In this document Roman Catholic Japanese are given express permission to consider these ceremonies as non-religious and to take part in them. The clergy are instructed to refrain from controversial discussions on this problem. A similar instruction has been given by the *Congregatio* to the Roman Catholic authorities in Manchukuo in regard to the Confucian problem.

The particularly distressing point in this decision is that the whole problem is treated as an important instance of adaptation and accommodation. This appears very clearly from Roman Catholic articles about this decision in leading Roman Catholic magazines such as, *Katholisches Jahrbuch*, *La Civilta Cattolica* and *Il Pensiero Missionario*. The writers connect it with the rites-controversy that raged in the seventeenth century in India and in the eighteenth century in China; and hence present it in the light of an important item of psychological and cultural accommodation, with studied neglect of the crucial religious problem. This is done in the teeth of the most patent facts, which have demonstrated for years that this Japanese religious nationalism claims to be the solely legitimate absolute for the Japanese people. The fundamental religious issue is the choice between God the Creator, the sole divine Object of absolute obedience and adoration, and the man-made pseudo-absolutes, State, Emperor and Nation. Its setting aside in this way is an extremely deplorable victory of the calculating politician-mind over the religious sensitiveness of the follower of Christ.

CHAPTER X

The Christian Mission in Relation to its Environment

THE task laid upon us is to state the fundamental position of the Christian Church as a witness-bearing body and to deal in detail with the evangelistic approach to the great non-Christian faiths. If these words were taken in the sense usually accorded to them, our task could be considered as finished. There are, however, some very important theoretical and practical reasons which induce us to take a wider view.

In the third chapter we explained the intrinsic unity of faith and ethics in the Christian revelation, on account of its theocentric character. God's revelation and redemptive Will is, according to Biblical realism, the creative ground of the Christian religious life, and at the same time the motive and inspiration of the Christian ethical life. Religion is ethics and ethics are religion. This means that speaking about the religious approach includes also its many-sided expression in relation to the different spheres of life. If we define the main utterances of the Christian Church as being worship, witness and ministry, it must constantly be kept in mind that these three terms must always be understood in such a wide and deep sense that each of them partakes of the essential nature of the other. So, worship has not to be interpreted exclusively in its strictly religious and liturgical significance, but witness and ministry must also be seen in the light of the worship of God. Similarly, witness has to be conceived as real ministry and ministry as real witness. Both things need to be said with great emphasis and earnestness, especially to-day. In some quarters witness, understood in the sense of direct evangelization, is theoretically maintained, but in fact it is disapproved of as " propaganda " and " proselytizing," and set over against " service " as the most Christian and disinterested witness in deeds. In other quarters " witness " and " announcement " are stressed so passionately as being the exclusive obligation of the Church that its ministry, its expression of the " way " that has become manifest through Jesus Christ in terms of life and action, if not theoretically, becomes practically of secondary or even minor importance. If bearing witness to God's saving acts and truth is not done in the spirit of the deep desire for " ministry " to the world and mankind, and if all that is usually comprised under the term " ministry " is not primarily motivated by the intention to do it as a real, though very imperfect, witness to the God and Father of Jesus Christ, in the long run we lose the essentially Christian basis of our work.

This view imposes itself irresistibly if we take seriously the prophetic and apostolic character of the Gospel, which has been constantly stressed in this book as the fundamental starting-point of all missionary thinking and of the Christian mission in the world. Whosoever pronounces the words " Christian mission " is necessarily deeply occupied with the world and, therefore, is already in vital touch with the whole range of problems concerning the relation of the Christian revelation and the Christian Church to the various spheres of life. In other words, the problems of the nature of the Church, of Christianity and culture in the widest sense of the word, of the social Christian ethic, present themselves imperiously to the minds of those who feel the obligation of executing the missionary task not only in faith and love, but also in *active, intelligent* faith and love.

A consideration of very great practical purport is that the Younger Churches as well as the missionary enterprise are facing everywhere the bewildering issues of cultural, social and national upheaval and reconstruction. Both stand in great need of guidance as to the meaning of the Christian faith and the obligation of the Christian Church in the midst of these burning issues. Hence it seems unwise to treat the subject of the Christian message in a non-Christian world and be silent about these issues and the underlying fundamental problems. Moreover, this silence would strengthen the tendency, already so fatally strong, to regard the religious and theological approach to the world of non-Christian religions as a matter of rather abstract theory, while the exact reverse ought to be true. If this religious and theological approach, as offered in the preceding pages, is not really fundamental but chiefly a perhaps interesting but abstract intellectual production, it indeed is but theory. If it is fundamental, however, in the sense of providing the right foundation for our action and of making it clear-sighted instead of blind, it is of the utmost practical importance. This practical importance manifests itself very distinctly when this approach is applied to the great issues with which the Younger Churches and missions are everywhere confronted and which we formulated at the end of our first chapter as the general, but always vital, problem of the relation of the Christian Church to the world and its spheres of life.

The two great subjects we have to deal with can be brought under the heading of the following topics—The nature of the Church, and The relation of Christianity to its material and cultural environment. As the attitude to such vital issues as social service, rural reconstruction, rebuilding of the nation in social and moral respects, working for a Christian social and international order and many other issues also, depends on our conception of the nature of the Church, this subject deserves to be dealt with first.

.   .   .   .

THE NATURE OF THE CHURCH

At the well-known conference in Shanghai in 1922 one of the cardinal topics of discussion was the necessity of getting an autonomous, indigenous Church freed from the leading-strings of foreign missions. The Chinese spokesmen at the Conference did not merely emphasize the fact that Chinese Christianity was dependent in financial matters on foreign missions, but pointed to the relation of theological, ecclesiastical and cultural dependence in which Chinese Christianity stood to the Western Churches.

In other words, the problem of the independent, autonomous, indigenous Church became a burning issue in the wake of the rising tide of nationalism. The spirit of nationalism and the awakening of Oriental self-consciousness caused an acute awareness of the " foreignness " of Christianity and of the way it had taken shape hitherto in the various mission fields. Since the Conference at Shanghai the problem of the Church in missionary discussions, therefore, has always stood in this light of the " foreignness " of Christianity and of the Christian Churches in the countries of Asia and Africa. The problem of the Church since then has always been conceived in terms of the problem of the indigenization of the Church. This is still so to-day. It is universally felt as true that the main task which faces the Younger Churches is that of becoming truly indigenous to the various nations in which they live and work. It is also almost universally expected that if the Younger Churches find a vital relation to their cultural, social and political environment, they will no longer be considered by their overwhelmingly non-Christian environments as factors of denationalizing propaganda, but as the bearers of a supra-national eternal Gospel.

The vehement complaint about the foreignness of Christianity and of the Christian Church is wholly justified. Taking into account the peculiar nature of the relation of East and West in the nineteenth and the first quarter of the present century, and also the kind of relation in which missionary agencies and native Christians stood to each other, the urgent demand for a truly indigenous Church adjusted to its environment was a crying need. It is rather strange that the urgency of this demand is of such comparatively recent date. One of the greatest services which the rising tide of nationalism has done to the cause of Christianity is to foster in many Oriental Christians this spirit of revolt against the " foreignness " of Christianity as it is brought to their peoples and countries, and to rouse the desire for a truly indigenous Church. At the same time it has spurred the missionary body towards a more energetic and intense occupation with the problem of how to render the most effective help in the process of making the native Churches indigenous and independent.

In the last ten years a great amount of progress has been made in this particular field of setting afoot autonomous, indigenous Churches. After the long period of dependence on foreign guidance and control, the creation of autonomous and indigenous Churches, led and controlled by their own indigenous organs, has come upon us like an avalanche. We are in the midst of all the new problems that arise from this new situation. To both sides, the indigenous Churches and the missionary agencies, it is an experiment, full of vicissitudes, dangers, fears, hopes and possibilities. The result, naturally, is a bewildering clash of opinions, differing in tone according to the various countries. From Japan, with its mainly urban Churches and its innate sensitivity towards independence, hopeful tones are heard, although of course the difficulties of adjustment to entirely new kinds of relation between missions and Churches are not absent. In China much has been achieved to bring more unity and steadiness of life and action in the various Churches, but opinions and impressions are much more divided in regard to this problem in China than in Japan. Along with the will towards independence and a new sense of responsibility one hears about the frequent tendency towards leaning on foreign support and guidance. The same is reported about India, and one can assume it as certain that the same conflicting impression can be gained on other mission fields. To a very large extent this new phase of creating indigenous, autonomous Churches is dominated in the discussions by the problem of financial self-support. The capacity or incapacity for financial self-support is largely taken as the true measure of the right of an indigenous Church to be autonomous and independent.

From China as well as from India voices are often heard that reject the whole conception of organized ecclesiastical life as being wholly foreign to the Chinese or Indian mind and therefore inimical to true indigenization. Such pronouncements as that the Christian Church should aim at the minimum of organization and dogma, and the maximum of the spirit of religion, are common and attract much sympathy. This attraction is the more intelligible because a complaint, heard for instance in India, finds wide approval. It is that missions, despite the policy of " devolution," still largely determine the life of the Church and represent still too much a duplicate of the political hold of the country.

The problem of self-support and independence leads everywhere to an entirely new investigation into the economic and social possibilities of the Orient in relation to the ideal of a truly indigenous and self-conscious Church.

We have selected at random these features of the situation, merely with the object in view of suggesting how natural it is that we should be in the midst of the difficulties and confusions of an important stage of transition, and how urgent it is to see the problem of the Younger Churches in the right perspective. The fact is that the creation of indigenous, autonomous Churches has set in a new light all the problems and activities that are connected with the Christian message in the non-Christian world. Missions must now face, much more clearly than was possible ever before, the problem whether their activity means the management of a spiritual enterprise in foreign parts or the stimulating support of and the cordial co-operation with a partner in the Universal Church for the sake of the expansion of Christianity. Missions and Oriental Christians alike have now an opportunity of considering with much greater equanimity than was possible in the past in what manner the contribution of the Western Churches and of Western missionaries towards the growth of the existing Churches and the spread of the Gospel in their respective countries can be most helpful, because equals meet in a different way from superiors and inferiors.

Above all things, however, the problem of the Church, its nature and its concrete function in the various concrete environments, gets a deeper touch of reality than it has had and could have in the past.

We have pointed already to the fact that the issue of the indigenous Church has become a burning one as a result of the rising spirit of nationalism. This and the Western, foreign character of missions are the two main reasons why the discussion about the Church and the mission field is chiefly approached from the side of the necessity to eradicate the foreign character of the Christian Church and to make it indigenous. We repeat with all possible emphasis that, seeing the weakness of the initiative towards a truly indigenous Christianity amongst missionaries and Oriental Christians, and the strong aversion that continues to dominate the minds of many missionaries to serious attempts towards realizing a truly indigenous Christianity, the concern for a truly indigenous Church is an obvious and urgent duty. Yet, at the present moment of conflicting opinions and sentiments, attention must be fixed on a point of still more central importance. The problem is, What is a church? What is its nature and what are its functions according to its nature? The way towards becoming an *indigenous* Church goes through becoming first a real *Church*.

To many ears this may sound a dangerous deviation of the mind from a burning and concrete issue towards a theoretical discussion, with all the attendant evils of theological hair-splitting and passion. Has it not always been the outspoken and clearly-defined aim of missions to found self-propagating, self-supporting and self-governing Churches, and to build up morally and religiously strong congregations? Have they not always been absorbed in the problem of what a Church is and should be, and is not the result rather disappointing in this respect, that the many Churches and congregations which have been the fruit of these labours are lacking so much in indigenous flavour? It is necessary to answer these questions, because this will introduce us to the heart of the matter.

Latourette in *Missions To-morrow* draws a comparison between Protestant and Roman Catholic missions in China. In that country Protestant missions in their methods of approach laid great stress on broadcasting the Message, attending to social and physical needs, and exercising wide cultural influence. Less stress was laid on building a continuing Christian community. According to Latourette's testimony Roman Catholic missions devoted their attention to the last-mentioned object but have been no more successful than Protestant missions in developing strong communities. It seems to me that, generally speaking, few Protestant mission fields where the building up of strong Christian communities has been one of the primary objects can be cited as producing examples of really Church-conscious communities. Now that so many mission fields have been converted from mission-controlled groupings of Christians into indigenous, self-governing Churches, there is a general impression prevailing that there is much uncertainty and ignorance as to what a Church really is and how it ought to function in order to reveal its peculiar nature.

These indications seem once more to point in the direction of showing how sterile and abstract it is to focus attention on the question of the nature of the Church as a right approach towards the concrete and vital problem of a truly indigenous Church. This would undoubtedly be true if statements and formulated ends could always be taken at their face-value and according to the good intentions by which they are inspired. This is, however, not the case, for more than one reason.

Missions in the past have been either evangelistically-minded, culturally-minded or Church-minded, according to the dominant interests of the supporters who were behind these different enterprises. Evangelistically-minded missions were wholly interested in the broadcasting of the Message, in organizing evangelistic campaigns, in winning converts and mobilizing them for the same evangelistic purposes. Culturally-minded missions grasped the opportunity of establishing useful and wide contacts and of permeating the minds open to alien influences with Christian ideas. Church-minded missions were chiefly occupied by the idea of building up congregations bound together in a well-knit and ordered ecclesiastical life, modelled on the pattern of the various home Churches.

These three tendencies have in practice never operated separately, but these distinctions are nevertheless justified if they are taken in the sense of denoting preponderating accents and tendencies in the different missionary agencies. Each of these tendencies expresses an aspect of the missionary urge and has had many good results. In the present situation, however, what are apparently their weak sides become exposed very clearly. By the present situation is meant the fact that now a new insight is continuously gaining ground. In the stage of Christianization to which the non-Christian world has come at present, and in the deeply altered relation of East and West which has become manifest after the World War, the future progress of Christianity in the non-Christian world depends as much, or even more, on the strength and vitality of the indigenous Churches as on those of the missionary movement from the West. Theoretically this has always been the conviction, as is evident from the well-known aim of missions to produce self-supporting, self-governing and self-propagating Churches. As, however, this is at present no longer a distant aim, but more or less a fact and a starting-point by which the whole movement is determined, our missionary thinking has in consequence to be revised. Christianity and the Christian Churches as established now in the different countries have a quite different status from that of the past. By the irresistible force of circumstances and conditions the indigenous Christian individuals and groups were in the past inevitably seen as instruments and factors in the total aspect of our missionary calculations and expectations. Ideas like Roland Allen's or such as are contained in the so-called Nevius method, dynamic and stimulating as they undoubtedly are, derived their main inspiration from the desire for a wide, successful and speedy expansion of Christianity, and they viewed the indigenous Christians wholly as instruments for the execution of this project. This desire is a good missionary one and the object is a very healthy one, namely, to avoid from the beginning the production of mission-controlled and mission-governed groups of Christians, and to treat them as independent and responsible Christian communities. The strong emphasis on self-support as the symbol of real independence and on evangelization obscured, however, a still more essential feature of a Christian community, namely, that it has to represent in faith, life and work the Christian conception of life, which means a well-ordered and Christ-centred fellowship.

In the past culturally-minded missions had great opportunities when the Eastern mind became eager to absorb Western knowledge, ideals and methods, and achieved important results. In their view indigenous Christianity was an adjunct to the great process of permeation, and the small significance that organized, indigenous Christianity then had in the total picture naturally aided in strengthening this conception.

Church-minded missions meant in the past at least two things. In the first place they were entirely determined by denominational points of view. The Western denominational divisions were transplanted without much self-criticism, and the sincerely-held ideal of establishing a really indigenous Church did not prevent the creation of indigenous copies of the different Church orders that have been a result of the history of Western Protestantism. In the second place, this denominational view-point, which (this ought not to be omitted) involved a great amount of spiritual care and organization, tended naturally towards imparting to the newly-created Christian congregations that spiritual and organizational drill which is the custom in our Western Churches. It achieved an ecclesiastical framework that was often splendid, but it built a Church without creating a real Church-consciousness, and so involuntarily fostered a conception of the Church in the minds of the indigenous Christians that is very congenial to ancient Eastern ideas but is alien to the real Christian idea, namely, the conception that a congregation is a human grouping of distinct social characteristics conditioned by a special religion.

The indigenous Church is no longer chiefly a factor in our missionary calculations and expectations ; it is an independent factor which has to be the most conspicuous representation of Christian faith and fellowship in a great non-Christian environment. Therefore, the problem of what Church-consciousness in the deep and wide sense of the word means becomes of central importance ; it is no abstract and theoretical matter but a very vital one. A more effective way of becoming an indigenous Church is to become conscious of what a real Church is rather than to attack the problem implied in the word " indigenous " without knowing what a Church is. This is so because one who thinks about the nature and the function of the Church in this world of concrete realities necessarily thinks about what is involved in the idea of an indigenous Church, but one who thinks about the problem of indigenization takes the nature and the function of the Church too easily for granted.

These statements about the central importance of starting from a clear vision of the nature and the functions of the Church are corroborated by other considerations. More than once in the argument of this book we have pointed out that the evangelization of the non-Christian world depends on two series of factors. The first series comprise all the means of purely moral and religious persuasion which stand at the disposal of missions. The second series are those outside the grasp of intentional missionary effort : the constantly shifting political, economic and cultural situation. A. W. Wasson in his book, *Church Growth in Korea*, calls these last factors the environmental ones, and continually calls attention to the influence that these two sets of factors, simultaneously or separately, have exercised on the expansion of Christianity in Korea. His illustrations make it very clear that, although the Church and Missions have to be alert to these environmental factors, a firm grasp of the nature of the purely moral and religious forms of expression is the most essential factor in relation to the Christian message in the non-Christian world, because there the Church is on its own ground.

.   .   .   .

Just as the prophetic religion of Biblical realism is a religion *sui generis*, so the Christian Church, according to the conception of the New Testament, is a community *sui generis*. The unique character of the Christian Church is entirely misunderstood if it is conceived as a welfare or goodwill society on a religious basis. In its mode of expression, in its ministry, it may make in some respects the same impression as such societies, but in reality it is something quite different. It is, as F. R. Barry says in *The Relevance of the Church*, not a voluntary society but God's act through Jesus Christ, called into being by His redemptive purpose. Thus, just as Christianity is a theocentric religion, the Church is a theocentric community. Our modern habit of viewing the Church as being *essentially* an association of religiously like-minded people is by its anthropocentric tendency a disavowal of this theocentric nature of the Church. This, it must again be stressed, is not a theoretical distinction that does not matter very much in practice, but it is a matter of life or death for the Christian Church. If this theocentric character of the Christian Church were taken seriously, it would dispel with its dynamic force many of our ecclesiastical and religious miseries, and dissolve many of our ecclesiastical idiosyncrasies into nothing.

The terms employed in the New Testament for describing the nature of the Church are not decorative figures of speech, but terms full of realism. The Church is, according to the New Testament, the *ecclesia*, the community and fellowship of those who are united in common faith, common love and common worship of Him who is their Life and Head, bound in loyalty towards Him, permeated, inspired and chastened by His Spirit. They are " called to be saints " (1 Cor. i. 2), " the royal priesthood, the consecrated nation, the People who belong to Him that you may proclaim the wondrous deeds of Him who has called you from darkness to His wonderful light, you who once were ' no people ' and now are God's people, you who once were unpitied and now are pitied " (1 Peter ii. 9, 10).

These terms do not at all denote that the Church is a society of the morally and religiously perfect, which *boast* of divine election. This conception would mean the most radical corruption of the meaning of the Bible. These terms are directed in the New Testament towards men and women of common clay, who are constantly reminded that they are to strive to purify themselves from great sins and very bad habits. The ground of their fellowship is not their striving and their objects and ends, but God's calling and grace. The Church, according to the New Testament, is the fellowship of those who live by the divine miracle of the forgiveness of sins. God's grace and forgiveness is the ground of their election, and therefore, although their strivings and objects and ends are not the ground of their fellowship, just because they are children of divine grace and divine salvation and born to a new life, the Spirit impels them towards strenuous moral effort in the spirit of deepest humility. Barry, in his book just quoted, rightly says that religion and Church in the essentially Christian sense of the words are no affirmations or apprehensions of absolute values, but express an act of trust and self-committal to the God and Father of our Lord Jesus Christ. The Church has in God its origin and its centre. This is expressed in the primitive Christian *credo* : Christ is Lord. The *sui generis* character of the Church, of which we have spoken, consists in the fact that Jesus Christ is its primal and ultimate King and Lord, whose authority transcends and conditions all other authority and loyalty. The fact of being governed by such a Head and of being obliged to obey Him above all other authorities, determines the unique character of the Church. From this fact is derived its priestly and prophetic character as being at the same time the servant and the critic of the world and all its spheres of life.

The Church is in the world, its members belong to the different spheres of life (family, nation, society, state) and have their obligations towards and relations with these spheres. The Church, however, as the fellowship of those who believe in Christ and love and worship Him, ought never to forget that this fellowship transcends all mundane relations by its loyalty to its Head and Lord. Another very vital aspect is that Christ inaugurated the Kingdom of God, and therefore the fellowship that centres around Him transcends the world by the peculiar nature of the expectation and hope that bind it together, namely, the *expectation* of the realization of God's Kingdom in Jesus Christ notwithstanding all human frustrations. This is what is called the eschatological character of the Church. The Church is not an ideal institution, but a fellowship that finds its origin and ends in God's redemptive Will for the world, and therefore enters fully into the need and peril of the world. If, however, it is true to its nature, it can never feel " at home " in the world because of its eschatological character, for it looks forward to a consummation which transcends our human strivings and achievements, the realization of the Kingdom of God by God Himself. By its expectation of the " Eternal City " it is essentially an interim-institution, living and working in this world between the time when it began its career through the effusion of the Holy Spirit and the time " which the Father has put in His own power " (Acts i. 7), or, in other words, between the time when God revealed in Christ His plan of re-creating this often so hopeless world and the time when this re-creation will become triumphantly evident. If the Church is unconscious of its eschatological nature, it loses one of its most essential characteristics.

Being a divinely-willed theocentric fellowship the Church, according to New Testament realism, lives by *charismata*, that is to say, gifts of divine grace, or gifts worked by the Spirit. Paul takes this so realistically that he makes no real distinction between what we would call spiritual gifts and business ability in connection with the Church. In I Corinthians xii. 28 amongst the members of the Body of Christ he promiscuously enumerates apostles, prophets, teachers, workers of miracles, healers, helpers, *administrators* and those speaking in tongues. It is a very impressive way of expressing the theocentric character of the Church.

In the faith that the peculiar nature of the Church is to be the divinely-willed fellowship of believers in and lovers of Christ, their Lord, lie the Church's inspiration and obligation. The empirical Church has to confront itself constantly with this mystery of its divinely-willed fellowship, and be cleansed and inspired by it in order to realize a kind of fellowship in the world that has its roots in eternity and thereby manifests a deeper quality than any other form of fellowship can. Another characteristic of this fellowship is that it does not exist for its own sake but for the sake of the world. To quote again Barry's book, " The Church is in the world to redeem it. A Church true to its character and mission will be looking outwards upon the world, not inwards upon its own system. An introverted Church has no future. The question is not, Which is the true Church ? It is rather, How can the Church come true ? "

In this dispensation the problem of the Church consists in the fact that it cannot be defined only by its essential nature. It does not exist in a vacuum but is also a part of this world, operating through our limited human instrumentality and tormented by our sins. It lives and functions in definite times and places, and is composed of human beings with their peculiar temperament and cultural predispositions. The New Testament, which portrays in such clear and forceful language the essential nature of the Church, leaves no doubt whatever on this point by the glimpses it affords as to the actual life of the first Christian communities. The Church, if aware of these two sides, must therefore always remain in tension between the triumphant recognition of its essential nature and the urge to penitence and constant renewal of its life. It is different from all other communities in the world because it is rooted in and governed and permeated by a personal transcendent Authority, subordination to whom is the only real freedom. To awaken this kind of Church-consciousness is to lay the right foundation for a vital Christian Church.

On the other hand, the Church is subject to the same laws and tendencies as all other forms of community in the world, just because it does not exist in a vacuum but in different concrete realities. It becomes entangled consequently in the same turmoil of right and wrong, better and worse, as other institutions. This is the ever-present problem of the Church in this world, under whatever circumstances it may exist. It is heavenly from the heavens and earthly from the earth. Here lie its dangers and temptations, as the whole course of Church history shows abundantly, and also its opportunities and duties. To be exclusively aware of its heavenly nature without evincing any consciousness of its prophetic and apostolic relation to the world ends in sterile dogmatism and in the denial of its dynamic religious nature. To lose the vision of this essential nature results in the Church's becoming a more or less good or bad segment of human society. The more conscious the Church is of its essential nature and of its obligation to realize this in the relative conditions of this complicated and confused world, the more alive and humble it will be. The more it loses this consciousness, the more it becomes concentrated on self-maintenance and self-interest, and the more de-christianized and secularized it becomes.

In regard to some points of vital interest we will indicate the conclusions that can be derived from this dynamic, prophetic-apostolic conception of the Church. Everyone who in his eagerness for so-called practical conclusions and directives persists in finding this conception theoretical must be aware of the fact, consciously or unconsciously, that he has at the back of his mind a certain conception of community which affords to him the inspiring impulse or the ideal end of his practical devices. It is required for the sober and realistic treatment of our subject that we take the Church according to the vision that is inherent in Biblical realism, because that is the only adequate and honest way of dealing with Christianity. It will be hard to find anywhere in the world a more dynamic idea of community and fellowship than we find in the Bible. Its theocentric character is the reason of its radically religious and ethical character.

The question will then arise, Why is this radically religious Biblical conception of the Church, of community and of fellowship, the most fruitful way towards an indigenous Church? At first sight this looks strange, and the better way seems to be to harmonize the nature of the Christian Church with the spirit and forms of indigenous sociological structure. Yet the situation in the case of the building of the Church is the same as in all problems of indigenization. In the case of indigenizing Christianity by expressing it in thought-forms and terms congenial to the environment, we found the rule that the radically religious and theocentric conception of Christianity as contained in Biblical realism gives freedom and courage to use the heritage and to use it creatively and critically. To do so is simply an act of obedience to the peculiar historical situation in which a new growing Christian Church is set, *provided the impelling and primary motive is to express the Gospel and its invariable essence.* This is the most energetic way of being Christian and indigenous. If the impelling motive is harmonization and accommodation, it results ultimately in an injury to the character of Christianity and a wrong indigenization.

The same reasoning can and must be applied to the case of the building of the Church, which pertains to the category of expressing Christianity in social forms. From the standpoint of the theocentric Christianity of Biblical realism there can be raised, therefore, an even stronger protest against imposing on Eastern Christians denominationalism, alien ecclesiastical forms of organization and alien methods of fostering spiritual life than from the purely psychological or sociological standpoint, although these two render great help in sharpening our powers of observation and insight. If the same fundamental condition is fulfilled of being primarily interested in the Church as the divinely-willed fellowship of the believers in Christ, the necessity of making a creative and critical, but free and courageous, use of existing and serviceable indigenous social forms and of methods of fostering spiritual life for the building of the Church, is at once self-evident and stringent. This is so, not because indigenous forms and methods are always the best and invariably the most serviceable to Christian life, but because the indigenous has the right to be considered seriously and sympathetically as the vehicle of life-expression before any other possible vehicle. Just as a man expresses himself best in his own language, however many other languages he may master, so communities and social groupings express their life best in forms congenial to their temperament and tradition, better than by the imposition of alien forms. The criterion for adoption or rejection lies in whether it serves to express or to frustrate, and this criterion applies alike to indigenous forms and methods and to alien. It ought to become a fundamental law in missionary work that alien forms and methods of spiritual and ecclesiastical life (which are to the Western missionary the indigenous ones) are viewed with the same scrutinizing criticism as indigenous forms and methods are usually subjected to.

The primary aim in building an indigenous Church, then, must be the fostering of a creative, spiritual life, so that the richness of the knowledge of Christ and the fruits of the Spirit may develop ever more fully. If the essential nature of the Church as depicted above is constantly kept before the mind when occupied with the important work of building a sound Church life, native and European leadership of an African or Asiatic Church should stoutly resist the temptation of considering Western ecclesiastical forms and Western methods of fostering spiritual life as the obvious and proper ones. Of course, there may be many cases in which the Western forms and methods are exceedingly serviceable, but the creative and critical use of the already existing and congenial forms must be stressed with all possible strength, because the natural aptitude of man, and of the missionary and the indigenous leader too, is to find the accustomed denominational forms the proper ones. From the standpoint of the theocentric conception of the nature of the Church the first missionary task is to discover what, according to God's pleasure, as evident also in the people's natural heritage and faculties, are for this people in regard to confession, worship, witness, propagation, administration and discipline the most fertile ways of expressing their *own* spiritual life and their *own* attainments in Christ.

It would seem that this line leads to a deeper and more natural kind of indigenization than when the *direct* and *exclusive* aim is to become truly indigenous. For the sake of the clarification of thought it is well, moreover, to consider that the programme of making an indigenous Church is often pressed in a way that is too much simplified. In the arguments about the " foreignness " of Christianity and of the Christian Church in many countries the leading idea is that by becoming truly indigenous in cultural, social and political respects, the Younger Churches will become " accepted " and " recognized " in the countries to which they belong. Maintaining with all possible emphasis the urgent necessity of thorough indigenization in the sense indicated above, we must remain realistic and never forget that in many cases there will remain a great difference between *being* truly indigenous in life and expression and being *recognized* as indigenous. A religious minority that does not conform to its environment in religious matters is not usually recognized as indigenous until the time when it is no longer a conspicuous minority. Now, a characteristic of Christianity is that it does not conform to its environment in religious and in socio-religious matters. Moreover, it is still a minority. However indigenous in the best and deepest sense of the word it becomes, the non-Christian environment will not cease to consider it objectionable until it has become at least a strong and impressive minority.

From the various mission fields one hears much about an anti-theological bias. Where this does not exist, the acceptance of theological formulas tends dangerously in the direction of creedalism or doctrinalism—religiously speaking a not less lamentable feature than an anti-theological bias. In the seventh chapter we ventured to offer an explanation of this anti-theological bias. One hears the same about an anti-ecclesiastical bias. Ecclesiastical life as commonly found in Christianity, with its strong predilection for regular pastoral care of souls and the employment of an appointed ministry, meets with much contradiction and is not infrequently deemed uncongenial to the Oriental mind. This anti-ecclesiastical bias has probably become more evident because the rise of self-governing indigenous Churches has made the problem of self-support very prominent in the discussions and deliberations. It would require a special investigation on the spot to discover the deepest roots of this anti-ecclesiastical bias, because without such a special investigation the danger of developing airy speculations is great.

Two opinions, however, on this point may be offered with reasonable confidence. In the first place, a great deal of this anti-ecclesiastical bias goes back, among the simple rural people, to economic reasons, and among many intellectual people (if reasons of purely religious conviction be omitted) to an unconsciously aristocratic attitude, which shrinks from identifying oneself with a community that consists largely of simple folk. About China, for instance, it is constantly repeated that the " practical-minded Chinese farmer " has an aversion from a "paid ministry " and therefore prefers laymen above well-trained ministers.

In the second place, this economic and social difficulty is a very real one, while the spiritual difficulty in many intellectuals is also real. Both must be taken very seriously, and the solution will certainly not be found without a full knowledge of the economic possibilities and of the right handling of people of such different mental make-up and social background as rural people and intellectuals are. Nevertheless, if the point of orientation is the dynamic vision of the nature of the Church, perseverance in order to find a solution will be much greater than in any other case. This perseverance requires primarily that this vision of the nature of the Church be impressed on the minds of the indigenous Christians themselves, because all our arguing and reasoning will never convince them of the truth that the systematic care for individual and communal spiritual life belongs to the essentials of Christianity, and that sacrificial giving is a natural consequence from it. Our arguments often appeal to reason and intellect, but these matters are not solved in the region of intellect but in that of a new religious apprehension, which can occur in simple and in intellectual people alike. It is extremely instructive to read the radical religious, social and economic effects achieved by Dr Keysser, to whose work we alluded in the preceding chapter, because he began at the beginning, perseveringly confronting the Papuans who had turned to Christianity with the vision of the " God-people," the Christian fellowship that is the essence of the Church.

Since Henry Venn formulated as the aim of all missionary work the establishment of self-supporting, self-governing and self-propagating Churches, the topic of self-support has been a very marked one in missionary discussions. As already remarked, the rise of the Younger Churches has made this problem still more acute. The will and the ability in a Church to achieve self-support are usually regarded as decisive indications that this Church has a right to become free from all missionary control. This is for another reason, too, an important point, namely, the inclination of many groups of Oriental Christians towards leaning on support. There are missionary agencies which, leaving apart this psychological trait, take the point of view that as long as an indigenous Church is living on money coming from foreign missionary sources, the missionary agencies have the right and the duty to control the way in which the money is spent. The motive for this attitude is that they are responsible for the spending of the gifts entrusted to them. As this matter causes much friction and misunderstanding between missions and Younger Churches and as it is ultimately not a practical or business problem but a deeply spiritual one, some remarks need to be made about it.

There are both practical and theoretical reasons for taking the standpoint that the measure of independence from missionary control should not depend on the amount of financial support that is still granted by missionary agencies to self-governing indigenous Churches. The necessity of continuing financial support is in various cases due to causes largely lying outside the responsibility of these Churches. They have been nursed by foreign missionary agencies ; their organizational machinery, although in many respects adjusted to their conditions, has been mainly conceived by European brains. We are, however, only beginning to learn the implications of adjustment to the economic and social conditions of Eastern life. The cost implied in self-support, therefore, is still partly determined by a machinery that has been set up without a thorough consideration of the indigenous economic foundations. On account of these practical considerations it is not at all to be marvelled at that in the period of transition from mission fields to self-governing Churches (for that is the situation in which we actually are) financial support is still needed in many cases.

Beside these practical considerations there are others, of a more theoretical character, that are of decisive importance. To connect the lesser or higher degree of independence from missionary control with the amount of financial support, and to distinguish mission money from Church money, has the psychological effect that the connection of missions and the indigenous Church becomes a source of irritation to the latter, and is spiritually unsound. The fellowship of Christians who together form an indigenous Church is, if we take seriously the idea of the nature of the Church that we have discussed, under any circumstances an independent body, whose only legitimate Head and Authority is Christ. It is the *fruit* of missionary labour, but not the *possession* of missions, and it is on the side of missions a serious and fatal misunderstanding of the nature of the Church to consider any indigenous Church in any stage of development to be in an inferior position because it receives financial support. The support given to one Church by another (in this case the support given by missionary agencies to indigenous Churches that are on the way to complete self-support, self-government and self-propagation) is no charity but fraternal help. The missionary agencies must act fully on the idea that Churches which are equal members of Christ's Body should receive fraternal help, which fact excludes the stipulation of rights, conditions or restrictions. Where rights are connected with support, the equal and fraternal members of Christ's Body easily take on the relation to each other of controlling benefactors to irritated recipients of charity. On the other hand, the Churches receiving this help recognize, in the same Christian spirit, the obligation of accounting for the support received.

The healthy growth of truly indigenous and vigorous Churches depends in a great measure on the kind of initiative which the Western missionary agencies take in this matter of financial support and on whether these agencies have a dynamic or a more or less static conception of the nature of the Church. This is the case also in the problem of denominationalism and unity. Especially at the present time the responsibility of the Western missionary agencies is very great. The Younger Churches and the missionary enterprise in the non-Christian world are vigorous forces, but they are very decidedly a minority in the midst of a world of increasingly aggressive non-Christian religions and forces. The Christian conscience all over the world is beginning to wake up to the necessity of a truly ecumenical spirit in the Christian Church. A truer vision of the fellowship the Church ought to represent, and the stupendous confusion of the present world contribute to this gradual awakening. The Christian Churches in the non-Christian world are by their many divisions much weaker than need be the case. These divisions are not of their making. It is certainly no exaggeration to say that one of the cardinal problems of the Christian mission in the non-Christian world is whether Western missionary agencies will find the faith and the courage to derive their orientation, in regard to these problems of denominationalism and unity in the mission field, neither from ecclesiastical indifference nor from ecclesiastical bias, but from confronting themselves with the dynamic conception of the Church as set before us in Biblical realism.

THE CHURCH IN RELATION TO ITS ENVIRONMENT

Max Weber in his famous studies on *Religionssoziologie* points out that in all soteriological religions in the world there is manifest a tension between the ideal of salvation that is their highest end, and the secular values and spheres of life. All these religions are characterized by an ethic that is highly individualistic, and conceive the relations of men to each other in the terms of fraternity. The tension with the spheres of art, politics and economics arises from the fact that artistic self-assertion has an open or secret conflict with the religious ideal of serving God or of exclusive concern about the life of the soul ; that the acquisitive urge in economics clashes with the norm of fraternity, and that the will to power stands in contrast to the ideal of love. In the present time the wide gulf between the ethos of soteriological religion and modern economic and political conditions is specially apparent, because the dominating capitalistic structure is exceedingly impersonal, and the complicated world-wide character of human relationships to-day results in various kinds of relationships that are inevitably impersonal. The old world of restricted, rural and patriarchal relationships is not nearly so necessarily impersonal as is the modern industrial world, ruled by world economics and world finance.

Christianity is also a soteriological religion with a personalist ethic of fraternity, but of a very specific kind. As has been explained in preceding pages [1] the prophetic religion of Biblical realism is, in contrast to the other soteriological religions, not anthropocentric but theocentric. This causes a radical difference. The well-known Asiatic soteriologies by their anthropocentric and eudæmonistic character all evince a strong world-denying tendency. Historical Christianity more than once has come under the influence of this same tendency, but even then its innate world-affirming tendency has often broken through triumphantly. The best illustration is West European monasticism and its activist, cultural tendencies.

Because the real centre of Christianity is God, the Living, the Creator and the Redeemer of the world and of man, its ethos, although deeply personalist, cannot adequately be described by this term, and its attitude towards the world and its spheres of life must necessarily be positive and not negative. God is the God of history. History is not a reproduction of the cyclic course of nature, but God's Will is the transcendent force and the end of history. The Kingdom of God, the reign of God in a fellowship of redeemed men, is the end of all human history, of which only God knows how it is to be realized. One of the essential and dynamic factors in the Christian attitude of faith is that it connotes the unshakable trust that the God and Father of the Lord Jesus Christ will realize this end through, and despite, human forces at the time of His pleasure. The primary mission of Christianity is to foster this attitude and awaken this faith ; hence its primary character is to testify to the religious realities of creation, sin, forgiveness, reconciliation and regeneration wrought in and through Christ. The vision that God is the God of creation, of redemption and of history, implies that God is also at work in man and the world, although because of the corruption and disorder of all spheres of life by sin, no human mind is able to indicate

[1] Cp. Chapters III and IV.

where exactly He is at work and where not. This means in practice that the urge towards a philosophy of history is always present in the Christian view of life, but that its actual production will for ever remain a fragmentary and passing attempt. The Christian view includes also the belief that God the Creator and Redeemer is at work in the human efforts to master life, which are called by a comprehensive term the cultural sphere in its various aspects, and in the human " values " that result from these endeavours. Human life, in all its manifestations has, as we have repeatedly said, a dual nature—that is to say, it is divine and demonic in indissoluble fusion. In all human culture there is a mixture of service to God and rebellion against God. To impart to these human " values " and spheres of life divine sanction by declaring them divine " orders " of life is to disregard their " relative " nature and greatly to underestimate the disorderliness of life through the corruption of sin. The Biblical view that the Will of God is at once the Law, the Crisis and the Judgment of nature and history, excludes the possibility of sanctifying any human sphere of life. Yet, although the spheres of life are vitiated and disfigured by sin and in their historical existence belong to the sphere of " relative " values, the Christian cannot surrender the view that God is somehow at work in the whole rich drama of human life, its productions and aspirations. The knowledge that, according to the Christian view, God has set us in this world to live our life in the different spheres of culture, economics, politics and society so as to find out His Will, imparts by its transcendental motivation and outlook a virile temper to the Christian attitude. All cultural, social and political attitudes are always ultimately rooted in definite assumptions regarding the nature and the Will of God and regarding the nature and destiny of man. In the problem of how the different spheres of life are related to Christianity and what its obligation is towards them, the Christian starts, of course, from the fundamental Christian assumptions regarding God and man as contained in Biblical realism.

In our third chapter it has been made plain that the

Kingdom of God is an operative but transcendental reality, and that therefore Christianity will not and cannot pretend to realize ideal cultural, social or political conditions. It has no revealed social or political or cultural programmes nor has it a ready-made set of eternal principles. There are mainly three reasons why this is so. The fundamental reason is that to identify the transcendental Kingdom of God and the realization of God's Will with some form of human society and culture, which by the nature of the case is relative, imperfect and transient, is a disastrous confusion of human " values " with divine standards. Ultimately this goes back to an idealist and not a Biblical conception of God and man. Second, the Church is called, on the ground of its theocentric ethic, to transform the world by witness and action, but it knows that the forces of evil are as real in the world as the working of the divine Will. It can never, therefore, make its obligation of transforming witness and action dependent on whether this witness and action are successful or not.

In the third place a sober estimate of reality teaches that the Church, however determined its will towards transforming witness and action may be, never can *promise* the solution of economic, social and political problems. It can put its influence in the scale and ought to do so, but it cannot guarantee a solution, for the simple reason that the Church cannot pretend to govern the economic and political factors that determine the outward course of the world at large. No earthly institution or organization can pretend to that, as the present time abundantly teaches. As A. W. Wasson has demonstrated in *Church Growth in Korea*, the unwarranted promise of solution necessarily breeds disillusionment. The Church therefore never can compete with communism or fascism or modern idealism, which offer and guarantee in their programmes ideal solutions of economic, social and political problems. It is very pertinent to the present situation of the Christian Church and of missions in the non-Christian world to state this solid fact, because it is natural that in the midst of terrible economic, social and political conditions many ardent young minds should raise the cry of the need for a socially-effective religion. The impatience that rings in this cry is of noble quality. Yet, it seems that the criticism which it contains of the Christian Church is laid at the wrong door. If the criticism means that in the Church the will to be socially effective is far too weak, it is more than justified. If it means, however (and it certainly does in many cases), that the Church ought to promise and guarantee the realization of an ideal social and political order, it derives from an entire misconception of the nature of the Church, and from a wrong view of the dual character of the world which is the battleground of divine and demonic forces. The promises and guarantees of communism and other social idealisms that they will realize an ideal social order are utterly unwarranted. At their best, they are well-meaning but deceitful illusions. To say this connotes no pessimism and quietism, for whoever really believes in the living God and the validity of His Will for all spheres of life is no pessimist and quietist. It is faithful realism.

It was necessary to make these general remarks in order to get the right perspective for the social and cultural activities of the Church and of missions. There is much discussion at present going on as to what is central in missions. H. Vernon White in his *A Theology for Christian Missions* devotes a whole chapter to it. " The service of man " is accepted there as the regulative aim of Christian missions. It is repeatedly defined as " man-centred." Much of what Dr White says is so full of prophetic and genuinely Christian moral fervour that one can heartily agree with it. His ardent plea, however, is blurred by some great defects, which tend to bring the discussion on this important problem to a deadlock, while it should be lifted to a new plane. The standpoint he recommends is too much conceived in an antithetical spirit. He contrasts with each other the programme of proselytizing with that of Christian service and nurture. By proselytism in this connection is meant " the desire to increase the geographical extent and the numerical strength " of the Church or of Christianity, and to have one's " religious beliefs accepted by ever larger numbers of people," " the passion for gaining more and more adherents to a creed for the honour of that creed and the cumulative proof of its truth and power." In these sentences a tone of moral indignation against dogmatism and doctrinalism is audible that finds much justification in present conditions. In the course of our argument we ourselves have frequently had occasion to expose the dangers of the dogmatic spirit. Nevertheless, if we bring back the discussion on this central problem of Christianity's concrete expression in life and work to the antithesis of either rabid and narrow-minded proselytism or service to humanity and activism, it will merely end in sterile exasperation on both sides, a very unhappy result. Dr White's characterization of proselytism not only contains an element of justified criticism, but in no less degree an entire disregard of the religious roots of true proselytism. As truly as Christianity is the prophetic and apostolic religion *par excellence* and as truly as missions can only endure on that basis, so also an essential element of Christianity and Christian missions is true proselytism. The bad repute in which this word stands must not make us hesitant in using it with all frankness. Dr White is entirely right in stressing with great fervour that Jesus has emphasized the " doing of God's Will " as a criterion, and that He likens a man who does so " to a sensible man who built his house on a rock." The spirit of mercy and helpfulness is as essential an element of the Christian faith as is faith in the forgiveness of sins. The New Testament does not know of distinctions, of higher and lower grades, in this respect. Yet, when Dr White in his eagerness to press his case declares that the spirit of service and ministry (which are, when rightly conceived, the spontaneous and indispensable *expressions* of the new mind in Christ) is the supreme meaning of the Christian revelation and of Christ, he remains, whether he likes it or not, eternally imprisoned in a pragmatist and humanist conception of religion and of Christianity, which unintentionally has lost touch with the religion of revelation which we find in the New Testament. It is no mistaken form of proselytism, but it belongs to the very essence of obedience to God, that a Christian and a missionary should live by the ardent desire that all men will surrender to Christ as the Lord of their lives. Whosoever does not stress that, does not sufficiently consider the passionately prophetic and apostolic spirit of the Gospel. The core of the Christian revelation is that Jesus Christ is the sole legitimate Lord of all human lives and that the failure to recognize this is the deepest religious error of mankind. Surrender to Christ does not mean to accept the only right religious tenets, but to accept the Lord, the only One who has a right to be the Lord. Seen in this light, not to recognize Him as the sole legitimate Lord is to serve false gods. To present Christ in this radically *religious* way is the deepest mode of expressing the well-known first commandment : " Thou shalt have none other gods before me."

All activities of the Christian Church and of missions in social service, in education, in rural reconstruction, in medical work and so many things more only get their right missionary foundation and perspective if they belong as intrinsically to the category of witness as preaching or evangelization. It depends, of course, on many factors how much a mission can do in these various fields, because considerations of precedence, of financial or technical possibility and other practical factors determine the actual shape or amount of action. We are at present only giving expression to the fundamental position. We repeat what has been said in the beginning of this chapter. When it is right to consider witness, ministry and worship to be the three natural expressions of the Church, they are only rightly understood if witness is also real ministry and worship, if ministry is also witness and worship, and if worship is also witness and ministry. These three sides must become saturated with the spirit that is the essential characteristic of each of the three. So the social and cultural activity of the Church are not *accessories* to its essential programme of witness and proclamation of the Gospel, but *expressions* of its nature.

Another consequence of this vision is that, however social or cultural the activity of Church and missions may appear, it can never be identified with cultural propaganda nor done in a spirit of utopianism. On the other hand, the opinion which is so often expressed in Continental missionary circles, that too great absorption in emancipating and civilizing action supplants the essential religious task of missions, has to be revised thoroughly in the light of this vision. It may be often true in practice, but it is not necessarily so. It is the case only when this vision fails to be the dominating force in the whole enterprise. To demonstrate in certain cases the absence of this vision does not justify a rather negative attitude towards its application. The denunciation of " activism " ought to give place to the right kind of activism. The theocentric fellowship of Christ, the Church, if true to its essential nature cannot but express its service of God in service to man, just as Jesus Christ expressed it. If it lives by this inspiration, all its social and cultural activities will come from a deeper source than direct social and cultural aims can provide. It is not fired by utopianism, because it knows the world and what is in it, but it lives and acts by the love of God and by the desire to fulfil His Will in a spirit of humility, longing for His Kingdom that transcends all kingdoms and societies. It does not shrink from emancipating or civilizing work, but loyally enters upon it when it is its obvious duty to do so. Harnack reminds us in his book, *Mission and Expansion of Christianity*, that the Christians of the Primitive Church showed themselves to be a new type of men by " almsgiving, support of widows or orphans, care of prisoners, care of poor people needing burial, care of slaves, care of those visited by great calamities, care of brethren on a journey and of Churches in poverty or in peril. The new language on the lips of the Christians was the language of love. But it was more than a language, it was a thing of power and action. The Christians really considered themselves brethren and sisters and their actions corresponded to this belief."

The concrete way in which Church and missions to-day have to express this same spirit and attitude is entirely different from that in the first centuries of the Christian era. We are living in a world widely different in all respects. Natural and social sciences have put at our disposal many means of tackling the problems of human life that were not available in that period of history, while on the other hand, as a consequence of technical evolution, the problems are of far greater dimensions. Our approach and methods differ accordingly. We cannot guarantee the cure of the world's evils by our man-made programmes, but the greater the evils the more is it incumbent upon us to battle strenuously against them, and especially so because the arms that are at our disposal are continuously on the increase through the ingenuity of the human mind.

Church and missions have to be in this respect zealous pupils of the world. Rural reconstruction, education, co-operation, and other activities that try to meet essential needs or glaring evils are in the present time as natural expressions of the Christian spirit of love and solidarity as almsgiving or the care of slaves was in the Ancient Church. In *Rethinking Missions* the wise remark is made that " the missionary enterprise cannot assume the responsibility for solving illiteracy or curing the ills of the women of rural Asia. But it can stimulate others to action and contribute to the solution of rural problems through demonstrating certain definite lines of rural welfare." [1] The need for reconstruction and for service to aid in this reconstruction is so terribly great in rural and industrial Asia and Africa that missions and the Christian Church cannot but play their part in it, however modest this contribution may appear in comparison with the hugeness of these needs. Not so long ago missions were the pioneers and leaders in many fields of social and cultural service. By their example they have stimulated Governments as well as indigenous agencies. This stage is definitely a matter of the past, for many reasons that are universally known. If missions in the future continue to participate in the various kinds of service that present themselves, their ambition must be to excel in creativeness of mind and in the quality of their work.

All these problems of Christian service and solidarity with

---

[1] The approach towards the problem of the Christian mission in the non-Christian world in this book is entirely different from that of the Laymen's Enquiry. Here, however, I avail myself of the opportunity to say with great emphasis that one of the detrimental effects of the discussion which centred around it is that the wealth of splendid practical advice and insight stored up in these reports remains so largely unused. Horror at the underlying " activism " and " syncretism " has blinded the eyes to some outstanding merits of these reports.

the environment are given a special note of urgency by the fact that the non-Christian world, in which the Christian task must be fulfilled, is going through a period of rapid change and transition, in which the old is in many respects vanishing and the new is still powerless to be born. Among many " primitive " peoples the crucial problem is how to help them (as far as strenuous human endeavour can do this) in achieving the very painful but necessary social and cultural readjustment which forces itself upon them. In this process the ancient cohesive forces are in danger of becoming shattered. By their fundamental religious attack on these societies missions are inevitably partners in producing the destructive tempest that has been let loose through the impact of Western civilization on these peoples. On the other hand, missions have also aided in widening their horizons, stimulating their desires, and creating new visions. These two reasons are already sufficient to make plain that missions have no right to evade the responsibility of aiding strenuously in strengthening the responsibility of the Christian and of the wider community by all means that experience, modern anthropological science and spiritual insight can furnish. Missions have to accept honestly and courageously their part in the task of rescue and education that arises out of this stupendous situation.

There is still another very stringent reason for intelligent and vigorous action. Missions make the claim, on account of their religious aim, that Christianity contains the forces of moral and spiritual regeneration, so sorely needed in this time of disintegration. It is encouraging to read twice, for instance, in Monica Hunter's *Reaction to Conquest*, that Christianity proves able to supply a new invigorating moral basis of life. Yet missions ought always to be mindful that this does not result *mechanically* from the acceptance of Christianity, but that to achieve it there is need for a constant application to the task of religious, moral, cultural and social education—and this must be inspired by the desire *to serve the true interest of the people*. This last principle has to be underlined, because missions are often accused of offering these things as baits. This accusation, probably, will never be entirely silenced, because there will always remain malevolent observers of missions. Missions, however, must not waste their time and energy in trying to court favour or escape disfavour, but, recognizing that this accusation is not wholly unsubstantiated, must become assured of the purity of their motives.

In closing we will make a series of short observations on some of the most important aspects of service at the present time.

In the mission field all over the world the problem of education is at an acute stage. Whether in colonially-governed non-Christian countries or in independent countries, the missionary system of schools and education, which was formerly an integral adjunct of the missionary enterprise, has, by the development of events, become an incorporated part of the colonial or national system of education. As to methods, aims and subject matter it is bound to programmes inspired and dictated by governmental and national aims. Everywhere the question becomes urgent how to preserve the vitally Christian character of the schools. There appear to be but two ways to find a satisfactory solution of this problem. In the countries where there is fortunately still a measure of freedom for experimentation as to methods and subject matter, missions and the Churches should be prominent in two directions. In the first place, great energy should be devoted to staffing the schools with a personnel imbued with a deep Christian spirit and developing an intensely Christian atmosphere in the schools. In the second place, as most of the peoples in those countries have to adjust themselves to a colossal change in outlook and circumstances, education should be used as one of the best means available to help them in this adjustment, and this presupposes an intimate knowledge of their structure of life as well as an intelligent grasp of the necessities of change and adaptation to new conditions.

In the countries where this freedom does not exist, all attention has to be focused on creating a personnel which is determined to live and work together as a fellowship of Christian workers in the real sense of the word Christian.

In these cases it is only the force of Christian personalities that can save the situation.

In medical work the outstanding problems are analogous and different at the same time. They are analogous, because the medical work of missions has become to a great extent co-ordinated to the govermental or national system of medical care and hygiene, with the ensuing danger of weakening the missionary character of the work. Medical care and hygiene, however, because of their philanthropic nature are not made the instruments of political ends of the State in the same way as to-day education is. Hence, the two universal problems of medical work in missions are to maintain an intensely Christian and missionary spirit, and to show eagerness in co-operating in effective ways with other agencies for the alleviation and prevention of the colossal amount of human suffering that prevails in Asia and Africa.

In the field of rural reconstruction there is one problem of great religious significance, which especially in America attracts more and more attention. There are everywhere in Africa and Asia rural Christians. Agriculture is the centre of their life. In their pre-Christian period their agricultural life was wholly intertwined with their religion. For two reasons their agricultural and social life is now becoming severed from religion. In the first place, because they have become Christians. In the second place, because the growth of self-reliance (in itself a very healthy thing), the use of modern means of cultivation and the spread of modern rational ideas kill the urge to take a religious view of life which imposed itself imperiously in their pre-Christian period when religious rites and devices were used to achieve economic and social ends. This can justly be interpreted as a much-needed purification of religion, but it should not be forgotten that both causes contribute also to a thorough secularization of life, a rather disquieting result of Christianization. In these simple rural environments the danger that Christianity should become merely a churchgoing-and-Sunday affair without relevance to real life is as great as it is in urban life and in Europe and America. Mr Reisner, the secretary of the Agricultural Missions Foundation in New York, very aptly remarks in one of his papers, " The Church has surrendered agriculture and the interpretation of its significance in human welfare to our scientific agencies and our commercial and industrial interests."

The urgent question is how to relate rural Christian life, in its agricultural and social aspects, to the realities of God the Creator and God the Redeemer, or in other words, how can man continue to live in genuine relation with God as the Prime Reality in the atmosphere of modern self-reliance and modern resourcefulness ? This end cannot be achieved by the way of exhortation in sermons, the expedient which the Church is always prone to use. Where our treasure lies there lies our heart. The great religious issue is whether God is the real treasure of our heart in the life of to-day, which by its trend of secularization seems so largely and successfully emancipated from God, or whether He is only theoretically " our treasure," while our real interests are wholly irrelevant to the sphere of God and His actions.

Christianity in Asia and Africa will be to a great extent a rural Christianity, and rural evangelism will have to play a preponderant rôle in the future. This is not said to minimize the importance of urban life and urban Christianity in Eastern countries, for that is continuously growing in significance and range. The bulk of the population, however, is rural, and all symptoms point in the direction of a growing rural Christianity and of increasing rural evangelism. By the desacralizing and secularizing influence of modern life, its inventions and attitudes, to which missions as parts of Western civilization also contribute, the ancient ties binding all spheres of life to religion have been destroyed. This is a great gain but also a loss. It is a great gain, because on the whole the intertwining of paganism and agriculture has meant a precarious bondage of the spirit and of life. It is a loss in this sense, that now a sterile secularism with its superficial and hollow view of life will invade the minds of numberless people. In this situation it is a great and difficult task to establish a vital and palpable relation between the eternal background contained in the Christian faith and the realities of rural life, which are so full of deep and suggestive meaning and which absorb such a great part of the interest of the people. In our modern age this must be done with more deliberate purpose than ever before. In former ages, for instance during the Christianization of Europe in the Middle Ages, there was no sphere of life that was secularized in the modern sense of the word. In the past, to connect rural life and certain elements of Christianity meant going along the well-trodden path of custom and often resulted in paganizing Christianity. At present, it requires a genuine deepening of religious life, a creative re-discovery of the relation of God's world with the spheres of human life to make this connection a reality. A huge task of religious pedagogy is awaiting the Christian Church in this field, and only the first tentative steps have been taken. Bishop Pickett's book on *Christian Mass Movements in India* contains many useful suggestions.

In the present initial stage of this great missionary problem we venture to mention three lines of action in regard to it. In the first and foremost place, as this problem is a religious one, the radical religious approach must be paramount. The only way to get in our modern age (whether one is a member of a rural or of an urban population) a new and vital grasp of the relevance of God to this de-religionized everyday world, is to live by the dynamic world of prophetic religion which we have called the world of Biblical realism. Its dominant conception is that God, the Creator and Redeemer, is the great Initiative-Taker and the absolute Lord of life, whose Lordship and activity has to be recognized in all things. This is the only way to prevent that fatal isolation of the domain of God and of religion, which so easily becomes a fact by the tendency to treat religion as a set of detached dogmas which, as is erroneously presumed, pertain exclusively to the life of the soul and the domain of private opinion. It is, too, the only way to counteract the pull of the pagan attitudes in religion, everywhere evident in nascent Christianity, the tendency to manipulate religious ceremonies for achieving material ends. In the second place, it is very important to devote great attention to elevating and purifying acts and forms of worship in family and community life. Here again Bishop Pickett's book is full of suggestions, and also H. P. Thompson's *Worship in other Lands*.

In the third place, our Christian festivals must become great moments of dramatic force in the yearly life of rural Christians. The great acts of God are celebrated in these festivals. The great themes of sin and victory over sin, of death and the triumph of life, of God's immediate concern with man and the world and of His abiding activity in the life of men, pervade them. Everywhere in the world there is much opportunity to mark these times in vivid and impressive ways through the great wealth of means for religious expression that have been inherited from the pre-Christian past.

EPILOGUE

WE are at the end of our journey. The problem of the fundamental position of the Church as a witness-bearing body and of the evangelistic approach to the great non-Christian faiths has been dealt with in a very incomplete way. We have purposely kept to fundamentals, for two reasons. First, because the primary need of the Christian Church in all its aspects, and also in missions, is for a radically religious re-orientation. Without that the Christian Church and the Christian mission in the present confusion get lost in nervous absorption into many important, but peripheral, activities. We have limited ourselves, therefore, to the religious and theological fundamentals of the witness and service that have to go out from the Church to the world. Many problems—such as nationalism, the race problem, the relation of the individual Christian and of the Christian community to the adherents of other religions in everyday human intercourse, the kind of missionary that is needed in the present period of transition, a detailed treatment of the approach to the non-Christian faiths, the problems that are connected with an adequately trained and spiritual indigenous ministry, and others besides—are very vital to the general subject of approach. Whosoever studies this book attentively will find the guiding ideas for these problems also, although they are not discussed ; but to treat them amply would have increased its size to an excessive extent.

Some concluding remarks may be permitted. In preparing and writing this book we have become strengthened in the opinion, already won by experience, that the urgent need of showing in broad outline and in detail to Western and to Eastern missionaries and pastors the most fruitful ways of approach to the great non-Christian faiths, can never be fulfilled by writing books. Books are able to stimulate and clarify thinking and to provoke fruitful discussion, but they can never effect a universal and abiding change in the methods of approach. This can only be done by the living voice and personal contact, because that is the only way in which the missionary body can voice its doubts and objections, and in which he who advocates definite insights and methods can have his approach constantly enlivened by the effects of criticism and contact with concrete situations. *Every important region needs some men who on account of their ability and knowledge regularly sow the seed of new principles and methods.* This proposal is seriously recommended to the responsible agencies.

The outlook of the Christian mission is at present hopeful as well as cloudy. The Forward Movements in Evangelism meet everywhere with gratifying response. On the other hand, gigantic forces of obstruction and enmity are arising, and make the future uncertain. The three main things that are needed are a deepening and vitalizing of the religious and theological background of missions and the Christian Churches, a determined effort to build everywhere strong indigenous Christian Churches that manifest the quality of fellowship which is peculiar to the community of believers in Christ, and a genuine evangelistic or apostolic spirit.

Much has been done, but nevertheless we are still at the beginning of the great discharge of apostolic obligation of the Christian Church towards the non-Christian world. The rise of the Younger Churches does not imply a gradual retreat of missionary activity on the part of so-called Older Churches, but it means a new start in co-operation with the Younger Churches. The great results of the labours of the past are the Christian forces and centres that are radiating now in the non-Christian world, and the more intelligent and realistic view we entertain at present of the structure and strength of the various non-Christian faiths and cultures, thanks to the labours of science and the exertions of past generations of missionaries. We know now that to persuade the non-Christian world to surrender to Christ as the sole Lord of Life is, as far as the direct activity of missions is concerned, a work of long and persevering moral and religious persuasion, because the hardest and most daring thing that can be done in the world is to invite great spiritual worlds of high antiquity to transplant their roots of life into soil entirely different from the soil to which they are accustomed.

It is very opportune in these times of great opportunities and great uncertainties to derive a heartening lesson from history. In the Middle Ages, when Christianity could recruit a great army of missionaries from the monasteries, it spread as a civilizing and religious power, despite the fact that there were many obstructive forces. In the first ages, when there was no systematic missionary work because the Roman State did not permit the preaching of the Gospel, and when there were no regular missionaries, Christianity worked its way by the courageous witness, the quality of life and the simple fact of maintaining a vigorous Christian community-life. The heartening lesson is that the Gospel can spread under *any* circumstances, provided a living and ardent faith burns in the hearts of men.

The Christian mission in the non-Christian world must be accomplished in the present complicated world with all the means that human intelligence, ingenuity and devotion put at our disposal, because it is our plain duty to make the hearing and expression of God's revelation and Message as palpable as possible. Theology, history, psychology, anthropology must be exploited to achieve one aim and one aim only : to be a better instrument in conveying the conviction that God is speaking in Jesus Christ His decisive Word to individuals, nations, peoples, cultures and races, without any distinction. The undying fire, however, without which all our endeavours are nothing and all our missionary enthusiasm is powerless, is only kindled by the faith and prayer which are born from the vision of the triumphant Divine Love that burns in the heart of the Universe and which became incarnated in Jesus Christ, our Lord.

INDEX

447